INDIA BEFORE MODI

T0333320

VINAY SITAPATI

India Before Modi

How the BJP Came to Power

HURST & COMPANY, LONDON

First published in the United Kingdom in 2021 by

C. Hurst & Co. (Publishers) Ltd.,

83 Torbay Road, London, NW6 7DT

© Vinay Sitapati, 2021

Printed in Great Britain by Bell and Bain Ltd, Glasgow

Typeset in Adobe Garamond Pro by Manipal Technologies Limited, Manipal

A Cataloguing-in-Publication data record for this book
is available from the British Library.

ISBN: 9781787385375

www.hurstpublishers.com

__Jugalbandi__ (जुगलबंदी) *means 'entwined twins' in Hindi.*
Typically used for an Indian classical concert
featuring two solo musicians,
usually with different instruments,
making music together.

Contents

PROLOGUE: PRIME MINISTER ADVANI (1995)

A tent city had been erected over the Mahalakshmi Race Course, playground of south Bombay's upper classes. A public rally was scheduled in Shivaji Park, maidan for middle Mumbai's middle classes. The three-day plenary session of the Bharatiya Janata Party had begun in Bombay on 10 November 1995, just months before the coming national elections.

Over 120,000 delegates attended, some even by ship from the Andaman and Nicobar Islands.[1] The freshly formed Shiv Sena–BJP state government deployed 6000 police personnel and four dog squads to shield participants.[2] A BJP functionary estimated that the three-day event had cost five crore rupees.[3] Brokers from the Bombay Stock Exchange had alone contributed one crore.[4] And a party insider speculates that long-time donor Nusli Wadia—grandson of Muhammad Ali Jinnah—made his own offerings.

Party bigwigs had their mugshots plastered onto the backdrop of the sprawling podium. But one picture loomed large—a balding dome, oval face, white moustache and black-rimmed glasses.[5] The sixty-eight-year-old Lal Krishna Advani had been party president for much of the past decade. He had remodelled the BJP in his radical image in these years, co-opting Rashtriya Swayamsevak Sangh (RSS) men like Narendra Modi as well as movements like the one for a Ram temple in Ayodhya.

The seventy-year-old Atal Bihari Vajpayee, meanwhile, had spent this past decade sidelined from a party travelling in the reverse direction from his preferred 'Gandhian socialism'. Vajpayee was a few inches shorter than Advani, with a face that was rounder, clean-shaven and full haired. This had been the face of political Hinduism since 1957, and Vajpayee had founded the BJP in this moderate image in 1980.

But ever since the RSS had removed him from party leadership in 1986,[6] Vajpayee had preferred prawn and alcohol-infused evenings in his house to orchestrating the rise of the BJP from party headquarters. He had become a relic to be revered rather than a front-runner to be followed. The crowd that had gathered in Bombay that November had no interest in him. As *India Today* magazine put it: 'For long, BJP cadres have looked upon their president, L.K. Advani as the prime-minister-in-waiting, confident as they were of the party's success in the next general election.'[7]

The backdrop of the stage additionally had a picture of the Red Fort in Delhi.[8] The depiction of the spot where Indian prime ministers ceremonially give their yearly Independence Day address was deliberate. Elections were scheduled for April–May 1996, and Advani's agenda this plenary was to ensure that on 15 August 1996, it would be a BJP prime minister who spoke from its ramparts.

There was no guarantee that this would happen. While the party had emerged as the second largest in the 1991 national elections, much had altered since then, including three domes of a mosque in central Uttar Pradesh. Confusingly, this demolition of the Babri Masjid in 1992 had slowed the ascent of the BJP. The party had done worse than expected in local and state elections held since.

These losses were aggravated by ego tussles in a party that prided itself on sticking together. The Rajasthan and Madhya Pradesh units were racked by the sort of infighting more common to the Congress.[9] Leaders in New Delhi were aligning themselves with factions,[10] what a leading magazine termed 'Lotus Wars'.[11] And worst of all, the BJP's winning score in Gujarat in March 1995—it had won 121 of the 182 assembly seats— was being levelled by self-goals.

Denied the position of Gujarat chief minister, the BJP's Shankersinh Vaghela had turned his wrath on the man who got the job, Keshubhai Patel, as well as his advisor, the forty-five-year-old Narendra Modi. Modi had managed to polarize the Gujarat unit of the party despite holding no elected position. Just a few months before the November 1995 Bombay plenary, Vaghela had shepherded rebel legislators to a resort in Khajuraho. When Vajpayee scurried to soothe him, Vaghela had just one demand: 'I want Narendrabhai moved out of Gujarat.'[12] Advani was forced to transfer Modi to Delhi that very November.

This was the same 'Congress culture' of factional fights that Advani had prided himself on staying away from. Indeed, this was the disunity that, in the RSS's telling, had been the historical source of Hindu weakness. *The Times of India* wrote on the eve of the plenary: 'Today, the party with a difference can hardly be distinguished from other political outfits ravaged by internal disputes and petty jealousies.'[13]

The first day of the plenary was dominated by these twin trepidations regarding party unity and electability. On day two, when party president Advani got up to address the public meeting at Shivaji Park, the crowd assumed that he would reiterate these twofold concerns and announce himself as the prime minister-in-waiting.

Instead, the audience began to hear a small section chant 'Vajpayee, Vajpayee'. Someone present remembers: 'One thing I can tell you about Advaniji. He controlled the party fully. Those [chants] would not have happened without his knowing . . . without his permitting.' And as if on cue, L.K. Advani announced the name of the party's prime ministerial candidate.

* * *

A few weeks earlier, Advani had visited a village in Madhya Pradesh. From this remote location, he had stated that it was Vajpayee, not he, who would be the next prime minister. So implausible was Advani's line and so obscure the platform that the cadre had not stirred. But Vajpayee had. He had called Advani to ask why his 'approval' had not first been sought. Advani had replied: 'Would you have said yes to my proposal had I consulted you?'[14]

The Bombay plenary that followed had provided Advani the loudspeaker to broadcast his decision: Vajpayee, not Advani, was the prime minister-in-waiting. Vajpayee spoke to the crowd after Advani, responding with characteristic mixed messaging. On the one hand, he was a 'soldier' who would accept 'any assignment.' But his candidature should not have been decided by Advani without discussion within the party. Vajpayee took care to sound self-effacing about being the next prime minister of India. '*Dilli to bahut duur hai*,' he said,[15] a play on the Sufi saint Hazrat Nizamuddin's classic line.[16] Delhi is still far away.

The rest of the party leadership were too angry to efface themselves. The BJP general secretary K.N. Govindacharya accompanied Advani to his hotel after the public address.[17] Along with Narendra Modi, the RSS functionary had been deputed to the BJP in the late 1980s to reduce Vajpayee's influence. 'How could you make this announcement without consulting the RSS?' Govindacharya asked Advani. An announcement of such magnitude required clearance from the mothership. But Advani replied: 'If I had told the *sangh* they would not have approved.'[18]

Even two decades after, an RSS leader remembers with an air of irritation: 'I have nothing to say about the 1995 Advani decision. Only thing I can say is that it was not decided formally.' The Vishva Hindu Parishad (VHP), which had ridden along with Advani on the back of the Ayodhya temple movement, was also mystified. Its leader Ashok Singhal confessed that very month: 'I didn't know that Advani was going to announce Vajpayee.'[19]

The RSS continued to argue for several days. But Advani refused to imagine himself as prime minister. He did not say if the love from his four-decade-friendship with Vajpayee had influenced his decision. He would only say: 'What I have done is not an act of sacrifice. It is the outcome of a rational assessment of what is right and what is in the best interest of the party and the nation.'[20]

* * *

'What prompted you?' the journalist Swapan Dasgupta asked Advani immediately after the announcement. Advani replied: 'We need the incremental votes. And for that, we need Atalji.'[21] A senior BJP leader of the time agrees: 'Advani announced Vajpayee as [the] PM candidate because Vajpayee was more acceptable to allies and coalition partners. We knew we needed coalition allies at that time [for the forthcoming elections].' Dinesh Trivedi, whose Trinamool Congress (TMC) would eventually ally with the BJP, admits: 'Advani was a shrewd politician.

I can tell you: Trinamool would not have supported BJP with Advani as PM.'[22]

The other reason for Advani's choice was that Vajpayee was better than he was at pacifying rebels within the party. A confidante of his says, 'Advaniji told me: "Why are we Hindus making [the same] mistakes as the past." He knew that the many factions [in the BJP] may not like Vajpayee, but they respected him. Only he could bring them together. Advani didn't have that skill.'

In the midst of such quarrels, Advani's decision stands out as a rare act of choosing party electability and unity over self-glory. This is all the more so given that Vajpayee did become the prime minister—first in 1996, once again in 1998, and finally in 1999. As a senior Congressman says: 'Maybe Advani thought Vajpayee was his senior so should be given a chance first. Or Advani felt that Vajpayee would be more acceptable to coalition allies. But it was certainly an act of putting organization above personal interest.' The BJP's Vasundhara Raje Scindia adds: 'Advani and Vajpayee complemented each other, they were both emotional men. There was something each could take from the other. A man like Advani could step back for Vajpayee. These people were big enough to step back.'[23]

* * *

It is this partnership between Vajpayee and Advani that this book employs as a vehicle to study the Bharatiya Janata Party: from an ideology in the early twentieth century, to a movement, then party, and finally government from 1998 to 2004. This first phase ends with the arrival of Narendra Modi on the national stage.

Picking a political relationship to analyse an ideology does come with blind spots. For one, the focus of this book is on electoral politics rather than social movements.[24] For another, the emphasis is on the Centre, rather than the states, since Vajpayee and Advani never held power outside of Delhi. But telling the tale through its parliamentary face and its party heart adds to several academic arguments—on what Hindu nationalism is; on whether power 'moderated' the BJP; on why it wins elections. Those interested in these debates may wish to first turn to the 'Scholarly Contribution' at the very end of this book before reading on.

These theoretical arguments, however, loiter in the background. The ensuing chapters weave a story of a relationship rather than prove a theorem. The music that runs through this book is the jugalbandi between Vajpayee and Advani, which reflected (in their early years) and shaped (in their later years) Hindu nationalism before Narendra Modi.

Vajpayee and Advani were able to upturn their internal hierarchies *not once but twice*. The 1995 decision of Advani to sacrifice for the sake of Vajpayee was not the first time they had switched places with each other. As this book shows, while Vajpayee controlled the party from 1968 onwards, he wordlessly stepped aside in 1986 and served under Advani for the next decade.

This ability to forgo for the other, complement the other—all the while maintaining distinctive dispositions and dogmas—showcases the BJP's nature *and* effectiveness. Even their births coincided with the origin of their political ideology. And so we begin this journey in the 1920s, with the births of Vajpayee, Advani and of Hindu nationalism itself.

PART I

THE PAST (1924–80)

1

HINDU FEVICOL (1924–45)

Atal Bihari Vajpayee was born in Gwalior to Krishna Devi and Krishna Bihari on 25 December 1924, the noon of British rule over the subcontinent. Atal's grandfather had migrated from Bateshwar in Uttar Pradesh to Gwalior, one of the 500-plus princely states that covered a third of colonial India.[1] This relocation, coupled with Gwalior's uncertain identity—Marathi or Hindi—meant that Vajpayee was never rooted to one place; he would contest elections from Gwalior, Uttar Pradesh, and New Delhi in later years.

At the time of Vajpayee's birth, Gwalior state covered 65,000 square kilometres and had a population of 3.5 million.[2] It had been carved out from the debris of the Mughal Empire by the ascendant Marathas in the eighteenth century, who had handed it over to one of their commanders, Ranoji Scindia. With the decline of the Maratha Empire, Scindia's descendants sided with the British. Though careful to never irk their overlords, their piety made Gwalior a hub for resurgent Hindu identity.[3]

Vajpayee was born into a poor *kanyakubja*[4] Brahmin family of the Gangetic plains. His father and grandfather were schooled in Sanskrit rituals, the women expected to take care of home, and conversations were conducted in Hindi rather than English. A family friend says: 'From an early age Vajpayee resented English-speaking Indians. But he was also fascinated by them. That's the story of his life.'

3

Like many other Brahmins during late colonial rule, the Vajpayees had converted ritual learning into a government job. Krishna Bihari became a teacher, an employee of the Scindias. He even fudged Atal's birthdate to 1926, in hope that his son would have a few more years if he joined government service.[5] Krishna Bihari was also a poet, writing in Hindi as well as its dialects. With a shock of grey hair and an eternally black moustache, he exuded bonhomie, an air his son would soon acquire.[6]

Three years after Atal's birth and 1128 kilometres due west, Lal Krishna Advani was born on 8 November 1927 in Karachi, in the western province of Sindh. Unlike the Gwalior of the 1920s, Karachi was directly ruled by the British. Its location by the Arabian Sea made Karachi, to quote its biographer: '. . . a destination for some of the most dramatic migrations of all.'[7] It was home to a mélange of Europeans, Hindus, Sindhi Muslims, Shias, Parsis and Pathans. The city of Advani's birth resembled that other metropolis of the British Empire: Bombay.

L.K. Advani's family had soaked up this ecumenical culture. They came from the educated Hindu Sindhi clan of 'Amils', taken from the Persian word for 'administrator'. It was a legacy of their selection as revenue collectors by a succession of Muslim kings.[8] One uncle was a civil servant—the mark of education in colonial India—another was a chemistry professor and yet another a lawyer.[9] Advani's own father Kishinchand worked as a trader in a family business with his oldest brother, while his mother Gyani Devi was a homemaker. They lived in an abundant bungalow located in Jamshed Quarters, a Parsi locality,[10] and owned a horse-driven Victoria carriage, an extravagance even in Karachi. A family friend says: 'Their house had a game room, only for games. I have seen it.'

The role of religion in the Advani family was layered. The grandfather was a scholar of Sanskrit, a religious marker made even more visible by the fact that Hindus made up only 25 per cent of Sindh.[11] The young Lal was conscious that the home of the Indus River was not some outpost of Hinduism, but essential to its sacred geography.[12] However, while Vajpayee was born into the orthodox strand of colonial-era Hinduism, Advani was born into its reformist variant. His family read from the Sikh holy book and visited gurudwaras. Advani remembers: '. . . it was also common for Hindus to pay homage at the shrines of Sufi saints and for Muslims to celebrate Hindu festivals.'[13] Ideas of the Arya Samaj were also popular in

Karachi, especially its criticism of caste. Years later, when Advani was a central minister in the Janata government, the politician Charan Singh would admonish him: 'You are from Sindh, you just cannot understand the caste motivations in this part of the country.'[14]

Had they been born at any other time, Vajpayee and Advani may have never met, let alone entered into a six-decade partnership. They had little in common: one poor, the other rich; one orthodox, the other freewheeling; one provincial, the other anglicized; one a Gangetic Brahmin, the other a Karachi Sindhi. But they were born in the decade in which a new political identity was covering these two contrasting characters under one single umbrella. They were born in the decade that birthed Hindu nationalism.

* * *

Perhaps the most enduring definition of 'nationalism' comes from the scholar Benedict Anderson. For him, nationalism requires a 'deep, horizontal comradeship' or 'imagined community', within territorial limits, and operating under a sovereign state.[15] While the first ingredient of Anderson's definition—'an imagined community'[16]—is well known, as important is his emphasis on a modern state with land boundaries, inside which this community conceives of itself.[17] To ask, therefore, when 'Hindu nationalism' was created, is to ask when the conception of a Hindu 'people' coincided with an idea of Hindu 'territory' and a Hindu 'state'. Let us look at the origins of these three ingredients, one after another.

The notion of a 'Hindu' territory has ancient antecedents. The Vishnu Purana, sacred literature put to writing in the fourth century AD,[18] states: 'The country that lies north of the ocean, and south of the snowy mountains, is called Bhárata . . .' This, the Vishnu Purana goes on to describe, '. . . is the land of works, in consequence of which men go to heaven, or obtain emancipation'.[19] This geographical imagination of a 'Hindu' India has since been congealed by pilgrimages to tirthas (or sacred locations) that are found between the oceans and the snowy mountain. The scholar of comparative religion Diana Eck says: 'For at least 2,000 years, pilgrimage to the *tirthas* (*tirthayatra*) has been one of the most widespread of the many streams of practice that have come to be called "Hindu".'[20]

While the notion of a religious terrain is age-old, what has been harder to harness has been a notion of a Hindu 'people'—an imagined religious community that shares 'deep, horizontal comradeship'. This is because Hinduism as a religion has lacked a canonical book (unlike the Koran) or an authoritative institution (unlike the Vatican).

The lack of a text or organization that has the final word has led to a plethora of cultural practices. India's 966 million Hindus constitute 80 per cent of the population. But they are distributed into 3000 castes, 25,000 sub-castes,[21] and more than 19,000 languages and dialects.[22]

Hindus are also separated by religious traditions or 'sects'. The sociologist A.M. Shah explains: 'When we enter the home of a member of a sect, we usually find in the front room pictures of only one principal deity . . . For example in the home of a follower of Pushti Marg . . . we find pictures only of Krishna . . . Even in the case of Krishna we may find a preference for one of his forms, particularly the child Krishna.'[23] In a non-sectarian house, '. . . we usually find pictures of a variety of deities of the Hindu pantheon hanging or pasted on the walls'.[24]

This cacophony of beliefs, organizations, texts and gods has led Marxist and postmodern scholars to argue that there was no such thing as a 'Hindu' consciousness before the nineteenth century. It was the modern, colonial state that created Hindu and Muslim identities. This claim, that Hinduism is a colonial invention, is disputed by other scholars who retrace a Hindu 'group' consciousness to the advent of Muslim rule from the eleventh century AD onwards.[25] Others go even further into the past, divining a recognizably 'Hindu' shape in the Puranas in the fourth century AD, which 'greatly expanded [the] mythology of the gods Vishnu, Siva and Devi'.[26]

Whatever be the source of a Hindu 'consciousness'—whether the fourth, tenth, or nineteenth century—there is scholarly consensus that by the late nineteenth century,[27] an imagined Hindu community was very much in evidence. Vivekananda, Bhudev Mukhopadhyay, Bankim Chandra and the Arya Samaj[28]—all aimed to establish a shared Hindu identity. What was lacking, however, was the third ingredient of Hindu nationalism—a conception of a Hindu 'state'.

Those looking for a model of a theocratic state in Islam, Christianity, or Judaism can find it. The Koran provides for the rule by a 'Caliph' according to the precepts of Islam.[29] The Hebrew Bible lays down the basis of a political structure,[30] as does the New Testament.[31]

Hinduism, in contrast, does not provide for a definitive model of a theocracy. As the political theorist Pratap Bhanu Mehta writes: '. . . politics, even when dependent upon religion for earthly legitimisation, has never in Hindu thought taken on messianic or apocalyptic significance.'[32] Even the concept of 'Ramarajya', as detailed by Valmiki in his Ramayana, conceives of a kingdom where, 'Every creature was full of joy and happiness. Everyone was engaged in the pursuit of *dharmic* actions or virtue.'[33] This is hardly a religious vision, let alone a theocratic one.

Perhaps the closest to a 'Hindu state' prior to the twentieth century was the king Shivaji and the Maratha Empire he founded. Shivaji was born in the seventeenth century near Pune in central India. His father was an estate holder for the Bijapur sultanate. Chafing at the domination of the Mughals in the north and the Bijapur and Golkonda sultanates in the south, Shivaji rebelled, formed an army by uniting various Marathi-speaking castes, kept three Muslim rulers at bay, and in 1674 crowned himself a sovereign king. His descendants (and their Peshwa advisors) widened this Maratha Empire, which at its high point in the eighteenth century controlled 25,00,000 square kilometres of territory.[34] It stretched from the Arabian Sea on the west to the Indian Ocean on the east, from Goa in the south to Delhi in the north. The Marathas, not the Mughals, were the paramount power when the British came to India.

This Maratha Empire Shivaji founded could have one day become a model for a Hindu state. Yet, and perhaps tellingly, the many 'Hindu' narratives of Shivaji stress his ability to unify Hindus, rather than run a government according to religion. The historian Sir Jadunath Sarkar even has an explanation for Shivaji's lack of vision for a state: 'For one thing, he never had peace to work out his political ideas . . . All his attention was necessarily devoted to meeting daily dangers with daily expedients and he had not the chance of peacefully building up a well-planned political edifice.'[35]

By the late nineteenth century, therefore, as a new Hindu identity began to develop alongside age-old notions of religious territory, what this proto-nationalism lacked was a theory of a 'state'. This void—the lack of a Hindu conception of power—began filling up from 1909 and reached fruition in the 1920s, the decade in which Vajpayee and Advani were born. And what filled this vacuum was the step-by-step introduction, by the British, of elections into colonial India.

* * *

The push towards a representative state, i.e., allowing Indians to select their own leaders, had begun after the 1857 revolt. That uprising had been fuelled, in part at least, by the callousness of the British towards Indian mores. Allowing some natives into the government would enable the British to hear their concerns.[36] The Indian National Congress (INC), set up in 1885, was part of this 'safety valve' logic.

By the late nineteenth century, however, the British rationale for permitting more natives into the colonial government was changing. The rise of liberal politics back home meant that the British had to come up with a 'liberal' justification for ruling India. The victory of the Liberal Party in Britain in 1906 deepened this commitment to self-representation in India.[37]

But what was this Indian 'self' and how would it 'represent' itself? In a society composed of individuals with interests, this would have resulted in the ideal of Western-style democracy. But in a society composed of groups with identities, the logic of democracy would be determined by demographics. Elections would provide incentives for groups to harden their own identities and view others with mistrust, all in order to form political vote banks. For the first time in Indian history, numbers would determine power.

The first group within India that understood this implication of elections was the landed Muslim aristocrats of what was then the United Provinces. They were overrepresented in the government, judiciary and bureaucracy. The introduction of some sort of regional elections in 1892 had halved the number of Muslims in the provincial bureaucracy, while doubling the Hindu number.[38]

The British intention to deepen elections at the national level in 1906 thus added to the panic among this Muslim intelligentsia. British India had approximately 67 million Muslims and 216 million Hindus.[39] For roughly one Indian Muslim, there were three Hindus. If political power followed this distribution—as groups voting as groups in a one-person-one-vote system would ensure—Muslims would forever be consigned to minority status.

The result of this alarm was the creation of the Muslim League that very year. Its aim was to lobby for electoral parity between Muslims and Hindus, irrespective of their numbers.

Three years later, the British introduced the Minto–Morley electoral reforms of 1909. They were, an American wrote at the time, '. . . the first step down that slippery slope at the bottom of which lies a parliamentary government for India'.[40] It enhanced the representation of natives in the central legislative assembly (akin to today's parliament) as well as the provincial councils (similar to today's state legislatures).[41] However, three years of lobbying by the Muslim League had led to a big departure from one-person-one-vote. Though the British did not concede to an equal number of Muslim and Hindu representatives, they created separate electorates, i.e., seats for Muslims to be elected by other Muslims alone. This concession was also in British self-interest. An India divided into incompatible communities would justify their presence as playing the role of umpire.

This opportunistic British response to Muslim trepidation over elections created, in turn, dread among Hindu politicians. The claim for electoral parity would mean that a single Hindu would have only one-third the voting power of a Muslim.

The result of this fear was the creation of the Hindu Mahasabha as a pressure group within the Congress party in 1915.[42] It was headed by Lala Lajpat Rai and Madan Mohan Malaviya, who, like Advani and Vajpayee, came from the reform and orthodox strands of traditional Hinduism. As Rai would presciently argue: 'Once you accept communal representation with separate electorates, there is no chance of its being abolished without a civil war.'[43]

The other group that balked at separate electorates was the Indian National Congress. Unlike the Hindu Mahasabha,[44] though, the Congress accepted the reality of separate electorates in 1916, in order to unite with the League against the British. And two years later, the Congress decided to join Muslims and oppose the abolition of the Caliphate in Turkey by the British. For the Congress, this 'Khilafat movement' was another strategy to erect a cohesive facade against the British. But it ended up allowing Muslim clergy to enter the national movement,[45] and alienated the Mahasabha even further.

The man responsible for these shifts in Congress policy was a forty-five-year-old South African lawyer who had returned to India in 1914 and was transforming a debating club into a mass movement. Scrawny and sun-baked, Mohandas Karamchand Gandhi had positioned himself as a representative of the largely Hindu peasantry—in garb and religious idiom. And to the Mahasabha's bafflement, he swiftly became the undisputed leader of India's Hindus. But his politics was not shaped in opposition to Muslims; on the contrary, he was willing to make concessions to the League in order to keep it within the Congress fold.

It was at this very time that the British announced yet another round of electoral changes. The 1919 Montague–Chelmsford reforms continued separate electorates for Muslims, though it acknowledged that 'The communal system stereotypes existing relations' and '. . . teaches men to think as partisans and not as citizens'.[46] They also pushed the idea of electoral benefits to Sikhs and Christians.[47] What made the 1919 reforms revolutionary was that it allowed for direct elections at all levels. The actual number of Indians who could vote was still minuscule,[48] and the British still held an effective majority. But the 1919 Act—and the three general elections of 1920, 1923 and 1926 that followed—marks, in some sense, the introduction of direct democracy into India.[49]

The limited electoral reforms of 1909 had, as one scholar put it, '. . . brought into sharper focus the emergence of the Hindus and the Muslims as distinct supra-local political communities'.[50] Now, with even deeper elections in 1919, the decade of Vajpayee and Advani's birth was set for even deeper communal clashes.

* * *

India's first general election was held in November 1920, four years before Vajpayee's birth.[51] The Congress boycotted these elections, as did the central Khilafat committee, who got a fatwa issued against Muslim participation.[52] What added to this lack of legitimacy were seats reserved for Whites, Muslims, Sikhs and Christians. This was all in addition to seats that would be directly nominated by the British. India's first elections froze the idea that Indians could not be viewed as individuals, but only through the lens of caste or religion.

It was just before these elections that Gandhi travelled to the Malabar region, in what is today northern Kerala, to speak in favour of the Khilafat movement.[53] Coming in the midst of an already communal campaign, the effect was the opposite of Gandhi's intention. Muslims of the region launched a violent rebellion against the British in September 1921. These Muslims were generally tenants to Hindu landlords (of the eighty-six large landowners in the Malabar, eighty-four were Hindu).[54] So, soon after rising against their political masters, these tenants turned on their economic masters. Rape, pillage and killings followed. Captured Hindus were offered the choice of Islam or death.[55]

This violence was followed with fear by a revolutionary fettered in Ratnagiri jail. It would forever mark him; he would even write a Marathi novel on the Malabar rebellion titled *How Do I Care*.[56] It is this man's face which would one day adorn the offices of Lal Krishna Advani and Amit Shah.

Thin, clean-shaven and sporting circular glasses that amplified the intensity of his eyes, Vinayak Damodar Savarkar was a Maharashtrian from the same Chitpavan Brahmin caste as the Peshwas. While in London in 1909, he had achieved fame for writing a revisionist account of the 1857 revolt. Where the British saw an uncoordinated mutiny, Savarkar portrayed a concerted war of independence. The young nationalist also translated a book on Giuseppe Mazzini, the unifier of Italy. Even at the age of twenty-six, Savarkar had identified the weakness of India: the lack of national unity.

He had then spent a decade in the torturous confines of cellular jail in the Andaman Islands for anti-British activities before moving to a prison on the west coast of India. His time in jail told him which Indians needed to be unified and which excluded. He began to see Muslims as adversaries out to weaken Hindus. He observed Dalit inmates being converted to Islam. He also noticed why: upper-caste prisoners were refusing to treat low-castes as equals.[57]

Savarkar would bring to bear these experiences in an essay he wrote two years after India's first general elections, and published secretly in 1923. His preoccupation was national power: how could India be as powerful as the West? His study of England had taught him that the race and ethnicity

of the majority undergird even their 'civic' nationalism.[58] His adaptation
of this insight to India is contained in a slim essay written in English.
'Essentials of Hindutva' would soon be published as *Hindutva: Who is a
Hindu?*.[59] It is carefully titled. In contrast to thinkers like Vivekananda
and Aurobindo, the atheist Savarkar was less concerned with 'What is
Hinduism?', more with 'Who is a Hindu?'

Savarkar answered the question by linking the ancient territorial idea
of Hinduism to a new imagined community bound by race. Seen this
way, all Indians were related by common blood.[60] But in contrast to Sikhs,
Dalits and Tribals, Savarkar suspected Muslim and Christian Indians,
since they looked outside of India's sacred geography, towards Mecca,
Jerusalem and Rome. Savarkar deemed them, not second-class citizens,
but traitors to their own race.

* * *

At the very time he was writing his essay, Savarkar was reading about the
elections being conducted.[61] This is perhaps why his preoccupation with
Hindus (as opposed to Hinduism) reflected a demographic obsession with
numbers. A theory that united 75 per cent of India was ripe for use in the
context of one-person-one-vote. That Savarkar realized the electoral value of
his ideas can be gauged from the fact that the moment the British permitted
him political activity, he became president of a political party.[62] He would
later say that what made India a 'Hindu state' was not religion but 'its
national majority . . . the Hindu state was not to be a theocratic state . . .'[63]

While Savarkar's own use of his theory was electoral, a walrus-
moustached doctor was reading *Hindutva: Who is a Hindu?* rather
differently. Keshav Baliram Hedgewar's family were Brahmins from
Telangana who had migrated to Nagpur, a city in the centre of India that,
like Gwalior, was both Marathi and Hindi-speaking. As a child, Hedgewar
had idolized Shivaji and the Marathas. He had spent time with the radicals
of Bengal and joined the Congress, but had become disenchanted with the
concessions that Gandhi was making to the Muslim League. The violence
in Malabar had also left a mark, as did Hindu–Muslim riots in the early
1920s in Nagpur.[64] Hindus, Hedgewar felt, were too fearful of Muslims to
defend themselves on the streets.

By 1922, Hedgewar was searching for an alternative form of public engagement when a handwritten copy of Savarkar's as yet unpublished essay was smuggled to him from prison.[65] What was needed, Hedgewar concluded, was not political agitation but a social organization dedicated to converting India's disparate Hindus into a unified Hinduism.

It was to act on this inference that Hedgewar met Savarkar in Ratnagiri,[66] and founded the Rashtriya Swayamsevak Sangh or 'National Volunteer Organization' in Nagpur in 1925. Its social location (Marathi-speaking Brahmins like Hedgewar) as well as its geographic location (not quite Hindi, not quite Marathi) would shape the RSS leadership for generations. While one would plant memories of the Maratha Empire, the other would cultivate a pan-Indian outlook.

Theirs was a slow start and it took three years for the first volunteers of the RSS to be sworn in—ninety-nine mostly upper-caste Maharashtrian men taking an oath before an effigy of the monkey God Hanuman.[67]

This nod to tradition disguised the fact that the RSS was a radical break from the past. While conventional Hinduism had emphasized sect and caste differences, the RSS saw this as the cause for Hindu vulnerability. Their solution was to invent a new, unified Hindu identity. The cultural grammar of this new Hinduism, 'Hindutva', was upper-caste (specifically Kshatriya). There was an emphasis on martial valour that could, if necessary, engage in defensive violence.[68] This was why the RSS was, from its very inception, an all-male club.

It was also, from the beginning, consciously defined against Muslims. In 1927 itself, uncomfortable with a Muslim shrine near Nagpur that attracted Hindu devotees, Hedgewar had it removed.[69] On the other hand, and unlike traditional Hinduism, the RSS from its very origin thought of low-castes, Dalits and Tribals as part of its family.

Through these early years, Hedgewar was insistent that the RSS stay away from politics. Where Savarkar wanted to weaponize Hindutva by creating an electoral majority, the RSS was content with morning calisthenics. This anti-political philosophy would infuriate Savarkar. As he would say mockingly of an RSS worker: 'He was born, he joined the RSS and he died without accomplishing anything.'[70]

Soon after the founding of the RSS, the third general elections of India were scheduled between October and November 1926. In anticipation, a flurry of religious and caste associations made their presence felt. The Khilafat conference morphed into a political party.[71] It was in this context that the all-India Hindu Mahasabha—created in the early 1920s as a knitting of regional mahasabhas[72]—decided to contest the upcoming elections.[73]

The 1920s was thus the age of elections as well as of Muslim and Hindu nationalisms. For Muslims, these elections presented a crisis, while for Hindu nationalists the distribution of power according to demographics was an opportunity.

This compatibility with electoral democracy was made easier by the fact that Hinduism does not provide a model of a religious state that can compete with democracy. As the scholars Farzana Shaikh and Venkat Dhulipala have shown, Islamic conceptions of self-representation did not allow a non-Muslim to 'represent' a Muslim individual.[74] There existed within Islamic tradition, ideas of an 'Islamic state' that the Muslim League would deploy in order to denounce the legitimacy of elections.

What is striking about the Hindutva politics of that era was that none of its politicians seriously considered a viable substitute to one-person-one-vote.[75] In the documents of the Hindu Mahasabha, RSS and Hindu leaders of that period, no alternative model to elections is genuinely discussed. The Hindu state, based on 'national majorities', was perfectly compatible with elections. While the ideology would, at best, be ambivalent about economic and social equality, it would be at ease with political equality. As Savarkar himself put it: 'The tenets of Hindutva were consistent with democracy.'[76]

* * *

While Hindu nationalism was on an upward trajectory in the 1920s and 1930s, so were the Vajpayees. Atal, his six siblings and two parents moved to lower-middle-class respectability as Krishna Bihari rose in the education bureaucracy. Vajpayee studied at the local Gorakhi School, a barebones establishment funded by the Maharaja of Gwalior.[77] Hindi was the medium of instruction, and the headmaster was Krishna Bihari.[78] It is a curse to study in a school one's parents are teaching in. Not for Vajpayee, who had begun to mimic his father's erudition and eloquence. He would later say: 'My father was a great speaker in English and Hindi. But didn't have the opportunity that I had. I am only his pocket edition.'[79]

Advani too was formed by his father, an impact augmented by his mother dying young. Advani's memory of Kishinchand is of a man marked by 'simplicity' and 'impeccable conduct',[80] with what must have been a trader's knack for logistics. Unlike the outgoing Krishna Bihari, Kishinchand was low-key, a trait he would hand over to his impressionable son.

While Vajpayee was spending his childhood in a mofussil milieu, Advani was being shaped by cosmopolitan indulgences. He enrolled in St Patricks, a Catholic school whose Latin motto was 'Per Aspera Ad Astra': Through Hardship to the Stars.[81] This English-medium education converted Advani into a *Macaulayputra*. The phrase literally means 'son of Macaulay', after the nineteenth-century British politician who had advocated teaching the natives English in order to create 'a class of persons Indian in blood and colour, but English in tastes, in opinions, in morals and in intellect'.[82] Hindu nationalists used the phrase as an abuse. Ironically, it was this very trait which would, as we shall soon see, boost Advani's career prospects.

St Patricks exposed the young Advani to the world of Christian missionaries,[83] their austerity, their single-mindedness. When Advani met Pakistan president Pervez Musharraf decades later, 'the first subject we discussed was our school and nearly 20 minutes of our 45-minute meeting were devoted to St Patrick's!'[84] When Advani returned to his alma mater in 2005, the students sang '*For he's a jolly good fellow*'. 'I was with him,' diplomat T.C.A. Raghavan says. 'I saw tears well up in his eyes.'[85]

While Advani was learning the affairs of modernity at St Patricks, Atal was learning the affairs of the heart. By 1941, Vajpayee had entered Victoria College, originally founded as a Muslim seminary called Lakshar Madrassa in 1846 before changing its name in honour of the British empress.[86] While the seventeen-year-old Vajpayee would sit in the back of the class, his attention fell on an arresting sixteen-year-old on the front benches.

Rajkumari Haksar was born in 1925 in Ujjain to a Kashmiri Pandit family which had since moved to Gwalior. Like Krishna Bihari, Rajkumari's father was employed by the education department. Rajkumari was also a second cousin of Indira Gandhi—her grandmother was Kamala Nehru's aunt. It is a fact that Vajpayee may not have known at the time.[87]

Years later, Rajkumari described that time to a friend: 'I met Atalji in Gwalior in college. We were in the same class. We were attracted to each other. But there was no formal affair. And things didn't go ahead because I felt my family may not agree. It was all very innocent . . . very harmless.' An RSS leader says: 'The issue was that Vajpayee was not a Kashmiri. And as a traditional Hindu girl, Rajkumari would have gone with what her parents wanted.' Vajpayee's biographer Vijai Trivedi speculates: 'Vajpayee was just seventeen, his family did not have money. What prospects did he provide as husband?'[88] Two other biographers have written that a possible marriage fell apart when her family didn't agree.[89] Rajkumari's small-town regard for Atal would have remained a postcard from her youth. Had they not, as we shall see, met two decades later.

Meanwhile, Britain had declared war on Nazi Germany in 1939, and had volunteered India without its permission. Over 2.5 million Indian troops would fight alongside the allies in World War II,[90] the largest volunteer army in the war.[91] Though opposed to fascism, the Gandhi-led Indian National Congress was furious that it had not been consulted. The Congress party had dominated the 1937 elections and formed governments in several states; it now resigned from these ministries in protest.

Gandhi demanded that in return for Indian support, Britain promise to free India after the war. When the British were unwilling to commit, the Congress party, in August of 1942, launched the Quit India movement.

Worried that this uprising would weaken their war effort, the British arrested the entire Congress leadership. The Muslim League, on the other hand, remained in government to curry favour. Assisting them was an improbable ally. Savarkar was by now heading the Hindu Mahasabha and believed in 'reasonable compromises'[92] to capture the centres of political power. His party also did not resign from the provincial assemblies and continued to run coalition governments with the Muslim League in three provinces, including Advani's Sindh.[93]

In the midst of this tumult, Vajpayee travelled to his ancestral village of Bateshwar on vacation. Vajpayee and his brother were in the bazaar watching a folk performance one day. He described what happened next in an article published in a Hindi newspaper in 1997: '. . . three young men arrived on the scene and stopped the performance. They informed the audience of Gandhiji's "Quit India" call of August 9 at Bombay, and exhorted the people to throw out the British imperialists.'[94] The gathering then attacked two forest outposts where the 'angry crowd demolished the structure'. The Vajpayee brothers were soon arrested, and Atal signed a confessional statement written in Urdu which named those who incited the crowd while denying rendering 'any assistance in demolishing the government building'.[95]

This confession would haunt his later career. Though the claim that Vajpayee was a turncoat is imprecise—the confessional statement was not used in the trial against the others accused—the propaganda that Vajpayee was a 'freedom fighter' rings hollow by his own admission.[96]

This incident reveals that Vajpayee's childhood, like Advani's, was not swept up by the anti-British struggle. What was keeping them busy instead was involvement in a 'cultural' organization that was expanding fast enough for the British to contemplate a ban.[97] It was membership in the RSS that would finally bring Vajpayee and Advani together.

* * *

By the late 1930s, the Rashtriya Swayamsevak Sangh had expanded to non-Marathi speaking areas and claimed a membership of 60,000.[98] Sometime around then, a functionary named Narayanrao Tarte came visiting Gwalior. He converted the teenage Vajpayee, who would later say: 'What I am today is the making of Sri Tarte.'[99] Vajpayee's entry into the RSS by 1939[100] was driven by location: Gwalior had a Marathi-speaking population and a Hindu king.[101] Had the Vajpayees persisted in the United Provinces, it is unlikely that Atal would have been exposed to the RSS at such a young age.

Atal's brother accompanied him into the RSS. Conscious of his caste status, this brother chose to cook his own food separately. But after a single day at the RSS, he joined the food line like the others.[102] Vajpayee himself entered wearing his sacred thread. But he soon removed it since he did not want any markers that distinguished him from other Hindus.

The other beneficiary of the RSS's expansion in this period came from a world far away from Gwalior. The fourteen-year-old Advani had just finished school in 1942. He was spending his vacation in Hyderabad (in Sindh) learning tennis. One day, right in the middle of a game, his partner told Advani: 'I am going.' Advani asked him: 'How can you go like this without even completing the set.' 'I have joined the RSS a few days ago,' his partner replied, 'I cannot be late for the *shakha* because punctuality is very important in that organisation.'[103] Advani joined a few days later, perhaps the only member to enter the RSS because of a tennis match.

Advani's wealth and background placed him at social odds with the RSS. And unlike Vajpayee, who knew Hindi and Marathi, Advani spoke only English and Sindhi. He would start 'reading, writing and conversing in Hindi' only after 1947[104] and would never learn Marathi. Despite these limitations, what endeared Advani to the RSS was his frugality, earnestness and zeal. Vajpayee, on the other hand, lacked discipline, an old-timer says. But he was noted even then for his felicity with Hindi.

The principal unit of the RSS is the shakha, modelled after the traditional akhara, a kind of gymnasium for young men. Shakhas typically consist of 50–100 male volunteers divided by age group.[105] These part-time volunteers are known as 'swayamsevaks' and can be children in school or family men who work for a living. As swayamsevaks, Vajpayee and Advani would regularly visit morning shakhas at open grounds in their cities, wearing the mandated white shirt, khaki shorts and black cap. Apart from synchronized stick wielding and team games such as kabaddi,[106] the focus of the one-hour meetings was on indoctrination.

Though attending shakhas more than a thousand kilometres apart, Vajpayee and Advani learnt the same version of Hindu history, one plagued by a lack of unity that rendered it vulnerable to invasions. The focus was on Shivaji, the Maratha Empire and the third battle of Panipat of 1761. The hefty losses that the Marathas suffered in that pivotal battle—which weakened them and paved the way for British rule—was attributed to Hindu disunity. Their Afghan enemy Ahmad Shah Abdali was able to rally Indian Muslim allies on the basis of religion. The Marathas, on the other hand, could not get Jats and Rajputs to side with them.[107]

These history lessons sparked in Advani a suspicion of Muslims, what his syncretic Sindhi childhood had scarcely countenanced. The sixteen-year-old travelled to Rajasthan in 1943, writing of his visit: 'On the walls of Chittorgarh Fort, I was pained to see thousands of idols of Hindu deities broken and defaced by intolerant Muslim invaders. Not one was left intact.'[108] Advani once read, at a stretch, five books on Shivaji. He also read K.M. Munshi's book on the sacking of the Somnath temple by Mahmud of Ghazni in 1024 AD.[109] The book's central point: Hindus were defeated because they were divided.

Vajpayee and Advani were also noticing that this historical lesson translated, within the RSS organization, into an ethic that valued teamwork. This was the focus of the bearded Rasputin lookalike who had succeeded Hedgewar as RSS head in 1940. M.S. Golwalkar's reading of history was typical: '[Over time] consciousness of the one Hindu Nationhood became musty and the race became vulnerable to attacks from outside . . .'[110] His solution was also characteristic of his ideology: 'Unless our society is cured of its internal malady of disunity and self-forgetfulness and made nationally alert and organised, it will remain incapable of enjoying prosperity in the world.'[111]

The RSS is a decentralized organization with a small team at the very top that operates out of Nagpur. At the bottom are lakhs of part-time volunteers or swayamsevaks who are organized around shakhas. Connecting these thousands of shakhas to Nagpur are 'pracharaks' or full-time officials who don't earn a salary, but whose needs are taken care of by the RSS. It was Golwalkar who created the position of pracharak, and it was Golwalkar who made it compulsory for them to be unmarried.[112] From his education at a Christian missionary college[113] and time working in the Ramakrishna Mission, he had learnt that traditional family ties could weaken the commitment to organization.

These pracharaks—the word literally means 'one who publicizes' or 'a missionary'—would eventually number more than 4000, and form the backbone of the RSS. They would serve in different parts of the country, learning multiple languages, while ceremoniously declaiming in Sanskritic Hindi. Over time, the top leadership would be staffed almost entirely by unmarried pracharaks. They would learn to love the RSS as their only family, and to stay united above all else.

Even though talented youngsters might be promoted out of turn in the RSS, ceremonial seniority is dictated by 'sangh aayu' or time spent in the organization—just one of the many techniques by which the RSS promotes merit even while assuaging the long-serving. One such old-timer points to another technique: 'This is an unwritten rule in the RSS. That if you have to say something good about anybody, say in front of everybody.

If you want to say something negative, say to his and your superior. Never to [an] equal.' Vajpayee and Advani were being taught that the organization tasked with uniting Hindu society had to stay united itself.

Advani and Vajpayee were yet to meet. But it is telling that they were so swayed by the RSS that they moved, around the same time, from being mere volunteers to pracharaks. To do this, they had to attend a three- to four-stage Officer's Training Camp or OTC.[114]

Each stage lasted for around a month, with the final OTC being a twenty-five-day camp conducted in Nagpur.[115] A long-time pracharak describes the daily routine: 'Four thirty in the morning to 10:30 at night, [there is a] combination of physical exercise and *baudhik* [ideological discussion]. Morning two hours physical, after breakfast group discussion or brainstorming, post-lunch baudhik by outsider. Then evening again 4:30–8 p.m. more physical.' Officers in training stayed together in sparse rooms. There was no privacy. The whole point was to emphasize the concord necessary to rejuvenate Hindu society.

* * *

Though Vajpayee and Advani were being given a new identity, their organization did not require that they join active politics. The RSS had internalized the significance of unifying Hindus socially. But the importance of coalescing Hindus politically would come to them only in 1951. Golwalkar in particular had a Brahmin's aversion to politics. He was also uncomfortable with the atheist and beef-eating Savarkar. Which is why when Savarkar, as president of the Hindu Mahasabha, asked for political help in 1942, Golwalkar declined. A jilted Savarkar sneered at the RSS: 'What will you organize all these people for. Will you make *achaar* [pickle] with them?'[116]

Meanwhile, L.K. Advani had, from 1944 onwards, started teaching English, history, maths and science to ten-year-olds at the Model High School in Karachi.[117] He showed no hint of electoral ambitions, immersing himself in English fiction, a passion that would persist through his life.

Vajpayee had graduated from Victoria College by then, and wanted to study further. But unlike the Advanis, the Vajpayees had to count their rupees. As Vajpayee later remembered: 'My father had retired from government service. My two sisters were of marriageable age. Dowry had assumed the shape of a curse. From where will I manage resources for post-graduation?'[118] Benevolence came in the form of a seventy-five-rupee monthly scholarship from the Maharaja of Gwalior. Armed with this amount, Vajpayee joined a law program at the DAV College in Kanpur in 1945.[119]

He was not alone. The now-retired school inspector Krishna Bihari decided to join his son in education once more, but this time as an equal. As Vajpayee later wrote in the college magazine: 'Whenever my father was late for the class, the professors amidst laughter, used to ask "tell where your father has disappeared. And when I was late, he used to be questioned as to "why your son is missing".'[120] A classmate recalls: 'Vajpayee virtually grew under the shadow of his father.'[121]

* * *

Vajpayee's entry into DAV College in 1945 coincided with the end of World War II. The war's finale brought renewed pressure on the British to leave India. This was amplified by the defeat of Winston Churchill's Conservative Party in July 1945. The victorious Labour Party was more responsive to Indian demands for Independence.[122]

Central elections were announced for December 1945, followed by provincial elections for January 1946. Some 41 million Indians (including 6 million women) were deemed to meet the educational and property qualifications to vote.[123] The British announced that these elections would be followed by a constituent assembly for a free India.[124]

The question of what form this freedom would take was open to negotiation. Forty years of telling Muslims they were distinct—through reserved seats and separate electorates—was not without consequences as Indians began to imagine life after Independence. For the Muslim League, that life would be permanent persecution by the Hindu majority. To pre-empt this fate, the League had demanded, in its 1940 Lahore resolution, the grouping of Muslim-majority provinces in the north-west and east of India to constitute 'independent states'. Population numbers would eventually draw the boundaries of this land of the pure: Pakistan.

Though such a division should have appealed to the Hindu Mahasabha and the RSS—given that it would have resulted in a bigger Hindu majority in India—what is notable is their unbending hostility to the creation of Pakistan.[125] Just days after the League's Lahore resolution, Savarkar said in a speech that his party 'could not tolerate and would oppose with all its might the Muslim idea of dividing India'.[126] The preservation of Hinduism's religious territory was plainly more important than demographics.

That same year, the leader of India's Dalits, B.R. Ambedkar—no fan of the Congress—wrote a book supporting the demand for Pakistan. He painted an image of Islam as a nation unto itself, incapable of living with other religions. He also pointed out that Gandhi's concessions to the League had only emboldened them. There was likely, Ambedkar clinically concluded, no solution to the Muslim question within an undivided India.[127]

Some scholars have claimed that Hindus in Punjab,[128] Bengal[129] and at the national level[130] favoured partition as a way of cutting Muslim numbers. Be that as it may, the political parties who claimed to represent India's Hindus—principally the Congress but also the Mahasabha—fervidly resisted partition.[131] The archives of the Mahasabha show an implacable opposition to the partition of India, including in a 1944 Akhand Hindustan Leaders Conference.[132] Savarkar dismissed Gandhi's attempts to reach any compromise with the Muslim League's Muhammad Ali Jinnah on this issue.[133]

In contrast, the party that claimed to speak for Muslims had made partition their one-point agenda. And whatever Jinnah's private mores, the pork-eating, south Bombay sophisticate was allowing himself to be portrayed as a new caliph.

Of the two strategies of Hindu nationalism that had emerged in these last decades—social unity and electoral unity—the RSS (the teenage Vajpayee and Advani included) was fixated only on the former. The result was that the Hindu Mahasabha, focussed on the latter, was being reduced to an electoral cipher. As the most important elections in Indian history approached in late 1945, British India's estimated 75 per cent Hindus were being drawn, in entirety almost, to Mohandas Gandhi and his Congress party.

Muslims, on the other hand, were less enamoured of the Congress. If Jinnah won the Muslim seats, he could prove to the British that he alone spoke for them. India's sacred geography would be defiled, and Advani's beloved Karachi would go to a new country. As the British prepared to conduct their last election in India, the stakes could not have been higher.

2

GHOSTS OF PARTITION (1945–50)

Elections to the central assembly, precursor to today's parliament, were scheduled for December 1945. Forty-eight seats were for 'Non-Mohammadan' voters and candidates and thirty for 'Mohammadan'.[1] In the elections to provincial assemblies (such as Bombay Presidency and the United Provinces) to be held a month later, seats were reserved for Muslims, non-Muslims as well as for Scheduled Castes.

As these elections came near, every party knew that the results would determine which of their 'ideas of India' the departing British would leave behind.

The Congress had by then conceded to some of the Muslim League's demands. These included near parity between India's 75 per cent Hindus and 25 per cent Muslims, and an exceedingly federal structure with all-powerful states and a crippled Centre.[2] This was as far as the Congress was willing to go; they refused to countenance a partitioned subcontinent.

But for the British to agree to this, the Congress needed to demonstrate that it spoke for all sections of the country. And for this, it needed to win not just an overall majority, but a lion's share of the general (i.e., non-Mohammedan) constituencies, the Scheduled Caste seats and among Muslims.

In each of these segments, the Congress faced challenger parties, each with their own ideas of Independence. It was battling for Muslim seats with the League, which had a single-point agenda of Pakistan. It was competing with B.R. Ambedkar's party for Scheduled Caste seats. And for the caste-Hindu seats, the Congress was pitted against the Hindu Mahasabha.

The face of the Mahasabha campaign was V.D. Savarkar, now sixty-two years old. His writings and lengthy incarceration had made him, as we read earlier, the ideologue of Hindu nationalism.

Joining him was a younger Syama Prasad Mookerjee, the son of a knight and high court judge. At the age of thirty-three, Mookerjee had become the youngest vice-chancellor in the history of Calcutta University. The Congress should have been the natural home for such a Macaulayputra. But Mookerjee had left the Congress, joined the Hindu Mahasabha and, by 1945, was one its most prominent politicians along with Savarkar.

The urbane Bengali and unbending Maharashtrian may have come from unalike social worlds, but their views on the Muslim question echoed the party line. Their Hindu Mahasabha was opposed to Pakistan of course, but also to any Congress concessions that 'deprive[d] the Hindus as Hindus of their due representation to such an extent as to compel three Hindus to have but one vote, while they offered one Muslim three votes'.[3]

Realizing the importance of these elections, the Mahasabha requested help from the RSS network of volunteers. The RSS refused.[4] An insider says: 'This was Golwalkar's biggest mistake. He continued to dislike Savarkar . . . He wanted nothing to do with politics.' Golwalkar ensured that the eighteen-year-old Advani and the twenty-one-year-old Vajpayee—who were yet to meet each other—were kept away from campaigning. It is not clear if either of these two even voted. What is known is that many in the RSS voted for the Congress as the party of Hindus. The Mahasabha was ignored.

When the results were announced, the Congress had swept the 'general' seats, winning 923 of 1585 seats in the provincial legislatures and fifty-nine out of 102 of the central seats. This latter figure included victories in all forty-nine caste-Hindu constituencies.[5] The Hindu Mahasabha did not win a single seat for the central assembly or the provincial assemblies.[6] Even B.R. Ambedkar's Scheduled Castes Federation was thoroughly defeated by the Congress.[7]

Gandhi's Congress could reasonably claim that they, not Savarkar and Ambedkar, were the sole spokesmen for Hindus high and low.

Where this claim could not extend was to Muslims. Of the thirty seats reserved for them in the central assembly, the League had won every single one.[8] Of the roughly 500 Muslim seats in the provincial assemblies, the League had gained 425.[9] Since the franchise was limited to those with property, money, or education, over 86 per cent of adult Muslims did not have the right to vote.[10] But the Muslim League interpreted the results conveniently. *All* Muslims, it declared, were behind its demand for Pakistan.

* * *

Vajpayee had continued studying law in Kanpur through this tumult. But soon after these elections in 1946, Vajpayee was asked by the RSS to leave his education and set up a Hindi newspaper in the United Provinces.[11] It meant leaving his father for the new paternal authority in his life. That same year, Advani completed his third Officer's Training Camp in Nagpur; he was now a full-grown functionary.[12] He returned to Karachi and was appointed city secretary of the RSS.[13]

Meanwhile, a national government had formed in New Delhi. But squabbles between the Congress and the League paralysed any chance of governance. The British prime minister declared that they would leave India no later than June 1948.[14]

Realizing that time was not on his side, Jinnah called on 'Direct Action' by Muslims on 16 August 1946 to force partition. He proclaimed that we shall have 'either a divided India or a destroyed India'.[15] He almost got both. Hindu–Muslim violence flowed across India, especially Calcutta, where more than 7000 died in just a few blood-splattered days.[16]

The RSS analysis of the violence was predictable. Golwalkar told Hindu merchants: 'The disunity of the Hindus in Punjab was the cause of the present calamity. The *Sangh* should unite the Hindus and the capitalists should help by funds.'[17] As the violence peaked in June 1947, delegates of the five Muslim-majority provinces left the constituent assembly. The British, desperate to leave, saw how Jinnah had proved his theorem on the ground: Hindus and Muslims were nations unto themselves, incapable of living in peace.

A new viceroy had been appointed in March of that year. Louis Mountbatten, the foppish nephew of the King of England, decided, in

June 1947, to advance Independence by almost a year—from June 1948 to August 1947. Just two months remained.[18] He also announced the final plan for Independence. The British would leave behind two sovereign states. The Muslim-majority provinces in the west would be part of Pakistan, while the religiously mixed states of Bengal and Punjab would be divided. The princely states would have the freedom to decide which country to join.[19]

The plan pleased no one. Congress had fought against partition its whole life, while Jinnah was enraged at the 'mutilated, moth-eaten'[20] Pakistan he would inherit. But such was the hurry produced by the baffling British decision to flee in two months that the Muslim League formally acquiesced to the partition plan on 9 June 1947,[21] and the Congress six days later.[22]

Wobbled by a turn of events they could not influence, the Hindu Mahasabha and RSS seethed on the sidelines. Syama Prasad Mookerjee wrote in the RSS journal: 'We have virtually given up a portion of our sacred territory without a fight . . . The Anglo-Muslim League conspiracy outmanoeuvred the Congress and the latter surrendered almost without a protest.'[23]

On 5 August, partition less than two weeks away, Golwalkar travelled to Karachi.[24] Advani received him at the railway station, and was part of the assembly of 100,000 jittery Hindus listening to the RSS chief speak. Advani was in charge of the 10,000 uniformed RSS men who marched to patriotic songs to calm the crowd. Advani's loyalty to Hindu nationalism would forever be bought by this show of support.

Nine days later, Pakistan was created as a Muslim-majority country, with Karachi as its capital. Advani remembers sweets being distributed; Hindu children refused to eat them.[25] India became independent the next day. 'What an accursed fate mine is,' the nineteen-year-old thought. He had looked forward to this day for the past five years,[26] only for his Sindhi soul to be partitioned into two. Through the next seven decades, through grassroots work, party-building, journalism and government service, Advani would remain haunted by the ghosts of partition. His life would be a quest to bandage himself back together.

* * *

That very day, 15 August 1947, the RSS launched a Hindi monthly called *Rashtradharma* in Lucknow. The twenty-two-year-old Atal Bihari Vajpayee was appointed its first joint-editor.[27] A few months later, he joined the weekly *Panchajanya* as editor.[28] He had finished his third Officer's Training Camp by then, and had even worked as a pracharak in Sitapur in the United Provinces.[29] But Vajpayee was unused to the hardships of this life. And his talent for Hindi ensured that he was soon moved to desk work. Though he did not know it then, he was already being marked as a communicator, a role he would play for the next six decades.

The *Panchajanya* of these months railed against partition, the culpability of the Muslim League and the connivance of the Congress. As editor, Vajpayee was well aware of the arguments. But sitting 800 kilometres from the international border, partition was a headline rather than a horror.

Meanwhile, an estimated 14.5 million Hindus, Sikhs and Muslims were being forced out of their homes to migrate to a new country.[30] More than ten million were rendered homeless.[31] As much as 2.7 million hectares of land were abandoned by Hindus and Sikhs in West Punjab, with 1.9 million hectares abandoned by Muslims in East Punjab.[32] The other macabre statistic was on sexual violence: 50,000 Muslim women were abducted as they attempted to flee, while for Hindu and Sikh women the number was 33,000.[33] The dead alone crossed a million.[34] Advani recalls motorcycling around Karachi soon after partition. 'I saw the body of a man who had been stabbed to death. A small distance ahead, I saw another corpse, and then a third . . . This was unusual and disturbing for me as it was the first time in my life that I had seen corpses lying on the street.'[35]

The emblems of this violence were trains—motifs of modern India—carrying refugees to the other side of Punjab. These trains would be stopped before the border, and the passengers methodically murdered. The trains would then chug along to the other side, delivering their silent cargo.

The Hindus of Karachi were sheltered from much of this initial violence. The family of Kamla Jagtiani—who would marry Advani in 1965—remained in Karachi for almost a year. She would tell a friend: 'I remember leaving Karachi only in 1948, and that too when we saw the gurudwara in front of our house burning.' On Advani's side, some relatives migrated to Mumbai, while his father moved to Kutch, across the border from Sindh. The cosmopolitan trader, owner of a palace, game room and horse carriage in Karachi was now reduced to working with the Sindhu resettlement corporation.[36]

Advani himself left Karachi for Delhi in September 1947, one of the few refugees who came by a propeller aircraft of the British Overseas Airways Corporation.[37] The loss of home and dispersal of family had traumatized Advani. But his RSS work had given him an extended family in India. He was taken care of by his new clan.

Two months on, he paid a visit to V.D. Savarkar in Bombay. Advani had been shaped by Savarkar's *Great War of Independence* as well as his essay on Hindutva. And in the aftermath of partition, Advani perhaps saw Savarkar as a clairvoyant whose decades-long warnings against Congress policies had turned out true. Advani remembers: 'As I sat in awe of his magnetic presence at his Shivaji park residence he asked me about the situation in Sindh and the conditions of Hindus after partition.'[38]

This awe did not extend to joining Savarkar's party. It says something about Advani's personality that faced with the suffering that turned others to street violence or hard-hitting politics, Advani chose quietism. He remained loyal to the RSS, to its anti-political ethic and to its emphasis on social change. This trait would remain with Advani through his life. The emotions that people ordinarily suffer—jealousy, anger, exuberance—would, in Advani, remain bottled up as silent stoicism.

Advani was soon sent to work as a pracharak in Rajasthan. His job was to supervise existing shakhas as well as standardize new ones. Given that shakhas bloom organically, have autonomy and even control their own bank account, Advani's role was that of a quality inspector ensuring a homogenous product. He would spend his day travelling from village to village, sometimes by bus, sometimes by cycle, sometimes by camel.[39] It was his way of making the subcontinent whole again.

Meanwhile, a national unity government had been formed in India. Gandhi had overruled the Congress cadre to anoint the 'foreign-educated' Jawaharlal Nehru, son of a Congress president, to be India's first prime minister. The cadre's preferred choice, 'Sardar' Vallabhbhai Patel, was made home minister and India's first deputy prime minister. Gandhi had also insisted that the first cabinet represent all parties, not just the dominant Congress. B.R. Ambedkar was made law minister, Syama Prasad Mookerjee industry minister.

For those Muslims who remained, partition had proved a cataclysm. From a confident minority being able to demand concessions, they were now evermore outnumbered, evermore fearful and wholly dependent on the Congress for protection. The RSS saw this as yet another ploy. In December 1947, Golwalkar told a meeting of 200 RSS full-timers that the remaining Muslims should quit India, whereas 'Mahatma Gandhi wanted to keep the Muslims in India so that the Congress may profit by their votes at the time of elections . . .'[40]

But with this Muslim percentage halved and waves of Hindu refugees flooding into India, the Hindu Mahasabha and RSS were witnessing a boost in their popularity. The former BJP member of parliament Prafull Goradia says: 'Many of us thought that with partition, we had a clear Hindu majority, and with partition violence, there would be a lot of sympathy for Hindu grievance. The moment seemed ripe for Indian people accepting Hindutva.'[41] All that changed at 5:17 p.m. on 30 January 1948 when a Hindu Mahasabha member who had worked in the RSS pumped three bullets into Mohandas Gandhi's chest.

* * *

Nathuram was born Ramachandra Godse in 1910 in Pune district. Three male children before him had died, and to ward of this curse, his parents brought him up as a girl for the first few years, even piercing his nose with a 'nath', the Marathi word for nose-ring. The teenage Nathuram Godse had been enamoured of the Mahatma, wore a Gandhi cap and shouted satyagraha slogans. But when his postmaster father was transferred to Ratnagiri in 1930, he came into contact with V.D. Savarkar.[42] Godse's bearing—chin shaven, eyes intense—began to mimic Savarkar's, as did his world view: the belief that Muslims were dividing Hindus, and that the Congress along with the British was assisting them. Godse, like Savarkar, was jealous of Gandhi's political skills in attracting Hindus to the Congress over the Mahasabha. It was envy mixed with the rage that Gandhi was blinding Hindus to their own interests. Godse coupled this with a critique of caste divisions. In his own words: 'I openly joined [the] RSS wing of anti-caste movements and maintained that all Hindus were of equal status as to rights, social and religious and should be considered high or low on merit alone and not through the accident of birth in a particular caste or profession.'[43]

Where Godse differed was in his penchant for violence. The RSS's preoccupation was Hindu unity. Its support for violence was, conceptually at least, only as a defence mechanism to protect Hindus during riots. But for Godse, pre-emptive violence was sometimes necessary. For the RSS, the lesson of Shivaji was that he had consolidated power by uniting Hindus. For Godse: 'It was absolutely correct tactics for Shivaji to kill Afzal Khan as the latter would otherwise have surely killed him.'[44] Gandhi was not just another politician leading Hindu voters astray, his non-violence mirrored the historic weakness of Hindu society.

In 1943, Godse started a Marathi paper, *Agrani*. The paper had a photograph of Savarkar on its masthead (in return, perhaps, for Savarkar's 15,000-rupee seed money).[45] The *Agrani* was critical of Gandhi's concessions to the Muslim League. It also had another, more unexpected, target.

'Godse used to abuse us,' the Rashtriya Swayamsevak Sangh's M.G. Vaidya says, 'he saw us as too slow and gradual.'[46] L.K. Advani later claimed that Godse's criticisms in these pages 'show how bitter he was to the RSS'. Godse felt that '. . . the RSS had sublimated the "militant spirit" among the Hindus making them incapable of aggressive action'.[47]

The partition of India's religious territory radicalized Godse further. On 12 January 1948, Gandhi announced another fast, to prod India to pay Pakistan its share of British India's finances.[48] This was the last straw for Godse: 'The accumulating provocation of 32 years culminating in his last pro Muslim fast at last goaded me to the conclusion that the existence of Gandhiji should be brought to an end immediately.'[49] Soon after, Nathuram Godse, along with his *Agrani* co-editor Narayan Apte and a Punjabi refugee called Madanlal Pahwa, decided to act.

On 20 January 1948, Pahwa ignited an explosive at Birla House in Delhi where Gandhi was staying.[50] The explosion did no damage and Pahwa was let off. Ten days later, Godse and Apte went to Birla House. Godse was carrying a Beretta 9mm semi-automatic[51] that had belonged to an employee of the Maharaja of Gwalior.[52]

The judge who heard Godse's crime describes what happened next: 'The prayer meeting had not yet started, but a crowd of about 200 persons was awaiting the arrival of Mahatma Gandhi. Godse was moving among the people apparently unconcerned. Suddenly, there was a stirring in the crowd, and everyone stood up to form a passage for Mahatma Gandhi, who was seen coming up slowly with his hands resting on the shoulders of two girls who were walking by his side. As he raised his hands to join them in the customary greeting, Godse took a quick step forward, pushed aside the girl on Gandhiji's right and, standing in front of him, fired three shots in quick succession at point-blank range.'[53] Gandhi's last words were 'Hey Ram, Hey Ram'.[54]

Godse was arrested along with nine others.[55] These included Narayan Apte and Digambar Badge—the latter helped the government's case against the others. It also included the pioneer of Hindutva, V.D. Savarkar.

The trial was conducted at the Red Fort in Delhi. The seat of Mughal power was chosen to signal continuity with the past as well as new India's secular credentials.[56] One hundred and forty-nine prosecution witnesses testified over a ten-month period. The judge convicted Godse and Apte and sentenced them to death. The others were sentenced to life in prison. Savarkar alone was let off for lack of evidence.[57] Godse was hung from Ambala jail on 15 November 1949. He walked to the gallows clutching a copy of the Bhagavadgita.[58]

There is no mystery about why Godse killed Gandhi. He provided a ninety-three-page explanation in court.[59] Apart from criticizing Gandhi's non-violence, Godse advocated his own vision of a Hindu state. It is an elected state based on what he termed 'joint electorates', i.e., one-person-one-vote. He was even willing to agree to 'the temporary introduction of separate electorates since the Muslims were keen on them'. He however 'insisted that representation should be granted in strict proportion to the number of every community and no more'.[60] His fury with the Mahatma was that he had bowed before the Muslim League's demands, in effect reducing the voting power of India's 75 per cent Hindus.

Godse was only mouthing the demographic anxieties born out of electoral competition that had plagued Savarkar, the Mahasabha and the RSS. There is no mystery about Godse's motives; they are the motives of Hindu nationalism.

More debatable, however, is the identity of all those who helped Godse kill Gandhi. Did it include the RSS, the Hindu Mahasabha and Savarkar?

Investigations revealed no link between the RSS leadership and Godse. A 1966 commission re-examined the conspiracy by scrutinizing 101 witnesses and 407 documents; it cleared the organization of any connection with the crime.[61] The most incisive critic of the RSS's role is the legal scholar A.G. Noorani. Even he says that the claim that the organization killed Gandhi is a straw man. The valid accusation, he says, is that Godse 'was a member of the RSS and shared its ideas'.[62]

That Godse had at one time been an RSS member is undisputed. It is less clear whether he was a member when he killed Gandhi. He himself denied it, as did Golwalkar.[63] The most detailed biographer of Gandhi, Ramachandra Guha, says that Godse had left the RSS by the time.[64] In 1992, L.K. Advani claimed that 'we have had nothing to do with Godse'.[65] In response, Gopal Godse said that his brother had never formally quit the RSS.[66]

The status of Godse's link to the RSS at the time he killed Gandhi will forever be debated. What is undebatable is that Godse did not share all of the ideas of the RSS. Far from supporting political violence, the RSS had wanted nothing to do with politics during this period. This is why Savarkar and Godse had publicly criticized the RSS through the mid-1940s. It is fair to conclude that the RSS played no institutional role in Gandhi's death.

The relationship of the Mahasabha to the killing is more convoluted. Gandhi's great-grandson, who has written a book on the assassination, says: 'Of the seven attempts on Gandhi's life, five involve the Pune unit of the Hindu Mahasabha.'[67] Immediately after the murder, Home Minister Vallabhbhai Patel wrote to Syama Prasad Mookerjee: 'There is no doubt in my mind that the extreme section of the Hindu Mahasabha was involved in this conspiracy.'[68] Godse and Apte were party members, and Savarkar was a former president. The current president spoke of a 'feeling of shame and humiliation, as the alleged assassin belonged to the Mahasabha'.[69] Yet, the Mahasabha was not banned after the killing. Nehru and Patel had realized that those involved were a splinter group unconnected with a Mahasabha leadership that included their own cabinet colleague.

What to make, however, of the role of Savarkar? Unlike the RSS and the Mahasabha, Savarkar was 'charge-sheeted' for the murder, i.e., the police and magistrate thought there was a strong enough case against him. Through the trial in the Red Fort,[70] he sat in the dock in the back row, avoiding Godse's eyes. The prosecution tried to establish that Godse and Apte had met Savarkar while planning the murder. But what was discussed remains unknown. When the judge asked Godse whether he was acting under the advice of Savarkar, Godse rejected this 'unjust and untrue charge'.[71] The prosecution case tying Savarkar to the conspiracy hinged on a single incident. Digambar Badge, who had turned 'approver' for the prosecution, told the court that after a meeting with Apte and Godse three days before the attempt on Gandhi's life on 20 January, Savarkar saw them off at the entrance with the Marathi words: 'Yashasvi hovun ya.'[72] Come back victorious.

But no witnesses could corroborate this. Savarkar was declared not guilty and spent the next eighteen years in Bombay. His family remained close to the Godses; his niece married Godse's nephew.

After Savarkar's death in 1966, a government-appointed commission reinvestigated Gandhi's murder. Savarkar's secretary and bodyguard testified that he had met Godse and Apte just before Gandhi was killed. This testimony had not been produced in the original trial. The commission concluded: 'All these facts taken together were destructive of any theory other than the conspiracy to murder by Savarkar and his group.'[73] This was only a commission finding, not a court judgment; Savarkar remains legally innocent. When the Supreme Court was asked to reinvestigate the murder fifty years later, the court-appointed lawyer examined the evidence and concluded: 'Since the late Vinayak D. Savarkar had been acquitted, at this stage, it would neither be advisable/desirable nor possible to come to a definitive finding with respect to Vinayak D. Savarkar's role in the assassination of Mahatma Gandhi.'[74]

In the immediate aftermath of the murder in January 1948, however, these fine distinctions were yet unknown. Apart from arresting Savarkar and eight others, the government turned its attention on the shadowy group that Godse had once been a member of. This organization had so far avoided politics, refusing to develop a theory on the state. But now, after the murder of Mohandas, it was the state that was developing a theory on the RSS.

* * *

M.S. Golwalkar was organizing in Madras when news reached him of Gandhi's death.[75] He immediately sent a wire to Nehru and Patel in Hindi. Golwalkar called Gandhi a 'great personality' and an 'unparalleled organiser'. He asked all RSS shakhas to observe a thirteen-day grieving period.[76] The next day he wrote to Nehru and Patel: 'My heart is filled with worries thinking of the future.'[77]

He was prescient. On 3 February 1948, the RSS leadership in Nagpur sent a terse message to shakhas across India: 'Guruji interned. Be calm at all costs.'[78] The next day, the government banned the RSS and arrested 20,000[79] of its five million members,[80] including almost every pracharak.[81] The RSS remembers this ban—which would last for the next seventeen months—as its most traumatic period. M.G. Vaidya, who was a member then, recalls: 'Everyone was against the RSS—*janata, sarkar, akhbar* [the people, government, press].'[82]

Ordinary Indians began to attack RSS men, burning their houses, vandalizing their offices. Irate crowds surrounded the RSS office in Delhi. Among those participating was the Congressman Jayaprakash Narayan,[83] who would ally with the RSS three decades later. The police even had to declare a curfew in Poona[84] to protect the RSS from an outraged mob. The Brahmins, who were seen as associated with the RSS and Godse, were specifically targeted. In Nagpur, a horde swarmed the office of an RSS weekly newspaper and smashed furniture. The Hindu Mahasabha office was also 'rifled' through. Another thousand-strong mob marched on the RSS headquarters and house of Golwalkar. Local Congress leaders had to intervene to protect them from physical harm.[85]

Its workers went into hiding. M.G. Vaidya remembers doing underground work—printing pamphlets, cyclostyling material—during the ban. 'I used to wear a necktie. The police did not think anyone with a necktie will be doing sangh work. So I was not suspected.'[86] Another RSS worker can still remember the ordeal. 'I was pracharak in what is today Washim zilla [district]. I was harassed. I found it hard to get food and drink as pracharaks depend on local people for that. So I ate *sev-chiwda* for four months. I did not even have a cycle. People were afraid to call me home for food since I was a *sangh ka aadmi.*'

L.K. Advani was in Alwar at the time. He was among the 'tens of thousands of RSS *swayamsevaks*, including most *pracharaks* [who] were put behind bars'.[87] Like the rest of his tribe, Advani had opposed Gandhi's negotiations with the Muslim League. But Gandhi's 'absolute honesty and the purity of his personality'[88] resonated with Advani. He spent the next three months in Alwar jail.

Advani was only allowed three thick rotis and tasteless dal, served just twice a day.[89] On release in August 1948, he spent the next several months moving from house to house to avoid detection. Advani's ordeal during this ban would mirror his tribulations the second time the RSS was banned, during the Emergency from 1975 to 1977.

Vajpayee's whereabouts during this ban would similarly echo his experience of the Emergency. The young editor was not arrested. It was just as well; unlike Advani, the epicurean would probably not have been able to survive the chunky rotis and insipid dal.

By February 1949, it was clear to the government that the RSS had no role in the killing of Gandhi. The ban was lifted in July 1949.[90] As barter, the government required the RSS to write a Constitution where it pledged loyalty to the Indian Constitution and flag, and vowed to remain apolitical.[91] The RSS adopted a Constitution two months later. It reiterated its original aim: 'unification of diverse groups within Hindu samaj', based on 'dharma' [religion] and 'sanskriti' [culture].[92]

The RSS Constitution also stressed its aversion to politics. But privately the RSS was rethinking this disavowal. Its leadership had noticed that few politicians had defended the RSS after Gandhi's death. Ravindra Bhagwat comes from an RSS family; his brother is the current head. He says: 'What I have heard is that after the illegal 1948 ban, there was not a single person in parliament talking against the ban.'[93]

Another RSS member points to another lesson learnt. 'We noticed that the Mahasabha was not banned.' This was despite Savarkar, Godse and Apte having been more active in the Mahasabha compared to the RSS. The reason for this, the RSS concluded, was that the Hindu Mahasabha had a footprint in parliament and the union cabinet. Political presence had protected the Mahasabha, while political absence had made the RSS vulnerable.

The RSS's turn towards politics was also being aided by changes in the Congress. Gandhi's death had left his party in the hands of his two lieutenants. Though sharing many dreams for a new India, Prime

Minister Jawaharlal Nehru and Deputy Prime Minister Vallabhbhai Patel had contrasting instincts towards Hindu nationalism. The RSS watched. Whose impulse triumphed would dictate whether the RSS would be content with being a social organization, or whether it would need a party of its own.

* * *

Born into a landowning family in Gujarat in 1875, Vallabhbhai Patel rose up as a lawyer in the judicial bureaucracy. He worked as a district pleader in Godhra, where a hundred years later, a burning train would end Vajpayee and Advani's careers and bring to life Narendra Modi and Amit Shah's. Older than Nehru and less anglicized, the balding Patel rarely smiled and only spoke after weighing his words. He enjoyed organizational work and had the devotion of the cadre.[94]

As India's first home minister, Patel integrated the 500-plus princely states into India, earning him the praise of Hindu nationalists still scarred by the partition of their sacred land.[95] Most of these states were ones where the ruler and the ruled were of the same religion, making it easy to integrate them into independent India. Three states, however, posed problems. Hindu-majority Hyderabad and Junagadh were ruled by Muslim kings. Kashmir on the other hand was a Muslim-majority province ruled by a Hindu king. Unlike the other two, Kashmir was also contiguous with West Pakistan. The logic of the two-nation theory dictated that it go to Pakistan.

That the Congress had reconciled itself to this can be seen from Patel's 'firm assurances' to Mountbatten, just before partition, that 'if [the Maharaja of Kashmir] acceded to Pakistan, India would not take it amiss'.[96] In a speech after independence, Patel said: 'Pakistan attempted to set off Kashmir against Junagadh. When we raised the question of settlement in a democratic way, they (Pakistan) at once told us that they would consider it if we applied that policy to Kashmir. Our reply was that we would agree to Kashmir if they agreed to Hyderabad.'[97] Had Pakistan given up Junagadh and Hyderabad state, the new Indian government would likely have accepted Pakistan's claim on Kashmir.

What surprised both Nehru and Patel was that on 15 August 1947, the Nawab of Junagadh, an eccentric devoted to his 400 dogs, announced that he was joining Pakistan. More infuriating for them, Pakistan accepted, even though Junagadh was a Hindu-majority province with no land connections to Pakistan.

Meanwhile in Kashmir, worried that the Hindu king would accede to India, Jinnah sent irregular troops to take over the state. A terrified Maharaja signed the accession treaty with India on 26 October 1947, and Indian troops pushed back the Pakistani irregulars. They soon seized Junagadh, as well as Hyderabad state. Jinnah's craving for all three princely states meant that he ended up having none.

What gave credence to the Indian claim on Kashmir was of course the agreed-upon partition principle that gave princes the power to decide for their state. But what lent legitimacy to the annexation was that Kashmir's most popular leader, Sheikh Abdullah, was in favour of India. The matter could have ended there, but for two decisions whose consequences play out to this day.

The most important of these was the government's choice, prodded by Mountbatten,[98] to agree to a ceasefire (Indian troops stopped at what is now referred to as the line of control) and ask the United Nations to mediate. UN Security Council Resolution 47, adopted in April 1948, provided a three-step process to solve the dispute, culminating in a plebiscite.[99] Both India and Pakistan rejected the UN resolution,[100] which has never been implemented. India argues that the conditions for a plebiscite have changed, and Pakistan never followed the first step, i.e., the withdrawal of its armed nationals from its part of Kashmir. Pakistan continues to insist that a plebiscite take place.

The other decision that has kept Kashmir unresolved was once again a choice by India's first prime minister. A scholar who has examined the original instrument of accession signed by the Kashmir king says: 'Every one of the 140 princely states that signed IoAs with the Dominion of India agreed to the same terms and conditions as J&K'.[101] These legal terms under which Kashmir acceded to India was under the Indian Independence Act and were not unique. What was singular was that the Nehru government thought that Muslim-majority Kashmir required constitutional provisions to protect its status. Nehru discussed the matter at length with his cabinet, and then the constituent assembly. The result: Article 370 of the Indian Constitution.[102]

The import of this article was to hold that Indian laws applied to Kashmir only with regard to defence, foreign affairs and communication. Like with some select parts of the country, Indians from other states required a special permit to enter Kashmir in the early years, and were banned from buying property in the state.[103] And unlike anywhere else, the state was allowed its own Constitution, prime minister, laws and flag.

These compromises were distasteful for a man who had effectively integrated all the other princely states into India. As Patel said in a speech in 1948: 'We have seen what price we have paid in Kashmir by going to that [United Nations] organisation.'[104] His biographer Rajmohan Gandhi says: 'Patel was unhappy with many of India's steps over Kashmir, including the offer of a plebiscite, the reference to the UN, the ceasefire that left a fair part of the State in Pakistani hands and the removal of the Maharaja. But though occasionally dropping a remark or a hint, he never spelt out his own solution.'[105]

The Hindu nationalists, on the other hand, spelt out their solution then, did so in manifesto after manifesto for the next seventy years, and finally got it written down in 2019. That was the year the Narendra Modi government used its parliamentary majority to pass legislation ending this special status for Kashmir.

* * *

If Kashmir showcases one disagreement between Nehru and Patel, their reactions to rebuilding the Somnath temple demonstrate another. The temple was located in the princely state of Junagadh and had been ravaged by Mahmud of Ghazni in the eleventh century. How critical this wound was to Hindu consciousness is contested.[106] What is clear is that K.M. Munshi's book on the ruin of Somnath, written in the early twentieth century, provided a rising Hindu nationalism with a parable to hold on to.[107]

With Junagadh annexed by November 1947, Somnath was now under Indian sovereignty. Patel travelled there three days later and declared that the Somnath temple would be rebuilt.[108] Nehru was uncomfortable with a secular state participating in a religious project. Funds for the reconstruction were collected privately and with help from the RSS.

Yet another 'Hindu' issue on which Nehru and Patel argued was the Babri mosque, built in 1528 by a courtier to the Mughal emperor who named it after his master. It was located in Ayodhya, which is revered in Hindu tradition as the birthplace of the god Ram.[109] Since at least the nineteenth century, there are records of violence between local Hindus and Muslims, with Hindus claiming the mosque stood atop a Hindu temple that marked the birthplace of Ram.

Now in 1949, a Hindu group placed idols inside the mosque.[110] A 'disturbed' Nehru demanded, via telegram, that the state chief minister 'undo the wrong'.[111] Patel saw the telegram and wrote his own letter to the chief minister. Though he deplored any use of force, Patel wrote: 'I realise there is a great deal of sentiment behind the move which has taken place.'[112] Fifty years later, Advani would depose before a judicial commission on the charge of obliterating the Babri mosque. He would stress this phrase in Patel's letter, adding: 'I would endorse every word of what he had said.'[113]

A final issue on which Nehru and Patel adopted opposing approaches was the question of Hindu refugees from East Bengal. Unlike Punjab where the ethnic cleansing of minorities on both sides was near total, there continued to be eleven million Hindus in East Pakistan (around 28 per cent of the population), while the five million Muslims in West Bengal constituted 24 per cent of the population.[114] Violence eventually flared up. In just the month of February 1950, anti-Hindu riots in East Pakistan killed 10,000. An estimated 860,000 Hindus crossed over,[115] while 650,000 Muslims left West Bengal for the other side.[116]

Patel warned Pakistan: 'If you are determined to turn out Hindus, you must part with sufficient land to enable us to settle down.'[117] Nehru on the other hand advocated a 'long distance dispassionate view . . . Any claim for territory is completely unreal.'[118] In the end, it was Nehru who won, avoiding war and signing an agreement with Pakistan's prime minister that listed mechanisms for both sides to protect minorities and stem the flow of refugees.[119]

Industry Minister Syama Prasad Mookerjee saw this as a sell-out. He had resigned from the Hindu Mahasabha over his party's reluctance to admit non-Hindus soon after Gandhi's assassination in 1948. Now, in April 1950, he resigned from Nehru's cabinet. The Mahasabha congratulated its prodigal son, as did the RSS. But even they realized that with Mookerjee's exit, their influence over the government was diminished.

This fear was amplified eight months later, when the seventy-five-year-old Vallabhbhai Patel died of a heart attack in Bombay. Patel had always been more sympathetic to the RSS than Nehru. He saw them as 'patriots who love their country. Only their trend of thought is diverted.'[120] Months before his death, he had ensured that the Congress passed a resolution allowing RSS workers to join. It took Nehru's personal intervention to scuttle the plan.[121]

The historian Ramachandra Guha writes: 'Nehru and Patel were colleagues not rivals, co-workers not adversaries. Working individually, and together, they united India and gave it a democratic template.'[122] But these differences on the RSS, Pakistan, Kashmir, Somnath and Ayodhya have led Hindu nationalists to see Patel as the first prime minister India never had.

Advani, who would eventually occupy Patel's office, would imitate India's first home minister. Vajpayee, on the other hand, would model himself after India's first premier. As we shall see through this book, he would maintain a distance from the RSS, and would follow his idol in making the most concessions any prime minister has made to Pakistan and Kashmir.

All that would come later. For now, with his deputy gone in December 1950, the prime minister was unfettered to shape his party, his government and his country. And he wanted that shape to be in opposition to the Rashtriya Swayamsevak Sangh and the Hindu Mahasabha. Faced with an unconstrained Jawaharlal Nehru, the RSS needed a new insurance policy.

3

IN NEHRU'S SHADOW (1951–67)

Some months before Sardar Patel's death, the recently resigned cabinet minister Syama Prasad Mookerjee travelled 1000 kilometres from Delhi to Nagpur. There he visited a bare brick-and-stone colonial bungalow that had previously lodged V.D. Savarkar.[1]

Waiting at the house was the bearded chief of the Rashtriya Swayamsevak Sangh. Free India's first elections were a year away, and Mookerjee asked M.S. Golwalkar for help to start a new party. It would compete for the Hindu vote against the Mahasabha, the party Mookerjee had left after it had refused to admit non-Hindus in the aftermath of Gandhi's assassination. Golwalkar refused. 'I warned him that [the] *sangh* will not become tail of any political party.'[2] '[Golwalkar's] aloofness from politics often bordered on aversion,' L.K. Advani remembers.[3]

Mookerjee was not discouraged. He knew that after the lacerations from the 1948 ban, there were enough within the RSS who wanted to buy 'political insurance'. So confident was Mookerjee that he met the Mahasabha president and told him 'to wind up the Hindoo Mahasabha and join his new party which he was going to establish under his own leadership with the help of Mr. Golwalkar of the [RSS]'.[4]

Four months later, and spurred by the death of Patel, Mookerjee called a meeting to plan the new party. He took care to ensure that leaders from the RSS were present.[5] A note to the draft Constitution suggested that 'Guruji [i.e., Golwalkar] should be persuaded to lend support of the organisation.'[6] It also explained why: 'The RSS has a strong volunteer organisation and a growing press under its management. It has a body of workers of startling merit.'[7] What is notable about this analysis, written in 1951, is that it continues to explain why the Bharatiya Janata Party needs the RSS today.

In order to escape the factionalism native to Hindu society, the RSS had given its head supreme, unhindered authority. But Golwalkar's order to stay away from politics was being flouted by his own deputies. In any other Indian group, such a rudimentary divergence would have resulted in rupture.

But Golwalkar decided to forgo self for unity. He decided to support Mookerjee in forming a new party. 'I will give you five gold pieces,' he promised Mookerjee. Soon after, a few RSS leaders were deputed to the new party. These included Deendayal Upadhyaya, Sunder Singh Bhandari, Nanaji Deshmukh, Bapusaheb Sohni and Balraj Madhok. Vajpayee and Advani were as yet too minor to have their worth weighed in gold.

At a meeting of 400 delegates a few months later, on 21 October 1951, the 'Bharatiya Jana Sangh' or 'Indian People's Organization' was founded. The 'fundamentals' of the party manifesto promised 'One country', 'One nation', 'One culture' and 'Dharma Rajya Not Theocracy But Rule Of Law'.[8] The election symbol was an earthen lamp with a burning flame.[9] Party president Mookerjee fuelled the fire in his presidential speech, holding that 'the partition of Bharat was a tragic folly' and blaming Jawaharlal Nehru. He took care, though, to deny the charge of communalism. Diverging from the Hindu Mahasabha he had abandoned in 1948, Mookerjee promised that membership of the new party would be open to all religions.[10]

Syama Prasad Mookerjee was deliberately made the face of the party, so that the light would not shine on an organization still recovering from a debilitating ban. But behind the scenes, the RSS took care to retain enough power. The all-powerful general secretary soon became an RSS man—someone reedy thin, with a thinner moustache, thick glasses and a flair for logistics.

This was Deendayal Upadhyaya, born in 1916 near Lord Krishna's birthplace of Mathura to parents who were poor, religious and Brahmin. Deendayal had been orphaned young, and had since lost several blood relatives.[11] Faced with such tragedy, he had found a lasting family in the RSS.

Unlike Mookerjee, Deendayal was uncomfortable with English, and unlike Vajpayee, he was uncomfortable with the limelight. And though he was a prolific writer,[12] he was not, as we shall see, an original one. What made Deendayal potent were not words or wisdom, but the discernment to spot and steer talent. It made him the ideal power behind the Jana Sangh throne.

This dual power structure of the party at the national level—where Mookerjee was the narrator and the RSS's Deendayal the scriptwriter—was mimicked at the regional level. A 'general secretary' was the formal head in the state. Technically below him, but in practice the holder of actual power, was the '*sanghatan mantri*' or organization secretary.[13] This latter post was always held by an RSS man. For instance, L.K. Advani, the pracharak for Rajasthan, was given 'organisational responsibility for the party in the state'.[14]

The other feature of the new party was a restrained role for religion. Though pictures of gods were displayed on stage during the October inaugural,[15] the Jana Sangh preferred its Hinduism to be a silhouette identity rather than overt belief. Mookerjee ensured that the word 'Hindu' did not appear in the party name.

These founding decisions caused ruptures, between Jana Sangh and RSS workers, between believers and atheists. Besides, there persisted within the RSS a strand that believed that Nehru would 'live to regret the failure of universal adult franchise in India'.[16] What stitched these slits back into one piece was an ethos of compromise, an ideology in itself. The RSS took care to avoid swaying policy, and Golwalkar decided to play down his piety in these early years.

This devotion to organizational unity meant that there were two kinds of politicians the new party did not need: prima donnas and ideologues. One would split the party through temperament, the other through theorems. On the other hand, it was clear from the opening pair of Mookerjee and Deendayal itself that there were two sorts of politicians they would need: orators who could pacify parliament; organizers who carry along the cadre. Vajpayee and Advani—yet to meet, yet to mature—would not have known it then. But their party was anticipating their dispositions.

* * *

Four days after the founding of the Jana Sangh in October 1951, voting began for the first free elections in Indian history.[17] These elections were based on the Westminster system of parliamentary democracy. The whole country was divided into constituencies, with parties selecting candidates for each of them. The candidate who won the most votes in each constituency would become its member of parliament or MP. The party with the most MPs could select the prime minister and form the government. Approximately 176 million Indians were eligible to cast their ballots in 224,000 polling booths supervised by 56,000 officers, 280,000 helpers and 224,000 policemen.[18]

The Congress had its own lubricated vote-gathering machine built by Vallabhbhai Patel. But the face of the party was without question Jawaharlal Nehru. And with the death of Patel in 1950, Nehru's vision for an Independent India—whether state-driven industrialization or the particular paranoia of the majority religion taking over the state—had become common sense in the central hall of parliament.

Taking on Nehru's Congress was Syama Prasad Mookerjee. His campaign speeches were able to draw crowds with his attacks on Jawaharlal Nehru and Pakistan. But he was well aware that the Jana Sangh, from an ideology tainted by the murder of the Mahatma, had to operate within the 'Nehruvian mainstream'. His party paid lip service to peasants, women and Scheduled Castes,[19] and did not oppose state intervention in the economy.[20] Its opposition to cow slaughter[21] as well as to the Hindu code bill[22] were subdued. Since the average voter in the 1950s operated within Nehru's idea of India, it made sense for Mookerjee to do so too.

Where Mookerjee made less sense was when he spoke Hindi, a prerequisite to canvass in the cow belt. The bhadralok politician was, in fact, disdainful of the attitude that 'India, that is Bharat, that is Uttar Pradesh'.[23] But UP was the heart of the Jana Sangh vote bank, and Deendayal Upadhyaya decided that Mookerjee needed a competent Hindi translator to accompany him there. His eyes fell on a twenty-seven-year-old currently editing an RSS magazine.

Atal Bihari Vajpayee had already distinguished himself as a Hindi orator, a skill he had picked up from his teacher father. His way with words had led Deendayal to place them on the pages of *Panchajanya*. And so it was that during the campaign for the 1951–52 elections, Vajpayee chaperoned Mookerjee as his Hindi translator.[24]

This is why Vajpayee travelled by train with Mookerjee to reach Kota in Rajasthan at the height of the campaign. The RSS was the backbone of the Jana Sangh campaign. And so it was entirely expected that the pracharak coordinating the election campaign in the state received them at the station.[25] There was chemistry right away.

This was the first time that Lal Krishna Advani met Atal Bihari Vajpayee, and the twenty-five-year-old was straightaway smitten. Nearly sixty years later, Advani could still recall his first impression of 'a poet who had drifted into politics . . . Something was smoldering within him, and the fire in his belly produced an unmistakable glow on his face.'[26]

It is telling that while Advani has discussed this first meeting in his biography, there is no record of Vajpayee ever having remembered it. Advani was still dealing with the demons of partition in the expanses of Rajasthan. Vajpayee, on the other hand, was naturally more outgoing and had not suffered the trauma of loss. His speech skills had made him the voice of the face of the movement. Advani would remain a star-struck fan for the rest of his life.

* * *

Vajpayee and Advani's campaigning had little effect on India's first election. They were an expected victory for Nehru's Congress, whose MPs formed an easy majority in parliament. The Jana Sangh won only three of the ninety-four seats it contested. But the 3.06 per cent vote share it won gave it the label of a national party. This vote share was higher than that of the Hindu Mahasabha or the Ram Rajya party, establishing the Jana Sangh as the *primary* party of political Hinduism.

Though Vajpayee's Hindi translations had not translated into many seats, Mookerjee kept him on, tasking him with parliamentary work and stenography.[27] While Advani continued operating in Rajasthani villages, Vajpayee's entry into Lutyens' Delhi had begun.

Contrary to the expectation that Mookerjee would now retreat to parliament, he expended his energy on the street.

In June 1953, he made yet another journey to Kashmir to protest what he deemed the non-applicability of the Indian Constitution to the state. Accompanying Mookerjee was a small group that included the by-now-indispensable Atal Bihari Vajpayee. When they reached the state border at Pathankot, Mookerjee was arrested.[28] He probably thought that the arrest would be brief, and sent Vajpayee back to Delhi to continue the agitation.[29] Mookerjee was moved to a house on the outskirts of Srinagar. It was in this 'house arrest' that Mookerjee complained of feeling uneasy. He was admitted to a government hospital on 22 June. Mookerjee sent a telegram to his brother saying that there was nothing to worry about; 'satisfactory arrangements had been made for his treatment'.[30]

Had Mookerjee's self-diagnosis been accurate, the fifty-one-year-old would have recovered and returned to parliament. Vajpayee would have likely remained his subordinate, with no opening presenting itself for at least a decade. Advani, on the other hand, could well have continued in Rajasthan, inching his way up the ranks. They may have continued to live parallel lives, and their ephemeral meeting in 1951 may have remained just that. All that changed on 23 June 1953, when Mookerjee's weak heart stopped beating.

* * *

When Syama Prasad Mookerjee's eighty-two-year-old mother heard of her son's death, she fainted.[31] The rest of his party reacted likewise. The death provided Hindu nationalism with yet another conspiracy to blame on Nehru. It also provided Vajpayee with the unexpected chance to succeed Mookerjee as the party's voice in parliament.

This opportunity first came a year later, in 1954, after Nehru's sister Vijayalakshmi Pandit resigned as member of parliament from Lucknow in order to become India's representative to the United Nations. Deendayal decided that the twenty-nine-year-old Vajpayee would contest on behalf of the Jana Sangh. It was a favour Vajpayee never forgot. The journalist and BJP politician Swapan Dasgupta says: 'Atalji's desk always had a photo of Deendayalji. I was very struck by that. Because Atalji would not normally do this kind of thing.'[32]

This first election of Vajpayee's was a fiasco. Not only did he lose, he placed third.[33] When Vajpayee heard the results, however, he chose to grieve by cycling to a nearby theatre to watch a film with his friend.[34]

Deendayal was as unfazed. Vajpayee had spoken hypnotically in that failed campaign, and Deendayal decided to redeploy his words throughout the Hindi heartland. Old-timers recall how, in these years, Vajpayee made a name for himself as a speaking replacement for Mookerjee.[35] And when the next general elections were scheduled for 1957, Vajpayee was given three Lok Sabha tickets to contest from: Balrampur, Lucknow and Mathura.[36] Though he lost from the latter two, he won Balrampur, formerly a princely state ruled during British times by a Hindu king.[37] It was a constituency where the landlords were Muslim, the peasants Hindu.[38] The man who would eventually cultivate a secular persona owed his first election victory to these realities of religion.

Vajpayee entered the Lok Sabha aged thirty-three.[39] Though three other Jana Sangh candidates had won, it was Vajpayee whom Deendayal made leader of the party in the Lok Sabha. It was a position that Vajpayee would most identify with for the next fifty-two years. He did not care who ran the party; he only cared that he spoke for it in parliament.

In his brief time in the Jana Sangh, Syama Prasad Mookerjee had demonstrated the value of parliamentary erudition. But Mookerjee had also revealed the merit of another trait: he was a westernized English speaker who could parlay with the media, with foreign diplomats, with those politicians who did not speak Hindi, and with Jawaharlal Nehru. An RSS man active during that period says: 'There are two types of Indians. Those who use Western toilets and those who use Indian toilets. We use Indian toilets. [But] we need some people who use Western toilets.'

If Vajpayee was an orator in Mookerjee's mould, L.K. Advani was very much from the cosmopolitan world of Karachi. Deendayal had always noticed this about Advani, and so, soon after the 1957 elections, Advani was moved to Delhi.[40] His job was to help the new parliamentarian Atal Bihari Vajpayee navigate the English-speaking elite of Lutyens' Delhi.

This was their first sustained interaction, and one that set the terms for the next six decades of their relationship. Vajpayee was already a star, someone who had become the face of the movement at an unusually early age. The thirty-year-old Advani, on the other hand, was a political nobody.

He had never given a public speech, and doubted he ever could. He was in awe of Vajpayee's talent, and anxious about the lack of his own. He was the ideal foil, Watson to Sherlock Holmes.

Advani first moved into Vajpayee's whitewashed government bungalow on 30 Rajendra Prasad Road near parliament and began to spend time with the new MP. They were joined by a twenty-year-old N.M. Ghatate, who was from RSS blueblood.

While lowly swayamsevaks emerged from a variety of backgrounds, the RSS leadership tended to come from a closely knit circle of lower-middle-class clans from the Nagpur region. Most of these families were not just Maharashtrian Brahmins, they were from the two specific sub-castes of Deshastha and Karhade. Ghatate's father, a Deshastha Brahmin, had been an RSS and Hindu Mahasabha pioneer. His family was held in esteem by the sangh parivar, the constellation of organizations around the RSS. And so it was but natural that when Ghatate left Nagpur to study law in Delhi in 1957, he was asked to meet the brand-new Jana Sangh member of parliament.

Vajpayee and Ghatate became immediate friends, at the very time Vajpayee and Advani were getting to know each other. It was a relationship that would last six decades; two of them politicians, one of them their lawyer, three of them friends.

Advani eventually moved to a modest room near the BJP office by the Ram Lila ground,[41] but continued to meet Vajpayee every day. 'They were softies at some level,' a family friend says. 'They understood this about each other.' 'From then on,' a later associate of Vajpayee and Advani, Sudheendra Kulkarni, says: 'I've heard from Namita [Vajpayee's daughter] that they were so close that hardly a day would pass without them speaking to each other on the phone.'[42]

Their relationship bloomed, even as it remained lopsided. Vajpayee was the guru, Advani the devotee. And friends they might be, but there was a spoken hierarchy between them that would persist through their six decades of camaraderie.

* * *

With just four of them in parliament, Jana Sangh MPs were allotted seats at the back, from where it was hard to catch the Speaker's eye. They were also entitled to minimal speaking time. Vajpayee bristled at these limitations; when once denied the chance to speak entirely, he told the Speaker: 'I am walking out as a protest.'[43] But in the few times that Vajpayee did get to speak, Advani remembers that he raised the profile of the Jana Sangh beyond its numbers.[44]

The new member of parliament developed a reputation for repartee. In an early speech he gave, Vajpayee began by attacking the left: 'Mr Speaker sir, the deputy leader of the communist party professor Hiren Mukherjee, for whom I have great respect . . .' Some MPs sarcastically interrupted him: 'Since when.' Without missing a beat, Vajpayee replied, 'For his learning and not for his views.'[45]

His biographer Ullekh N.P. has studied his speeches before and after he entered the Lok Sabha. Ullekh says, 'After Vajpayee began to attend parliament, the nature of his speeches changed. He began to speak in more parliamentary ways. The effect of parliament on his thinking was clear.'[46] When parliament was on, Vajpayee would spend evenings at home waiting for the uncorrected script of that day's parliamentary session to arrive on motorcycle. From the moment Vajpayee heard the motorcycle stop outside, usually around 5:30 p.m., all activity in the house would cease while Vajpayee rectified the script.[47]

A reputed Hindi poet judges Vajpayee's own poetry to be mediocre. 'But he had a sense of the sound of sentences [that was] better than politicians. So even though his poetry was not good, his speech was very good.'[48]

Just a year after Vajpayee entered parliament, Prime Minister Jawaharlal Nehru replied to Vajpayee's foreign policy opinions in Hindi, singling him out for praise.[49] When Soviet premier Nikita Khrushchev visited India around then, Nehru made sure to invite Vajpayee. When Nehru was introducing Vajpayee, he said: 'This is one of our future prime ministers.' Khrushchev replied: 'Then what is he doing here? In our country, we send them to the Gulag.'[50]

Advani, meanwhile, was assisting Vajpayee research his speeches as well as working with the Delhi unit of the Jana Sangh. He saw how the party of Hindus entered into an alliance with the communists for the 1958 Delhi municipal elections.[51] From being used to the certitude of the field, Advani was learning the give-and-take of politics. Some of Vajpayee's outlook was also rubbing off on the stolid Advani. When they lost that election, they decided to go see a film starring Raj Kapoor and Mala Sinha named *Phir Subah Hogi* or 'Morning Will Dawn Again'.[52] It is unlikely that the political theme of the film—the lead song, by Sahir Ludhianvi, was a critique of the unfilled promises of Nehruvian India—was why they chose to see it. The more likely explanation was that of two friends relishing an evening out, taking pleasure in other's company.

While films were a pastime for Vajpayee, they were a passion for Advani. In 1960, K.R. Malkani, the editor of *Organiser*, asked Advani to review films for the magazine. Advani would analyse Hindi films under the pen-name 'Netra' or 'Eye'. Even here, politics would intrude. 'Netra', for instance, expressed disapproval at Nehru's encouragement of the British producer Richard Attenborough's attempts to make a film on Gandhi (released in 1982, the film would eventually win eight Oscars). 'Netra' saw this as a slight on Indian film makers: 'Distrust of local talent and a fawning, unreasonable reliance on "foreign" experts has been the bane of all activities of our government.'[53]

This was the first time that Advani was earning a salary, a princely sum of 350 rupees a month.[54] To make up for abysmal pay, senior journalists were eligible for housing assistance from the Nehruvian state. It was thus that Advani was allotted a small apartment in R.K. Puram under the quota for journalists. After he had fled his mansion in Karachi thirteen years ago, this was Advani's first real accommodation. His neighbour was R. Rangarajan of *The Indian Express*. Every morning, Advani would drive his scooter to the RSS city headquarters in Jhandewalan, while Rangarajan rode pillion up to Bahadur Shah Zafar Marg. When Rangarajan got a car, his son, the historian Mahesh Rangarajan, says, 'The roles were reversed and the film critic got off and took a bus to Jhandewalan.'[55]

* * *

The third general elections in India were scheduled for February 1962. Vajpayee contested from Balrampur once again, and was pitted against the Congress candidate and freedom fighter Subhadra Joshi. But Vajpayee's real opponent was the colossus of parliament, who travelled all the way from Delhi to Balrampur to give a speech. Nehru's words ensured that

Vajpayee lost his Lok Sabha seat by a narrow margin.[56] His career was rescued once again by Deendayal, who gave Vajpayee a Rajya Sabha ticket, ensuring his unbroken presence in parliament.

Meanwhile, tensions between India and China, simmering for a while, had begun to boil.[57] Border fisticuffs between the two through the summer of 1962 expanded into a full-blown invasion by China. The result was defeat for the Indian army—unprepared, outmanned, and ill-led.

The RSS cast the response to the invasion as a '*dharmayudh*', i.e., a religious war to recover India's holy lands.[58] It triggered the RSS's instinct for 'defensive violence', which, along with Hindu unity, had been its founding rationale. When Nehru dismissed the loss of territory with, 'we have only lost some rocks, not fertile land,' Vajpayee replied, 'our country is not a piece of land, it's a living breathing national person'.[59] And when China tested its nuclear bomb a few years later, Vajpayee declared: 'What is the answer to the atom bomb? The answer to an atom bomb is an atom bomb, nothing else.'[60]

The war, a threat to Hindutva's holy map, proved a blessing to its legitimacy. The RSS had supported the war effort, even offering its cadre to assist the troops. As reward, Prime Minister Nehru did the unthinkable by permitting uniformed RSS cadre to march on Rajpath as part of the 1963 Republic Day parade.[61] As the *Organiser* reported, 'More than 2,000 Swayamsevaks in Delhi, in their full organisation uniform, white shirt, khaki knickers, belt, black cap and full boots took part in the parade and formed the major highlight of the Delhi Citizens group.'[62]

Contrary to those who see the 1975 Emergency as the mainstreaming of the RSS, it was the 1963 Republic Day that did that. The Congress party understood this then itself, as a meeting held soon after makes clear. To irate Congressmen, Nehru replied generically that all citizens had been called upon to participate and so the RSS also took part. A senior Congressmen asked: 'Why did not the Delhi Congress seva dal also take part in the parade?' The reply: 'Well, we had just 250 uniforms, and knowing that the RSS strength would be much greater, we thought that, in contrast, the seva dal would make a poor showing?'[63]

The increasing acceptance of Hindutva by Nehruvian India was spurred by the China war, no doubt. But it was also because the Jana Sangh had taken care to stay within the political consensus of the period.

There were three core beliefs on which they would not compromise: Hindu demographic concerns (in Assam), threats to religious territory (represented through Pakistan and China), and worries of unequal political rights (in Kashmir). Other than these, their guiding aim was to appeal to the average voter.[64]

Even as the Jana Sangh was moving closer to the prime minister, the seventy-four-year-old was moving closer to death. Nehru finally died in May 1964, of 'an internal haemorrhage, a paralytic stroke, and a heart attack'.[65] Vajpayee's condolence speech was pointed: 'The loss to Parliament is irreparable . . . In spite of a difference of opinion we have nothing but respect for his great ideals, his integrity, his love for the country and his indomitable courage.'[66]

The voice was Vajpayee of course, but the brain was Deendayal Upadhyaya. Without his concurrence, the RSS would never have allowed the Jana Sangh to project such a moderate air. Advani watched and took notes. As Sudheendra Kulkarni says, '[Advani] worked very closely with Deendayalji. He saw how Deendayalji had changed over the years. Advani used to very often refer to a book by the American academic Craig Baxter[67] that aggregation and social integration were as important as being an ideological party. He learnt [these views] by watching Deendayalji.'[68]

By 1964, therefore, the Jana Sangh was behaving less like a movement and more like a party, alive to the compromises that expanding a coalition demanded. The bleak nationalism of Savarkar and Golwalkar was concerned with what connected Hindus to each other. But it had never mapped out views on governance and policies *once* it came to power. Now, with its popularity rising, the time had come for it to articulate a governing ideology. And that articulation took place for the first time in the southern town of Vijayawada, where Deendayal Upadhyaya referred to the phrase 'Integral Humanism'.

* * *

Few present at the Jana Sangh's conclave that January 1965 grasped that the phrase would one day become its official ideology. 'I was present in Vijayawada. I was a sanghathan mantri,' M.G. Vaidya remembers. 'At the time, I didn't realize that it would be such a big thing.'[69] That realization would come three months later, when Deendayal gave four speeches in Bombay between 22 and 25 April, explaining exactly what 'Integral Humanism' meant.

Three features are noteworthy. First, he makes an earnest attempt to appear non-communal. 'There is freedom to worship according to one's religion . . . We called it a "Secular State" to contrast it with Pakistan.' He also dismisses the argument that India should uproot a thousand years of Muslim and British rule: 'The task of turning the waters of Ganga back to some previous point would not be wise.' A second feature of Deendayal's concept is that it is acrobatic on policy particulars. Deendayal is critical of the Congress 'system' with its multiple ideologies: 'If there can be a magic box which contains a cobra and a mongoose living together, it is Congress.' But his own definitions have room for the entire animal kingdom to reside within. The third feature of 'Integral Humanism' is its belief that a set of cultural norms (what Deendayal calls '*chitta*' or soul, based on dharma) predate the Indian state and the individual. It is these norms that bound Indians together.

The title and ideas in Deendayal's four speeches bear remarkable resemblance—without attribution—to a book published in 1936. It was titled *Integral Humanism: Temporal and Spiritual Problems of a New Christendom* by the Catholic thinker Jacques Maritain.[70] While Maritain's 'Integral Humanism' has since become the guide for the Christian Democratic parties of Europe, Deendayal's 'Integral Humanism' is the stated ideology of the BJP. Its flexibility in justifying any policy makes it the ideal election manifesto.

* * *

When he heard Deendayal Upadhyaya mention 'Integral Humanism' in Vijayawada in January 1965, Lal Krishna Advani was a thirty-seven-year-old bachelor. It is unlikely that those words left much of an impression, since Advani had something else on his mind.

At the end of the session, he left Vijayawada for Bombay, not his home in Delhi. It was about a girl.[71] Advani had fled Karachi aged nineteen, when men of means of the time considered marriage. He had spent the next decade in Rajasthan's villages and small towns, with neither means nor inclination. And as long as Advani was a pracharak, marriage was out of the question. But he had since moved into active politics in a large city, and now possessed an apartment, a salary and a position. His younger sister, who lived in Bombay, was keen that her brother get married. And since, as Advani put it, 'I had never befriended any lady in my life', his sister suggested a young girl from south Bombay.

The Jagtianis, like the Advanis, were a wealthy family from Karachi who had fled to Bombay during Partition. Their daughter, Kamla, was forced to work in the local post office. This was the story of many Sindhis, and it gave Lal and Kamla a shared identity, hardened by expulsion, even before they met.

When they did meet, they hit it off. A common friend who knew the Jagtianis at the time says: 'Kamla liked Advani for his sincerity. He came across as naïve . . . for a politician.' Advani was attracted to Kamla's matter-of-fact worldliness; she was the kind of sturdy harbour that could shelter a bobbing boat.

They were married that very month, with a reception held on the terrace of the Sindhi-owned K.C. College near Churchgate railway station.[72] For a man who has railed against special laws for minorities, there is some irony that L.K. Advani's wedding reception took place at a constitutionally sanctioned 'minority' educational institution.

Kamla would continue to work for the next few years in Delhi, and would be the dominant figure in Advani's life for the next fifty-one years. She was the primary breadwinner in those early years, while also bringing up their two children, Jayant and Pratibha. 'She would always refer to her husband as "Advani". It was an equal relationship,' says the journalist Karan Thapar, who knew the family well.[73] The BJP's Harin Pathak says: 'Mrs Advani kept all the accounts, all the income tax returns.'[74] He adds: 'I remember, there are so many photos in Advani's house. There is one on the dining table where Mrs Advani is staring at Advani, with piercing eyes. When guests would come, Advani would say, "If you see this photo, you can see whose raj runs in this house."'[75]

Advani's marriage—a steady, monogamous partnership—says much about the man. Vajpayee's personal life similarly says much about him. As Vajpayee himself put it, '*Mein avivahit hoon, kunwara nahin.*'[76] I am a bachelor, not a celibate.

Soon after he became a Lok Sabha MP, Vajpayee was invited to Ramjas College by some RSS students to give a talk. Present in the audience was a middle-aged philosophy professor, Brij Nath Kaul, along with his younger wife, Rajkumari. As we read earlier, Rajkumari and Vajpayee had been classmates in Gwalior in 1941, but the attraction had fizzled and they had lost touch for the next sixteen years. The Ramjas talk rekindled the flame.

From then on—and through the 1960s—the Kauls and Vajpayee were constantly in each other's homes. When B.N. Kaul became warden of Ramjas hostel, students would know that Vajpayee was visiting by an official black Ambassador car parked outside.[77] Kaul's children soon became Vajpayee's. He developed a special affection for the younger daughter, Namita, who was called Gunu.

Rajkumari Kaul acquired a reputation for helpfulness even then. When there was a milk shortage and MPs had extra coupons, 'Mrs Kaul gave the coupons to my wife for my children,' N.M. Ghatate remembers. 'She would also help with medicines and recommending doctors.'[78] The journalist Virendra Kapoor, who was then a student at Ramjas, says: 'I remember a young Ashok Saikia spending the money his father gave him on alcohol, so he didn't have enough for his fees. When Mr Kaul threatened to remove him, it was Mrs Kaul who gave him money to pay his fees.' Another former student remembers Gunu learning to walk, waddling barefoot in the corridors of the hostel. Years later, when he spoke sharply to Gunu about her influence in Prime Minister Vajpayee's office, she retorted, 'You don't see me as an adult. You still think of me that way [as a child].'

The heart of the relationship between Vajpayee and Rajkumari was intellectual. From a provincial north Indian milieu, Vajpayee was both perplexed by as well as attracted to an educated woman who could hold her own. Friends remember Rajkumari arguing with Vajpayee on politics, her persistent yet soft sentences a contrast with Vajpayee's commanding words. Rajkumari was fluent in English, well read and, unlike Vajpayee, came from an urbane family. As a Kashmiri Pandit in the Delhi of the 1960s, she had got to know the 'Kashmiri Mafia', i.e., the Pandit bureaucrats and officials who surrounded first Nehru, then his daughter— Rajkumari Kaul was after all a blood relation of Indira Gandhi. All this added up to a confident liberal.

This presented the RSS with a hurdle. As a family friend of the Kauls says: 'The RSS had a huge problem with aunty Kaul. Vajpayee was a show-boy and they were proud of him. But they were very scared of aunty Kaul. Aunty Kaul had a huge influence on Vajpayee. She was a very, very powerful woman. She also made Vajpayee far more mellow, secular, cosmopolitan than he initially was. He was quite a provincial politician before he met her.'

If Mr Kaul had an objection to the relationship, he never articulated it. 'He was a philosopher . . . self-absorbed,' another family friend says, '[he made] hardly any conversation, he had a wry sense of humour. He was always very proper.'

While Mr Kaul raised no objections, the party did. Balraj Madhok, whom we shall read about in the next chapter, claims that he called Vajpayee to his room in the 1960s after another Jana Sangh leader complained about the women in Vajpayee's life. Madhok was a founder of the Jana Sangh and considered himself Vajpayee's senior. Madhok claims he told Vajpayee: 'You should marry, otherwise you will be defamed and the image of Jana Sangh will also take a hit.'[79]

Sometime around 1965, Golwalkar travelled by train from Nagpur to Delhi, headed straight to the RSS office in Jhandewalan, and called a meeting with one item on the agenda: What was to be done about Mrs Kaul? Bhausaheb Deoras, the UP *pranth pracharak*, voiced his opinion: 'As long as there is no publicity, it's ok.' Jana Sangh treasurer Nanaji Deshmukh disagreed, saying, 'He [Vajpayee] should marry Rajkumari Kaul.' Nanaji had separately told Vajpayee this at a hotel in Patna. 'Nanaji was a matchmaker. He liked match making,' R.V. Pandit, a long-timer donor to the Jana Sangh and BJP, remembers. 'He had introduced Shatrughan Sinha to his wife Poonam. He did this all the time.'[80]

Golwalkar listened to these opinions before pronouncing his own. He told Vajpayee to break off the relationship with Mrs Kaul. 'Vajpayee, to his credit, refused to do so,' Dattopant Thengadi, who was present, later told an aide. Faced with a choice, Golwalkar decided not to punish Vajpayee. A Yadav politician from Bihar says: 'Vajpayee was let off because he was a Brahmin. Only Brahmins are allowed to break brahminical rules.'

But it was also decided that Vajpayee would be removed from the inner circle of the RSS. Until now, Vajpayee had always done what the

RSS had asked of him. But from now on, they would be at arm's length, each needing the other, each never trusting the other. Vajpayee's political journey from here on would be in tension with the sangh; sometimes that strain would be managed, sometimes it would cause rupture. As a pracharak says: 'This was the beginning of Atalji getting a psychological distance [from the RSS].'

* * *

It is perhaps no coincidence that just at the time Golwalkar was handling Vajpayee's non-traditional lifestyle, he was also thinking deeply about the virtues of traditional Hinduism. As we read earlier, the RSS was a radical break from Hindu custom. But the former Ramakrishna Mission monk was shaped by a religious world view. Aware that the Jana Sangh needed to appear Nehruvian, he had not imposed this world view thus far. But Golwalkar now felt that perhaps Hindutva needed more of Hinduism. He also had a sweet spot for the Hindu sadhus and peeths that the RSS had shied away from. And starting from the mid-1960s, Golwalkar began to introduce them to Hindu nationalism.

Powai today is a temple of modern India, home to an Indian Institute of Technology, Internet start-ups, a civic movement trying to clean the lake and pimpled eruptions designed by the architect Hafeez Contractor. But on 29 August 1964, it hosted a very different vision of India. It was on this day that Golwalkar and Chinmayananda—the men who ran the RSS and Chinmaya Mission respectively—called a meeting along with S.S. Apte, to set up a World Hindu Council. In Hindi, it would be known as the Vishva Hindu Parishad. VHP.

The VHP's core mission was 'to bring sadhus, sants and mahatmas of various sects on one platform',[81] thus uniting all those 'sampradayas [religious denomination and sects] that originated in India'.[82] Like with Savarkar's formulation of Hindutva, this included traditional Hinduism as well as Sikhism, Buddhism and Jainism, but excluded Christianity and Islam. The aim was to solve the problem of 'authority' in Hinduism by creating, for the first time, a Hindu Vatican.

The Vishva Hindu Parishad resolved, at this very first gathering, that the 'ancient glory and social standing [of temples] be restored'.[83] While that resolution would take two decades to morph into the Ayodhya movement, more immediate was the VHP's resolution to push the government to pass a law banning cow slaughter. Such a demand had been made in a muted manner for some decades. But it was the creation of the VHP—with its consolidation of religious heads—that gave this movement fillip.

The apogee of this anti-cow slaughter movement was a march on parliament two months later, on 7 November 1966, by over three lakh people.[84] These included members of the Jana Sangh and Hindu Mahasabha mingling with saffron-robed sadhus and Arya Samajis. The mob turned violent, burning cars, setting fire to government buildings and attempting to storm parliament.[85] The police opened fire, killing seven people and injuring over a 100 outside parliament.

Inside parliament, Vajpayee played the part of a defence lawyer, a role he would re-enact after 6 December 1992. When a Congress MP alleged that the demonstrating leaders had incited the crowd to burn ministers for not protecting the cow, Vajpayee was 'quick to refute his allegation'.[86]

The agitation ended soon, but its legacy persists to this day. The protests changed the original character of the party, since the RSS and Jana Sangh worked with religious figures and institutions for the first time. This union not only provided the palette for a new shade of saffron, it also offered a model for the movement that would one day pickaxe the Babri Masjid.

* * *

The Jana Sangh fought the 1967 elections on the tailwind of the anti-cow slaughter agitation—perhaps the first time it was stepping outside the Nehruvian consensus. Vajpayee contested from Balrampur against Subhadra Joshi, whom he had lost to in 1962. This time, Vajpayee made sure to deploy the 'cow issue and appeals to the sentiment of the people'.[87]

What added ballast to this religious rhetoric was the entry of Vijayaraje Scindia into the party. The dowager queen of one of India's largest princely states, Gwalior, was a pious Hindu, constantly fasting for one *vrat* or the other.[88] She would soon become a trustee of the VHP. The queen of Gwalior brought with her money the extent of which the

Jana Sangh had never seen before. Her daughter Vasundhara Raje says: 'In the late 1960s, she was the single biggest funder. She is the one who gave money to Nanaji.' Another source says: 'The 1967 campaign was paid for by Vijayaraje. Without her, the results would have been different.'

The invigorated Jana Sangh was facing a Congress in coma. After twenty years of dominating Indian politics, the Congress 'system', wracked with infighting, was malfunctioning. Nehru's death had eventually brought his daughter to power in 1966. But the new prime minister, Indira Gandhi, was unable to deal with food shortages, the aftermath of an inconclusive war with Pakistan, and, above all, factions within her party. She had yet to discover her populist touch. Her party sought to counter the Jana Sangh with smear rather than substance: '*Vote nahin denge hum, Gandhi ke hatyaaron ko.*'[89] We will not give votes to the killers of Gandhi.

When the results were announced in February 1967, the Congress seats in the Lok Sabha had reduced by seventy-eight to 283. In the state elections held in parallel, the Jana Sangh had won an estimated 266 MLAs from over sixteen states.[90] Their thirty-five members of parliament included Vajpayee, who had won Balrampur, as well as his competitor for the number two spot in the party, Balraj Madhok.

While the campaign against cow slaughter seems to have anticipated the national mood, the more pertinent reason for the Jana Sangh's success is showcased in how they were able to form the government in Madhya Pradesh in 1967.

Vijayaraje Scindia had woven an anti-Congress coalition for the state elections. But the Congress still won a comfortable majority. What should have been an easy return to power, however, was stymied by infighting. Incensed with the chief minister-designate D.P. Mishra, Congressman Govind Narayan Singh—the dynastic son of a former Congress chief minister—left the party along with thirty legislators. Though Vijayaraje could have laid claim to chief ministership, 'she told Govind Singh to become the CM in order to form a stable government'.[91]

Twenty months later, Singh would rejoin the Congress on condition that he remain chief minister.[92] Vijayaraje, on the other hand, would remain in the Jana Sangh, continuing to finance and campaign for it, continuing to abjure power. Their contrasting sense of loyalty showcases the organizational difference between the Jana Sangh and the Congress party.

* * *

While 1967 was an ambiguous year for Vajpayee—winning him a Lok Sabha seat but also increasing competition from within—it was an unambiguous triumph for Advani. Under his supervision, the Jana Sangh had swept the three near simultaneous polls held in Delhi: for the Lok Sabha, for the municipal corporation and for the metropolitan council (deemed a state legislature, since Delhi was not technically a state at the time).[93]

Forty-year-old Advani was elected chairman of the council, in effect the Speaker of the Delhi assembly. For a man who, only a decade ago, had been a lowly secretary to a first-time MP, Advani had come a long way. He shifted to a comfortable government house in Pandara Road,[94] in what would become his perch in Lutyens' Delhi for the next several decades.

Lal Krishna and Kamla Advani began to develop their own circle. Visitors would include Deendayal Upadhyaya, Dattopant Thengadi, Rajendra Sharma, N.M. Ghatate and his wife Sheela.[95] The most frequent visitor, of course, was Atal Bihari Vajpayee. Though Vajpayee still treated Advani as a subordinate whose company he enjoyed rather than an equal whose skills he needed, he had taken care to develop a cordial relationship with Kamla Advani. Their common friend R.V. Pandit says: 'Kamla Advani played a big role in solving tensions. She was the dominating figure in the Advani household, and she was an admirer of Atalji.'[96]

Advani's sudden rise mirrored his party's. The Jana Sangh was now the second-largest party in parliament by vote share, the third-largest by seats. But it was facing the challenges that come with political success.

At the ideological level, the Jana Sangh had to choose whether to continue within the Nehruvian consensus, or to follow a more strident Hinduism. This ideological schizophrenia translated into a simmering personal feud between the Indira-leaning Vajpayee and the right-leaning Madhok. At the level of organization, newly gained power threatened an ethos of abnegation in a way that struggling in the margins never had. The discipline of its thirty-five MPs and 266 MLAs risked being corrupted.

And, an ailing Golwalkar meant that changes in the RSS were in the offing, and with it, changes to the Jana Sangh.

What held all these tensions together was Deendayal Upadhyaya, unquestioned arbiter of political Hinduism. His personal integrity aided his acceptance as the sangh parivar's referee. An old-timer remembers meeting Deendayal in late 1967 and watching him waving his kurta in the wind. Deendayal explained that he had just two kurtas, and had spilt coffee on one of them. He needed to wash and dry that kurta straightaway to ensure he had something to wear the next day.

It was this very Deendayal who had delicately displaced Madhok as party president in December 1967. As long as the harmonizing fifty-one-year-old was in control, the unity of the party seemed assured. That is, until one cold morning two months later, when a dead body was found near Mughalsarai station.

4

PARTNERSHIP FORGED BY FIRE (1968–73)

The body had fallen by the tracks, 100 yards from the station platform in Mughalsarai, a small town near Varanasi. It was 2:20 a.m. on 11 February 1968. An ankle was broken, the head injured, and right arm marked with blood. The clenched fist enclosed a five-rupee note. A body search revealed twenty-six more rupees and a watch.[1]

It says something about the nature of the Rashtriya Swayamsevak Sangh that most of its leaders were organizing at the time. M.S. Golwalkar was in Allahabad, 160 kilometres away, conducting an RSS *shivir* (camp) when he heard the news. 'Guruji asked me to take a car and go to Varanasi, saying do not conduct [the] post-mortem without me,' an RSS leader of the time remembers after all these years. '[Golwalkar] said I will finish the shivir and come.'

While the RSS men were in the trenches that morning, their legislative counterparts in the Jana Sangh, Balraj Madhok and Atal Bihari Vajpayee, were attending a parliamentary meeting in Delhi. They instantly left in an air force plane for Varanasi. From there, Madhok says he made his way to Mughalsarai, while Vajpayee, his rival within the party, disappeared on arrival.[2] The Jana Sangh deputy chief minister of Uttar Pradesh—the party was part of the state government by 1967— was in Lucknow when he heard the news. He pressed the entire state's resources to solve the murder, straightaway flying a high-ranking official to Mughalsarai.[3]

For the man killed was not ordinary. As the previous chapter showed, Deendayal Upadhyaya had run the Jana Sangh for the last fifteen years. Though president only briefly, his unchanging position as general secretary gave him power behind the throne. He had been travelling from Lucknow to Patna. When the train left Mughalsarai station at 2:10 a.m., he was not in his coach, and was noticed ten minutes later by the tracks.[4]

Deendayal's death was investigated by the Central Bureau of Investigation (CBI) as well as a judicial commission. Both concluded that the murderers were petty thieves.[5]

Balraj Madhok was having none of it. When he reached Mughalsarai that afternoon, he was shown the banian, kurta and woollen sweater that Deendayal was wearing at the time of death. Madhok saw no blood on the clothes.[6] The post-mortem was conducted that evening in Varanasi. Madhok later claimed he inspected the body there, and noticed a small bloodied clot behind the neck, which he interpreted as having been caused by a poisoned needle.[7] Adding two and two to make five, he announced to a baffled press that Deendayal Upadhyaya's death was 'cold-blooded murder' and 'politically motivated'.[8] Madhok claims that Vajpayee confronted him, saying: 'Upadhyaya was a fighter cock. He must have got into a fight in the train . . . don't call it a murder.'[9]

Madhok's depiction is disputed not just by Vajpayee and government reports, but by the RSS leader who had been with Golwalkar in Allahabad and was now present at the post-mortem. 'I went and saw the body. I don't think there was any poisoning. I did not see any puncture marks in the neck. By evening, it had become quite dark when the post-mortem was conducted. By then, Guruji had come. Madhok was not present. I didn't see Vajpayeeji either. There was no light, just one petromax [lamp] in the room. So I was tasked with lifting Deendayalji's body to make sure that his face could be seen for the post-mortem. Seeing his face, Guruji said, "*Hey prabhu, agar aapko unhe lena hi thaa, to diya kyun?*" [Oh Lord, if you had wanted to take him, why did you give him to us in the first place?].'

The stench from this body would linger within the organization for decades, adding to a historical sense of Hindu victimhood. But the immediate effect was on the leadership of the Jana Sangh. Forever sensitive to organizational harmony, Deendayal had avoided naming an inheritor. As long as he was alive, the second rung he had built—K.L. Sharma, M.L.

Sondhi, Nanaji Deshmukh, Vajpayee, and Madhok—had deferred to him. But with the patriarch gone in 1968, his children began to squabble. And the first stone was thrown by Balraj Madhok, who accused Atal Bihari Vajpayee of murdering Deendayal Upadhyaya.

* * *

Balraj Madhok was born in 1920 to an Arya Samaj family based in Jammu. Like most other Hindu nationalists, he came from a lower middle-class, non-English-speaking background. He had joined the RSS a few years before Vajpayee and Advani, and assisted Hindu refugees fleeing Pakistan in 1947, many of them Punjabis like him. Thin, with an elongated face, a pencil moustache, and eyes that looked hunted, Madhok was a mix of the eclectic and the dogmatic. He taught in Srinagar and later Delhi, and wrote on topics as varied as Syama Prasad Mookerjee, foreign policy, and the lack of Indian-ness among Muslims. When Vajpayee was still an editor with *Panchajanya* in 1951, Madhok was considered important enough in the RSS to be one of the gold coins loaned to Mookerjee to found the Jana Sangh. He had become president of the party in 1966, before Vajpayee was bestowed that honour. All this gave Madhok the sense that he was the natural inheritor to Deendayal's legacy.

But Madhok had missed the warning signs. After just a couple of years as party president, he had been replaced by Deendayal. L.K. Advani provides an explanation in his biography—Madhok's tenure was so damaging that repair was needed.[10]

Balraj Madhok was too much of an individualist to fit into an organization that required sublimation of the self. His personality is best described by his associate Prafull Goradia. 'Madhok was a very clean-hearted person. But he could put his own views above the organization. I don't refute that. He was not a practical politician.'[11] Govindacharya is a Tamil Brahmin whose father moved to Banaras to teach Sanskrit. Decades in the RSS and then BJP have given him an unmatched institutional memory. He remembers: 'I really respected Madhokji. But he used to get "mood off" once in a while. He did not care about his language when shouting'[12]—behaviour that was rare within the sangh parivar.

Nowhere was this more evident than in the days following Deendayal's killing. Prafull Goradia recalls Madhok telling him: 'It was Vajpayee and [senior RSS leader] Balasaheb Deoras who did it.' When he met Govindacharya in Patna, Madhok floated a conspiracy that sounded like a Hindi film. 'There was a meeting in Nepal. Murder plan was hatched to make Vajpayee the party president.'[13] But Govindacharya, no admirer of Vajpayee, found that no such meeting had taken place. Govindacharya argued with Madhok, who replied angrily: 'When you go to [the RSS headquarters in] Nagpur, they take the key from your brain, and throw it in the Naaga *nadi*', a reference to the river running through the city.[14]

On seeing Deendayal's body in Varanasi that February, Madhok claimed that a crying Golwalkar had told him: 'The responsibility of the Jana Sangh is now with you.'[15] So imagine his astonishment when Vajpayee was unanimously elected president of the party just a few days later. The RSS also threw its weight behind Vajpayee. Golwalkar, who a few years ago had considered Vajpayee's relationship with Rajkumari Kaul a liability, had come around. Soon after, for example, he wrote a solicitous letter to Vajpayee counselling him on his health, especially the ulcers in his stomach, and advocating ayurvedic instead of allopathic treatment.[16]

When Deendayal's body was brought back to Delhi, it was to Vajpayee's official bungalow that the body was taken. Prime Minister Indira Gandhi came to pay her respects there,[17] with a sombre Vajpayee playing host. Advani was too junior to have to play politics at the cremation. He had the luxury of giving expression to his emotions by bursting into tears at the funeral.[18] Without this luxury, Vajpayee had to put on an act. In parliament on 12 February 1968, Vajpayee made sure that he was the one to pay the evocative tribute. 'He was not a member of parliament, but if any one individual could be given credit for those Bharatiya Jana Sangh members of parliament who are sitting in this and the other House . . . it is Upadhyayaji.'[19] And soon after the murder, it was only Vajpayee who was provided with a bodyguard—the imperial-moustachioed Shiv Kumar, who would remain with him till death. Manoeuvring without appearing to exert himself, Vajpayee had supplanted Madhok as Deendayal's successor.

* * *

While Vajpayee was subtly taking control of his party, Prime Minister Indira Gandhi was less subtly doing the same to her own. Like Madhok, she too imagined enemies everywhere. As Vajpayee put it: 'Whenever I met Smt. Indira Gandhi, I felt she was in the grip of some unknown fear. There was a deep sense of insecurity in some corner of her mind.'[20] What Indira Gandhi had—but Madhok did not—was a preternatural sense of the national mood. Historian Srinath Raghavan says, 'Indira correctly read the 1967 results as a mandate against the Congress establishment. So she began to place herself as an insurgent against that very establishment.'[21] She did this by accusing the Congress of turning conservative and splitting the party in 1969. Painting herself as a messiah of the poor, Indira proceeded to nationalize banks, abolish privy purses and impose controls on economic production.

Balraj Madhok wanted the Jana Sangh to respond with a frontal assault on Indira's economics and merge with the pro-business Swatantra, the party beloved of maharajas and landlords who detested their property being redistributed. After a visit to the Tata factory in Jamshedpur, he had realized 'that even in a socialist economy, private producers are profiteering and the loss-making factory's loss is being transferred to the public . . . nationalization is not in everybody's interest. Bureaucrats and politicians use this for themselves.'[22]

Madhok travelled to Germany in 1970, home of the Christian Democratic Union (CDU). Deendayal Upadhyaya's 'Integral Humanism' had been lifted from Christian Democratic thinker Jacques Maritain's 1936 book of the same name.[23] The definition too that Deendayal had taken—of the need for a spiritual counter to the materialism of capitalism and communism—had been concretized by Christian Democratic parties into policies that advocated a free market, welfare programmes and social conservatism.[24]

Madhok saw the need for Integral Humanism to be similarly translated in India. He even met with Helmut Kohl, eventually Christian Democratic chancellor of a reunited Germany. Madhok says in his memoirs that Kohl told him: 'Mr Madhok, based on my information, you are a leader of India's Hindu Democratic Party . . . communist, socialist and liberal parties of different countries each have their own international organizations . . . Christian Democratic Party and Hindu Democratic Party should also form their own international organizations.'[25]

* * *

Balraj Madhok was not the only one within his party critiquing state controls of the economy. By 1970, the economist Subramanian Swamy had been influenced enough by opposition leader Jayaprakash Narayan to give up a faculty position at Harvard University, and return to India. His essay in favour of India acquiring a nuclear bomb impressed the Hindu nationalists, for whom this had been an ideological fixture.[26] Just thirty-one years of age at the time, Swamy says he soon became beloved of the RSS, and was asked to draft an economic plan for the Jana Sangh.[27] His plan envisaged a reduction in state controls, but in a nod to the party's indigenous hankerings, was called the 'Swadeshi' plan.

In these early years, Vajpayee and Swamy were not the antagonists they would later become; it was Vajpayee who first taught the 'foreign educated' Swamy to wear a dhoti.[28] Swamy remembers: 'In 1970 and [the] first quarter of 1971, Vajpayee couldn't spend one day without calling me. He was living in 1 Feroze Shah Road. Mrs Kaul also liked me, because she was thinking, "Since he is from the West, he will understand our relationship."'[29] But Swamy's rapid rise began to threaten a Vajpayee who was still consolidating his grip over the party. Vajpayee's insecurities were heightened by Swamy's tendency to speak rashly and promote himself relentlessly.

Yet another factor pushing the Jana Sangh in favour of a strong line against Indira's socialism were the Bombay-based industrialists who were now funding the party. They were culturally and financially unlike the shopkeepers and traders (and even Rajmata Scindia) who had funded the party in the 1960s. They were against Indira Gandhi's economics, and had read the 1967 elections as heralding the Jana Sangh as a national alternative to the Congress. These Bombay corporates were, however, motivated by self-interest rather than principle. While supporting free enterprise for domestic entrepreneurs like themselves, they lobbied to keep the external controls that prevented multinationals from entering.

The credit for bringing these Bombay businessmen into contact with the northern Indian Jana Sangh lay with Chandikadas Amritrao 'Nanaji' Deshmukh, the incorruptible treasurer of the Jana Sangh. His legend was built on relentless pursuit of lucre for the party, including running on foot after a horse-riding prince to entice him to give money. Nanaji was also uncommonly honest, so much so that the party would send him alone to collect money. 'After him, two people go now. To make sure,' N.M. Ghatate says. '[But] with Nanaji there was never any doubt.'[30]

Through the early 1970s, Nanaji cultivated the Tatas, Mafatlals and other industrial houses. He also got to know R.V. Pandit. Pandit would himself part with much money for the party—cheque only, since he was against black money[31]—and would become one of Vajpayee and Advani's closest friends. 'I used to give the cheque directly to Advaniji and Atalji and George and Jaswant,' Pandit says, providing his bank statements as evidence for this.[32]

Of all these patrician industrialists who gave money to the party, the most prominent was also the most unusual. At the time one of the richest groups in India, the Wadias were Parsis who had made their money during colonial rule. Their flagship Bombay Dyeing textiles was a household name. The scion of the Wadia group, Nusli, wasn't just uncommonly rich, he was also the grandson of Muhammad Ali Jinnah.

The founder of Pakistan had disinherited his daughter Dina when she had married the non-Muslim Neville Wadia. When partition came, Jinnah had moved to Pakistan, leaving behind Dina and grandson Nusli. 'As long as Nusli's father was alive he forbade him from politics,' a friend of Nusli Wadia says. 'Basically, he [Nusli's father] felt that one politician in the family had caused enough problems. But once he died, Nusli began links with [the] Jana Sangh.'

Nusli Wadia became acquainted with Nanaji in the late 1960s when they were introduced by a businessman friend.[33] It was Nusli who then introduced Nanaji to J.R.D. Tata.[34] And by the 1970s, Jinnah's grandson was funding large parts of the Jana Sangh. One illustration provides a sense of his influence.

Nanaji Deshmukh understood early that newspapers and magazines could prove a potent weapon, since radio and television were controlled by the Congress government. The RSS already ran the Hindi weekly

Panchajanya, the Marathi daily *Tarun Bharat* and the English fortnightly *Organiser*. But Nanaji was convinced that an English daily was required to reach the influential urban Indian who was repulsed by the Jana Sangh. Virendra and Coomi Kapoor were two of the first journalists to join this newspaper, *Motherland*, housed in the first two floors of the Deendayal Research Institute in north Delhi. Nanaji would live above the shop on the fifth floor, while K.R. Malkani edited the paper. Virendra Kapoor says: 'A newspaper depended on patronage. No advertisement was possible since Congress was in power, and no industrialist wanted to cross them. But I saw Bombay Dyeing ads in *Motherland*, and I remember Nusli Wadia visiting the offices once before going up to see Nanaji.' Kapoor says that it was brave to fund a Jana Sangh newspaper in those days. 'Once, an industrialist offered to pay us cash. Malkani [the editor] said no, buy an advertisement. So he put an ad. A few days later, at a party, a Congressman said to him, "Oh! I remembered you the other day . . . when I saw your ad in *Motherland*." The point was made. The industrialist never gave any more money to us.'[35]

* * *

With pressure to oppose Indira's socialism coming from Madhok and Subramanian Swamy within, and corporate funders without, it stands to logic that the Jana Sangh should have merged with the Swatantra Party and articulated a capitalist position. That this did not happen owes something to the class background of Hindu nationalists—lower middle-class men just one step removed from poverty and suspicious of unbridled capitalism. But the primary reason why the Jana Sangh declined to oppose Indira's economics was neither ideology nor class background. As the party's internal debate over bank nationalization shows, the answer was much simpler.

By the late 1960s, India had several private banks, apart from government-owned ones. For a variety of reasons, credit was scarce for rural areas as well as for small urban enterprises. Sensing an opportunity, Indira Gandhi began advocating state control over those private banks to extend credit to a wider swathe of Indians. When the bank nationalization bill came to parliament, Madhok opposed it, saying that 'people taking loans will have to do bootlicking of officers'.[36] In the same parliament, Vajpayee was more conciliatory. 'Sir, Bharatiya Jan Sangh is not opposed to nationalisation in principle. It can be done if it is in the public interest . . .'[37] The Jana Sangh's final resolution on nationalization strove for a middle path, supporting the principle but opposing a policy made without 'due thought and without preparing any blue-print'.[38] And when the matter came up to vote, Jana Sangh members conveniently absented themselves.[39] An incensed Madhok gave a public statement questioning the Jana Sangh leadership[40]—a not-so-subtle dig at its president.

In refusing to oppose Indira's economics, Vajpayee was joined by L.K. Advani, who since 1970 had become a parliamentarian in the Rajya Sabha or the unelected Upper House. Thus far, Advani had been Vajpayee's devotee. But now, confronted by Madhok, Vajpayee needed more than just an admirer; he needed an equal partner.

Joining them were many others in the party, who realized that bank nationalization was the consensus in parliament. An aide to Vajpayee says: 'Atalji knew which way the wind was blowing. The Indian public supported Indira's socialism. The Jana Sangh realized that.'

The party's economic socialism at this time must be contrasted with Prime Minister Vajpayee's market economics in the first decade of the new millennium, and Narendra Modi's heavy-handed intervention in the economy in recent years. The ease with which Hindu nationalists can spout opposing economics suggests they do not have a principled view on the subject. And that their economics in the 1970s also went against their funders points to the fact that money power alone does not explain their policies. Instead, the deciding factor in choosing to not confront Indira Gandhi was an analysis of what it took to win elections. It was votes, not ideology or money, that shaped Jana Sangh economics.

* * *

The Jana Sangh's reluctance to confront Indira Gandhi was borne out by the 1971 election results. The prime minister recovered her father's mandate, which she had lost in 1967, gaining more than sixty-nine seats, and giving the Congress a commanding majority. The anti-Congress alliance, of which Jana Sangh was a part, was routed. The party itself was

reduced to two-thirds of its previous tally—to just twenty-two seats.[41] One
of those was from Gwalior, won by Atal Bihari Vajpayee.[42] Madhok lost
his elections from Delhi. He attributed this to yet another conspiracy, this
one hatched by Indira Gandhi, the Indian communists, the Soviet Union
and Atal Bihari Vajpayee.[43]

With his rival defeated, Vajpayee was once again elected head of
the party in parliament in 1971. While Vajpayee had tactically become
president of the Jana Sangh in 1968 to ward off the threat from Madhok,
being its main spokesman in parliament was what he identified with more
than anything else.

* * *

Indira Gandhi followed her electoral success in March 1971 with a
calibrated war with Pakistan. India's nemesis was at the time divided
into two wings. As Bengali-speaking East Pakistan smarted under the
dominance of West Pakistan and Punjabi Muslim troops committed
atrocities, millions of Bengali Hindu and Muslim refugees fled for India.
The crisis provided Indira the excuse to act. Her initial strategy was to
train East Pakistanis to form a militia called Mukti Bahini. This militia
would assist the Indian army's eventual liberation of Bangladesh. It would
also provide the Pakistanis with a model to train disgruntled Kashmiris in
the early 1990s.[44]

India's 1971 victory not just redeemed its army after the loss of 1962
and stalemate of 1965, it split into half the religious logic for Pakistan.
Vajpayee was all praise for Indira Gandhi—though, contrary to public
belief, he did not liken her to Goddess Durga and had to spend much of
his later life denying this.[45]

Indira's domestic dominance after the Bangladesh war, her populist
turn and the 1971 election results had an acute impact on Vajpayee. He
was taking control of the party at a time when the Jana Sangh's rise in
1967 seemed to have tapered off. He thought deeply about the relationship
between ideology and electoral victory. His conclusion, forged in this
crucible, would shape Hindu nationalism for decades to come.

Soon after the 1971 elections, an innocuous article appeared in an
English newspaper, written by 'A Swayamsevak', a reference to a lowly

RSS volunteer.[46] It said that there were two roads ahead for the RSS and Jana Sangh. They could remain an ideological party and become a pressure group. Or they could compromise on ideology, and come to power.

So obvious was the actual author that Vajpayee was summoned by Golwalkar to a meeting at Hedgewar Bhavan in Nagpur. Asked to elaborate, Vajpayee explained that Hindus were moderates, and would not agree to an ideological party. Many in the RSS opposed this. Lunch was served, a vegetarian meal that was eaten in communion.[47] Guruji spoke after lunch. 'I agree with Atalji that an ideological party will find it difficult to come to power and won't come to power quickly. But I disagree that it will never happen.' He gave the example of how 'the Labour party came to power in England, despite a Westminster system made by conservatives'. But for the moment, Golwalkar and the RSS were willing to be led by Vajpayee and his ideological moderation.

It is hard to overestimate the impact of this 'deal'. For the next three decades, political Hinduism would run its politics based on this presumption—that while Hindutva would energize the cadre, the party needed to dilute its ideology to appeal to moderate Hindus and win power. Even when frustrated at this strategy, as the RSS and VHP frequently were, they would never overturn it. This was the strategy responsible for the first bloom of the Bharatiya Janata Party, expiring only after the 2002 Gujarat state elections, when, as we shall see later, Chief Minister Narendra Modi proved that it was possible to have your cake and eat it too.

* * *

The 1971 'deal' between the RSS and Vajpayee ended any possibility of a free-market party line. And Advani, by now in thrall of his mentor, took Vajpayee's side. Madhok, however, saw this not so much as a pragmatic choice, but as a sell-out. He turned to personal attacks.

He complained to Golwalkar about the women in Vajpayee's life. Golwalkar replied: 'I know about the weakness and character of these people. But I have to run the organization. I have to take everyone along. Hence every day I consume poison like Shiva.'[48]

While Madhok was conjuring an array of reasons why Vajpayee was winning the ideological argument, the obvious one seems to have eluded him. Vajpayee's easy charm drew more converts than Madhok's intensity. As Congress politician Jairam Ramesh says: 'Vajpayee was the only party figure acceptable to all factions of his party. He was also the only figure whom the entire opposition was comfortable with.'[49] Vajpayee also knew how to ingratiate himself to the press in a way that Madhok did not. The journalist H.K. Dua was once travelling by scooter to the Jana Sangh office to attend a press conference thrown by president Vajpayee. On the way, he saw Vajpayee waiting outside his house in Feroze Shah Road for a taxi to take him to that very meeting. When Dua offered, Vajpayee happily rode pillion to reach the venue where he spoke, while Dua took notes.[50] Ullekh N.P. adds: 'Vajpayee was very close to editors of sangh newspapers. So [during press coverage] for any sangh function, he would always get prominence in the reportage.'[51]

While Vajpayee loved this spotlight, he was careful to be seen as a team player, necessary to remain in Hindu nationalism. When he did not get his way—as his disagreement with his party on the Ayodhya movement or on Gujarat chief minister Narendra Modi's ouster will show—he would sulk on mute. When Madhok did not get his way, he saw conspiracies and voiced them to the press. Even Madhok's friends could tire of him. Madhuri Sondhi remembers him coming over to talk with her husband M.L. Sondhi, eventually a Jana Sangh MP. 'My husband would try to hide from Madhok. But he would find my husband in the house . . . and they would then have a discussion . . . It was like a joint family.'[52]

Madhok's critics trace his individualism to imperfect socialization in the RSS. Govindacharya points to the fact that Madhok perhaps did not complete the OTC training, the three-step course where aspiring pracharaks are taught about team building and RSS ideology.[53] It is a charge his family denies.[54]

As Madhok became progressively distanced from the Jana Sangh and RSS, he hung on, hoping that Vajpayee's tenure as president would end soon. Madhok wanted Rajmata Scindia to be the next president.[55] Madhok must have calculated that the party under her would be more aligned to his beliefs.

Imagine Madhok's surprise, therefore, when Lal Krishna Advani's name was floated in early 1973.

Though he had been head of the Delhi metropolitan council and was at the time a Rajya Sabha MP, several others in the party were senior to Advani. He had also not distinguished himself as a parliamentary orator (unlike Madhok), as a national organizer (unlike Nanaji Deshmukh), or as a mass politician (unlike Rajmata Scindia). He looked every inch the common man from R.K. Laxman's cartoons, an everyday spectator who silently took in the larger currents around him. Madhok referred to Advani as a 'boneless wonder' who 'does not have his own character or opinion'.[56] There was nothing to recommend Advani as the head. Except for one attribute.

By the early 1970s, Advani and Vajpayee were inseparable. The flamboyant Vajpayee enjoyed the company of the quieter man. They would go out to watch films, a shared passion, followed by pani puri.[57] Apart from personal chemistry, Vajpayee's cultivation of Advani had a political end. A Jana Sangh leader at the time says: 'Vajpayee picked Advani since he spoke good English, was trustworthy and perceived as a man who could never win a Lok Sabha election.' Madhok was more direct. 'Advani was very close to Vajpayee. He had no independent existence and he lacked confidence.'[58]

Advani later told an aide: 'I was politically junior to several others, and I was not even an orator in public rallies. This is the most elementary requirement for a mass leader and president of a party. But Vajpayeeji told me: "You will acquire this."'

Advani insisted that others be asked first—prominent amongst them Rajmata Vijayaraje Scindia. But she refused, a reluctance to hold a post that would be her hallmark. Her contribution to the party far exceeded the vice-presidency she would eventually ascend to in 1986. When asked about her mother's distaste for party posts, Vasundhara Raje smiles. She brings the fingers of her right hand together and points downwards in the gesture for giving. 'She was used to doing this,' she says. She then inverts her hand to form a begging bowl. 'Not this.' [59]

With the Rajmata refusing, Advani agreed to be president. The public announcement was to be made in Kanpur in February 1973. It was perhaps the single most important session for the party. For it would mark the end of Madhok and the beginning of Vajpayee–Advani's control.

* * *

The Kanpur session of the Jana Sangh was held between 9 and 11 February 1973. Like all sessions, arrangements were thorough but spartan. Even senior leaders would have to share tents or rooms, and hospitality was provided by local businessmen sympathetic to the Jana Sangh.

Madhok was coaxed to attend—in what he later claimed was a set-up.[60] At a private meeting just before the public session, Madhok was questioned about a twenty-two-page note he had circulated.[61] Madhok was worried about a small cabal dictating policy—the RSS in cahoots with Vajpayee, Advani and Nanaji. He had wanted top party posts to be elected, and the 'selection of party candidates should be made by a larger body'.[62]

Madhok was particularly critical of what he considered the direct influence of the RSS over the Jana Sangh. Since all organizing secretaries up to the district level were appointed by the RSS, Madhok argued that they would not answer to the Jana Sangh leadership.[63] Madhok's concern is borne out by data. In a detailed survey of three constituencies conducted between 1968 and 1971, the scholars Walter Anderson and Shridhar Damle found that only 10 per cent of Jana Sangh posts were occupied by non-RSS men. At senior levels, in fact, there was no one without RSS links.[64]

At the meeting, Madhok claims he was told: 'Muslims don't like you, are repelled by you, don't want to join Jana Sangh because of you. In order to get them to join, you must resign.'[65] Vajpayee asked that he resign from the party.[66] An angry Madhok made plans to leave Kanpur immediately. Aware that Madhok's departure would be permanent, an RSS pracharak of the time remembers telling him to accept that his ideas had not found purchase, and remain through the session. It was the right advice, since Vajpayee would avoid expulsion from the party a decade later by protesting Ayodhya but never leaving in a huff. But Madhok was not Vajpayee. He left Kanpur for Delhi that very day, an event widely reported in the press.[67]

At the start of the public session, outgoing president Atal Bihari Vajpayee criticized Madhok by name—unheard of in an organization that prided unity over all else. He said that Madhok was alone in the view that the party should 'opt for a rightist front'. The Jana Sangh, he swore, was a 'centrist forward-looking' party and would not 'function as a lobby for vested interests'.[68] Having rejected the challenge from Madhok, Vajpayee went on to seal his hold on the party. He announced—in what had only been a rumour until then—the name of Lal Krishna Advani as the new president of the party.

Harin Pathak, the long-time MP from Gujarat, attended the Kanpur session. He remembers the reaction of the crowd to the announcement. 'Everybody was shocked . . . Dada [Advani] was not so much popular among the people. Everybody was little bit astonished.'[69] Noticing the disquiet, Vajpayee ended his speech by saying, 'Today you say Atalji Atalji. One day, you will say Advaniji Advaniji.'[70]

Closing the session, Advani gave what was perhaps his first public speech. He left no one in any doubt about what the party stood for and who spoke for it. While attacking 'monopoly houses' and import controls,[71] he also referred to the upcoming Uttar Pradesh elections, and announced that Vajpayee would direct 'the strategy and campaigning in the state'.[72] Soon after, Advani declared: 'Presidents may come, presidents may go, but Atalji will always be our leader.'[73]

With the end of the session, the Jana Sangh was left to deal with the largest crisis since its creation. Unlike in the fractious Congress, no ranking leader had been threatened with disciplinary action,[74] let alone a co-founder and past president of the party. In a meeting that included the RSS, Madhok was accused of anti-party activities and expelled for three years.[75]

Advani was uncomfortable, later telling his confidante Swapan Dasgupta: 'I was forced to be the executioner.'[76] He had no dislike of Madhok, and left to himself may not have taken this step. Madhok later wrote: 'They [Vajpayee and Balasaheb Deoras] used Advani's shoulder to put a gun and end my political career and planned my political murder. If Advani had some confidence and self-strength, he would not have played their game.'[77]

* * *

The removal of Balraj Madhok was followed by M.L. Sondhi leaving the party. The Rhodes scholar and former diplomat had tried to contest against party president Vajpayee in 1971. Govindacharya says, 'M.L. Sondhi did not know the grammar and dynamics of the sangh parivar relationship. Almost 85 per cent of Jana Sangh cadre were linked to the RSS. Only 15 per cent were like Sondhi, with no RSS connection. How could he win?'[78]

By 1973, Vajpayee had waded through the succession crisis created in the wake of Deendayal's murder. He had outmanoeuvred two rivals; two more (Nanaji and Subramanian Swamy) would follow. It was never hardliners who made him insecure; he needed them to justify his own existence. It was the orators who could replace him in parliament who threatened Vajpayee the most.

The expulsion of Madhok reveals another trait of Hindu nationalism: its reluctance to break organizational unity. It had taken the party a full five years after Madhok had accused Jana Sangh leaders of killing Deendayal to banish him. And when he was finally expelled, the bitterness created had the texture of a family drama.

These years also reveal the conversion of a friendship into a partnership. Vajpayee and Advani never let the party presidency out of their hands from 1968 all the way to 1998, with only a two-year gap in between. Advani's rise from a cautious backroom operative to head of the party was entirely due to Vajpayee, and Advani never forgot the favour.

* * *

The ascendancy of Vajpayee and Advani to power in the Jana Sangh coincided with a change of leadership in the RSS. In liberal circles, Golwalkar is known as a bearded fundamentalist given to racist writing. But those within the 'family' saw him as a gentle patriarch loathe to play personal politics. By June 1973, after thirty-three years of running the RSS, he lay dying of cancer in Nagpur. An assortment of politicians came visiting, including the Congress chief minister of Maharashtra.[79] Years later, Vajpayee would recall spending time with Golwalkar the day before his death.[80] Even in his last hours, Guruji was catering to his family.

Golwalkar left behind a supple ideology and volunteer force, 30,000 of whom saluted at his funeral in Nagpur.[81] In his three decades as head, he had moved Hindutva from the sidelines it had been relegated to after Gandhi's murder, to the middle of the national road.

Guruji's replacement could not have been better suited to this new reality. Along with his brother Bhaurao, Balasaheb Deoras had spent his life in the RSS. Like much of the founding families of the RSS, the Deorases were Brahmins from Nagpur, from the Deshastha sub-caste. Both brothers were easy to work with, an RSS pracharak says. 'They knew how to work together in an organization. They were practical people . . . in that sense they were political animals, you can say.' Another former pracharak, Seshadri Chari, does say: 'Balasaheb Deoras believed that we cannot keep political calculations totally out of consideration while going about the day-to-day activities of RSS. This is starkly in contrast to Golwalkar.'[82] Deoras had already set a precedent by being the first RSS leader to address the annual conference of the Jana Sangh.[83] He had also, as we read earlier in this chapter, played a role in Madhok's ouster. Balasaheb Deoras was, like Vajpayee and Advani, a politician.

By 1973, therefore, the leadership of the Jana Sangh and RSS had both gone to realists rather than ideologues. As the next three chapters will reveal, these leaders took their organizations on a particular trajectory from 1973 to 1984.

But it might be interesting to pause for a moment to consider a counterfactual: What if Deendayal Upadhyaya had lived on, and, as some speculate, replaced Golwalkar as the head of the RSS? And what if it was Madhok who had grasped the leadership of Jana Sangh, rather than Advani and Vajpayee?

The first departure would have been in ideological opposition to Indira Gandhi. Madhok would have merged the Jana Sangh with the Swatantra Party to create a 'conservative' coalition, one opposed to bank nationalisation and the abolition of privy purses, and advocating more open markets. He would have also followed a radical Hindu agenda, adopting the Ayodhya movement, or some such provocation, far sooner than Vajpayee did.

In the short term, such a strategy might have hurt Hindu nationalists electorally. As we shall see in the next chapter, the opposition to Indira Gandhi took the form of a socialist alliance, and Vajpayee was prescient in moving his party in that direction. The 1970s were not a good time for Madhok's politics.

Yet, in a prophetic way, Madhok's support for capitalism, his frontal assault on the Nehru–Gandhis, criticisms of Islam and his overtures to the US and Israel would resonate with a man versed with Madhok's writings. When Madhok died in 2016, this man, Prime Minister Narendra Modi, would pay respects to his dead body in west Delhi.

It would take Modi another four decades to dominate India. For now, it was Indira Gandhi who towered over her country's politics. But though she was at her peak, the Congress's long decline had begun. By 1973, gloom from the grassroots was coalescing, as were opposition parties. For Vajpayee and Advani, who had just manoeuvred their way to control their party, this turmoil provided them the opportunity to merge with other opposition parties—and finally gain the respectability they craved. But for this to happen, they would first have to go to jail.

5

PERKS OF PRISON (1974–77)

As a national movement taking on the British, the Congress had brought diverse religious, caste, language and regional groups under one umbrella.[1] After independence, the Nehru-led Congress continued to win with 'nation-building' appeals at the macro level while pandering to singular castes, religions and regions within the 'Congress system' at the micro level.[2] What added to this dominance, the political scientist Atul Kohli argues, was the persistence of a caste hierarchy that channelled votes to the Congress.[3] But with a loosening of this social order, the passing of Nehru, and quite simply the passing of time, the 'Congress system' began to decline.

Indians started to seek parties that catered exclusively to their identities: the Jana Sangh for Hindus, Akali Dal for Sikhs, the DMK for Tamils. Fuelling their anxieties was a sense that the Nehruvian model of rapid development had failed, and a new kind of politics was required.[4] The rise of these parties and this politics, first seen in the 1967 elections, threatened Indira Gandhi's hold over power.

The prime minister could have accepted this decline in Congress dominance as inevitable, and striven for democratic stability. Instead, she amplified the crisis by splitting her party, labelling her competitors as anti-national and playing left-populism to retain voters.

To add to this political volatility in the early 1970s was an economy nearing catastrophe. Successive droughts impoverished the majority of

Indians who were dependent on agriculture.[5] The Bangladesh war drained the exchequer. State control produced low growth. Unemployment increased by 100 per cent between 1956 and 1972.[6] And in the year 1973, there were 12,000 strikes in the city of Bombay alone.[7]

Faced with instability that had been a long time in the making, Indira Gandhi had only made it worse. And with her adversaries refusing to budge, the year 1974 was ripe for revolution.

* * *

The first blow, in January 1974, was struck by students in Gujarat. The price of food grains there had doubled in 1973 and hostel bills had swollen by 40 per cent in the month of December alone.[8] The student marches and police backlash snowballed into a critique of the Congress state government. More than 100 were killed, over 3000 injured and 8000 arrested in the turmoil.[9] The Congress government in Gujarat was forced to resign in March 1974. Inspired by this feat, students in Bihar began protesting against their own Congress state government.

In the initial months, the demonstrations were not the coordinated conspiracy that Indira Gandhi alleged. They were unprompted and diffuse, with parties and groups watching from the side. This leadership void was soon filled by the only student body that was anti-Congress as well as fighting fit. The Akhil Bharatiya Vidyarthi Parishad (All India Students' Organization) or ABVP had been created as a front for the RSS when the latter was banned in 1948. Though partnering with non-communists like Lalu Prasad Yadav[10] and careful to never advertise ownership of the protests, they came to dominate the organization behind it.[11]

Working in Bihar were RSS leaders like Govindacharya, who would one day run the 1989 and 1991 election campaigns for the BJP. Leadership of the protests in Gujarat also fell to RSS workers, including a newly minted pracharak named Narendra Damodardas Modi.[12]

The son of a tea-stall owner, Modi was part of a new breed of non-upper castes who were becoming functionaries of the RSS. Modi had started visiting shakhas when he was eight years old in 1957, but it was only in 1972 that he became a full-time pracharak.[13] He was too young to remember the RSS's distaste for politics before Independence, or its existential suffering after Gandhi's murder. He lacked both the anti-politics or the moderation of the older pracharaks. Instead, the twenty-four-year-old Modi's imagination of politics was being shaped by these student protests of 1974. It was giving him his understanding of state power as well as of Congress weakness.

These student demonstrations in early 1974 were accompanied by the largest working-class mobilization in Indian history. More than a million railway workers went on strike in May 1974,[14] led by a Catholic seminarian turned rumpled street fighter from Bombay named George Fernandes.[15] The railways were the largest employers in India (and one of the largest in the world); they were the veins through which administration flowed through the country. Cultural critic Sadanand Menon worked with the strikers at the time. He says: 'For the first time, trade unions across India coordinated. It was a big deal. That could have led to some kind of working-class solidarity at the national level.'[16]

The strike would immobilize India, but would amount to nothing, soon merging with the larger agitation. The historian Bipan Chandra explains this implosion by pointing to a divided working class, most of which was unorganized and not even part of the formal union structure.[17]

While the Jana Sangh kept its distance from the railway strike, it had become the spine of the student protests. This backing was due to the initiative of local workers, rather than commands from the top. For, Atal Bihari Vajpayee's instinct remained what it had been during his quarrel with Balraj Madhok: Indira Gandhi was too popular to be confronted head-on. He advocated a middle path, requesting the government in April 1974: 'Instead of solving problems with police brutality, build bridges with the students, with the new generation.'[18]

But others who had concurred with Vajpayee earlier were now having second thoughts. Through 1974, L.K. Advani, Balasaheb Deoras and Nanaji Deshmukh travelled to Bihar to engage with the students.[19] Unlike Vajpayee, all three had worked at the grassroots before, and sensed that Indira's popularity was in decline. Nanaji especially plunged into the protests, and was propped up by the media as a hero.[20]

This was a time when Vajpayee was insecure about his leadership of the party. He now saw Nanaji as a threat, as he did Subramanian Swamy, to whom Nanaji had given a Rajya Sabha ticket in 1974. Swamy says:

'Vajpayee told me not to move with Nanaji. That's where my problems with Vajpayee started.'[21] For his part, Nanaji resented Vajpayee's knack of capturing the limelight with minimal exertion, once complaining: *'Bheed ham laate hain, dari hum bichaate hain. Saara shrey Atalji ley jaate hain.'* We get the crowd. We spread the carpet. But it is Atalji who takes the entire credit.[22]

* * *

Hindu nationalists alone could not have transformed the protests of 1974 into a national movement. They still repelled many who were otherwise hostile to Indira Gandhi. What the protests needed was a face that was universally respected.

Born in Bihar in 1902, Jayaprakash Narayan, or 'JP' as he was known, had returned from the University of Wisconsin in 1929, a steadfast Marxist and Congress activist. He admired the 'socialist' Nehru and disagreed with the 'conservative' Vallabhbhai Patel.[23] He was also repulsed by the 'communal' RSS, even staging a demonstration outside the *Organiser* office after Gandhi's murder in 1948.[24]

'Inside every thinking Indian there is a Gandhian and a Marxist struggling for supremacy,' writes historian Ramachandra Guha.[25] Wrestling with that very struggle after independence, JP left politics in 1954[26] and chose to work with local movements for land reform in Bihar.[27] This was a communitarian vision embodied not just by Gandhi, but also by the RSS. This was why JP was working closely with the RSS by the late 1960s.[28] And by the middle of 1974, JP had taken leadership of and lent his initials to the inchoate movement that was arising from student protests, the railway strike and opposition support.

The Jana Sangh backed him from the beginning. When JP was 'lathi charged' by the police during a protest in Patna in late 1974, it was Nanaji Deshmukh who came to his defence.[29] The RSS supported JP's call for a 'total revolution',[30] and its head Balasaheb Deoras called him a 'saint' who had 'come to rescue society in dark and critical times'.[31]

This support culminated in JP telling Advani and Vajpayee: 'I need your cooperation. You should join me in my movement.'[32] Party president L.K. Advani sprang at the chance to turn informal help into formal association. He had by now internalized his guru Atal Bihari Vajpayee's view that to mainstream itself, the Jana Sangh had to first become one with the parliamentary opposition.

These connections allowed Indira Gandhi to portray the entire 'JP movement' as right wing. As many as 116 Congress and communist MPs signed a letter saying that the RSS and other fascist organizations should be banned.[33] Even supporters of JP, such as the Communist Party of India (Marxist), wanted no tie-up with 'communal and capitalist groups'.[34] But JP was unmoved, even attending a Jana Sangh national executive session in early 1975.[35] In his speech to around 40,000 assembled party delegates, he declared: 'If the Jana Sangh is fascist, then Jayaprakash Narayan is also fascist.'[36]

Jayaprakash Narayan's doggedness in including the Jana Sangh in his movement compelled other opposition parties to work with them. The peasant leader Charan Singh ran the Bharatiya Lok Dal (BLD) party and represented the agrarian interests of the Jat, Rajput, Ahir and Gujjar castes of northern India.[37] An unwavering vegetarian and religious Hindu, Charan Singh had aligned with the Jana Sangh in UP before. But he was worried even then about RSS influence on the party, a concern he would voice over and over again until breaking point in 1979.[38] A second ally was the Socialist Party, composed of urbane activists like George Fernandes. The third party willing to work with the Jana Sangh was the Congress (O), headed by the 'right-wing' Morarji Desai and other Congress renegades. These alliances would be the kernel of the Janata Party, eventually formed in 1977.

They seemed to be paying off even by 1975. In the assembly elections in Gujarat in June of that year, the newly formed 'Janata Front', an alliance that included the Jana Sangh, came to power.[39] The Congress had been unable to secure a majority in the Gujarat assembly for the first time.[40] That same day, 12 June 1975, the Allahabad High Court dismissed Indira Gandhi as prime minister for corrupt electoral practices.[41] The Supreme Court soon granted a stay on her dismissal, but ruled that the prime minister could not vote in parliament.[42] It was an unparalleled censure of the head of government.

On 22 June, a nationwide 'Janata Front' was set up to agitate for Mrs Gandhi's resignation,[43] with an action plan drawn up by Nanaji

Deshmukh.[44] They met at JP's house on 25 June to form a 'coordination body'. Nanaji, not Vajpayee, was named its general secretary.[45] That evening, this body, virtually one party now, organized a rally of more than 100,000 in the Ram Lila grounds in north Delhi. Vajpayee spoke, along with other opposition leaders. But it was Jayaprakash Narayan who made the crowd delirious by declaring Indira Gandhi's prime ministership unlawful, and asking the police and army to disobey her 'illegal orders'.[46]

At 10 p.m., Indira Gandhi informed her press secretary H.Y. Sharada Prasad: 'I have decided to declare an Emergency. The President has agreed. I will have to inform the Cabinet tomorrow.'[47]

The 'Emergency' Mrs Gandhi was referring to was provided for in Article 352 of the Indian Constitution. When the President of India (a placeholder for the union cabinet headed by the prime minister) declared an internal Emergency, elections were suspended, government ran via prime ministerial decree and the fundamental rights assured to every Indian were not even guaranteed on paper.

Indira Gandhi summoned her cabinet early the next morning. She told them that JP's incitement to the army and police the previous night, along with the bedlam spread by his movement, threatened the security of the nation. In reality, the only threat was to her own power. But none of her bleary-eyed ministers were willing to make this point. They were an afterthought anyway; orders had already been given to disconnect the electricity from newspaper printers and arrest opposition leaders. The Emergency had begun.

* * *

Vajpayee and Advani woke up that morning, 26 June 1975, clueless about what was unfolding. They were in Bangalore, scheduled to attend a parliamentary commission on the anti-defection law. Given that June is the hottest month in Delhi, they were relieved to have travelled to the garden city.[48]

At 7:30 a.m., the local Jana Sangh office called Advani to tell him that opposition leaders were being arrested in Delhi. 'The police may shortly come to arrest Atalji and you.'[49] An hour later, still a free man, Advani listened to Prime Minister Indira Gandhi's unscheduled voice on the radio. She justified the Emergency[50] in order to save the country from a 'deep and widespread conspiracy which has been brewing ever since I began to introduce certain progressive measures'.[51] Vajpayee arrived, and the two decided to head to the canteen for breakfast while they awaited the police.[52]

They were arrested at 10 a.m. and taken to Bangalore central jail, where they were provided a large, oblong-shaped room to share;[53] the Congress (O) leader Shyambabu Mishra and Madhu Dandavate were given the other room.[54]

The jail manual divides daily duties between inmates, and Vajpayee was tasked with cooking.[55] Something of an epicurean, he must have relished this, though it is doubtful if he was allowed to prepare his beloved prawn curry. Advani's recollection is telling: 'The food he cooked was simple but wholesome.'[56] Prison would provide the chance for Vajpayee and Advani, whose original camaraderie was being overshadowed by an instrumental partnership, to rekindle their early intimacy.

Advani straightaway wrote to their lawyer N.M. Ghatate, who had since returned to India with a PhD from the American University in Washington DC and had worked as a legal junior to the Congressman V.K. Krishna Menon.[57] Meanwhile, opposition leaders from across India, including Jayaprakash Narayan, had been arrested.[58] Nanaji Deshmukh had escaped after receiving a call on the night of 25 June itself. A female voice had told him that he had an hour to get away: 'The police will surround your place around one o'clock.' Nanaji made calls to warn others while his assistant packed a couple of shirts and dhotis into a briefcase. While the rest of Delhi slept, he fled to a secret location.[59] He would soon find himself in south Bombay, squirreled away in the home of Nusli Wadia.

Over the next two years, an estimated 36,000 people would be jailed,[60] almost all on rickety charges that would not have stood in a democracy. Indira Gandhi seemed to delight in humiliating those who thought they were her equals. The maharanis of Gwalior and Jaipur, Vijayaraje Scindia and Gayatri Devi, were both arrested under the Kafka-esque COFEPOSA law for economic crimes and lodged in Delhi's Tihar jail. Gayatri Devi's beauty made her as much a global figure as Indira Gandhi. The Rajmata remembers having to share a toilet with Gayatri Devi. 'There was no tap there; only a hole existed on the ground; the jail sweeper would pour a few buckets of water twice a day in that hole.'[61] Jail authorities would visit them to ogle at Gayatri Devi 'as if she was an animal in a zoo'.[62]

The Rajmata's loyalty to her new family caused a rift with her old one. Her son Madhavrao Scindia—young, handsome and responsible for bringing in its wealthiest funder, Nusli Wadia—was at the time the star of the Jana Sangh. 'When Emergency was declared, Madhavrao ran away to Nepal. He was a coward,' says an angry BJP leader. Madhavrao eventually left the party for the Congress, sparking an unrelenting feud between mother and son.

Unlike Madhavrao, Nusli Wadia refused to give in. He and his wife Maureen considered Nanaji part of their household; Nusli remembers even working with Nanaji to collect money from Bombay businessmen for the party.[63] The Jana Sangh treasurer would reciprocate with spicy pickles for the Wadias every time he visited Bombay.[64] Jinnah's grandson was not about to betray this new family of his. Though industrialists were vulnerable to state expropriation, Nusli continued to back the Jana Sangh during their darkest days.[65] Vasundhara Raje followed her mother, not her brother, in weathering the Emergency. She says: 'Nusli spent money during the Emergency. He was the one who kept us afloat. Nusli really helped our family.'[66]

* * *

The RSS chief Balasaheb Deoras was arrested a few days after the Emergency was imposed. His organization was banned four days later, on 4 July 1975. Though Indira had also banned twenty-five other groups, the RSS was her principal target. Raids were carried out in cities across India, and the two-storey RSS headquarters in Nagpur was sealed.[67] A search of these premises revealed fifty-three swords, seventy-four daggers, an old double-barrelled pistol and a bayonet—hardly adequate to take on the Indian state. Also seized were fifty-one leather shields, fifty-eight canes, 788 lathis, 510 belts, 626 caps and 844 pairs of socks.[68]

This was the second time the RSS had been banned. As we read earlier, the ban after Gandhi's murder had shaken the organization. With memories of that torment perhaps, Deoras wrote two conciliatory letters to Indira Gandhi, even offering to put the RSS at the service of her development activities.[69] These letters were later used as proof of his cowardice.[70]

The impact of this ban on the RSS, however, was less severe than before. They were able to tap into money from overseas Indians. The cadre was also left mostly intact: only 186 of its 1356 pracharaks were arrested.[71] The rest went into hiding.

Narendra Modi began travelling across Gujarat incognito, growing a thick beard that covered much of his face.[72] A month after the Emergency was declared, he was instructed to meet George Fernandes, and help with travel plans.[73] With his fearless attacks on the Congress, George had become a working-class hero for Modi. And since the socialists were members of the Janata Front, the RSS considered Fernandes part of their extended 'family'.

The Emergency was a period in which Modi's horizons expanded, he later told his biographer Nilanjan Mukhopadhyay. He came into contact with two university professors who encouraged him to write about his ordeals. Narendra Modi's first book, *Apatkalme Gujarat* or 'Gujarat during the Emergency', was published soon after.[74]

Modi's experiences were indicative of the spread-out saffron network during the Emergency. Leaders were provided shelter and food in the houses of sympathizers, often at risk to their families. When Ghatate flew to Bangalore to meet Vajpayee and Advani, Nanaji simply told him: 'Someone will come to pick you up.' From the airport, an RSS man took Ghatate to his home where Ghatate stayed and ate. 'No questions were asked,' he remembers. 'What people don't realize is that it is like a family.'[75]

The RSS was not the only secretive network during the Emergency. But so effective were they that Indira Gandhi complained six months after the ban that there was no 'let-up in the RSS activities. They were functioning now in an organised underground manner.'[76]

* * *

Vajpayee was unused to spartan living, and Advani worried that his friend would be unable to survive the jail conditions. On 1 July 1975, just a week into the Emergency, Advani sent Ghatate a telegram asking him to bring

woollens from 'the residence of Atalji . . . Also Atalji's medical reports.'[77]
When Ghatate visited Bangalore jail, Vajpayee was wearing warm prison
clothes. He joked: 'Now Indira Gandhi will feed me and Indira Gandhi
will give me clothes. I am not going to spend a penny from my pocket.'[78]

Twelve days later, Vajpayee was shifted to Victoria Hospital in
Bangalore with appendix pain.[79] He was then moved to the AIIMS in
Delhi where his spine was operated upon. Vajpayee kept his humour
through his recovery. He was able to drink whisky and eat chicken at the
hospital,[80] and when told that there was a Parsi specialist in Bombay who
cured back problems through calculated kicks, Vajpayee replied: 'Indira
Gandhi is already kicking me. Why do you want one more person to kick
me?'[81]

Few outside the sangh parivar—the family of organizations such as
the Jana Sangh and VHP revolving around the RSS—dared visit Vajpayee.
An exception was the bureaucrat Ashok Saikia, who had been Mr Kaul's
student in Ramjas College in the 1960s; he would later be a vital member
of Prime Minister Vajpayee's office.

By this time, B.N. Kaul had retired from Ramjas College. A family
friend remembers, 'The Kauls had definitely moved in [to Vajpayee's
official bungalow] by then.' From then on, the Kauls would live with
Vajpayee until the end of their lives. During the Emergency, Vajpayee's
room at the AIIMS hospital was considered a prison, with jail rules
applying. Rajkumari Kaul would visit every week, even waiting for hours
to get government permission every single time.[82]

L.K. Advani had meanwhile adapted to prison life. He took to reading
in the small library located beneath the circular watchtower,[83] and playing
table tennis.[84] He even successfully contested for a Rajya Sabha seat from
Gujarat in 1976.[85] His many letters written to his lawyer from jail—on
a censorship pro-forma sheet titled FORM B (see clause 15[2])—reveal
constant courtesy: 'Regards for Sheela and love for the kids.' Advani wrote
on another such sheet: 'Sorry for this shoddy scrap. We are required to
write on these pro-formas. Always yours Lal.'[86]

After Advani had begun working for Vajpayee in 1957, the two would
speak with each other almost every day. Now, after eighteen years of daily
contact, Advani missed Vajpayee, and longed for news of his closest friend.
'How is Atalji?' he wrote in one of many letters to Ghatate. 'Nothing has

been appearing lately even in the parliamentary bulletins. Hope he has recovered completely from the operation. Give him my warm regards.'[87]

During this period, Vajpayee was keenly aware that leadership of the party, which he had wrested from Madhok with help from Advani, was slipping away. Nanaji had directed the opposition and led the resistance before being arrested. Subramanian Swamy, who had fled abroad, made a dramatic reappearance in parliament in August 1976, before escaping. They were both outshining Vajpayee.

Vajpayee complained from hospital in a letter to Advani: 'No one listens to me in the underground.' Advani's reply exhibited just a touch of exasperation. 'I am inside jail. You are outside. For all practical purposes, you are president. You decide.'

* * *

The imposition of the Emergency had quietened the daily demonstrations that preceded it. Those around Indira Gandhi painted this as evidence that the JP movement had not been all that popular to begin with, and that 'the hard core of the movement was confined to the Jana Sangh and its RSS cadres'.[88] Such an explanation discounted the thousands silenced through incarceration, or the millions terrorized by the blunt tools of the state.

The bluntest of these tools was the male sterilization ('*nasbandi*' in Hindi) programme the government began promoting to control the population. It became an instrument of oppression—in Haryana, for instance, an entire village was surrounded and its men forced to undergo vasectomy.[89] It evoked such dread that people hid when they saw even an ordinary van.[90] Censorship of the press—editors had to submit any news item critical of the government for clearance[91]—ensured this popular rage never made its way to those in power. Editors who refused to comply were fired, and some magazines chose to shut shop rather than submit to censorship. Around 7000 people were arrested just for circulating uncensored political material.[92]

All Indians were allowed to hear was propaganda praising a return to order from the chaos of democracy. The prime minister's twenty-point programme promised the efficient implementation of a range of populist schemes: from reduction in the prices of essential commodities to land reforms to lower taxes for the middle class.[93] And with the parliamentary opposition in jail, Indira Gandhi easily passed legislation emasculating the judiciary and removing constitutional limits on the parliament she now dominated.

Lawyers and judges began to fight back. Thousands of political prisoners filed petitions in courts challenging their confinement without trial. Vajpayee and Advani asked the Bombay lawyer M.C. Chagla to argue for them in the Karnataka High Court. Chagla was a Muslim and had been Muhammad Ali Jinnah's junior in legal practice; he was a telling choice for these two princes of Hindu nationalism.

Chagla argued for two full days, with Advani sitting by his side. 'I missed the presence of Vajpayee as he was confined to his home with a slipped disc,' Chagla later wrote.[94] He nonetheless won.[95] The government went on appeal to the Supreme Court. This appeal was combined with others originating from high courts across the country. Every single case had been decided in favour of the prisoners.

Five judges of the Supreme Court pronounced judgment on these appeals in April 1976. Four of them held that the Emergency made it legal for detainees such as Advani and Vajpayee to be denied the right to a fair trial. A lone judge, H.R. Khanna, dissented, arguing that such a right could never be smothered by any law. He added: 'In a purely formal sense, even the organised mass murders of the Nazi regime qualify as law.'[96]

The majority judgment is widely considered the nadir of the Supreme Court of India. *The New York Times* wrote a withering editorial titled 'Fading Hope in India', while quoting glowingly from H.R. Khanna's dissent.[97] When Ghatate went to inform Vajpayee about the outcome, he replied: 'Political battle cannot be won by legal means.' On hearing Vajpayee's comment, Advani replied: 'Atalji is very right'.[98]

The Emergency was to have a lasting impact on Hindu nationalism. For thousands of RSS and Jana Sangh workers, their incarceration made real the rights that only democracies guarantee; they learnt the value of civil liberties and freedoms.

For Vajpayee, the Emergency fulfilled his cherished aim of mainstreaming the Jana Sangh and accommodating it within the broader opposition to the Congress. For Advani, who endured jail for its entirety, the Emergency was more personal; he even converted his prison diaries into a 287-page hardback, *A Prisoner's Scrap-Book*.[99] The former journalist in him galled at how the press had complied with their own censorship. He would later say, 'You were asked to bend, but you began to crawl.'[100]

On its fortieth anniversary in 2015, Advani was asked whether the Emergency could happen again. By now sidelined within the party by the prime minister, Narendra Modi, he chose his words with care. 'I don't think anything has been done that gives me the assurance that civil liberties will not be suspended or destroyed again. Not at all.'[101]

* * *

On 18 January 1977, Indira Gandhi once again took India by surprise. She announced the release of political prisoners, and fresh elections in March.[102] In ending the Emergency, Indira blamed the opposition and asked them 'to admit their anti-democratic mistakes'.[103] It is a measure of the times that the press reported this statement without underlining its irony.

Vajpayee had spent the final months of the Emergency working to merge the opposition into a single party, even writing to Jayaprakash Narayan: 'The question of unification awaits your decision . . . those who do not agree; leave them to face the ire of the public.'[104] He now seized on the chance provided by Indira's call for elections. When asked about his conditions for joining an anti-Congress front, Vajpayee replied: 'We have no conditions.'[105]

The day after Indira's announcement, on 19 January 1977, leaders from the original 'Janata Front'—the Congress (O), Bharatiya Lok Dal, Socialist Party and Jana Sangh—met.[106] It was Vajpayee who represented his party, though he was neither president nor its Emergency-era face. The fact that leaders from these four parties had shared prison time made for a convivial discussion. Four days later, they formally announced a united 'Janata Party' to fight the Congress in the coming elections. Curiously, L.K. Advani—not Nanaji, who had been general secretary of the pre-Emergency 'Janata Front'—was made general secretary. The hand behind this switch is not hard to identify.

The newly formed Janata Party got a boost on 2 February 1977 when Indira Gandhi's right-hand man, Jagjivan Ram, joined them.[107] It had taken him until the end of the Emergency to notice the 'civil liberties violation and the decline of intra-party democracy' in the Congress.[108] The Akali Dal in Punjab, the Dravida Munnetra Khazagam (DMK) in Tamil Nadu, and CPM in Bengal, all entered into seat adjustments with the Janata Party. The Shahi Imam of the Jama Masjid in Delhi, who joined them, even asked for the ban on the RSS to be lifted.[109]

But amidst these shows of unity, there were auguries of the final break-up. The Janata manifesto was beset with contradictions. It advocated 'Gandhian socialism' and abolishing the right to property, despite some of its constituents leaning right.[110] Its leaders also began to bicker about who should helm the party. These fissures were on display during discussions over a common party flag. Charan Singh wanted it to be green, as a token to the farmers who were his party's bedrock. L.K. Advani favoured the Hindu holy colour of saffron. The final Indian-style consensus was a flag two-thirds saffron and one-third green, with an image of a plough-carrying farmer on the saffron side.[111]

* * *

The 1977 election campaign was like no other in Indian history. Since censorship persisted, the press foretold a Congress victory. The ruling party responded with overconfidence, pasting posters on bus stands, noticeboards and even urinals terming the Janata party 'a conglomeration of rats'.[112] Another poster asked them the valid question: 'Who will be your prime minister when you are fighting each other on the distribution of tickets?'[113] The Janata responded in kind. One of their posters said: 'When the Congress asks for votes, ask for a sterilization certificate.' Another had a suggestion for Indira Gandhi's election symbol: 'A bulldozer.'[114]

Contesting from New Delhi, Vajpayee campaigned wearing 'a spotless, neatly creased white *dhoti* and *kurta*, with a brick-coloured Nehru jacket left open'.[115] His health seems to have magically recovered. A magazine report covering his campaign noticed that Vajpayee came alive on-stage, tailoring his message to the audience and leaving them spellbound. Off-stage, Vajpayee retreated to his normal self. His home was not bustling with supporters; 'the atmosphere was quiet, unruffled, unlike any politician's house'.[116]

Advani, meanwhile, chose to remain a member of the Rajya Sabha rather than contest these Lok Sabha elections. He remained too much in thrall of Vajpayee's speaking skills and too little of his own, to emerge as a politician in his own right. Instead, he chose to follow orders from Vajpayee and worked behind the scenes to get Janata candidates elected.

Assisting them was the most resilient of organizations in the country. Ravindra Bhagwat is a lawyer in eastern Maharashtra who comes from an RSS family; apart from his brother being the current chief, his father was an early mentor to L.K. Advani. He says: 'Generally, the RSS does not give orders from the top. But 1977 is the only election where RSS workers directly campaigned. This was because of the ban on the RSS and suspension of democracy by Indira Gandhi. So a change in government was the only solution. I myself campaigned.'[117]

The Congress noticed and responded with ads portraying the RSS as the driving force behind the Janata Party. It hoped that the Indian voter would consider the party too extreme to countenance.

This could not have been more wrong. The results were announced on 22 March 1977. The Janata Party had won 43 per cent of the national vote, which translated into 298 seats, a snug majority. The Congress was reduced to 154 of the 542 seats in parliament. Indira and Sanjay Gandhi lost their seats. The Congress was annihilated in the Hindi-speaking belt where it won only two of the 237 seats on offer.[118] It had done better in the south where the Emergency had been less severe, and where many feared that the Janata Party would revive Hindi chauvinism.[119]

Jana Sangh candidates had won ninety-three seats, making them the largest among the Janata constituents. For a group that many felt was weighing the Janata Party down, it was an unqualified victory.

This success, however, came with new challenges. The prime minister in the new government should logically have been from the Jana Sangh, as should a plurality of ministers. But this might not have been acceptable to the others. Another problem was Vajpayee and Advani's grip on the party, weakened as it had become during the Emergency. Then there was the Janata itself. Though legally a single party with a majority in parliament, it was in fact a loose confederation of warring tribes with each chieftain wanting to be crowned prime minister. Besides, each of these constituent parties catered to select slices of India—landowning north Indian peasants, urban socialists, middle-class upper castes and disgruntled Congress workers. The Janata Party was, in Jayaprakash Narayan's own words, a 'hotchpotch'.[120]

Facing such challenges, how would Vajpayee, Advani and Hindu nationalism navigate their first taste of power?

6

PRUDENT IN POWER (1977–80)

Right from the start, the Jana Sangh was determined not to rock the Janata boat. Despite winning more seats than the other four constituents of the Janata party in the 1977 elections, they did not throw their hat in the prime ministerial ring. 'We were happy that we were part of the government. Others in Janata did not like our connection to RSS. We did not want [the] government to be seen as run by us,' says a former BJP minister.

This team spirit was in contrast to that of the other Janata constituents, as the race for prime minister devolved into a brawl between Morarji Desai, Charan Singh and Jagjivan Ram.

Dubbed 'conservative' for his pro-business and Hindu-lite politics,[1] Morarji had almost become prime minister in 1964 and again in 1967. Better known for drinking his urine, Morarji had handled every lever of the Indian state: he had served as a civil servant, state chief minister and then central minister for years.

The Jana Sangh's preferred candidate was Jagjivan Ram, from the 'Congress for Democracy' or CFD. The Sanskrit-speaking son of a priest from the Shiv Narayani sect,[2] Jagjivan Ram had been Indira's defence minister during the popular Bangladesh war. He was especially experienced—he would hold a world record for being an elected parliamentarian for fifty straight years. But it was his Dalit caste that seemed to matter more than all these skills.[3] 'He was a Harijan. If we worked under him, it would show Hindus as united,' a former BJP minister says. It was also for this very reason that Charan Singh 'refused under any conditions to support Jagjivan Ram'.[4]

Singh was a Jat from western Uttar Pradesh, an 'organic intellectual of the rich and middle peasantry'.[5] He represented the political rise of farmers in north India; 36 per cent of all MPs in the 1977 Lok Sabha came from farming backgrounds, up from 22 per cent in 1952.[6] Charan Singh's middle-caste status led to a grudge against Brahmins such as Morarji; it also triggered derision for Dalits such as Jagjivan Ram.'[7]

Charan Singh demanded the post of prime minister, since his Bharatiya Lok Dal (BLD) had more seats than Morarji's Congress (O), an argument which, if taken to its logical end, would have made for a Jana Sangh PM. The matter was resolved when Jayaprakash Narayan chose Morarji Desai. And in March 1977, Morarji was sworn in as the first non-Congress prime minister of India.

Hours later at midnight, newspaper offices announced to cheering crowds that Morarji had picked nineteen people to be in his cabinet.[8] Vajpayee was given the foreign ministry, while Advani was made minister of Information and Broadcasting. Jagjivan Ram and Charan Singh were placated with the defence and home ministries. They were both made deputy prime ministers.

Care had been taken to include all factions of the Janata Party in the cabinet. There was one minister for every seven Socialist members of parliament, every thirteen CFD MPs, every seven Congress (O) MPs, and every eighteen BLD MPs.[9] However, the ninety-three Jana Sangh MPs were represented by just three ministers, a ratio of 1:31.

Some have argued that this underrepresentation was because the taste of power had made Jana Sangh leaders 'breathless at the bargaining table'.[10] But the primary reason is likely more insidious.

Then Jana Sangh MP Subramanian Swamy complains, 'Morarji told me that you will be finance minister. But Vajpayee told him a lie that I had been slated for organizational work. The reason there were only few ministers from Jana Sangh was because of Vajpayee. He was insecure.'[11] There is no way to verify Swamy's charges, but we do know that Swamy made the same allegations to the press.[12] Virendra Kapoor is both a journalist as well as Swamy's brother-in-law. He says: 'I told him not to do it. I told him, as long as you are a member of a party, fight your battles within.'[13] Swamy was making the same mistake that Madhok had; in response to backseat steering by Vajpayee, he had broadcast his quarrel, something that was anathema to the sangh parivar.

The other unexpected omission from the cabinet was Nanaji Deshmukh. Nanaji, after all, had been the hero of the Emergency underground. The new prime minister had first offered him the industry ministry. But that very day, Nanaji received a surprise visitor. Rajendra Singh, then the number 2 in the RSS and eventually number 1. Singh told Nanaji: '[As party treasurer] you have very good relations with industrialists. But if you are industry minister, questions will be raised [about these connections]. You will spoil your image and that of the party.'[14] Govindacharya sees in this direction a not-so-hidden hand. 'Rajju Bhaiyya [i.e., Rajendra Singh] was Vajpayee's mentor. They were very close.'[15]

As Vajpayee and Advani moved to be the only representatives of their ideology in government, Nanaji wordlessly acquiesced. Unlike Swamy, he was too much of a Hindu nationalist to publicly break with party unity.

* * *

Soon after being sworn in, foreign minister Atal Bihari Vajpayee visited his office in South Block on Raisina Hill. He had visited as an MP before, but this time he noticed something amiss. The wall that usually carried a portrait of India's first foreign minister, Jawaharlal Nehru, was bare.[16] An overzealous bureaucrat had removed it to curry favour with the new dispensation. Vajpayee right away ordered that the painting be put back.

In interview after interview, he said, 'Foreign policy is neither decided nor conducted on party lines.'[17] Natwar Singh, who would one day become the Congress's foreign minister, was then a diplomat. He says, 'As external affairs minister, Vajpayee did not fundamentally depart from Nehru's foreign policy. He did not reject non-alignment, but unlike Indira Gandhi he avoided a tilt towards the Soviet Union.'

Where this continuity was most evident was in dealings with Pakistan, bugbear of Hindu nationalists since the early twentieth century. 'The Pakistanis saw Vajpayee as a votary of Akhand Bharat [the concept of a Hindu India that included the territory of Pakistan and Afghanistan] and someone who had opposed the Shimla agreement,' T.C.A. Raghavan remembers.[18] But the former high commissioner to Pakistan adds that Vajpayee placated these fears when he visited in February 1978, a journey every bit as important as his bus ride to Lahore in 1999 as prime minister.[19] He charmed Pakistani dictator Zia-ul-Haq,[20] and even ensured that Kashmir—that perennial barrier—did not derail discussions.[21]

Vajpayee agreed to be chief guest at a music concert by the Pakistani ghazal singer Mehdi Hasan, organized by the Pakistan High Commission in Delhi. Indira Gandhi was also in attendance. The once-towering figure in Indian politics was now being made to feel small by the Janata government. When a Pakistani at the venue invited her to Lahore, Indira Gandhi looked at Vajpayee and sarcastically said, 'First please ask him to return my passport.'[22]

In perhaps one of the few breaks from Congress foreign policy, Prime Minister Morarji Desai invited the Israeli defence minister Moshe Dayan for consultations in 1977.[23] India at that time did not have full diplomatic relations with Israel. The Nehruvian consensus had depicted Israel as an illegal colonial settlement, an attitude backed up by the more prosaic concerns of Arab oil and domestic Muslim votes. 'We tried to hide Dayan, but there was one thing we could not hide—he wore a black eye patch,' the Intelligence Bureau official in charge of the visit remembers after all these years.[24] The trip was kept hidden from even Vajpayee, who, unlike others in his party, was 'not a big fan of Israel'. But when Vajpayee visited the Prime Minister's Office and recognized the man with the eye patch, he told a friend in anger, '*Yeh kahaan se aaya*?' Where has this one come from?

These courtesies to the views of opponents from other parties ran parallel to Vajpayee's discourtesies to rivals *within* his party. It is a trait that pervades this book: not only was Vajpayee capable of being heard in multiple registers, he was capable of containing within himself multitudes.

This is perhaps why he coupled a largely Nehruvian foreign policy with just enough nods to Hindutva ideology.

He travelled twice to Afghanistan. Vajpayee wanted to see where Mahmud of Ghazni 'who had always pricked my heart like a cactus' had come from. Both Vajpayee and Advani were brought up on tales of the eleventh-century sacking of the Somnath temple. But Vajpayee was told by his hosts that there was nothing to see in Ghazni; there was not even a 'five-star hotel'. This hurt Vajpayee even more. In his words: 'Ghazni was a small village . . . with shanty huts . . . but a looter [from there] got a collection of looters and came to loot the golden bird.' He succeeded, Vajpayee concluded, because of 'our internal splits . . . the king will fight, the kshatriya will fight . . . [but] we have banned the big section of our society from fighting . . .'[25]

The other foray into ideology that the foreign minister undertook was when he visited the United States in June 1978 along with Prime Minister Desai. He spoke in Hindi to a diaspora crowd of 10,000, despite objections from those who did not know the language.[26] More celebrated is another speech of Vajpayee's, to the United Nations in New York. It was the first such in Hindi.[27] It was during these trips that Vajpayee would get to know a diplomat who, as we shall see later, would one day supplant Advani as his guide on governance.

Brajesh Mishra was then India's permanent representative to the UN. Slightly younger than Vajpayee but with much less hair, Mishra was both a Macaulayputra as well as from the Hindi heartland. While he himself spoke in clipped English and always wore a suit, his father was D.P. Mishra,[28] the former Congress chief minister of Madhya Pradesh and Indira loyalist. Just as the father had served one prime minister, the son would serve another prime minister with that same devotion.

While Vajpayee's term was a success, it was marred by his visit to China in 1979, the first by a foreign minister since India's 1962 defeat.[29] The Chinese attacked Vietnam, a friend of India, while Vajpayee was in China. The charm that he had turned on Pakistan seemed to have come to naught with this neighbour. An embarrassed Vajpayee cut short his trip. He returned home to brickbats from the Mandarin-speaking Subramanian Swamy,[30] as well as the press who decried it as a 'wrecked China visit'.[31]

While Vajpayee ignored Swamy and the press, he took parliament more seriously. The diplomat Shivshankar Menon remembers Vajpayee allowing other MPs to speak for ten minutes during the debate, not just those within his own party. This way the issue seemed bipartisan. 'I'll say this for Vajpayee's visit . . . if you get out of the media stuff, this trip is where the mending began. All this about Kailash Mansarovar, not allowing [the] rest of the relationship to be held hostage by the boundary [dispute]. It all began then.'[32]

* * *

While minister Vajpayee was making a mark by largely sticking to the Nehruvian consensus, Lal Krishna Advani was doing the same, but in his more subdued style. He had by now acquired his first car—an old blue Fiat—which was an improvement on his rickety scooter. 'These are people who lived simple, middle-class lives,' the journalist Virendra Kapoor says. 'By and large, Advani was very clean.'[33]

Though the information and broadcasting ministry—in charge of regulating newspapers, radio, television and films—was not customarily considered influential, the Emergency with its censorship routine had changed that. There were those in the Janata party who did not want to expose this post to the nascent fascism of a Hindu nationalist. They could not have been more wrong.

Lal Krishna Advani reaccredited journalists who had been blacklisted by the Indira government. Laws that stifled the press were rescinded[34] and the Press Council was revived.[35] He also introduced a law that provided modest autonomy to Doordarshan and All India Radio (AIR) from government control.[36]

N. Ram, then an investigative journalist who would one day become editor of *The Hindu*, remembers that 'Advani was relatively pro-press during the period after Emergency. So he made a relatively good impression among journalists.'[37]

While minister Advani was a civil libertarian, there was some controversy over whether his ministry had provided a platform for RSS propaganda. A Socialist MP alleged that 'several officials were transferred and key positions were given to RSS sympathisers. We also saw a subtle change in the programmes of All India Radio.'[38] Even Advani admits asking film-makers in Bombay to make 'movies based on our great epics Ramayana and Mahabharata', similar to the 'best Hollywood films on biblical themes'.[39] His advice wasn't heeded then. But as we will see, the serialization of these two epics a decade later would take place during the first bloom of the BJP.

These anecdotes aside, there is no evidence of systematic manipulation of the media, the way it was done by the Congress during the Emergency. In fact, Balraj Madhok, now estranged, accused Advani of allowing far too much coverage of Indira Gandhi.[40]

* * *

Vajpayee and Advani's reluctance to impose their party agenda was probably why almost no Hindutva causes made their way into law under the Janata government.

Take, for example, education policy, which the RSS saw as reflecting the hegemony, first of British, and then of Marxist historians. Their immediate concern was the propaganda of the Congress party through the 1970s, especially by its Marxist education minister Nurul Hasan, who had ensured that state educational and cultural institutions reflected a 'progressive tone'.[41]

The RSS was keen to replace this bias with its own. Its chief told the press in May 1977 that education was an area where the RSS would 'cooperate' with the government.[42] Textbooks written by the historians Romila Thapar and Bipan Chandra were considered for withdrawal,[43] leading to an outcry. In the end, the Jana Sangh did not want to draw attention to itself, and the government only pulled back one book.[44] Unlike when the BJP was in power from 1998 to 2004, the 'Janata government did not initiate attempts to influence the writing and teaching of history'.[45]

The other area where Janata policies did not run on RSS lines was reservations. While caste quotas in government education and employment had existed for Scheduled Castes and Tribes since Independence, quotas for middle castes, known by the technical phrase 'Other Backward Classes' or OBCs, were a constitutional afterthought.[46] Several southern states had enacted reservations for these middle castes soon after Independence, and in early 1978, the Janata Party in Bihar introduced 26 per cent 'backward caste' quotas in government jobs (in addition to the 24 per cent reserved for SCs and STs).[47]

The push for quotas for these 'backward castes' was driven by demographic changes in the profile of politicians. In the 1977 national parliament, upper castes comprised less than 50 per cent of all north

Indian MPs for the first time.[48] Their place was taken by a surge in 'OBC' legislators.

Pressure from these MPs led Prime Minister Desai to appoint a commission headed by Bindeshwari Prasad Mandal to recommend policy benefits for backward castes.[49] While this Mandal commission would eventually change the trajectory of both India and Hindutva, the Jana Sangh supported its appointment. It did not wish to split the Janata Party or alienate middle castes from the Hindu fold.

It is thus clear that the Jana Sangh and the RSS chose not to promote their agenda through government. Their actions outside of the state, however, were a different matter.

* * *

Unlike after Gandhi's murder, the RSS had survived the Emergency ban with its morale enhanced. Between 1975 and 1977, the number of RSS shakhas expanded by 30 per cent, from 8500 to 11,000.[50] It now had fifty-three organizations linked to it, an annual budget of rupees two crores and over 2000 pracharaks.[51] This was the fastest expansion of the RSS till that date,[52] a 25 per cent growth in membership, which now stood at one million.[53]

This enlargement of the RSS alarmed other politicians. Janata Party leaders turned on the RSS.[54] They argued that the RSS was not a cultural, but a political body. This meant that the Janata MPs formerly from the Jana Sangh had 'dual membership' in two political associations, i.e., the Janata Party and the RSS. They demanded the ending of these RSS links.

Vajpayee responded with time-tested skills. He publicly supported the RSS and refused to renounce his membership; he also chafed at being treated like a 'second class citizen' by others in the Janata Party.[55] But, during the annual-day celebrations of the RSS in March 1979, Vajpayee made it a point to sit in the back row, despite being asked to sit in front.[56] He also went out of the way to 'fraternise' with RSS-baiters in the Janata.[57] This double-speak seems to have bought temporary calm. When Morarji termed the RSS a cultural organization[58] that was compatible with political membership in the Janata Party, others chose not to precipitate the matter for the time being.

During this period of respite, the prime minister and his foreign minister visited India's global patron, the Soviet Union. Perhaps exhausted from the attacks back home, Vajpayee dozed off during the second half of a ballet performance hosted for their benefit.[59] He returned home, in June 1979, to a government about to be put to sleep.

* * *

Charan Singh had resented not being made prime minister, and it was left to Vajpayee and George Fernandes to mediate the many disputes that arose.[60] The camaraderie from these years would be the stencil for the time when Fernandes would become Prime Minister Vajpayee's improbable defence minister, two decades later.

Yet, no amount of diplomacy could quench Charan Singh's ambition. By July 1979, the Janata government had unravelled, with Charan Singh and some others leaving. Reduced to a minority in parliament, the Morarji government was forced to resign, as the rules of the Westminster system dictated. That Charan Singh's departure was not entirely principled was seen immediately after, when Indira Gandhi added her MPs to his tally in parliament.[61]

Charan Singh was sworn in as the fifth prime minister of India; he had finally gained the title for which he had wrecked so much. The glory was all title only. As journalist B.G. Verghese put it, 'Charan Singh is in office but Mrs Gandhi is in power.'[62] Indira Gandhi soon withdrew support, ensuring Charan Singh's resignation and her ultimate aim of fresh elections. The Janata experiment was over.

Through this ordeal, Vajpayee and Advani were dismayed at how egos had squandered a political fortune. Their own partnership had been crafted, not just for personal fortune, but for a loftier goal. The same was true of the sangh parivar. Even though they were beset by as much differences as the rest of the Janata Party, they had stayed united in deciding to take a back seat in government. Since their ideology was anchored in organizational unity, they were particularly maddened at the Janata Party's conduct. Even Balraj Madhok wrote a letter to JP about the lack of a common thread in the Janata Party.[63]

Which is why, soon after the fall of the Morarji Desai government, Vajpayee wrote an op-ed in *The Indian Express* titled 'All Responsible for the Janata Crisis'. Vajpayee did not fault ideological incompatibility. Instead, he blamed 'factional quarrels within the party and public airing of grievances'.[64]

The other lesson Vajpayee and Advani had learnt from their short-lived stint in power was that their RSS affiliation was a roadblock. Though it had not been the reason for the downfall of the government, allegations of 'dual membership' had dogged them throughout. So, in that very same op-ed, Vajpayee complained that 'the RSS . . . should have taken greater pains to demonstrate that they did not seek a political role'.[65] His article, unparalleled in its public condemnation of the RSS, also had a suggestion: the RSS should formally disavow the concept of 'Hindu Rashtra' and replace it with 'Bharatiya Rashtra'.[66]

* * *

Elections were set for January 1980. With Charan Singh gone and Morarji Desai unavailable, the Hindu nationalists did not hesitate in supporting Jagjivan Ram as their prime ministerial candidate. Once more, they downplayed their own dreams in order to project Hindu unity between the Dalit leader and their upper-caste base.[67] Vajpayee contested from New Delhi, while Advani remained a Rajya Sabha MP.

In the midst of this campaign, an ailing Jayaprakash Narayan died on 8 October 1979. He had lived long enough to see his dream birthed, then murdered, but not long enough to attend the funeral. Vajpayee was distraught,[68] and as we shall see in the next chapter, JP's legacy would remain in his mind long after.

The campaigning saw an invigorated Indira Gandhi taking on an enervated Janata. The woman who had lorded over Indian politics until two years ago still retained her feel for the public mood. Persecution by the Janata government had also given her the aura of a martyr. As importantly, the disunity of the Janata government had reminded voters that authoritarianism had its pluses.

When the results were announced, the Congress had won 362 out of 520 seats.[69] The Janata Party was reduced to just thirty-two seats; the Jana Sangh tally had shrunk from ninety-three to sixteen.[70] It was Prime Minister Indira Gandhi once more.

Knives began turning for the Jana Sangh within the Janata Party. Jagjivan Ram wrote a letter blaming them for the election defeat.[71] Advani and Vajpayee sensed where the denouement was heading. When the Janata Party decided to meet on 4 April 1980 to take a final decision on 'dual membership', Vajpayee and Advani scheduled a Jana Sangh rally on 5 and 6 April.

The meeting concluded as they had anticipated. On the basis of a 17:14 vote majority, the national executive of the Janata Party decreed that no party member could also be part of the RSS.[72] The Jana Sangh viewed this as a 'virtual expulsion' and decided to leave the party rather than abandon the mothership.[73]

The Jana Sangh met the next day, 5 April 1980, in Feroze Shah Kotla. Though only 1500 were expected, 3683 party delegates made it a point to attend.[74] Garlanded portraits of Deendayal Upadhyaya shared space with that of Mohandas Gandhi and Jayaprakash Narayan. On stage and giving speeches were those who were not affiliated with the RSS, from lawyers Shanti Bhushan and Ram Jethmalani to the Muslim politician Sikander Bakht.[75]

L.K. Advani announced the creation of a new party.[76] In his speech on 6 April, Vajpayee, who had been declared the new president, declared that 'there was nothing wrong with the Janata party's policies and programmes. It was the behaviour of the politicians which the people had voted against.'[77] The party agenda would be announced later, as would its symbol. But before the day ended on 6 April 1980, the name was announced. Instead of reverting to Jana Sangh, the new party wanted to be seen as heir to the Janata Party. It was christened Bharatiya Janata Party. BJP.

* * *

Vajpayee and Advani's decision to form a new party rather than renounce the RSS bought them its gratitude. The 13 April 1980 editorial of the *Organiser* claimed, 'Although many would like to give the old Jana Sangh name to the new party, it was but appropriate that the new party should get a new name . . . there are significant new elements which can only broaden its base.'[78]

While Vajpayee had shown a warm heart by staying loyal to the RSS, he was simultaneously cold-blooded in denuding the new party of any remaining competition. He met RSS chief Balasaheb Deoras and said, 'It's either [Subramanian] Swamy or me in the new party.'[79] R.V. Pandit says 'Atalji did a slight injustice to Swamy. He was cleverer than Atalji. And he tried to show-off. Whereas Atal and Advaniji are not show-offs at all.'

Pandit's comments echo the condemnation that Hindu nationalism faces for being hostile to intellectuals. While some hold that a shallow ideology cannot attract brainpower, the more likely answer is that brilliant people tend to have outsized egos—as Subramanian Swamy, Balraj Madhok and M.L. Sondhi all had. An ideology that places teambuilding above all else is unsuited to solo performers.

The one man Vajpayee found hard to expunge was Nanaji Deshmukh. The co-founder of the Jana Sangh was older than Vajpayee, and perhaps the only man remaining in the party who could call him 'Atal' without the honorific '*ji*' at the end.[80] But Nanaji was by now disillusioned with the way the Janata Party had put ambition before principle. Equally, he resented how methodically Vajpayee had demoted him. Nanaji could have made a public scene, as was standard in other parties. Instead, he announced his retirement from politics, claiming that he had turned sixty and wanted to set an example.[81]

Nanaji decided to move to rural India. He would eventually settle in Chitrakoot, a forested area in central India, and work with tribals. Such a move typified Mohandas Gandhi's idiom of social change, illustrated by his 'ashrams' in South Africa, Ahmedabad and Wardha. For all the RSS's fury at Gandhi in the lead-up to partition, their glorification of village life was quite similar.

There was also symbolism in the location of Chitrakoot, given that in the Ramayana, it was in these forests that Ram, his brother Lakshman and wife Sita spent a part of their fourteen-year 'vanvaas' or banishment from the throne. It was here in Chitrakoot that Nanaji chose to spend his own 'vanvaas'.

With this exit, the final competitor to Vajpayee and Advani's partnership had been subdued. And with the RSS still grateful, they were now entirely free to decide what their new party would stand for.

Jugalbandis are concerts where two musicians perform together in a way in which it is not clear who the main performer is, who the accompanist. After decades in which Advani was subordinate to Vajpayee, by 1980 their relationship had become more equal. While Advani had always needed Vajpayee, he was now as needed. They were now a classical jugalbandi.

This was why, in thinking about what the new BJP should stand for, Vajpayee made sure that Advani was as involved in drawing lessons from the failed Janata experiment. Reflecting together, they came to the conclusion that the Janata government had articulated a distinct ideology of civil liberties, socialism and decentralization. And both of them believed that Indian voters were more receptive to this than to Hindutva. What voters had rejected in the 1980 elections was not JP's ideological inheritance; it was his squabbling executors.

The new-fangled Bharatiya Janata Party, Vajpayee and Advani concluded, would need to couple Hindu nationalist discipline with the policies of Jayaprakash Narayan. It would also have to keep the RSS at arm's length. Crafting such a 'moderate' party required nimble footwork by Vajpayee and Advani. But they both had long become adept at working together to balance parliament, party, movement and voters. They were now confident they could do it again. Or so they thought.

PART II

THE PARTY (1980–98)

7

RADICAL HINDUS,
MODERATE VAJPAYEE (1980–84)

A temporary township had been implanted in Bandra Reclamation, Bombay, to house the BJP's inaugural convention in December 1980. More than 7000 party workers were responsible for three kilometres of water lines, 1000 taps, 1500 tube lights and 600 kilowatts of electricity. Just five states—Maharashtra, Madhya Pradesh, Rajasthan, Uttar Pradesh and Bihar—accounted for 73 per cent of the 54,632 eventual delegates.[1]

The convention began on 28 December, and arrangements had been made to feed and house 40,000. By noon, 44,000 delegates had arrived with trainloads still expected. The new party's new general secretary, L.K. Advani, was reduced to requesting those who could eat out to do so.[2]

The new flag fluttered everywhere. It was one-third green and two-thirds saffron, like the Janata flag. But the plough-carrying farmer had been replaced by a lotus, a holy flower capable of blooming in murky waters. The lotus had first made its appearance in the April 1980 founding in Delhi.[3] In the eight months since, the Election Commission had agreed to make it the party symbol.[4]

That evening, a session open to the public, was held in the twenty-eight-acre Shivaji Park in central Bombay. The new president Atal Bihari Vajpayee rode the four kilometres from one venue to the other in an open jeep, cheered by thousands. In a nod to the locale as well as Hindu nationalism's venerated warrior, men dressed as Maratha soldiers rode horseback in front. Trucks followed, carrying giant portraits of Deendayal Upadhyaya and Jayaprakash 'JP' Narayan.[5] The new party's new motto was also on display. It was a phrase popularized by JP: 'Gandhian Socialism'.

To show gratitude to Vajpayee and Advani for leaving the Janata Party rather than the RSS, Bhaurao Deoras, brother of the chief, marked his presence at the convention.[6] While Deoras kept his views to himself, a reporter present wrote that 'younger elements in the Bharatiya Janata Party, especially those belonging to the RSS school, are opposed to the party's economic policy being termed "Gandhian socialism"'.[7] The RSS's Seshadri Chari was in attendance. 'Jayaprakash Narayan's *Gandhiwadi Samajwad* was difficult for us to digest,' he confesses. 'Many of us in the Jana Sangh and RSS were unhappy in 1980. That is for sure.'[8] The VHP's Pravin Togadia remembers: 'In 1980, the majority of people of the Jana Sangh were not in agreement [with] Gandhian Socialism, and [the] change of flag. I know because I was a swayamsevak then.'[9]

While this unease was widespread, it was hushed. What added to the reticence was that L.K. Advani, whose years working with the party cadre had earned him their respect, supported the shift in ideology.[10]

The one person who refused to hush her unease was Vijayaraje Scindia. It was Indira Gandhi's 'socialism' that had dispossessed royalty, including the House of Gwalior. Her daughter Vasundhara Raje Scindia remembers: 'She told me: How can the two words go together?'[11] Vijayaraje later wrote, 'I protested against this deviation, but in the Bombay convention of the party it was adopted as one of the guiding principles.'[12] Govindacharya credits her subordination before the party consensus to that very Hindu nationalist of ideals: '*aatma vilopan*', dissolving the self.[13]

Having branded the BJP, Vajpayee went about creating distance with the RSS: 'Our party was born in 1980; the Jana Sangh in 1951; the RSS in 1925. These are separate events. No one can be the other.'[14]Advani promised that the new party would have no relationship with the RSS, though individuals were free to associate.[15] The new party had also imported leaders from outside the RSS network,[16] ironically, the very change that Balraj Madhok had demanded in 1973. The lawyer Ram Jethmalani was made party vice president; Jaswant Singh, from the Swatantra Party, became the national secretary; and the party's Muslim face Sikander Bakht was also inducted.[17] These appointments caused murmurs in the halls of

Hedgewar Bhavan in Nagpur. An RSS pracharak present remembers: 'The RSS was not at all happy with what Vajpayee was doing. But Vajpayee was the most popular man [across India] from the party. So we decided not to protest.'

Coming from a man known for his speeches, Vajpayee's speech at the convention on the night of 30 December was one of his most famous. He stood on stage behind a brown lectern decked with wires and mikes. His cross-legged deputies huddled on the stage floor, angled like sunflowers toward the lectern. L.K. Advani sat right in front, wearing heavy black glasses and listening, head bowed.

Vajpayee's voice boomed on multiple loudspeakers, some with a lag, giving his words the halo of echoes. He vowed: 'The Janata Party was broken, but we will not allow Jayaprakash's dream to break.' While the new party would continue JP's legacy, it would not inherit the culture of the Janata Party. 'We have no space for those after money or status.' He refuted newspaper reports that there were differences in the party on 'Gandhian socialism'. All that the phrase meant was the rejection of those 'twin brothers', capitalism and communism, 'one of which ends equality and the other freedom, but both of which increase centralization'.[18]

Many Bangladeshi migrants lived in the slums sprawled to the south of the venue in Bandra Reclamation. To the west lay dingy rain-beaten buildings where middle-class Maharashtrian Hindus nervously preserved status. Theirs were the apprehensions of the Hindu nationalist voter. But Vajpayee's speech ignored their fears. Instead, he ended with hope. 'Standing on the shores of this ocean beneath the Western Ghats, I can say with confidence about the future. The darkness will end. The sun will rise. The lotus will bloom.'[19]

* * *

Presiding over this speech as chief guest was someone who had been Advani and Vajpayee's lawyer during the Emergency. Owl faced, with the perpetual stoop of the arguing counsel, Mohamedali Currim Chagla had served as the first chief justice of the post-Independence Bombay High Court. But he had his bones set as Muhammad Ali Jinnah's legal junior in pre-partition Bombay. 'Jinnah was in those days my *beau ideal*, both in politics and in law,' he wrote in his memoirs. 'So long as Jinnah remained a nationalist . . . I remained with Jinnah . . . But as soon as Jinnah became communal-minded and started his two-nation theory, I parted company . . .' The Gujarati Muslim told Jinnah that Pakistan was mainly 'in the interest of the Muslim-majority states. But what happens to the Muslims in the states where they are a small minority?' 'They will look after themselves,' Jinnah replied. 'I am not interested in their fate.'[20]

Chagla had endeared himself to Hindu nationalists by being their beau ideal of an Indian Muslim. In the September 1979 issue of the *Bhavan's Journal*, Chagla wrote: 'I am a Hindu because I trace my ancestry to my Aryan forefathers.' He added, '. . . it is wrong to look upon real Hinduism as a religion. It is more a philosophy and a way of life.'[21]

Chagla was thus the ideal fit for chief guest at the launch of the BJP. Vajpayee welcomed him by telling the audience that Chagla was the symbol of secularism. Despite working for Jinnah, he had opposed the two-nation theory.[22] Chagla returned the compliment, calling Vajpayee a future prime minister. He also requested the assembled delegates to, 'Tell the people you are not a communal party, not the Jana Sangh in a new garb, but a national party that can replace Mrs Indira Gandhi in the next elections, or before that.'[23]

If the chief guest was one way through which Jinnah was connected to the proceedings, the other way was through the money. The entire convention had cost 20 lakh rupees, a tidy sum at the time. A BJP leader involved says that the primary donor was Nusli Wadia.

Jinnah's grandson through his daughter Dina had become its principal funder by the late 1970s. This continued even after his godfather Nanaji Deshmukh left for Chitrakoot. A friend of Nusli says that, by then, he was paying individual BJP leaders in cash and cheque, 'especially Vajpayee and Jaswant Singh'. Wadia's close friend R.V. Pandit says: 'Nusli had an equation with Advani, but more with Vajpayee.'[24] Pandit himself contributed to the new party, and has with him bank statements recording payments to 'Vajpayee', 'J. Singh', 'M.M. Joshi'. 'By the early 1980s, I paid two crores to the BJP, but cheque only,' Pandit says. He adds: 'For each of the elections Atalji and Advaniji fought, I gave them rupees 250,000 each. Much of this was to get Indira Gandhi removed because of her illegally declared Emergency.'

While Nusli had been a funder long before the Hindu nationalists were fashionable, his sponsorship in the 1980s was also self-serving. He was by then locked in a corporate battle with Dhirubhai Ambani for control of the textile market. Nusli accused the ruling Congress of bending rules for Ambani's Reliance Industries. He was to later reflect on this struggle: 'To some extent, yes (I did miss the bus), but that's because I chose not to manipulate the system . . .'[25] This was only somewhat true. As Pandit says: 'Nusli's involvement [with the BJP] was really political. He felt that in Delhi you have to have friends because of his battle with the Ambanis.'[26]

His munificence would be returned, with interest. As later chapters reveal, Nusli Wadia was in and out of the prime minister's office when the BJP was in power from 1998 to 2004. But by the 1980s itself, he was making his presence felt.

It was around this time that one BJP MP in the Rajya Sabha made a statement defending the Ambanis, while another party MP, Jaswant Singh, stood up to defend Nusli Wadia. Vajpayee was angry. A friend remembers Vajpayee telling Advani: 'Two businessmen are fighting, and our party is defending both. Why should the BJP get involved?'

More than the veneer of 'Gandhian socialism', the involvement of an associate as well as grandson of the founder of Pakistan signalled the road Vajpayee and Advani wanted to take. This route, from radical to moderate, Hindu to Indian, was their reading of where voters had headed in the 1970s.

* * *

By the early 1980s, however, India's 550 million Hindus, 82.6 per cent of the country's population,[27] were displaying signs of journeying in the opposite direction. For, the evidence points to incipient anxieties during this period, which in turn was propelling the assertion of a common Hindu identity.

These ground-up anxieties were partly driven by economic difficulties not limited to Hindus alone. Inflation, the way ordinary Indians sense price rise, had increased from 3 per cent in 1978–79 to 22 per cent in 1979–80.[28] Farm distress, a dry monsoon, and infrastructure and energy shortages were pushing India to bankruptcy.[29] In 1981, the Indian government took a five-billion-dollar loan from the International Monetary Fund,[30] the largest in IMF history at the time. These tribulations were illustrated by a year-long strike in 1982 in that bastion of the Indian working class, Bombay's textile mills. Working for the mill owners was the Shiv Sena, which was successfully converting the class anxiety of the workers into ethnic (i.e., Maharashtrian Hindu) solidarity.

If the Hinduization of Bombay's working class showed how economic distress fuelled identity politics, more direct radicalization occurred in states in north and western India, where upper-caste Hindus began to feel a threat to their traditional domination.

Reservations in postgraduate medical colleges led to an agitation by upper-caste medical students in Gujarat. Sixteen people died in the police firing. Protesting students anointed Gandhi's statute with a red tilak of blood. Hours later, Dalit protestors ritually washed the statue. They were led by local Congress politicians.[31]

This is because, unlike in other parts of north India, the Gujarat Congress had accepted the electoral ascendency of lower-caste voters, and had abandoned its traditional Brahmin–Bania–Patel base. The Congress had constructed, instead, an arithmetically broader coalition of communities known by the acronym KHAM: Kshatriyas, Harijans, Adivasis and Muslims. This alliance of Muslims with low castes threatened to squeeze out upper-caste Hindus.

The other state where Hindus of all castes began to feel victimized was in Punjab.[32] Unlike material differences between upper and lower castes in Gujarat, Sikhs and Hindus were bound by intricate weaves. An example of this was L.K. Advani himself. A Hindu Sindhi born in Karachi, he says that 'there was a *Granth Sahib* in the house and we would be reverential towards it. I occasionally participated in the *akhand paath kirtan* [the continuous recitation of Sikh religious texts] which took place.'[33]

By the early 1980s, however, separatists were turning Sikhs against Hindus.[34] Widening the rupture was a tall man with a flowing beard and pyjamas that ended well above his ankles. Jarnail Singh Bhindranwale had begun as a lay preacher against drugs and pornography to disaffected young men. He soon morphed into a violent separatist targeting the state's Hindus, and demanding a separate country for Sikhs: Khalistan.

If Gujarat and Punjab invoked dangers to Hindu unity and sacred geography, the problems of Assam were related to the third pillar of Hindu nationalism: demographics and elections. In the run-up to the 1971 Bangladesh war, an estimated 8.3 million refugees from East Bengal, both Hindu and Muslim, had sought refuge in states in eastern India, including Assam. Many remained even after the creation of Bangladesh, while a steady influx had continued since.[35] Within Assam, indigenous students feared being reduced to a demographic (and hence electoral) minority. They began agitating, from 1979 onwards, for the expulsion of these migrants.

These concerns reflected a general demographic anxiety that characterizes Hindutva. The first census, administered by the British in 1909, had led to the influential book titled *Hindus a Dying Race*.[36] Census conducted every decade since had generally revealed a higher Muslim birth rate compared to Hindus. The 1981 census continued the pattern, revealing a slight dip in the Hindu percentage compared to an increase for Muslims.

Demographic changes coupled with threats to territorial unity had triggered Hindu fear previously, notably in the 1920s[37] (after the first general elections) and the 1940s (in the lead up to partition). But on both these occasions, a moderate Hindu leader, i.e., Mohandas Gandhi, had calmed these concerns while still claiming to speak for Hindus. As important as his leadership was a capacious 'Congress system' that was able to represent Hindus while taming their fears. What was different about the early 1980s was that Indira was no Gandhi, and the 'Congress system' had since malfunctioned.

It was also at this very time that the new BJP was disassociating itself from its Hindu roots. Vajpayee was still too invested in the parliament of the 1970s to sense that the voter was shifting right in the 1980s. Contrary to those who think that the rise of the BJP in the 1980s was top-down, it actually began as inchoate 'demand-driven' anger at the ground level. And with no national party willing to absorb and thereby moderate these grass-root worries, the field was left open to provocateurs from outside the mainstream. And they got their opportunity one morning in a hamlet called Meenakshipuram.

* * *

On 19 February 1981, the town of Meenakshipuram in southern Tamil Nadu wore celebratory attire. A feast had been organized, and Muslims from nearby villages came in festive dress; 558 of the 945 Dalits from the village had decided to convert to Islam.[38] In preparation for the ceremony, 'most of the Harijans were seen tonsured, and some sported well-groomed beards. And they repeated the *kalima* and prayed to Allah by kneeling down towards the west.'[39] Muslim League leaders, under whose auspices the conversion took place, laid the foundation stone for the village mosque soon after.[40]

The conversions had been driven by the oppression of local Dalits by Thevars, middle-caste Hindus landowners in the village. Dalits complained that 'they could not wear chappals while passing through caste Hindu localities. Nor could they wear shirts or any sort of upper garment.'[41] The social mobility of these 945 Dalits, with two doctors and an engineer in their midst, irritated the Thevars. When a Dalit set up a teashop, the Thevars shut it down; when a Dalit set up a barber shop, the Thevars shut it down.[42]

This was a familiar sequence. Cruelty to Dalits had spilt over well into the twentieth century, as had their conversions to escape from it. B.R. Ambedkar along with lakhs of his Dalit followers had rejected Hinduism for Buddhism in 1956, just a few miles from the RSS headquarters in Nagpur.[43] Over the years, other Dalits had converted to Christianity and Islam. But they had caused local tensions and little more. The fallout from this conversion in an isolated village should similarly have been contained. But Hindu anxiety was in the air at this very moment, triggered by apprehensions regarding reservations, demographics and the Khalistan movement. Meenakshipuram became the stage on which this nationwide Hindu fear gathered, congealed and demanded political expression.

* * *

The first party to sense this was the Congress. G.K. Moopanar, a Congress MLA from the area, immediately responded that he regretted the attitude of such Harijans who embraced Islam without looking deeply into Hindu doctrine.[44] He formulated a plan to stop conversions, claiming that he reflected Prime Minister Indira Gandhi's sentiments.[45] The union home minister, Zail Singh, said that the conversions 'is a matter of concern to all', and that a central government probe was on.[46] Another Congress minister cited the role of rupees three crores from an Arab country.[47]

Two academic studies conducted in Meenakshipuram reject the notion that money played a role.[48] As Hindus, the Dalits of Meenakshipuram were eligible for Scheduled Caste scholarships, as well as quotas in education and employment. On converting to Islam, they lost these benefits, since Muslim Dalits are not considered Scheduled Castes. 'But for the community now,' one study noted, 'human dignity was more valuable than concessions.'[49]

The fact that the Congress chose to ignore this evidence was part of Indira Gandhi's larger strategy to woo Hindus from the 1980s onwards. The most visible illustration of this was the Virat Hindu Samaj (VHS), created by Karan Singh, son of the last Hindu king of Kashmir, after the Meenakshipuram conversions. Karan Singh was on a break from the Congress (I) at the time, but had been with them earlier and would join them again soon. The VHS planned a well-attended rally in Delhi against proselytization. The city's 550 RSS shakhas worked to ensure its success.[50]

The conversions did more than play up a Hindu fault-line. Thevars were at the forefront of the middle-caste dominated Dravidian movement, and the conversions threatened 'non-Brahmin' unity. The state chief minister, M.G. Ramachandran of the AIADMK, announced that he would go back to Meenakshipuram with his entire cabinet, and share a meal with Dalits. A state Dalit leader dismissed this as posturing. 'Keep these community feasts to yourself, come and share a wedding feast with us.'[51]

The party of the Hindus, not the Congress or AIADMK, should have been the rightful recipient of these fears crystallized by Meenakshipuram. But Vajpayee was still mesmerized by the Janata politics of the mid-1970s. It took him five full months after the conversions to lead a team of volunteers to Meenakshipuram.[52] Vajpayee's attitude was to blame 'basically the failure of Hindu society'.[53]

Instead of rallying the base, the BJP chose to expand it by appealing to non-Hindus, especially in the south of India.[54] It also reached out to Pakistan. 'You could say we sound almost pro-Pakistan,' said a party leader, adding, 'this is because of Atalji's influence.'[55]

The RSS was watching. From 1971 all the way until now, it had not blocked Vajpayee and Advani's journey to cleanse the party of its Hindu past. But the passions unleashed after Meenakshipuram presented the RSS with a fork in the road: to follow the BJP's moderation or to follow its own instincts.

* * *

The World Hindu Organization or Vishva Hindu Parishad (VHP) had been created in 1964 to bring 'sadhus, sants and mahatmas of various sects and orders on one platform'.[56] As we read earlier, this was meant to create a central religious power that could mobilize Hindus. But after agitating for a ban on cow slaughter, the VHP had retreated from the public glare from 1967 to 1981. Perhaps Golwalkar had realized that Vajpayee was right about the 1970s—the route to Hindu votes was through moderation. But the 1980s were already proving a different decade, and the VHP noticed. To quote Subramanian Swamy, 'The VHP was resurrected by the RSS after Meenakshipuram because they felt that it was necessary to create a Hindu movement and the BJP wasn't able to do it.'[57]

The technique by which they resurrected the VHP reveals much about the way in which the RSS exercises power. Like with the global consultancy company McKinsey, the RSS's most precious resource are its workers. It regularly farms out its middle-level managers (pracharaks) to lead groups that promote specific agendas. This creates a constellation of organizations around the RSS, the sangh parivar, that may move in distinctive circles, while trying to keep Nagpur in the centre of their orbit. The RSS does not then need to issue diktats; its pracharaks, ideology hardwired, already know what to do.

So it was in 1951 that the RSS sent its best to found, and thus shape, the Jana Sangh. So it would be, as we shall see, that the RSS would send Narendra Modi to the BJP in 1987 to reduce the sway of Vajpayee. And so it was now, in 1981, that the RSS decided to counter the BJP by deputing a pracharak to awaken the VHP.

Ashok Singhal was a metallurgical engineer[58] from a wealthy baniya family in Allahabad, close to Nehru's ancestral house. He had joined the RSS in 1942, around the same time as Vajpayee and Advani. Unlike the other two, however, he had continued as a functionary and was not contaminated by parliament.

The Vishva Hindu Parishad under Singhal took up the Meenakshipuram cause with gusto. In 1981 itself, it organized its first programme to combat Christian and Muslim proselytizing.[59] The VHP (along with the RSS) adopted a two-pronged strategy to deal with conversions: welcoming Dalits, while excluding and demonizing Muslims and Christians.

Attempts to include Dalits were on display when an ecclesiastical Hindu conference held in Meenakshipuram the very month of the conversions declared: 'We, the religious heads assembled today at Meenakshipuram solemnly declare that our *vedas* and *shastras* have not mentioned untouchability in any form.'[60] The top decision-making body of the RSS called 'upon the entire Hindu society to bury deep the internal caste dissensions and the pernicious practice of untouchability and stand up as one homogenous family'.[61]

This encompassing attitude urging Hindus to look within was coupled with pointing blame outwards. As the VHP and RSS began to establish a presence in the area, newspapers reported an increase in religious violence. By June 1982, a mosque had been burnt down in Meenakshipuram.[62] A year later, the makeshift mosque was blaring Allah's name for five minutes at dawn and dusk through loudspeakers. The newly hired priest in the refurbished Kaliamma temple blasted chants of the Gayatri Mantra on his loudspeaker. The only thing that paused this rivalry, a journalist wryly pointed out, was 'the erratic power supply in the state'.[63]

It is perhaps no coincidence that the months soon after Meenakshipuram saw an expansion in violence between Hindus and Muslims in cities as far apart as Meerut in north India,[64] Hyderabad in central India,[65] and Kanyakumari in the southern tip.[66]

This militant line was mimicked in a Gujarat divided over caste reservations. While the national BJP cold-shouldered upper castes abandoned by the Congress, the VHP and the RSS channelled anger against quotas into Islamophobia, an umbrella under which upper- and lower-caste Hindus could stand united. Ahmed Patel was a young Congressman in Gujarat at the time. His own treatment testifies to this new strategy of the VHP–RSS, as journalist Sheela Bhatt, who writes for both Gujarati and English newspapers, explains. 'Ahmed Patel is known as "Babubhai" Patel in Gujarat. He was always called that. But after 1980, the VHP–RSS started calling him "Ahmed" Patel. I remember an election campaign against Ahmedbhai in Bharuch at that time. I was told they had put graffiti on the wall saying "Babubhai Patel". And they drew a cross line across it and wrote "Ahmed Patel".'[67]

These were the strategies of the RSS–VHP that Narendra Modi was part of at the time. Modi's biographer Nilanjan Mukhopadhyay says that soon after Meenakshipuram, Modi was given added responsibility. As the RSS prepared for agitation, he was tasked with coordinating between various sangh parivar outfits.[68] And in reaching out within the family, he met for the first time an eighteen-year-old who had just joined the Akhil Bharatiya Vidyarthi Parishad, the student wing of the RSS. The teenager's name was Amit Anilchandra Shah.

* * *

Amit Shah was born into a wealthy family. Like with Lal Krishna Advani, it was a class background unusual for an RSS volunteer. His father was a trader in PVC pipes in Mansa in north Gujarat, his mother a Gandhian who only wore khadi. The family house had a large library, which stocked Gujarati historical novels by writers such as K.M. Munshi and Dhumketu (the pen name of Gaurishankar Govardhanram Joshi). The young Amit Shah grew up with these novels. Like Vajpayee, Advani, and Modi before him, he read Munshi's book on the sacking of Somnath. He also read the three-part 'Patan trilogy' by Munshi on the last Hindu king of Gujarat, Siddhraj Jaysinh, and his artful advisor Munjal Mehta.[69] He developed a version of history in which Hindus had been invaded because of infighting. It was only natural for a boy with such a world-view to be attracted to the RSS.

This makes the reason for Amit Shah joining the Rashtriya Swayamsevak Sangh different from those before him. Vajpayee had been attracted to the RSS by his Brahmin background as well as his location in Marathi-speaking Gwalior. Advani had likely been spurred by a wave of Sindhi anxiety produced by the possibility of partition. Modi, poorer than Advani and even Vajpayee, had sought a sense of belonging and social mobility. It was Amit Shah alone who seems to have joined because of ideology.

Be that as it may, by the early 1980s, Amit Shah was visiting shakhas, swallowing the same physical and ideological doses that Vajpayee and Advani had gulped in the 1940s and Modi in the 1960s. Shah's family had since moved to Ahmedabad, and he soon joined the ABVP. It was here, in 1982, that Narendra Modi met Amit Shah for the first time.[70]

They quickly became inseparable, so much so that they were referred to as 'Jai-Veeru' after the entwined twins in the hit film *Sholay*.[71] Like with Vajpayee–Advani, Modi–Shah were schooled in the necessity of winning elections and importance of staying united. Where they applied these lessons, though, was to the caste churning of 1980s Gujarat. Their organizations worked closely during these years, with the RSS and ABVP jointly seeking to convert Hindu anxiety into votes, by preaching caste equality along with a united front against Muslims. It was the reverse of where Vajpayee–Advani were taking the national BJP at this time. When we compare Modi–Shah with Vajpayee–Advani at the end of this book, this divergence between the national BJP and Gujarat BJP in the early 1980s is where that story will begin.

This divergence was being perceived even at the time, and no one was more alarmed than the chief of the RSS. Balasaheb Deoras had always understood the compulsions of politics but worried about its corrupting influence. 'Politics is like a dirty bathroom,' he used to say. 'There is oil, there is dirty water. If you are not resolved of mind and heart, you will slip.' But Deoras had also internalized the ideology of Hindu nationalism: of staying together *despite* differences. This was why, though he had been discomfited with the trajectory taken by the new party, he had held his tongue. But now, patience exhausted, Deoras concluded that the slipperiness of power had tripped up Vajpayee and his Advani. The time had come to teach them a lesson.

* * *

The RSS had customarily coordinated with the Jana Sangh for election campaigning; its permanent cadre providing muscle, information and goodwill. But, starting from the Delhi elections in 1983, RSS workers pointedly did not campaign for the BJP. A newspaper report from the time states that 'So stringent were its instructions, that even RSS activists who had earlier held elected posts were unwilling to participate'.[72] While there is no evidence of any formal arrangement between the Congress and the RSS, 'more swayamsevaks were clearly voting for the Congress'.[73] The result was that the BJP lost control of both the metropolitan council and the municipal corporation.[74] This was ominous, given that Delhi, particularly the Punjabi Hindus now voting for Indira,[75] had long been the Jana Sangh's safety deposit box.

Vajpayee announced his resignation as party president, noting bleakly: 'Organisational weaknesses came to the fore during the campaign, especially on the polling day.'[76] Even general secretary Advani saw what the RSS had done, saying: 'There was something very wrong with our organisation.'[77]

Though Vajpayee's resignation was rejected and he continued as president, the Rubicon had been crossed; Nagpur would not be taken for granted anymore.

Eight months later, in October 1983, state elections were held in Jammu and Kashmir. BJP candidates (in their earlier avatar) had won twelve seats from the Hindu-majority Jammu region in the last state elections.[78] But this time, the RSS refused to campaign for the BJP. Indira Gandhi also played the Hindu card, promising to protect the state's Hindus against the Muslims from the Valley. The result was that Farooq Abdullah's National Conference took the Muslim vote in Kashmir, while the Congress won the Hindu vote in Jammu.[79] The BJP did not win a single seat.[80]

These losses, along with defeats in the Madhya Pradesh and Uttar Pradesh local body elections, woke up the BJP ranks. Some complained of Vajpayee's readiness to 'placate' Pakistan; others felt that 'minority cells' for Muslims were 'creating confusion' in the new party.[81] It was left to the ever-dutiful Advani to defend Vajpayee, saying that 'a few irresponsible elements here and there may be trying to blackmail the BJP with these charges'.

For an ideology that prides unity over all else, the divides were out in the open by 1983. This, counterintuitively, liberated the RSS and VHP. They were now free, free to make an audacious opening move. One that would alter the very notion of India.

* * *

Recorded history reveals that from the late nineteenth century, there have been clashes in the temple town of Ayodhya in Uttar Pradesh over the Babri mosque.[82] Local Hindus alleged that the mosque was built atop a destroyed temple, and that this temple marked the birthplace of their god Ram. The colonial administration had refused to alter the status quo. That changed, as we read earlier, on the night of 22 December 1949, when a local Hindu crowd surreptitiously installed idols inside the mosque.[83] The Congress government decided to keep the idols in place, and a judge permitted Hindu pilgrims to enter the compound and pray.[84] But they could only worship from a distance, behind locked gates. In the meantime, civil suits filed by both Hindus and Muslims dragged on in the courts, unresolved. Thus remained the situation until now, the early 1980s.

This was when Dau Dayal Khanna, a former Congress state minister, came up with demands regarding three north Indian mosques that, he claimed, had been built above the vestiges of shattered temples.[85] The temples Khanna alluded to were supposed to have been built for different deities: Mathura to mark Krishna's birth, Kashi for Shiva and Ayodhya to signify Ram's birthplace. He demanded that the temples be rebuilt after demolishing the mosques. There was no pressing cause for this revision of history, and ordinarily, it would have died unmourned.

But these were no ordinary times, and the RSS and VHP sensed they had a winner. And of the three demands, they latched on to the one to build a Ram temple in Ayodhya in place of the Babri mosque. It quickly became their call to arms.

Much scholarship has asked why such a focus on Ram over all other gods, with some answering that the Ramayana was unique among Hindu legends in heralding a 'divine political order' in which a just king vanquished 'a fully demonised Other'.[86] Given that Hinduism mostly does not have a conception of state power, the Ramayana had the potential for political mobilization that other Hindu mythologies did not. The Sanskrit scholar Sheldon Pollock points out that while the Ramayana dates back to antiquity, it 'came alive in the realm of public political discourse in western and central India in the eleventh to fourteenth centuries in dramatic and unparalleled ways'.[87] This period coincided with the early part of Muslim rule. The most popular version of the Ramayana was in fact composed by Tulsidas in the sixteenth century, at the apogee of Mughal power.

The Ramayana seemed to offer the same mobilization advantages 400 years later, when the VHP organized a 'Hindu sammelan' in Muzaffarnagar in 1983. Dau Dayal Khanna, fashioning himself into a twentieth-century avatar of Tulsidas, was the star speaker.[88] In the presence of another Congressman, Gulzarilal Nanda, as well as the RSS,[89] Khanna reiterated his idea, with emphasis on building a Ram temple in Ayodhya.

The Ayodhya movement had begun in earnest, and between November and December 1983, the VHP organized a procession with trucks carrying pots of water from the Ganga traversing the breadth of the country.[90] This holy water was 'distributed in villages on the way, while the pots were refilled with water' from local rivers or temple tanks.[91] The symbolism was to unite diverse Hindu rituals and geographies. This procession, the first such holy pilgrimage or 'yatra' ever conducted for the Ram temple at Ayodhya, was so successful that it set the template for many other yatras, most famously the one in 1990.

Through this period, the fear uppermost in the Hindu mind were the killings in Punjab. Jarnail Singh Bhindranwale had retreated along with his admirers to the Golden Temple, the holiest site of the Sikhs. From here, lists were drawn and hits plotted for across the state.[92] To protect against assassination, Delhi resembled an armed camp. Security was provided to 150 leaders including Atal Bihari Vajpayee, who joked, 'With a police camp at my doorstep, my house looks like a temporary jail now.'[93]

On 7 April 1984, the VHP organized its first meeting of the *dharma sansad*, a kind of Hindu Vatican council consisting of 600 religious leaders from various sects and denominations. The religious leaders asked gurudwaras to turn away extremists, claiming that 'there was no direct clash between Hindus and Sikhs in Punjab but politically-vested interests were trying to exploit the situation by promoting hatred'.[94] The gathering also resolved to 'liberate' Ram in Ayodhya from Muslim confinement.[95]

The BJP's reaction was a study in contrast. It ignored the call to break the Babri Masjid, and the president of its Punjab unit refused to commit to 'police entry into the Golden temple', where Bhindranwale and his militant followers were holed up. He told the press that 'the BJP did not take up the cause of the Hindus [in Punjab] because a national party could not afford to conduct itself on communal lines . . .'[96]

While the BJP was dilly-dallying, Prime Minister Indira Gandhi had had enough. In late May 1984, she called up Vajpayee to tell him that she was sending troops into the Golden Temple. Vajpayee and Advani had always supported sending the army into Punjab, but ordering troops into the Golden Temple was a bridge too far. Though Vajpayee disagreed with the prime minister,[97] she ordered the army to enter on 1 June 1984. By the time the military operation ended five days later, 700 soldiers and at least 2000 others including Bhindranwale had been killed.[98] Images of the bulleted dome were transmitted across the world, provoking Sikh fury.

The RSS and BJP cadre supported the operation, codenamed 'Blue Star'. A BJP leader, who was then part of the Delhi unit, remembers: 'We had been agitating for years for [the] Hindus of Punjab. What Indira did was required. We supported it.' Vajpayee, on the other hand, told parliament: 'The army was entrusted a very difficult and delicate task. It should be congratulated for discharging that responsibility with skill and courage.' But, he added, '. . . This was the first occasion when the army was sent into any religious shrine, and it should be the last.'[99]

A month after Operation Blue Star, reprisals against Hindus in Punjab unending, the VHP constituted a committee to liberate Ram's birthplace. While Dau Dayal Khanna was the general secretary, leadership vested in the head of the Gorakhpur monastery, Avaidyanath, predecessor of the UP chief minister Yogi Adityanath as of 2020. In September 1984, the committee launched another yatra, from Sitamarhi in Bihar to Ayodhya 400 kilometres west, accompanied by a lorry carrying idols of Ram and Sita.

The procession ended on the bridge over the Sarayu on the evening of 6 October 1984. It was small, 'only a few trucks with shouting people and some private cars crammed with sadhus'.[100] The next day, a programme attended by 60,000 was held on the banks of the Sarayu.[101] The dais was dominated by a hoarding showing Muslims with swords confronting unarmed sadhus.[102] Speaker after speaker demanded that Muslims hand over the property 'in the interest of national unity and integrity'. Disregarding Vajpayee's plea that the movement be non-political, one of the speakers declared, 'Whosoever helps in the liberation of this and the other two sacred places will get the Hindu votes in the coming elections.'[103]

The next day, 8 October, the VHP announced the creation of the Bajrang Dal, named after the army of monkeys who helped Ram free his wife and destroy Lanka. Its aim, millennia later, was to destroy the Babri Masjid and free Ram himself.

The involvement of Hindu religious heads in what was obviously a political movement was rare. V.D. Savarkar, for example, was a 'hardboiled atheist'[104] who declared the cow to be 'a useless animal with no sacredness in it'.[105] He cast Hinduism in racial rather than religious terms. Both Advani and Vajpayee were also not religious in the way the word is traditionally used. 'Atalji was not very much a practising Hindu, you know,' R.V. Pandit says.[106] Sheila Ghatate, Advani's long-time parliamentary assistant, adds, 'Advani's family is a not a ritualistic family. Once in a while, you have something, a puja. But I wouldn't call them religious in a ritual sense.'[107]

This lack of religious leaders had led to an ideology that drew on material anxieties rather than transcendent passions. India's sadhus—from the Shankaracharyas to the Sai Babas —had kept their distance. 'But after 1984, sadhu sants had a major role,' a VHP leader says.

Sadhus were able to use their popular stature to attract millions to the movement. 'If a pracharak tells a common man something, he may not listen,' Ravindra Bhagwat says. 'If a sadhu says, he will.'[108] But they had their down sides. Sadhus are conceptually beholden to neither caste nor kin—a safety valve from the rigid everyday of Hinduism.[109] Academic Rajesh Pradhan interviewed thirty senior sadhus involved in the Ayodhya movement. He found that theirs was a religious motivation with a 'commitment to common transcendental causes'.[110] They were also 'free and independent spiritual agents',[111] unlikely to adhere to a political script. In two words, they were unpredictable and undisciplined, words taboo for Hindu nationalism.

* * *

Like with Meenakshipuram, the Congress was the first political party to encourage the Ayodhya movement. It is no coincidence that two former Congress ministers, Dau Dayal Khanna and Gulzarilal Nanda, were at the founding in 1983. A Congressman who declines to be named says he heard rumours that Indira Gandhi was planning to open the locks of the Babri Masjid for Hindu prayer as far back as 1983. Even Advani admits to Congress's initial backing for the Ayodhya movement.[112]

In contrast, the BJP stayed away. Vajpayee told a friend, 'We should never let *sadhus* into Parliament.'[113] Pravin Togadia says, 'It is true that Vajpayee did not participate in [a] single Ayodhya-related movement.'[114]

Advani, on the other hand, was facing the first test of loyalty in his life. Unlike Vajpayee who spent his days in the central hall of parliament, Advani was a fixture at party headquarters, listening to the cadre, meeting voters and parlaying with other organizations in the sangh parivar. While Vajpayee and he had jointly set up the BJP as a moderate party, he was now hearing what Vajpayee was deaf to—that the Hindu voter was being radicalized and it made electoral sense for the BJP to move in that direction. Advani also realized that the Ram temple movement could be the way in which the BJP could attract these radicalizing voters. In his memoirs, he even cites the Ayodhya issue as one of the few instances 'when significant differences arose between Atalji and me'.[115] But while Advani's brain advised a break from Vajpayee, his heart refused. He had also internalized the history lessons the RSS had taught him from a young age: if party leaders fought with each other, they would repeat the historical cause of Hindu weakness.

And so Advani continued to publicly support Vajpayee's BJP, as it chased the chimera of non-Congress coalitions for the national elections scheduled for December that year. M.L. Sondhi, the Rhodes scholar who had left the party in part because of Vajpayee in the 1970s, had by now returned. He described the atmosphere of a party meeting in Poona around then to his wife, who then relayed it via a letter to their son in the US. 'The dominant mood was one of throwing out I.G. [Indira Gandhi],' she wrote, adding, 'They have also decided to overcome their objections to the Communists and ally with them.'[116]

Not everyone within the BJP agreed. At a meeting soon after, a party worker complained to Vajpayee, 'I don't agree with the policy of coalition . . . It is like a child being forced to play in the company of bad children.' Vajpayee replied, 'If only bad boys are available what should we do?'[117]

By October 1984, however, Hindu nationalists had decided that it was Vajpayee who was the bad boy. The Ayodhya movement had acquired a life, a mind, of its own. The political aim of Hindu unity had been to win votes, but the social aim had always been more ambiguous.[118] And with the Ram temple movement escaping the confines of the political and percolating into society, no one quite knew where it would lead, what sort of violence it would unleash. Nothing, it seemed, could break its momentum.

Until, that is, at 9:20 a.m. on the 31st of that month, when Prime Minister Indira Gandhi was shot dead by her Sikh bodyguards.

* * *

The murder of Indira Gandhi halted the Ayodhya juggernaut; the sadhus and VHP workers quietly dissipated. One supporter explained that it was 'not correct to organise anything against the government in these difficult days'.[119] And as Peter Van Der Veer, an academic who was also eyewitness, put it: 'The "Us" and "Them" identification changed overnight from Hindus against Muslims to Indians against Sikhs.'[120] In Faizabad (near Ayodhya), Hindus and Muslims jointly attacked Sikh property.[121]

Indira's Hindu turn in the early 1980s had energized the Rashtriya Swayamsevak Sangh. She had proven more adept than Vajpayee at divining the direction of the political winds. Her ambivalence towards the Ayodhya movement, when contrasted with Vajpayee's resolute disapproval, made her all the more palatable. For an organization defined by its opposition to Nehru, it is ironic that the RSS mourned his daughter's death as one of their own.

Meanwhile, the dawn after the murder unveiled a four-day pogrom in the capital city. As many as 2733 Sikhs were killed while Congress leaders led angry mobs and the police looked on.[122] One such mob surrounded the Sikh-run taxi stand outside Vajpayee's house. When a Sikh driver escaped and took shelter inside his bungalow, Vajpayee emerged and stood protectively at the gate until the police arrived.[123] Vajpayee and Advani even visited Home Minister Narasimha Rao to ask him to activate the government machinery. What they did not know was that Rao had been bypassed by a direct order from the prime minister's office.[124]

The new prime minister was Indira's son Rajiv Gandhi. While personally secular, his non-action during those three days remains his original sin. He was to describe the violence with: 'Whenever a mighty tree falls, it is only natural that the earth around it does shake a little.'[125]

The state television channel, Doordarshan, repeated the phrase '*khoon ka badla khoon*'.[126] Blood in exchange for blood.

In the elections held a month later, in December 1984, the Congress scapegoated the Sikhs. 'India could be your vote away from unity or separation,' posters warned.[127] The party put out a full-page advertisement in newspapers: 'Will the country's borders finally be moved to your doorstep?'[128]

On the campaign trail, the Congress accused the BJP, along with other opposition parties, of having links to Sikh extremists in Britain.[129] It accused the BJP of backing the Anandpur Sahib resolution,[130] which had demanded more autonomy for Punjab, as well as the recognition of Sikhism as separate from Hinduism.

While the Congress caricatured the BJP as anti-Hindu, the BJP skirted religion. There was only a single reference to the word 'Hindu' in its election manifesto, and that too in the context of preventing 'any harm being done to innocent people, Hindu or Sikh' in Punjab.[131] Instead, it sought to encash the popularity of Vajpayee, distributing cassettes of his speeches.[132] The BJP even got a Catholic leader to join on election eve.[133]

Faced with one party that pandered to Hindu identity and another which ran away from it, the RSS knew which to support. Govindacharya was an RSS pracharak in Patna. He remembers: 'Before the 1984 elections, there was coordination between RSS and BJP. But for [the] 1984 [elections] this stopped.'[134] Even Nanaji Deshmukh, that old antagonist of Vajpayee, came out of retirement to endorse Rajiv's Congress over Vajpayee's BJP.

The Congress thanked Nanaji Deshmukh.[135] And while campaigning, Rajiv Gandhi did not attack the RSS as vehemently as his mother had. When asked why, the Congress spokesperson replied, 'the situation has changed'; the focus was now on the Sikhs.

L.K. Advani, still in the Rajya Sabha, sensed where the elections were heading. He was worried that his best friend was so blinded by his own radiance that he was about to trip. Advani wanted Vajpayee to contest from two seats as insurance: his home town Gwalior as well as Kota in Rajasthan. Advani had heard that the Congress was putting up Madhavrao Scindia from Gwalior. The estranged son of the Rajmata was heir to the abolished throne of Gwalior. But Vajpayee brushed this aside, saying that

Madhavrao had told him that he was contesting from elsewhere. Vajpayee filed his nomination papers from Gwalior alone.[136]

Madhavrao Scindia filed his candidacy papers from Gwalior immediately after. The Congress had purposely waited until the last minute.[137] As Vajpayee later wrote, 'The secrecy and cleverness with which the whole strategy to tie me down to Gwalior was planned came to light only after . . .'[138]

Vajpayee cast the fight in David–Goliath terms. '*Yeh to raja aur rank ki ladai hai,*' he claimed.[139] This is a fight between the prince and the pauper. The prince was clearly the more alluring draw. Centuries of patronage had made his lineage revered in the constituency; even the teenage Vajpayee had benefitted from a scholarship given by Madhavrao's father.[140] A journalist accompanying Scindia wrote: 'His cavalcade of cars and jeeps is repeatedly stopped by men, women, children, all anxious to get the blessings . . .'[141]

Though the Congress was expected to do well, few had anticipated that it would be chosen by 115 million of India's 241 million voters in 1984. In India's first-past-the-post system, that translated into 403 seats out of 515 in the Lok Sabha.[142] Rajiv Gandhi had received a mandate greater than what his grandfather or mother had ever earned.

The Bharatiya Janata Party had been crushed. Only two of the BJP's candidates had won, the lowest the Jana Sangh or BJP had ever got. Advani bitterly called it an election to the '*shokh sabha*',[143] a sympathy wave. The RSS's *Organiser* interpreted the results differently, calling it a 'massive Hindu mandate' for Rajiv Gandhi. 'It was a conscious Hindu vote, consciously and deliberately solicited by the Congress party as a Hindu party. And this is what . . . decimated the "revisionist" BJP and reincarnated Congress (I) as BJP.'[144]

Vajpayee was in his constituency in Gwalior when the results were announced. He had gambled that the path to power lay in moderation, not grasping that the inchoate Hindu anxiety of that era was rewarding politicians prepared to travel in a more radical direction. The VHP–RSS, then the Congress, and finally even Advani, had understood this before Vajpayee had. The result: not only had his party been crushed, he had lost in his constituency. The *Times of India* placed Vajpayee's photograph in a series of mugshots of 'Some Prominent Losers'.[145]

Vajpayee decided to drive the 363 kilometres from Gwalior back to Delhi. He cut a sorry figure, right hand in a sling and leg fractured from injuries sustained during the campaign.[146] The journalist Ajoy Bose accompanied him for part of his journey. Bose remembers: 'Vajpayee was so overwhelmed, he would not speak. He felt that this was the end of politics for him. He was really depressed. It was not just a personal humiliation. He felt that the entire politics he had crafted was over.'[147]

It was darker than ever. The sun had set. The lotus had failed to bloom.

8

ADVANI'S BJP (1985–89)

In order to analyse their annihilation in the 1984 elections, the Bharatiya Janata Party held multiple national executive meetings in the space of ten months. M.L. Sondhi attended all of them. He noted that 'in spite of its two forlorn MPs in the Lok Sabha . . . its primary activity seems to be to go from one national executive meeting to the other!' These gatherings, he added, 'turned into a breast beating and mutual castigation affair . . . I don't think these fellows have any idea of what needs to be done'.[1]

Such bustle was an end in itself. Since toilets in these hurriedly erected tent cities were rudimentary, workers would venture out to defecate in a group. They slept huddled on sheets stretched on the ground, and even senior leaders had to share cots. The urbane M.L. Sondhi, for instance, shared a room in which the 'bed linen was soiled' and 'carpeting—full of dust'. 'Sanitation near feudal, but in this respect [I] was probably better off than where the jamboree had assembled itself for communal living.'[2] This 'communal living' made for discomfort, but ensured that Hindu nationalists considered each other family, and avoided the public squabbling prevalent in other parties.

Now, in the aftermath of its worst defeat in memory, these mechanisms to prevent intra-party conflict were being tested. Those who had protested Vajpayee's leftward tilt felt vindicated, though they took care to speak only within party walls. Pravin Togadia was then a young man in the RSS. He recalls his resentment. 'When the BJP under Vajpayee abandoned ideology . . . they got only two seats in 1984. Whenever they abandon ideology, they lose power.'[3] Many felt, in private of course, that the BJP should be put to death and the Jana Sangh resurrected.[4]

Party president Vajpayee was having none of it. He made clear that reviving the Jana Sangh 'will amount to a slide-back, and we cannot afford to do that if we are to make progress'.[5] He was proud that the new party had Muslim leaders, and that it had 'no truck with the Vishva Hindu Parishad'.[6]

But some appearance of introspection was unavoidable. And so, Vajpayee constituted a twelve-member 'working group' to analyse the 1984 election loss. '. . . Atalji and I were consciously left out [of the working group],' Advani recalls, 'to facilitate free and open discussion.'[7]

Whatever his private views, Advani publicly claims that the report of the working group 'is the most in-depth and useful of all the review documents in the party's history'.[8] Its principal conclusion was that 'the notion that there has been a very serious erosion in our electoral base is not quite correct'.[9] Vajpayee's own analysis was, unsurprisingly, the same. 'The Bharatiya Janata Party, in terms of the percentage of votes polled in its favour received the same public support as it had received in 1971.' The main difference was that 'the wave of sympathy towards the Congress uprooted the Opposition'.[10]

This was a specious reading of the 1984 election results since much had changed in India *between* the 1980 and 1984 national elections. As the previous chapter has revealed, anxiety over Khalistan, reservations and conversions had expanded the Hindu vote bank. The more likely account for the 1984 results is that this vote bank simply transferred to the Congress out of sympathy for Indira and apathy for Vajpayee.

While Vajpayee was able to spin his way out of this analysis and once more get the party and Advani behind him, the RSS was another matter.

The working group's report was discussed at the Gandhinagar National Executive held that October. Amit Shah, then a twenty-one-year-old worker with the student wing of the RSS, was deputed to help. Shah has recounted to a friend that he remembers standing outside a room where Vajpayee and Rajmata Vijayaraje Scindia were resting. His job was to pound betel nuts into powder, and take it inside so that the Rajmata could chew on it. While darting in and out of the room delivering betelnut powder in the cup of his hand, Amit Shah remembers overhearing an RSS man deliver a message from Balasaheb Deoras. The RSS chief was ordering Vajpayee to resign and Vijayaraje to be made interim president. The party flag was to be raised that day—the prerogative of the party president—and Deoras insisted that Vijayaraje, not Vajpayee, raise it. Amit Shah recalls a tense room: Vajpayee sullen, Vijayaraje uncertain. The matter ended with Vijayaraje walking out and proclaiming in the earshot of Shah and others: 'I am raising the flag after the party president has instructed me.' Her gingerly assembled sentence signalled that Vajpayee was still her boss; it also indicated that this would not be for long.[11]

And so, with the end of the session, the hunt began for a new president. Vijayaraje was the frontrunner. Her daughter says: 'She kept giving parts of her palace to the RSS. She felt that it was one family, and we should all feel the same way.'[12] And, as we saw in the previous chapter, Vijayaraje had opposed the new party's secular frontage in 1980 and had supported the Ayodhya movement in 1983. Vijayaraje Scindia offered the clearest ideological counter to Vajpayee.

The hitch for the RSS was that Vijayaraje considered Vajpayee to be family. A friend of Scindia says: 'After 1984, most of the people ganged up on Atalji. But Vijayarajeji did not. She said: 'I have beliefs in [the] Ram temple. But I also believe in Atalji and Advaniji.' And so, when mulling whether to accept the BJP presidency, Vijayaraje sought guidance from her religious guru. The guru was silent for a while before leaving the room saying: 'I have to take a bath.'[13] Vijayaraje interpreted this as the counsel she wanted to hear; she told Vajpayee she had no wish to replace him.

With the Rajmata declaring herself unavailable—and others of Vajpayee's stature either suspended, expelled, or self-exiled—there was only one leader who could become the new party president. Vajpayee had known this all along.

He was thus left free to announce, in May 1986, that it was L.K. Advani who would succeed him. Nagpur acquiesced. 'Advani is considered closer to the RSS than Vajpayee,' the journalist Shekhar Gupta wrote at the time by way of explanation.[14] Advani was not enamoured by parliament or even of any particular ideology. But he was a consummate party man, always listening to the cadre. This, ironically, gave the Macaulayputra the image of a 'hardliner'. It was an image that Vajpayee was happy to nurture as a foil to his own 'moderation'. They could play both the instruments that Hindu nationalism needed, so Vajpayee thought, while still allowing him to pick the tune.

Sheila Ghatate was Advani's parliamentary assistant from 1979 to 1989. She says: 'I spent a decade researching speeches for both Advaniji and Vajpayeeji. Vajpayee would say, *"Kuch Assam key bare mein lao"* [Get something on Assam]. Now *"kuch lao"* means what? Then I would go to Advaniji and ask, "Atalji is saying this, what to do?" Advani would know exactly what Atalji meant. Advani would tell me: "Look at the immigrant population . . . how many over eighteen . . . what is the mortality rate." Advaniji knew Vajpayee's wavelength.'[15]

* * *

In anointing Advani in 1986, Vajpayee was using the same strategy he had deployed in picking Advani as his replacement as party president in 1973. On the one hand, the move would placate the RSS. One the other, his personal chemistry with Advani would allow Vajpayee to steer the party in his preferred direction of opposition unity and secular nationalism.

But Vajpayee was once again underestimating the height of the waves washing up against India in the 1980s, with sprays so powerful that they would even shake Advani's loyalty to him.

As we saw in the last chapter, Hindu anxiety had since translated into a Hindu vote bank, nurtured first by the VHP–RSS and then by the Congress. What was making this vote bank even more nervous was the proliferation of parties that were re-measuring upper-caste Hindus as a minority against which electoral majorities could be cobbled up.

The bloodiest example of this was in Punjab. The state's Sikhs, though constituting 60 per cent, are divided into different castes. Yet, separatists had effectively preached unity *between* Sikh castes, while demonizing Hindus as the 'other'. Jarnail Singh Bhindranwale would refer to Indira Gandhi as *'Panditan di dhee* or *Bahmani*, that Pandit's daughter or the Brahmin woman'.[16] He would exhort every Sikh to kill exactly thirty-two Hindus,[17] the precise demographic ratio between the two communities in India. Violence continued even after his death. In 1985, Sikh terrorists placed a bomb in an Air India flight from Canada, killing 329. The Hindu general who had headed operation Blue Star was shot dead in August 1986. Two months later, a Sikh assassin fired at the president and prime minister when they were visiting the samadhi of Mohandas Gandhi.[18]

The RSS and VHP, who regarded Sikhs as Hindus, were exasperated by this violence, but were taking notes. What had enabled Sikhs to unite thus were a set of cultural markers (a common book, common language, common script) as well as a unified religious authority (the Akal Takht),[19] all of which traditional Hinduism lacked.

The other state where a political coalition was forming against upper-caste Hindus was in Gujarat. As we saw in the last chapter, the state Congress had cemented an electoral alliance between low castes and Muslims, known as KHAM. This had isolated the upper castes of the state who were a minority of the population. The common grammar of this KHAM alliance was reservations. The Congress chief minister of Gujarat, Madhav Singh Solanki, had pushed for an expansion in Dalit quotas in 1981; now, in 1985, Solanki increased backward-caste quotas in government jobs and education. The result was electoral triumph—the Congress won 149 of the 182 seats in the Gujarat state legislature in 1985.[20]

This anti-upper-caste coalition in Gujarat was sought to be replicated in India's two most populous states by Mulayam Singh Yadav and Lalu Prasad Yadav who, by 1985, had become leaders of the opposition in Uttar Pradesh and Bihar. They traced their politics to Ram Manohar Lohia, who was the first to grasp the demographic power of middle-caste Hindus[21] (by one estimate, numbering 52 per cent of the national population).[22] He had demanded: '*Picchre payein sau mein saatth.*' Backwards and Dalits should get 60 per cent.[23] However, while Lohia was withering towards upper-caste Hinduism, his counter-narratives were also from within Hinduism. He would, for instance, contrast 'Ram's *maryada*' [limits] to 'Krishna's *amaryadit*' [limitlessness].[24] His ointment to the injuries of Hinduism could be found within Hinduism itself.

Lohia's pupils would remain content with an arithmetic critique of Hindutva (rather than an ideological one). The disciples of Ambedkar, on the other hand, would follow their mentor in articulating a thorough break from Hinduism.

The most prominent of these Ambedkarites was a Dalit Sikh employee of India's most sensitive nuclear plant. Round-faced and with slices of white hair combed to the side, Kanshi Ram would dress in the attire of educated officials—trousers with shirt tucked out—rather than the kurta-pyjamas favoured by politicians. He had first attempted to organize Dalit, Muslim and middle-caste employees within the government. From this bureaucratic coalition, Kanshi Ram began to imagine a political partnership against upper-caste Hindus across the country.

On 14 April 1984, Ambedkar's birth anniversary, he announced the creation of the Bahujan Samaj Party.[25] The word 'bahujan' had a precise meaning in his lexicon: non-upper-castes. Unlike Lohiaites (and like the Hindu nationalists), Kanshi Ram understood that uniting social groups required a common culture. He emphasized low-caste saints (such as Kabir and Ravidas) as well as reformers (like Ambedkar and Phule). He was also keen to avoid being typecast as just a Dalit leader. The BSP's first agitation, in the mid-1980s, was over the implementation of the Mandal Commission report,[26] whose recommendations contained no new benefits for Dalits.

These attempts at building partnerships had a majoritarian logic. As Kanshi Ram once explained to a journalist through the visual aid of a ballpoint pen: 'The Brahminical social order is like this dot pen held vertically with the Brahmins, Kshatriyas and Vaishyas dominating the top. The rest is dominated by the Shudras, the Ati-Shudras (lowest castes) and the Bahujan Samaj. And see the manipulation of the Brahminical order. The Shudras and Ati-Shudras are further divided into 6,000 castes. It is time this pen is held horizontally.'[27]

* * *

If the growth of these anti upper-caste parties was the primary reason the new BJP president L.K. Advani was rethinking Vajpayee's approach, the other was a Congress under Rajiv Gandhi threatening to steal the BJP's vote bank.

The forty-year-old prime minister initially resolved to modernize party and country. At a famous speech in December 1985 in Bombay, he promised to rid the party of 'power brokers'. His first budget was also the most liberalizing India had seen till then.[28] 'I must admit here that Rajiv Gandhi endeared himself phenomenally to the people of India in the first year of his premiership,' Advani remembers.[29] When Advani's father, that millionaire left penniless by partition, died in 1986, the new prime minister paid Advani a condolence visit at his Pandara Park house.[30]

The irony of India was that this original Rajiv—genteel, liberal, reformist—eventually produced an epic of corruption and communalism not seen until then.

The corruption saga began theatrically on 16 April 1987, when a Swedish radio broadcast announced that bribes had been paid by a Sweden-based company to Indian politicians and officials during the purchase of the Bofors artillery gun. Fingers would soon point towards the prime minister's friends and family. Rajiv Gandhi's lieutenant V.P. Singh stubbornly scrutinized these charges. When he was finally fired, Singh became the focal point for Congress dissidents disenchanted with Rajiv. As we shall see, this organizational split would have repercussions on the Congress's electoral performance in the next elections.

Rajiv's tryst with communalism began with a Supreme Court verdict[31] that obliged the former husband of Shah Bano, a Muslim divorcee with five children, to pay her 179 rupees every month as alimony.[32] In doing so, the judges held that the Code of Criminal Procedure superseded the sharia laws that confined alimony to just a few months. The court also reinterpreted the Quran to demonstrate that there was no clash between secular and religious laws.[33] This was hardly a new technique for their lordships. Over the years, the Indian Supreme Court had conveniently redefined the 'essential practices' of Hinduism to harmonize religious belief with constitutional norms.[34] But the application of this technique to the Quran set off protests from Muslim clergy.[35] Worried about losing the Muslim vote bank, Rajiv Gandhi used his parliamentary majority to pass a law nullifying the Supreme Court verdict.[36]

Having thus pandered to Muslims, Rajiv sought to placate Hindus by ensuring that the locks on the Babri Masjid were opened for Hindu prayer. Then, trying to contain the Muslim reaction, he had Salman Rushdie's *Satanic Verses* banned, the first government anywhere in the world to do so.[37] This was also around the time Rajiv Gandhi acquiesced in the rigging of the Jammu and Kashmir state elections to ensure that a Congress ally won. These 1987 state elections would provide a pool of disgruntled Kashmiris at the very time the Afghanistan war was winding down, and Pakistan had surplus militants to turn east. Former cabinet secretary Naresh Chandra remembers: 'All those who are terrorists now were trying to become MLAs then. After the fraud elections, they all turned to Pakistan . . . Sayeed Salahudeen [head of the terror group Hizbul Mujahideen] was standing for MLA [then]. Now look where he is.'[38]

This was what the party of Nehru had reduced itself to by the 1980s. It was countering the proliferation of identity politics, not with high-minded liberalism, but by pandering to extremism. And it was this Congress party that was directing L.K. Advani's new course of action.

As we saw earlier, Hindu nationalism had been constituted by elections; by the need to win power under conditions of one-person-one-vote. From 1971 onwards, Advani had followed his mentor in believing that this route to a parliamentary majority lay in appealing to the 'moderate' voter. But by now, 1986, Advani had realized that the BJP needed to change if it had to win. Though his personal devotion to Vajpayee remained intact, he owed another loyalty—to the party and to the sangh parivar. These clashing allegiances must have surely upset a man whose life had been defined by obedience. But eventually Advani chose. While he would never desert Vajpayee the man, he had to abandon Vajpayee the ideology.

* * *

The new president's decision to break from the old began with his choice of personnel. Soon after becoming BJP head in 1986, L.K. Advani named three RSS men as general secretaries, the most prominent of whom would be the physics lecturer Murli Manohar Joshi.[39] A Brahmin from Uttar Pradesh who dabbed a vermilion dot between his eyebrows, Joshi had done his PhD in physics at Allahabad University. His thesis topic was on spectroscopy and his advisor, the eventual head of the RSS, Rajendra Singh. Joshi was just seven years younger than Advani, and had similarly been moved to the Jana Sangh by that talent spotter, Deendayal Upadhyaya.

RSS workers continued to move laterally into the BJP through the late 1980s. At the lower levels, they included Amit Shah, who was shifted from the ABVP in 1987. At the senior levels, they included men like Seshadri Chari. Govindacharya, another transferred pracharak, remembers: 'If you want to know why Vajpayee always disliked me, go back to when the RSS was sending members to [the] BJP to make it less like Vajpayee's party. I didn't understand why I was sent . . . [but] he knew why.'[40]

Along with these pracharaks, one other was moved to the BJP. Chari remembers, 'It was around 1987. I had just been made Mumbai pradesh general secretary [of the BJP]. I was in my office when a young pracharak came to meet me. He had also been seconded to [the] BJP. He asked me: "What is being in the BJP like? What are the things I should keep in mind about politics?" His name was Narendra Damodardas Modi.'[41]

Of those inducted into the BJP at that time, it is Narendra Modi whom history will remember. His biographer Nilanjan Mukhopadhyay says that he was chosen mainly because he came from Gujarat, the laboratory of a novel, virulent strain of Hindu politics.[42] Both he and Amit Shah had been critical of Vajpayee's 'Gandhian socialism' and were fine-tuning a strategy of uniting high- and low-caste Hindus by using Muslims as scapegoats. 'I knew Modi then,' journalist Sheela Bhatt says. 'He knew the caste [breakup] of every village in Gujarat. His understanding of the traditions and colloquial language of each caste is deep.'[43]

Their takeover of the BJP would come later, but by the late 1980s, it was Advani who had steadily seized control of the party.

If, on the one hand, he assuaged the RSS by allowing their own into the BJP, he also promoted middle-rung operatives who were his protégés alone. These included Arun Jaitley, Venkaiah Naidu, Rajnath Singh, Sushma Swaraj[44] and Pramod Mahajan. A Congress leader says: 'Advani had mentored so many politicians. It shows that he was not a "political" person. In the sense that he was not insecure.'

Insecure he was not, but Advani 2.0 was a changed man. Finally emerging from the shadow of his mentor, he gave speeches pushing for a cow slaughter ban, a uniform civil code so that Muslims and Hindus would have the same personal laws, and the removal of Article 370 of the Constitution that granted special status to Kashmir. These were pet issues of the Jana Sangh, but ones that Vajpayee's BJP had downplayed.[45] Advani began to dwell on the 'problem of foreign nationals in Assam'.[46] He even demanded that a 'national register of citizens should be prepared',[47] something that was finally done in 2018 under a BJP state government.

Advani's ascension also ended any distance between the RSS–VHP and the BJP on the Muslim question. Violence against Muslims began to play a role in binding backward to upper castes, as Ornit Shani has shown in her study of Gujarat.[48] The most notorious of these incidents was in Meerut in Uttar Pradesh in 1987; 150 people died, over a 1000 were injured and 13,000 security forces were deployed to keep the peace.[49]

If the BJP was now overtly hostile towards Muslims, it was becoming more hospitable towards Hindus of all castes. Middle-caste politicians such as Uma Bharti and Kalyan Singh were promoted to leadership positions; they would soon become chief ministers of their states. Religious organizations, led by the VHP, made efforts to reach out to low castes.[50] The BJP even demanded that the Mandal report be implemented, though balancing this with quotas for the upper-caste poor.[51] Govindacharya, the architect of this outreach, calls it 'social engineering'. 'For us, Hindu unity meant that backwards and forwards would think of themselves as Hindu.'[52]

By the late 1980s, therefore, every arm of the sangh parivar was swinging in tandem. Electoral coordination between the RSS and BJP had resumed at the booth level, the lack of which had cost the party the 1984 elections. An RSS worker remembers being part of these meetings around then. '[These] coordination committees were created after the 1984 elections. One or two of them are RSS members, the rest six to eight are from BJP. [There is a] lot of going house to house and giving pamphlets. We [RSS] do that. We are the ones who are working through the year. We know which house is what.'

This reappearance of Hindu nationalist unity after the fissures of the Vajpayee era had an electoral effect. The BJP alliance won in Haryana in November 1987,[53] and began to win local elections in Maharashtra.[54] A string of local election victories in the late 1980s was seen as a mood predictor for the coming national elections. A grateful party decided to give Advani a second term as president in 1988.[55] He had by now replaced Vajpayee: on television, in newspapers, and most hurtful of all to his guru: in parliament.

* * *

It took more than a year for Vajpayee, who had lost his elections to the lower house of parliament in 1984, to be made a member of the Rajya

Sabha. Unwanted in Delhi, he began to frequent the United States to treat his worsening kidneys, staying at the house of a friend, the New York doctor Mukund Modi.[56] He would not stay with Namrata, the daughter of Mr and Mrs Kaul, who had married a software engineer and become a doctor in the United States. 'He had a different relationship with Namrata compared to Namita,' Vajpayee's biographer Vijai Trivedi says.[57]

Since foreign travel was expensive, Prime Minister Rajiv Gandhi made sure to include Vajpayee in government delegations to the US, something which even Vajpayee acknowledged.[58] Rajiv was continuing a tradition set by his mother. A senior bureaucrat close to the Congress explains why. 'Vajpayee was the only one from their side whom the Congress could talk to. He had to be kept in good humour.'

Removed from political relevance, access to money dried up. Jairam Ramesh says that during this period, 'It was widely believed that Vajpayee was kept afloat by the Hindujas.'[59] Subramanian Swamy concurs. 'Vajpayee's medical treatment abroad was paid for by the Hindujas.'[60] A family friend reveals another source of sustenance: 'Through the 1980s, Nusli [Wadia] would send 30,000 rupees to the Vajpayee household. BJP leaders were quite honest then . . . they didn't have a lot of savings. Vajpayee needed the money.'

Vajpayee began to spend his freed-up time with family. A BJP leader who was also a family friend remembers witnessing long conversations between Rajkumari Kaul and Vajpayee on the Babri Masjid.[61] Mrs Kaul would also keep in touch with BJP workers, helping those who needed medical care get admission into the AIIMS hospital. She was playing a double role in Vajpayee's life, heightening his liberal instincts while ensuring that his personal ties to the party never severed.

Though she took care to never appear in the press herself, Rajkumari Kaul would ensure that the Hindi-speaking Vajpayee reached out to the English-speaking media. Karan Thapar remembers calling up Vajpayee's house number to schedule an interview. 'Mrs Kaul picked up and very sweetly asked us to come. When we came on schedule, Vajpayee was waiting. "You have spoken to the high command," he told us.'[62] A BJP leader says: 'If anyone had a problem with Vajpayee, if he was rude or anything, Mrs Kaul would calm things . . . Without her, he was nothing.'[63]

The younger daughter Namita, Gunu, lived with Vajpayee along with the Kauls. In 1983, she had married Ranjan Bhattacharya, a Bengali from Patna who worked in the Oberoi hotel. Since Ranjan had lost both parents, he moved in, and like Namita, called Vajpayee 'Baapji'. Vajpayee, who lacked the politician's knack for names, would refer to Ranjan variously as 'Banerjee', 'Mukherjee', or even 'Bengali babu'.[64]

Apart from spending time with family, Vajpayee would while away evenings with friends, snacks and drinks. Brajesh Mishra, whom Vajpayee had known from the late 1970s in New York, had since retired from the Foreign Service. A relative of his remembers, 'First, Brajesh went to the Congress. But Rajiv already had his whiz kids around him. There was no space.'[65] Mishra then began to call on Vajpayee. The jazz-loving and formally dressed Mishra—he who was never seen without a suit or Nehru jacket—enjoyed his alcohol.[66] But, says someone present at these evenings, 'Brajesh knew how to hold his drink. He would never have more than two [glasses of] scotch.' Contrary to popular perception, Vajpayee was also not much of a drinker. 'I actually never saw him holding a glass of alcohol, truth be told,' his relative by marriage and future private secretary Shakti Sinha remembers. 'He was a rustic man. What he would enjoy most were bhaang [opium-laced] pakodas.'[67] The one person who would drink a lot was the former army major Jaswant Singh. 'My father enjoyed Black Label,' Manvendra Singh says.[68] Bhairon Singh Shekhawat and N.M. Ghatate, along with the journalist Virendra Kapoor and IAS officer Ashok Saikia—the last two of whom had studied under Mr Kaul at Ramjas Collage—would also drop in. Shiv Kumar, now more friend than bodyguard, would also be present. Rajkumari Kaul would produce plate after plate of Kashmiri food, including mutton rogan josh and saffron chicken, while Camelot's court would sit around the table, talking politics.

As we shall see in later chapters, it is these knights who would form the nucleus of Prime Minister Vajpayee's office. They had stuck with ex-party president Vajpayee when he was down. He did not forget the favour.

Vajpayee and Advani's personal equation should have been imbalanced during this period of professional estrangement. But they continued meeting, continued sharing notes, agreeing to disagree. A friend of both says: 'Advani went out of the way when he was party president to make

Vajpayee feel respected . . . they were good friends.' Vajpayee would have also realized that Advani was hardly alone in distancing himself from his politics. Virtually every leader in the BJP and RSS wanted nothing to do with Vajpayee. In this political wilderness, Advani was Vajpayee's one insurance against being completely discarded.

Other parties sensed Vajpayee's isolation during this period. V.P. Singh later claimed that Vajpayee wanted to break away from the BJP.[69] The Congress also came fishing. 'Rajiv wanted the Hindu vote, and Vajpayee was the kind of person who may have been able to get it without . . . [antagonizing] Muslims,' a senior Congress leader who met Vajpayee to entice him remembers. But, this leader adds, '[Vajpayee] would listen, and then laugh. He would not say anything . . . [but] we knew. He was not going to come.' When asked by journalists about leaving Advani's BJP, Vajpayee would reply, '*Jaayein to jaayein kahan?*'[70] If one were to leave, leave for where?

* * *

Self-interest alone does not explain why Vajpayee did not leave during this period. Nor does Vajpayee's disposition, as his ruthlessness to rivals within the party attests. The more likely explanation is the argument of this book. From an early age, Vajpayee had been brought up on the RSS's emphasis on organizational unity. He had learnt from the ousting of Balraj Madhok and Subramanian Swamy—differences of opinion would be tolerated, but never rebellion. As Ravindra Bhagwat says, 'We are told, "As many men there are, there are points of view." So express it. But once a decision is made by all, you have to go by the decision.'[71]

This emphasis on unity derived from a reading of history in which Indians had been vanquished because they did not work together. This history lesson weighed into Vajpayee's decision to not leave the BJP, as seen from a speech he gave at the height of his estrangement, in 1988.

Vajpayee referred to the battle between the East India Company and the Nawab of Bengal in 1757 which marked the beginning of British rule. 'In the Battle of Plassey, as many people were fighting as were standing outside the battlefield and seeing the entertainment. They were waiting to hear the results of the battle. The future of the country was being decided, but the entire country was not involved in this decision.'[72]

Vajpayee's fear of division was not just moored in history; it was anchored in the rifts that were tearing apart the Congress right then. He made a trip to England in the late 1980s to attend an academic conference in Oxfordshire. Here he met the Princeton political scientist Atul Kohli who had written lengthily on the de-institutionalization of the Congress. 'I have read your books,' Vajpayee told him during their evening walks. 'That is what we are worried about. That's why organization matters so much for us.'[73]

* * *

Vajpayee's decision not to depart ensured that his party remained together through the turmoil of the late 1980s, projecting a united face to the voter. What added to their fortune during this period was the Congress decision to telecast Hindu epics on the state-run Doordarshan at that very time.

The seventy-eight-episode *Ramayan* ran from 1987 to 1988, while the ninety-four-episode *Mahabharat* ran from 1988 to 1990.[74] Deploying religion in state media was not new. The Congress government had broadcast a daily recital from Tulsidas's *Ramcharitmanas* from radio stations in the Hindi belt during the Emergency.[75] What was new about the broadcast of these two serials in the late 1980s, however, was their impact.

Though the production and acting of *Ramayan* had 'all the finesse of a high school function',[76] it became the most watched programme on Indian television, earning a record-breaking 40 million dollars every week in advertising revenue.[77] Temples were deserted on Sunday mornings,[78] as worshippers chose a different kind of darshan. Arun Govil, the actor playing Ram, became so popular that villagers would drop on their knees in respect.[79] A mother wrote that she made her blind son touch the screen every time the serial was playing in hopes of getting his eyesight back.[80] When 'load shedding' took place in Meerut on Sunday mornings, the residents agitated and got power back so that they could watch their beloved serial.[81] As the serial was winding down in July 1988, sweepers in

Jalandhar went on strike demanding that the show be extended.[82] A few months later, Doordarshan began screening *Mahabharat*.

The serials portrayed the common culture required to nourish a Hindu vote bank. Muslim personal law board member and MP Syed Shahabuddin argued that 'most people watch it for religious reasons. It actually amounts to pampering the religious ethos of the majority community.'[83] The Dravidian leader M. Karunanidhi saw the serial as a ploy to 'impose Hindi on the country's non-Hindi speaking population'. Since people loved the epic, he said, they would be forced to see it despite the language.[84]

The decision to make and air these epics was made by the party of Nehru, not the party of Hindus.[85] Rajiv Gandhi, the first senior politician to support the Ayodhya movement, perhaps thought this was another way to get the Hindu masses on his side. He even made actor Arun Govil campaign for his party. With the benefit of hindsight, it is clear that this gambit flopped; *Ramayan* and *Mahabharat* did not reap Rajiv Gandhi any electoral benefits. The opposition even turned the tables on him, describing Arun Govil's campaign as: '*Ram chala hai Raavan ke liye vote maangne.*' Ram is asking for votes on Ravan's behalf.[86]

While the serials did not sanctify the Congress in any way, the question is whether they blessed the BJP. Did the record viewership help strengthen the Hindu vote bank (i.e., *cause* the electoral rise of the BJP), or was this TV phenomenon a *consequence* of a Hindu vote bank already created by then?

Even the pre-eminent academic on the subject, Arvind Rajagopal, admits, 'I neither uncover nor confirm any simple causal mechanisms of media effect.'[87] In the absence of proof, the most plausible explanation is that the electoral rise of the Bharatiya Janata Party took place because of factors that came together *before* the screening of *Ramayan* and *Mahabharat* (dealt with in this and the previous chapter). The popularity of these serials was evidence of a vote bank, fully formed and inflated. And, as the 1989 national elections approached, this Hindu vote bank stood waiting to be encashed.

* * *

It was in this atmosphere that the BJP formally supported the Ayodhya movement in its Palampur session held in June 1989. The only surprise was why it had taken so long. The session signalled the tone for the coming national elections, scheduled for November. The party's campaign manager Govindacharya recalls: 'It was the first elections where we directly mentioned Hindutva.'[88] To make the signal even clearer, Advani agreed to a tie-up with the Shiv Sena. While Vajpayee was once again quiet, his friend Jaswant Singh expressed both their rage when he stormed out of the session, walking kilometres to the nearest railway station to leave the city.[89]

The BJP's formal endorsement of the Ayodhya movement made Rajiv Gandhi engage in competitive communalism yet again. He allowed the VHP to organize a foundation ceremony for a temple in Ayodhya.[90] And so, on 9 November 1989, just days before the elections, 10,000 VHP and Bajrang Dal activists performed a brick-laying ritual near the Babri mosque. Gorakhpur's Mahant Avaidyanath declared that this amounted to laying the foundation of a 'unified Hindu society'.[91]

The BSP's Kanshi Ram, meanwhile, was attempting a unification of his own. Through September and October 1989, he held rallies in Moradabad for Muslims, Delhi for Scheduled Castes, Kanpur for backward castes, Ludhiana for Sikhs and Bangalore for Christians.[92] Each of these 'bahujan' groups were linked, in his telling, by resentment at upper-caste Hindu domination.

While Kanshi Ram was conjuring a demographic majority by expanding his *social* coalition, V.P. Singh was attempting his own majority through *political* coalitions.

A year earlier, he had merged his Congress splinter group with the backward-caste Lok Dal and former socialists to form the Janata Dal. Now, with elections approaching, he brought still more parties together, forming a National Front coalition that included Andhra Pradesh's Telugu Desam Party (TDP), Tamil Nadu's DMK and Assam's Asom Gana Parishad (AGP). The one party barred was the BJP. V.P. Singh instead chose a two-faced 'seat-sharing' arrangement where both parties coordinated to defeat Congress candidates without formally presenting voters with a united coalition.[93]

In a telling reversal of roles, Advani contested from the Lok Sabha for the first time (from New Delhi), while Vajpayee continued in the Rajya Sabha. Helping Advani make the transition was his wife. While Kamla never had a say in party politics, she was the apolitical rock to Advani that Rajkumari Kaul was to Vajpayee. Advani's nomination was 'proposed' by the writer Khushwant Singh,[94] who would later tell Advani at a public gathering. 'You are a clean man, you don't drink, you don't smoke, you don't womanise . . . But such men are dangerous.'[95]

Opinion polls prophesised a hung parliament and they were right. A simple majority required 263 seats, and Rajiv's Congress had been reduced to 196, down from 414. The BSP won only three seats. V.P. Singh's Janata Dal won 139 seats; they had expected 200.[96]

The BJP, on the other hand, gained eighty-five seats, forty times more than the two seats they had won five years earlier. This was all the more creditable since the party had contested only 225 of the 545 seats, mainly in the north and west of the country. With Advani deciding that the BJP would support a V.P. Singh-led government from the outside, a majority was cobbled up, and Singh became prime minister.

The Congress vote share had declined from 49 to 39 per cent, while the Janata Dal had won 18 per cent of the vote share,[97] at least some of that earned by renegade Congressmen. Had they not split their party, the Congress could well have come back to power.

A similar story of loss stemming from leadership squabbles was playing out in the BSP. Kanshi Ram had carefully selected his deputies to represent the range of 'bahujan' communities. Dr Masood Ahmad, a doctorate from Aligarh Muslim University, was a founder. Mayawati was a civil service aspirant from the Jatav caste of UP. Dr R.K. Chaudhary, a lawyer from the Pasi community, the largest Dalit group in UP after the Jatavs, would be inducted soon.[98] Yet, even by 1989, insiders were grumbling that Kanshi Ram was favouring Mayawati over others.

Kanshi Ram could have created his own version of history and learnt from it, just as Hindu nationalism had. He could have surmised that the problem of India's low castes was that they were historically disunited and prone to internal squabbles—between Pasis and Jatavs, for example, or between Dalits and Yadavs. He could then have made keeping various castes united the *central* preoccupation of his politics, just as Hindu nationalism had. Instead, the inability of the BSP leadership to unite as one—a breakdown accelerated by Mayawati's lack of team spirit—would prevent the BSP from becoming a truly national party.

In contrast to the Congress and BSP's failure to manage their flock, the BJP had remained together despite ideological and personality differences. Vajpayee continued in the party, while Advani–RSS–VHP–Bajrang Dal marched in tandem. And though Vajpayee and Advani's political partnership had frayed, their personal friendship remained intact. More than any single fact, it is this unity that allowed the Hindu vote bank to transfer to the BJP in 1989.

Academics have explained the rise of the BJP as resulting from a range of causes.[99] These include: the decline of the Congress system, a reaction to backward-caste reservations, polarization caused by the Ayodhya movement, Hindu epics shown on television, the inevitability of a Hindu party winning in a Hindu-majority country, and economic liberalization and a growing middle-class. These manifold theories, however, do not account for how competing explanations interacted with each other.

In contrast, this chapter has laid out the sequence of the BJP's rise: how incipient Hindu anxiety in the early 1980s was converted into a vote bank, originally by the RSS–VHP, then by the Congress, and finally by the BJP. How, in an era when other parties conceived coalitions that conjured up majorities, what set the BJP apart was not demographics or ideology, but organizational unity. Despite experiencing the political and personality differences that were tearing other parties asunder, Hindu nationalism coordinated to present the voter with a synchronized performance. The result was the quickest electoral expansion in its history.

But while eighty-five was a substantial number, it was still far from the 250-odd MPs required to rule Delhi. The 1989 elections had heralded what the political scientist Yogendra Yadav calls 'India's third electoral system', i.e., one characterized by an increase in the effective number of parties, a drop in the Congress vote share and a reduction in the number of states ruled by the Congress.[100] Advani entered the new Lok Sabha as a man wielding considerable influence over the new prime minister, V.P. Singh, who was dependent on the BJP's support. But Advani wanted power, not just influence. And as he aimed to move the BJP from third biggest to single largest, three roadblocks awaited him. His responses to Mandal, Mandir and Market would shape the BJP for decades to come.

9

MANDAL, MANDIR, MARKET (1990–91)

Vishwanath Pratap Singh took oath as prime minister in December 1989. His 'National Front' was a brittle coalition between the Janata Dal and smaller parties such as the DMK and TDP. The Janata Dal itself was a loveless marriage between middle-caste leaders such as Mulayam Singh and Lalu Prasad Yadav and Congress defectors such as V.P. Singh himself. Dinesh Trivedi, another such renegade from the Congress, says: 'It was like Indian Airlines and Air India merger . . . there was no compatibility . . . one was Lohiaite the other Gandhian.'[1] There was also the habitual Indian headache of egos. Many of his cabinet colleagues daydreamed of supplanting the new prime minister.

To add to this ricketiness was the government's dependence on eighty-five MPs from the Bharatiya Janata Party. Its president Lal Krishna Advani may not have had the appetite to devour V.P. Singh. But, as we read in the past chapter, the party had just formalized its support for a Ram temple in Ayodhya, something the prime minister's other partners—especially the left parties—were dead against.

And so, when the Vishva Hindu Parishad announced that they would begin construction of an Ayodhya temple by February 1990,[2] the government's stability was straightaway tested. Advani himself, however, represented 'those [within the BJP] who do not wish the government to collapse at this stage'.[3] The VHP was weighed upon to delay temple construction[4] until 30 October 1990. No one foresaw what all would take place between now and then.

154

These tensions over the Ram temple soured negotiations between the BJP and Janata Dal for seat sharing in the coming elections to six north Indian states. Narendra Modi, whom Advani had recently moved from the RSS to the Gujarat BJP, complained: 'Though the Janata Dal leaders talk of defeating the Congress(I), they are no less power hungry.'[5] Nevertheless, Modi worked hard to stitch not just the alliance, but also a new coalition of Hindus, high and low. Helping him inadvertently was a Congress up to its old tricks. The journalist Harish Khare spent many years reporting from Gujarat. He remembers: 'The Congress had a group of six to seven very strong leaders behind the KHAM alliance. They were Adivasi, Rajputs and OBCs . . . But these guys kept fighting with each other. The Congress even put its own Adivasi leader in jail. Can you believe it?'[6]

When the results for these state elections were announced in February 1990, the BJP had won four out of six: in Himachal and Madhya Pradesh on their own, and in Rajasthan and Gujarat in partnership with the Janata Dal.[7]

These victories finally put its president on the national map. *India Today* juxtaposed Advani with a photo of a blooming lotus on its cover. He was introduced thus: 'You've seen him somewhere . . . Bang in the middle of [R.K.] Laxman's daily cartoon, the bristle-brush moustached little common man peeping at the political world in bemused befuddlement . . . In life, Advani sports not only the moustache but also the quizzical countenance of the little old fellow.'[8]

The other major figure in the party at the time was Murli Manohar Joshi. He was neither a Nehruvian liberal masquerading as a Hindu nationalist, nor a Sindhi cosmopolitan radicalized by partition. This made him beloved of the Rashtriya Swayamsevak Sangh. Four years after Advani had made him general secretary of the party in 1986, Joshi was emerging as Advani's competitor. N. Ram remembers: 'By the early 1990s, Murli Manohar Joshi was the big rival to Advani, so every time they said anything, we tried to read between the lines.'[9]

Just as the throne was being contested inside the BJP, this was also the case inside the government. The National Front was endlessly unsettled by claimants to the prime minister's post.

The weightiest of these was the 6-foot-2 inch-105-kilogram Devi Lal. He had inherited Charan Singh's mantle of both Jat peasant leader as well as deputy prime minister. He had also inherited Charan Singh's pursuit of self-glory, no matter the cost. His attempts to reinstall his son as chief minister of Haryana despite corruption allegations led to resignations from Janata Dal members. V.P. Singh had to remove Devi Lal from the government.[10] Lal's response was to announce a farmer rally in Delhi on 9 August 1990. A few lakh farmers would come out against the prime minister.

The V.P. Singh government was about to end before it had begun. The prime minister needed a magic rabbit. On 7 August 1990, two days before the farmer protests, he pulled one out of his hat. Its name was Mandal.

* * *

Quotas were part of the original Indian Constitution, aimed at redressing centuries of oppression of Dalits and Tribals. In accordance with their population estimates, they amounted to 22.5 per cent of seats reserved in state and central employment and higher education. In addition to these, several southern states had introduced quotas for middle castes, known by the constitutional moniker 'Other Backward Classes' or OBC.[11] But it was only in the 1980s that northern states began to introduce OBC quotas. These reservations were spurred by the political ascendancy of the more dominant of these middle castes—Yadavs, for example—who wanted to convert political power into educational and employment opportunities.[12]

Backward-caste quotas were as yet absent in the 100,000[13] central government jobs, including for IAS, IPS and IFS recruitments. These elite services were staffed largely by upper-caste Hindus. The Janata government, which Vajpayee and Advani were part of, had set up the Mandal commission. Its report, submitted in 1980, had recommended 27 per cent quotas for 3743 backward castes that made up 52 per cent of the population.[14] But the prime minister at the time, Indira Gandhi, had shelved the report, as had her son when he succeeded her.

By 1989, however, the composition of parliament had changed. The new Lok Sabha, which brought in V.P. Singh as prime minister, had seen a doubling of 'backward' MPs, from 11 to 21 per cent.[15] The Janata

Dal housed many of them, and even the party manifesto had vowed to implement the Mandal report. A slogan of the times was: '*Vote se liya CM, PM; Mandal se lenge SP, DM.*'[16] Middle castes had become politicians though votes; Mandal would give them bureaucrats.

But manifestos and jingles are storage spaces for ideas that will never make it to policy, and no one expected the report to be implemented until V.P. Singh's announcement on 7 August 1990. Around half of central government jobs would now be reserved on the basis of caste.

That Mandal was a rushed counter to Devi Lal's call to arms is proven by the fact that Singh informed even his own cabinet just one day before. Advani was told only that evening.[17]

The move check-ed the prime minister's rivals. Given that middle castes were a demographic majority, the Janata Dal was forced to rally around Singh. And though Devi Lal nitpicked that it was a political move to counter his farmer's rally, even he could not criticize the caste quotas themselves. The left parties and the Congress were privately downcast but publicly had to confine themselves to demanding a class element to this caste quota.

These nuanced reactions were at odds with the mood on the street. While middle castes supported the decision, upper castes were noisily against it.[18] A government job was seen as one of the few paths to social mobility. And faced with reduced avenues, upper-caste students, many from poor backgrounds, brought cities to a standstill. One study chronicled violence in 'various small towns in Gujarat, Madhya Pradesh, Rajasthan, and even as far afield as Hospet in Karnataka—claiming lives at the rate of one or two every day. It flared up in Indore on October 14, claiming over 40 lives. It then spread slowly across the Hindi heartland, neglected by the state, ignored by the press, and fanned by prejudice, until it broke out violently again in Bihar.'[19] The figure of the protests was Rajeev Goswami, son of a Brahmin clerk from Punjab. After failing to draw attention to a nine-day hunger strike against the Mandal quotas, Goswami poured kerosene all over his body and set himself on fire.[20]

The RSS now demanded a suspension of the report.[21] It argued in the pages of the *Organiser*: 'What V.P. Singh through Mandalisation of the society intends to achieve is a division of Hindus on forward, backward and Harijan lines.'[22]

The BJP's mostly upper-caste leadership agreed in private. In public, however, Advani chose not to stand up to Mandal, calculating that alienating middle castes would reduce his party's potential voters to a numerical minority. He, therefore, sought a balancing act: his party would not oppose Mandal but wanted sub-categorization of castes and promised that the total reservations would not exceed 50 per cent.

The party's upper-caste 'base' saw through this sleight of hand. Students surrounded Advani to demand that he protest the report.[23] Some BJP leaders were even roughed up.

The party had been here before, in the upper-caste riots protesting reservations in Gujarat some years ago. Its response—manufactured by men like Narendra Modi and Amit Shah—was to unite Hindus of all castes by targeting Muslims. That diversion had succeeded. But India is more than Gujarat, and Advani needed an even bigger smokescreen than what Modi and Shah had crafted.

On 26 August 1990, nineteen days after Mandal, the RSS called a meeting to coordinate support for the VHP's ceremony to inaugurate the Ayodhya temple in two months. Though OBC reservations was barely cited, it was the elephant in the room without which the RSS would not have called this meeting.[24] Advani was present and sensed both the current of 'Mandir' (i.e., temple) and the undercurrent of Mandal.

It took him a few more weeks to put the two together. Advani was at home with his wife, talking to Pramod Mahajan, the ever-smiling former journalist who had quickly become the chief trend-spotter of the BJP. It was in the course of this discussion that it struck Advani what the diversion from Mandal would look like.

It would be a 'mini-bus or mini-truck' designed to look like a chariot. Advani would travel on it for 10,000-kilometres from Somnath to Ayodhya. This 'rath yatra' – or chariot procession – would begin on 25 September, travel through ten states, and reach Ayodhya in time for the VHP's ceremony on 30 October 1990.[25] It sounded offbeat, this smokescreen, but from its haze would emerge, in Advani's words, 'the greatest mass movement in history'.[26]

* * *

Advani and his wife began 25 September 1990 by praying at the Somnath temple, restored with government help in 1951. As Nehru had feared, that support was now being cited as a precedent. Advani asked the assembled sea of saffron: having recreated Somnath after centuries of pillage, why was the government unwilling to rebuild at Ayodhya?[27] He then got onto his Toyota chariot fitted with a wireless telephone, air-conditioned cabin and electronic microphone.[28] Like with Hindu nationalism, this modern device was dressed up in tradition: the canopy resembled the ones used in in the TV series, *Mahabharat*.[29]

His cavalcade surrounded by trishuls and saffron bands,[30] Advani set out to a tight schedule. In just Gujarat, 600 villages were traversed and fifty meetings held in the space of a few days.[31] This composition had been arranged by Pramod Mahajan. Helping him for the Gujarat limb of this pilgrimage was the forty-year-old Narendra Modi.

They had their ears to the ground, both. But neither Mahajan nor Narendra Modi had imagined the reception to Advani's chariot. The journalist M.K. Venu was accompanying the procession. He remembers how 'a lot of womenfolk got mobilized and lined up on either side of the road with a copper plate and with ritual materials like lamp, flowers and coins which were thrown at the DCM Toyota rath. Advani's rath got expensive offerings, like received in temples, which included coins.'[32] These hurled coins were like pellets. Narendra Modi complained: 'It tends to cause injury to persons on the *rath*. If declined, it hurts the sentiment of the people who like to give.'[33]

As the yatra drove from village to village, it united Hindus divided over Mandal. One middle-caste villager told the political scientist Christophe Jaffrelot that he did not support 'the BJP as such but sympathised with its commitment to build a Ram temple at Ayodhya. He might abandon the party if it betrayed this cause.'[34] Cheering alongside him were upper castes, many of whom had been agitated by Mandal.[35] Advani's equivocation on Mandal had infuriated them a month ago. But now, riding a chariot and carrying a bow, Advani was infallible. One young man even stabbed his hand and smeared the blood on Advani's forehead as a tilak. 'Advani blanched, his discomfort evident . . .'[36]

This public response finally gave Advani, still emerging from Vajpayee's shadow, the confidence to believe in his own appeal. Swapan

Dasgupta says: 'Advani was a different man when he got into the rath yatra and when he stepped out.'[37] He was finally capable of standing on his own feet, a mass politician in his own right. As Advani himself told his associate Harin Pathak: 'I was a party apparatchik until Ayodhya.'[38]

Advani's ascent annoyed the VHP, which had started the Ayodhya movement a decade earlier with no support from the BJP. Its leader Ashok Singhal told Subramanian Swamy: 'Who is Advani? We never invited him. He was never asked to lead the rath yatra.'[39] Pravin Togadia says: 'Now I can tell that Advani participated in Ram temple movement, but he did not have deep-rooted conviction.'[40] Sudheendra Kulkarni, a former communist and journalist, had by then become a vocal defender of the Ayodhya movement. He counters: 'Togadia's anger is misplaced as Ram Janmabhoomi would never have taken on a mass character without the BJP taking it up, with Advani at the helm.'[41]

* * *

The one man who watched all this with unease was Atal Bihari Vajpayee. He had opposed the Ayodhya movement in 1983 and its formal adoption by the party in 1989. But here was his protégé using the party podium, or chariot, to broadcast the Ram temple across the country. Far earlier than Advani, Vajpayee had understood that if Hindutva moved from a political project to a religious movement, the passions stirred would not be confined to votes. 'The difficulty of the *rath*,' he would later say, is that 'once you ride it you do not feel like getting down from it.'[42]

Soon after Advani rolled out from Somnath, Intelligence Bureau officials met Vajpayee in Delhi and showed him videos of Hindu–Muslim violence breaking out in parts of India. Vajpayee immediately called up Advani and asked him to abandon his chariot. 'You are riding a lion,' someone present remembers Vajpayee pleading with Advani over the phone. Advani refused to listen; he chose to continue his journey.

The rath yatra marked the first time Vajpayee's fondness for Advani was tested. He complained about Advani in private, sensing that his best friend was undergoing a personality change. But in public, Vajpayee used wordplay to communicate without saying: 'Advani is going to Ayodhya to do penance, not fight Ravan. But many times the *vanarsena* [the monkey army] that followed Ram did not know where they were going.' Vajpayee travelled to Somnath as part of a parliamentary delegation some weeks after. Yashwant Sinha was with him. He recalls: 'Vajpayee was extremely unhappy with what was going on. He was considering leaving the party. For him, it appeared that Advani was upstaging him.'[43]

But even Vajpayee was incredulous at how successful the yatra was proving. He later wrote: 'As the *rath* rolled on, it became increasingly clear that the question of building a Ram Temple deeply touches the emotional chords of the majority of the community.'[44]

Midway to Ayodhya, Advani got off his chariot to attend a BJP meeting in Delhi. The only question discussed at the 17 October 1990 meeting was what the party would do if Advani was arrested en route. The V.P. Singh government must not fall, Vajpayee said.[45] There was silence. Then speaker after speaker got up to praise Advani. Vajpayee was drowned out as his party decided that if Advani was forced to step down from his chariot, the prime minister would have to step down from his.

Advani recommenced his yatra. The convoy could have travelled due east and reached Ayodhya in a matter of days. But this was an electoral journey not a geographic one, and the procession first travelled east of Ayodhya, to Bihar. The state's chief minister, the Janata Dal's Lalu Yadav, had come to power on the basis of a Yadav–Muslim coalition against upper castes. In meeting after meeting, Lalu had wanted Advani arrested, while Prime Minister V.P. Singh urged caution, not wanting to risk the BJP's electoral support. But on 22 October, the left parties gave an ultimatum to the prime minister: arrest Advani or risk losing *their* electoral support.[46] Advani was doing to Singh on Mandir what the prime minister had done to him on Mandal: Singh was being forced to take a stand.

Advani reached Samastipur in Bihar on the night of 22 October. Officials reached there by helicopter in the early hours of the morning. They woke up Advani as he was sleeping in the circuit house and told him that he was being arrested under the National Security Act.[47] Advani was flown out instantly. Neither the 100 journalists staying nearby nor even party MPs sleeping in the floor above Advani realized what was happening.[48] Lalu Yadav explained the BJP president's arrest with: 'The Government took this extreme measure to save humanity.'[49]

L.K. Advani was flown to a scenic guest house by a lake near Dumka, in what is today Jharkhand.[50] Used to hardy jails during the RSS ban in 1948 and during the Emergency, this was a holiday in comparison. In a replay of the Emergency, his lawyer N.M. Ghatate visited Advani. He says: 'By this time Advani [had] realized that what he had done was so momentous. He had seen the response to the yatra. He did not expect . . . the whole country was talking about it.'[51]

Advani is at pains to point out that no anti-Muslim violence erupted on his route.[52] A survey of the newspapers of the day seem to bear out this claim,[53] though the parallel VHP mobilization did result in violence in Uttar Pradesh, Rajasthan and Karnataka.[54] And the riots after Advani's arrest killed sixty-one.[55]

Advani's chariot was pure opportunism, short-term politicking rather than long-held belief. It must, however, be conceded that, having radicalized a Hindu vote bank like never before, Advani stepped back from the brink. He refused to denounce Muslims; he refused to advocate violence.

Vijai Trivedi was covering the rath yatra. He says: 'The kind of response was more than [Narendra] Modi has ever got. People were falling at Advani's feet. Advani at that time was the leader of Hindus. Modi has never come close. But Advani didn't want to encash it. He never criticized Muslims directly.'[56]

During the 2019 election campaign, Amit Shah was asked in private what the difference was between him and Modi on the one hand, and Vajpayee–Advani on the other. He replied: 'They never believed that fully waving Hindutva flag could win them votes. This is the difference between us and them.'[57]

* * *

Hours after Advani's midnight arrest in Samastipur and 1144 kilometres away, Atal Bihari Vajpayee presented his party's letter withdrawing support to the V.P. Singh government to the president of India. A BJP leader says: 'Vajpayeeji was deliberately sent even though there were others. He had opposed withdrawing support. We wanted to send a message that [the] party is united.'

Meanwhile, as the 30 October deadline neared, 75,000 activists reached Ayodhya. The state Janata Dal government headed by Mulayam Singh Yadav relocated 20,000 policemen to protect the mosque.[58] As if to make up for lost time, Vajpayee arrived in Ayodhya the day before the event to assume leadership of that which he had opposed.[59] This was a drama Vajpayee would re-enact many times, including in the aftermath of the 2002 Gujarat riots: he would initially oppose his party on principle, then overcompensate when he felt his position threatened.

The next morning, 40,000 kar sevaks or religious workers gathered at the bridge leading to the entrance of the old town of Ayodhya.[60] They included sadhus who had been mobilized along with half-pant wearing RSS volunteers. The VHP had sworn to confine their ceremony to the land next to the mosque. Instead, and as feared, activists scaled the Babri mosque to bring it down. The chief minister of Uttar Pradesh ordered his police to fire. Several activists died, but the mosque remained standing.

Back in Delhi, the government lost a no-confidence motion triggered by the withdrawal of the BJP's support. V.P. Singh had to step down. By this time, his party, racked with personal ambitions, had also split. Chandra Shekhar and Devi Lal walked out with fifty-eight other MPs. And with outside support from the Congress, Chandra Shekhar became prime minister in November 1990.

A leadership change was also in the works in the BJP. The second consecutive term of party president Advani, free again after his third spell in jail, was nearing its end. Since Hindu nationalism abhorred personality cults, the party president was expected to change every two terms. Vajpayee and Advani had overcome that hurdle by stepping down for the other every six years or so, between them controlling the party all the way from 1968. But now, Vajpayee was no more a force, and the BJP had to look for another person to replace Advani.

That person was Murli Manohar Joshi, the former physicist beloved of the RSS. He was made party president in February 1991.

To come out of Advani's shadow perhaps, the new president decided to conduct a yatra of his own. The 'charioteer' for this journey was Narendra Modi, the same role that Pramod Mahajan had played for Advani's rath yatra. But Joshi had not bargained for the fact that Advani had now become a wily politician in his own right, with its virtues as well as vices.

Attracting few cadre and fewer crowds, this yatra was less than successful. Sudheendra Kulkarni was a confidante of Advani. He says: 'Joshi's yatra did not have the full backing of Advani and Vajpayee.'[61] Govindacharya remembers: 'To be fair to him, Joshiji thought when he became president in 1991, he would have his own team. He even made a list in February 1991. Then Advani said, this is not how it happens. You have to talk to the sangh.' Advani ensured that the RSS chose his own men, including Govindacharya.[62]

While this infighting within the Bharatiya Janata Party was rare, it was of a piece with the internal struggles taking place in the Janata Dal and the Congress. What set the BJP apart was that these divisions did not result in open sabotage. Neither Advani nor Joshi said a word against each other in public.

An example of the mechanisms the BJP possessed to bring together factions can be gleaned from a story found in M.L. Sondhi's private archives. As we read earlier, the urbane Sondhi had been evicted from the party by Vajpayee in 1973, only to return years later. But any chance of a second shot as New Delhi's MP was being thwarted by the state heavyweight Madanlal Khurana. Now, in 1991, when Sondhi travelled to Jaipur for a party event, he was given the keys to his guest room. He went to his room and slept off, only to wake up 'in the middle of the night to find [Madanlal] Khurana getting into the next bed'.[63] Perhaps it was a coincidence. Perhaps it was the BJP's way of conjuring family-like ties to keep the party united.

* * *

This unity was in vivid display in the campaign for the May 1991 national elections, necessitated after the Congress withdrew support to Chandra Shekhar's fledgling government. Advani, Joshi and Vajpayee all worked as one Hindu undivided family, even though it was clear that Advani was the prime ministerial candidate. The BJP even set up a nine-member committee of advertisers and journalists with a two-crore budget to help package Advani.[64]

In the previous elections, in 1989, the BJP had contested just 225 seats; this time they put up candidates in more than 425 seats, a sign of confidence.[65] Advani contested two of these: New Delhi (where he was pitted against the actor Rajesh Khanna) and Gandhinagar in Gujarat.

He travelled to Gandhinagar to file his nomination papers. Sitting next to him, with a groomed black beard but wild hair, was Narendra Modi. It is clear, from a photograph of the event, that Modi is in charge, pointing to where Advani has to sign.[66] Positioned respectfully behind them, along with other junior leaders, was the twenty-six-year-old Amit Shah, Advani's campaign manager for Gandhinagar.[67]

The national campaign was more overtly religious than any before. The new Advani urged every voter to mail postcards to their relatives asking them to vote for the BJP. 'And write on top [of the postcard], *Jai Siya Ram*.'[68]

Like what Modi and Amit Shah had executed in Gujarat in the mid-1980s, the BJP campaign's refined Islamophobia was coupled with unsubtle allurements to low-caste Hindus. The BJP's nominee profile for the Uttar Pradesh state elections, being held in sync, offers a glimpse of this approach. In addition to the approximately 22 per cent candidates in seats reserved for Scheduled Castes and Tribes, the party ensured that 26 per cent of its candidates were OBCs[69]—a potent figure given that the Mandal Commission had recommended 27 per cent reservations. The party's candidate for chief minister was Kalyan Singh, from the 'backward' Lodh community.

Two lakh RSS workers campaigned door to door for the BJP.[70] Having learnt from 1984, Advani was careful to pay his respects this time around. While electioneering near Nagpur, home of the RSS, Advani visited his old mentor Madhukar Rao Bhagwat. His son Ravindra Bhagwat says: '[Advani] directly went to the rally. After that, he came to our home. It was a formal talk.'[71]

Away from the summit of the party, Vajpayee had pitched his tent in the Rajya Sabha. The journalist Neena Vyas asked him in February 1991 whether he had been marginalized. Vajpayee's reply is revealing: 'Sometimes corrections happen only in the margins.'[72]

But his luck was turning. Riding on the rath yatra and the firing on activists, the BJP had detected a wave in Uttar Pradesh.[73] Vajpayee remembers: 'I had announced that I would not contest the elections for the Lok Sabha [but] the party wanted to form its government in

Uttar Pradesh. To boost the election campaign, it was very necessary to field from there a person who could muster more public support for the party.[74] He was asked to contest from Lucknow, where he had last stood twice before. As precaution, he also stood from Vidisha in Madhya Pradesh.

The election was divided into three phases, with the first scheduled for 20 May 1991. The day after, the Congress's Rajiv Gandhi travelled to Tamil Nadu for the second phase. He was in Sriperumbudur outside Chennai when a woman from the Liberation Tigers of Tamil Eelam (LTTE) mingled with the crowd. As prime minister, Rajiv Gandhi had sent troops to Sri Lanka to enforce a peace treaty; the LTTE was worried that if re-elected he would do so again. The woman made her way to the former prime minister. As she bent down to touch his feet, she detonated a bomb attached to her body.

* * *

Rajiv's murder provided the Congress, so far caught between VP Singh's 'Mandal' and the BJP's 'Mandir', with an emotive issue of its own. When the election was eventually completed and the results announced, the Congress had won 232 of the 524 seats, a near majority.[75] The BJP came second with 120 seats, a 40 per cent jump from its past election. It had almost doubled its vote share, from 11 to 20 per cent.[76] Advani won from both his seats and chose to retain Gandhinagar; he would contest and win from here another five times. Vajpayee won from both his seats and chose to retain Lucknow. He would contest and win from here another four times.

The BJP believes that Rajiv's murderer slowed its juggernaut. Seshadri Chari says: 'In 1991, had Rajiv not died, BJP may have got 200 seats. In that case, Advani would have been PM. How stable it would have been is a different question.'[77] An analysis of the election results somewhat bear him out. One statistical survey estimated that the Congress gained twenty-five seats because of the assassination—the difference between forming government and being in opposition.[78]

An elderly Congress insider, P.V. Narasimha Rao, became prime minister in May 1991, and the BJP the principal opposition party. It was now entitled to the post of leader of the opposition. Ever since Vajpayee had joined parliament in 1957, he had represented his party in parliament. It was only natural, he assumed, that he be made leader of the opposition. But the RSS had other plans. They demanded that Advani be given that post.

Though flattered at the elevation, Advani still had feelings for his former mentor. He knew just how much Vajpayee cherished leading the party in parliament. Advani sent the RSS a simple message: 'The leader of opposition has a status. It befits Atalji.' But he was told: 'Issue is closed, don't reopen. When it was a small party, it can be Atal. And you made the movement.' On hearing this rejection, Advani 'hit his [own] head'. He said: 'Don't they realize the problems this will create'.[79]

But as Lal Krishna Advani took his place in the front row facing Prime Minister Narasimha Rao, Vajpayee's hurt ego was perhaps not the first thing on his mind. India was in the midst of a balance of payment crisis and lacked the money to pay. Drastic reforms were required, and as the prime minister grappled with a response, his counterpart in the opposition did too. Having adroitly navigated Mandal and Mandir, the two 'M's that continue to define the BJP today, how was Advani going to navigate the 'Market'?

* * *

The immediate cause of the economic crisis was that India did not have enough money to repay its external loans; if it defaulted, it would become an international outcaste. The International Monetary Fund, the global loan agency, was only willing to help if the government promised to undertake economic reforms.

The deeper problem however was an economy that had been mismanaged by decades of state intervention. Myriad rules dictated which sectors entrepreneurs could enter, and on what terms; manifold barriers kept foreign capital away. Private companies were also intentionally kept from growing big. All of these were part of a 'socialist' ideology that the Congress had inherited from Nehru partly, but his daughter mainly. To overturn economic policy, Prime Minister Narasimha Rao had to overturn Congress ideology.

Lal Krishna Advani was in a similar bind. The trader base of his party was all for the removal of restrictions on their own businesses, but they wanted to limit competition from foreign companies and capital. The RSS had its own axe to grind: the worry that globalization would swamp Indian culture.

As long as economic liberalization was a distant demand, the BJP enjoyed the safe perch of the fence. That changed through July 1991 as Prime Minister Narasimha Rao, aided by his finance minister, Manmohan Singh, and principal secretary, Amarnath Varma, transformed the economy. The rupee was devalued in two secretive steps, and the new industrial policy abolished licensing (except for a few industries). Industrialists could now set up businesses in most sectors without first buying approval. Public sector monopolies were now limited to just a few sectors, and the web of laws that kept companies entangled were unspun. Finally, foreign direct investment was permitted to reach 51 per cent (i.e., a controlling stake) in many industries, and barriers to foreign trade were trimmed. These ideas had already been sketched out by policy makers a decade prior. But it took a Machiavelli to rush them past party, parliament and the bureaucracy.[80]

Narasimha Rao's reforms placed the BJP in a bind. As the principle party of opposition, how would it respond?

In his memoir, Advani says that his BJP supported the end of the licence–permit–quota raj.[81] The facts tell another story. A particularly angry voice was Murli Manohar Joshi's. Demanding 'economic independence', he provided a dire description of other countries that had fallen prey to foreign loans: 'In the Philippines young boys were working in the Gulf while young girls took to prostitution to earn foreign exchange for the country.'[82] Vajpayee, who still commanded respect in parliament, was as critical within its walls. So harsh was his denigration of the government's economic reforms that Finance Minister Manmohan Singh even complained to Rao. Vajpayee was decent enough to apologize, but only in private. Contrary to Advani's claims, the BJP's parliamentary response to liberalization was political posturing.

Within the walls of the sangh parivar, however, Rao's policies spurred a more nuanced conversation. Most in the party supported the end to the domestic controls that had plagued its small trader base. Where the party was divided was on outward liberalization.

While marginalized on Mandir, the BJP's dominant view on Markets was mouthed by Vajpayee: '. . . Cable TV, Star TV are coming—have come. They will sell luxury articles. People will watch them in their huts. Even if the children do not have milk to drink, shampoo will be bought.'[83] An MP in the house misheard shampoo as champagne. Vajpayee replied: 'I did not say champagne. Those who love champagne thought I said champagne.' He added, quoting Tulsidas: '*Jaki rahi bhawana jaisi, Prabhu moorat dekhi tin taisi.*'[84] A devotee sees God in the image he wants to see.

This critique of liberalization was rehashed in a BJP national executive meeting in Trivandram in September 1991. A private record of the discussion makes for absorbing reading. The party produced an initial 'anti-IMF draft, heavily critical of the government's policies'. Vajpayee and Murli Manohar Joshi's influence seemed to pervade it. 'How could India become a *pithoo* [subordinate] of the USA,' Vajpayee asked.[85] It seemed certain that the BJP would officially oppose liberalization.

Then Advani spoke, in Hindi. He opposed the draft, supported the need for liberalization, and reserved praise for Manmohan Singh. 'This encouraged other speakers from the floor to say that they were all for the IMF loan, and for all the measures the govt had taken!'[86] The boss had spoken; the minions fell in line.

By the end of the meeting, the BJP had adopted a stand more favourable to liberalization. Had Advani not spoken, his party would not have either.

The RSS could not stomach this equivocal stance to the entry of foreign capital, commodities and companies. In November 1991, they created the Swadeshi Jagran Manch which aimed to counter the BJP's tolerance of liberalization. This strategy of the RSS mimicked its resurrection of the VHP in 1981: When it felt that the BJP was not toeing the line, it would prop up another organization to put pressure. But this time, its target was not Atal Bihari Vajpayee; it was Lal Krishna Advani.

Advani's against-the-grain decision on Markets mirrors his resolve on Mandal and Mandir. All three involved a fog-laden path for the BJP. On Mandal, the BJP was torn between its upper-caste base, the electoral power of lower castes, and the imperatives of Hindu unity. Likewise, on Mandir, the BJP was dithering between electoral moderation and the need to unite Hindus after Mandal. And on Markets, the BJP was caught between support for internal and opposition to external liberalization.

It is to Advani's credit that, looking ahead into low visibility and without Vajpayee as navigator, he changed the direction of his party. It was not ordained that the BJP would be the party of pro-OBC reservations, pro-Ram temple and pro-liberalization. But for better or worse, these choices, Advani's all, continue to guide his party to this day.

10

TOO MANY GENERALS (1992)[1]

The third battle of Panipat was fought in 1761 between the Maratha confederacy and the Afghan warlord Ahmad Shah Abdali.[2] With the Mughal Empire in decline, the Marathas were the ascendant national power. Had they won at Panipat—86 kilometres north of Delhi—the Marathas could have ended the fledgling British presence in India before it ballooned into Empire. And, who knows, the Indian elite could today be speaking Marathi instead of English. The results of the third battle of Panipat would shape modern India like no other.

Though Ahmad Shah Abdali was from another country, he was able to gather local support. The Rohillas from Doab and the Nawab of Awadh rallied around him in the name of Islam. On the other side, the Marathas failed to entice the Rajputs, Jats and Sikhs to fight with them. Add to this the fact that a top general in the Maratha army was a Muslim, and you get a war where only one side could deploy religion for battlefield unity.

The other problem the Marathas faced was a weak chain of command. Rather than ruled wholly by the Peshwas, they were structured as a confederacy of chieftains: the Holkars from Indore, Gaekwads of Baroda, Bhonsles of Satara and the Scindias from Gwalior. This meant that, while the royal guard of the Peshwas supplied 11,000 cavalrymen for the battle, Jankoji Scindia, whose progeny would one day fund the teenage Vajpayee's education, alone contributed 10,000 men on horses.[3] The

100,000 Marathas at Panipat on the morning of 14 January 1761 were not a single army; they were a mishmash of militias.

This was on prompt display the moment fighting began. As one historian writes: 'In the absence of a coherent and disciplined force under a unified commander . . . control over the various Maratha cavalry was at best weak.'[4] The cavalry disobeyed orders, and attacked without coordinating with the infantry. The result was that 30,000 Marathas died in battle and 10,000 in retreat, while 10,000 went missing and 50,000 were enslaved or slaughtered.[5] Twenty-seven Maratha commanders were killed in combat, along with the Peshwa's son.[6]

The war extinguished the dream of a pan-Indian Maratha empire. It also proved a stalemate for Abdali, whose exhausted soldiers forced him to leave India. Into this power vacuum crept the British. As BJP president Amit Shah put it in 2019: 'The Marathas lost this one battle after winning 131, but had to pay a heavy price and we faced 200 years of colonial slavery.'[7]

Whatever be the truth to this narrative, this was what the RSS leadership, Maharashtrian Brahmins in the main, had told its own from a young age. Atal Bihari Vajpayee, Lal Krishna Advani, Narendra Modi and Amit Shah had all grown up believing that the cause of Hindu defeat in Panipat still persisted in present-day India. As the longest-serving RSS chief M.S. Golwalkar explained: 'People say that there is now a change in circumstances, that since the British have left this country there is no need for an organisation of this type. We, on the other hand, view the problem differently. We say, the Hindus were here and they continue to be here. They were disunited and are still disunited. We see the same disintegrated, mute Hindu Society letting itself to be trampled upon without a murmur of protest. And when it does speak, it is with so many voices that what it says sounds like gibberish.'[8]

Hindu nationalism had spent decades attempting to not just get Hindu voters to speak in unison, but its organizations (the BJP, VHP, RSS, etc.) to speak in one voice. But as the sangh parivar entered 1992 after having nimbly navigated Mandal, Mandir and Market, it seemed to be forgetting its own lessons from Panipat.

* * *

At the level of organization, Advani and Murli Manohar Joshi were humming different tunes. As we read in the last chapter, though Joshi had replaced Advani as party president, Advani had been able to appoint his own within the BJP. But Joshi did manage to place some of his supporters to favoured positions. The most significant of these was the selection, in June 1991, of Kalyan Singh as the first BJP leader of India's largest state. Not only did the new Uttar Pradesh chief minister formally report to the new party president, he was also beholden to him.

This crack within the BJP's chain of command was made worse by the other groups that had coalesced around the Ayodhya movement. These were not just from Hindu nationalism, they were from traditional Hinduism.

The theological unit of the Hindu religion is the sect, also known as a *sampradaya* or tradition. The celibate monks within each of these sects are known as sadhus or sants. In popular imagination, they are bearded men clad in saffron robes, smeared in grey ash. These ascetics typically belong to the Shaivite or Vaishnavite tradition.[9] Attached to these sects are militant ascetic groups, known as akharas, the Sanskrit word for mud pits where they practise wrestling. These warrior ascetics came to prominence in the eighteenth century, working as mercenaries for various empires.[10] But by the twentieth century their most public role was in the organization of the kumbh mela, a gigantic religious congregation that rotates, in twelve-year cycles, between the pilgrimage sites of Haridwar, Ujjain, Nashik and Allahabad.

Though the RSS shakha is modelled after the akhara, Savarkar and Hedgewar had kept away from these religious men—seeing them as too disorganized, and simply too religious, to contribute to the creation of a modern, unified, Hindu identity. As we read earlier, this had begun to change with the formation of the Vishva Hindu Parishad in 1964, the 1966 anti-cow slaughter agitation, and the creation of the Ayodhya movement in 1983. By the early 1990s, the akharas were not just part of the political movement, some sadhus even came from RSS backgrounds.[11]

The presence of these religious figures created an Ayodhya movement that was as disjointed as the Maratha Empire. While Hindu nationalists were driven by electoral considerations, these sadhus were driven by transcendent passion. They *believed* that Ram was born on the ground where the Babri Masjid stood. They were making their voices heard through the VHP and Bajrang Dal, but were too individualist to be ordered around by even these groups.[12]

A united BJP could perhaps have controlled them. But by late 1991, Advani was too busy sparring with Murli Manohar Joshi and Kalyan Singh to keep an eye on the rest of the movement. As Hindu nationalism once more prepared for battle over the Ram temple at Ayodhya, their in-house Peshwas, Bhonsles, Scindias and Holkars were each marching to their own tunes.

* * *

The first actions of the UP chief minister illustrated this disconnect. Soon after his appointment in 1991, Kalyan Singh visited Ayodhya. He was accompanied by his mentor Murli Manohar Joshi. Amidst slogans of '*Mandir Yahin Banayenge*' [i.e., the temple will be built above the mosque, not adjacent to it], Singh and Joshi took an oath 'for the construction of the temple at the disputed site'.[13]

The state government soon acquired 2.77 acres of land around the Babri Masjid, handed it over to the VHP, and began to demolish ancient Hindu structures in the outer courtyard (though they left the main mosque untouched). It was only when the Supreme Court forbade this that Kalyan Singh stopped.[14] Prime Minister Narasimha Rao's own Intelligence Bureau reported to him that 'notwithstanding the present impasse on account of legal obstacles, the BJP government in U.P. is considering how best to circumvent those hurdles that are standing in the way of the construction of the temple'.[15]

Even as Kalyan Singh and Murli Manohar Joshi worked in tandem with the VHP, they were being outdone by even more radical opponents. The sadhus were unwilling to countenance any solution other than destroying the Babri Masjid and building a temple above it. They began to launch an agitation, not against the Narasimha Rao government or even Advani and Vajpayee, but against the Kalyan Singh government! Singh's counter to this bullying: 'The question of pressurising (sic) me doesn't arise when I am myself committed to building the temple.'[16]

Just as Indira and Rajiv Gandhi had sensed a mobile Hindu vote bank unhappy with the BJP in the 1980s, the Congress prime minister, Narasimha Rao, now saw an opportunity to reclaim the Hindu voter. He kept negotiating with a variety of sages and *peeth* heads, hoping that the institutions of traditional Hinduism could be detached from the institutions of Hindu nationalism. Rao had to balance this Hindu outreach with charges from his own cabinet ministers, from men like Arjun Singh, that he was ignoring Muslims. His solution to please Hindus without upsetting Muslims: 'It is our desire that a grand temple be built there, but the mosque must remain intact.' He ensured that Hindu and Muslim groups met around ninety times in late 1991[17] and through 1992.

These meetings produced nothing. Someone present says: 'The VHP had no interest in a solution. They wanted the problem to keep going on. That's why they insisted that *Mandir Wahin Banayenge*.'

Under pressure from his right flank, Kalyan Singh once again resumed construction around the mosque in July 1992, in violation of the Supreme Court. Narasimha Rao panicked and considered dismissing the Uttar Pradesh government, halting only when Kalyan Singh finally listened to a fresh Supreme Court order.[18]

A nervous prime minister called Advani, Joshi and Vajpayee for a meeting. Vajpayee 'suggested that the prime minister should call the sadhus and the sants and talk to them about the construction'. The RSS also told the prime minister to 'talk to the sants and sadhus for this'.[19] This was a revealing request. Even the discipline-worshipping RSS was admitting they were not in control anymore.

Of all the 'sants and sadhus' who seemed to have taken over the movement, the most famous was Mahant Ramachandra Das Paramhans. With thick spools of hair on his head, in his beard, and on his eyebrows, all that would be visible were his dreamy eyes and a shrunken mouth. Born in Bihar in 1910, Paramhans had felt a sense of detachment from the material world at the age of twelve and had abandoned home.[20] He had wandered in the company of other sadhus before settling in Ayodhya and running an akhara. Paramhans had made the Ram temple there his life's mission. From placing the idol inside the mosque in 1949 to arranging a brick-laying ceremony in 1989,[21] Paramhans *was*, in some sense, the

Ayodhya movement. Now aged eighty-one and still on fire, he had no interest in negotiating with mere mortals. Neither the BJP nor RSS nor even the VHP fully controlled him.

Some months later, on 30 October 1992, the VHP announced they would begin temple construction on the land next to the mosque. They would erect a 116-foot by 138-foot by 6-foot platform[22] on which their new Hinduism could stand. This would violate the Supreme Court order. But the saffron-clad men couldn't care less. They even gave a date for when they would disrespect the law. It would be a month from now, the sixth of December.

* * *

This fresh provocation led Narasimha Rao to once again contemplate imposing central rule in Uttar Pradesh. In a top-secret memo, his home secretary laid out how the Centre could take over the disputed structure: A strike force of 'CRPF: 90 Coys [companies]; RPF 25 Coys; CISF 54 Coys. Total 169 coys' would fly from Delhi to Lucknow and then make their way by a road convoy to Ayodhya. The home secretary pointed out that the mosque could be attacked once the crowd realized the convoy was on its way. For this reason, the home secretary recommended that if the prime minister chose to impose central rule, it be done well before 6 December, i.e., before the lakhs of kar sevaks gathered around the mosque. The note said, '[A] date prior to 24 November 1992 may be considered.'[23]

It was under this looming shadow that Narasimha Rao decided to repeatedly meet with Lal Krishna Advani, to convince him to protect the mosque. Rao would have liked to negotiate with his friend Atal Bihari Vajpayee instead. But he realized that no one within the movement cared to listen to Vajpayee. Where he erred was in assuming they would listen to Advani.

Vajpayee had predicted a long time ago that the Ayodhya movement would one day make even Advani irrelevant. He had always understood that Hindutva needed to be confined to parliament and subjected to its compromises in order for it to remain within their control. Advani, greener than Vajpayee, was convinced that he could ride the tiger without being eaten.

It was under this joint delusion that Rao and Advani met three times that November.[24] This was in addition to Advani's many meetings with senior Congress intermediaries in the months prior. Rao thought Advani was speaking on behalf of the movement. Little did he know that Advani had met the VHP probably only once through November,[25] and likely had no contact with either the Bajrang Dal or the Shiv Sena.

The 24 November deadline came and went. Rao was now powerless to physically protect the mosque without risking the integrity of the structure. The only solution seemed to lie in negotiations.

In a secret meeting around 25 November 1992, held in bungalow number 5 in the prime minister's house, Advani and Vajpayee met Rao along with Kalyan Singh. They assured him that the mosque would be intact.[26]

Vajpayee meanwhile avoided being identified with the movement, sticking to his favourite role in parliament. The fifth session of the tenth Lok Sabha was scheduled from 24 November to 23 December.[27] Records of the proceedings reveal that the main issue discussed was the impending kar seva. As MP after MP expressed fury, it was left to Vajpayee to use his three decades of contacts within parliament to sell the line that 'the BJP was trying to avoid a confrontation and wanted the temple issue to be solved amicably'.[28]

* * *

The Supreme Court seemed to provide this very 'amicable solution' on 28 November 1992, when it took note of the sangh parivar's assurance, and subsequently allowed a kar seva on 6 December in the land in front of the mosque.[29] It sought to balance this concession to the VHP by ordering that the event be limited to liturgy and chanting, rather than any construction activity that could threaten the mosque.

This court intervention allowed the BJP to support the 6 December kar seva without being seen to break the law. Advani's response, however, lacked Vajpayee's ability to say without saying. He swore that the kar seva—far from being symbolic, as the court had ordered—would end with the construction of the temple.[30]

The next day, 2 December 1992, parliament was in uproar over Advani's statement. Tempers ran high and the air was thick with cries of 'shame, shame'.[31] It was left to Vajpayee, whose role was now reduced to being Advani's advocate, to calm parliament. He claimed that newspaper reports carrying these statements were erroneous. The situation, Vajpayee artfully replied, 'was not so serious or alarming as made out by press reports'.[32]

Meanwhile, the real theatrics were taking place elsewhere. In anticipation of 6 December, Bajrang Dal and Shiv Sena cadre were 'vying with each for the fame of blowing up the disputed structure and this fact was within the knowledge of VHP'.[33] They even took an oath by the Sarayu river to destroy the structure.[34] The Intelligence Bureau sent the prime minister a top-secret report that a VHP suicide squad was training to blow up the Babri Masjid. The report was, however, careful to stress that this was an unverified rumour. This was a typical Intelligence Bureau ploy, a confidante of Narasimha Rao says. 'All IB reports present both arguments. If the mosque fell, they would say we predicted. If it didn't, they would say we predicted.'

Meanwhile, Advani and Joshi were travelling across Uttar Pradesh, whipping up support for the kar seva. They reached Lucknow, three hours from Ayodhya, on 5 December. They planned to speak at an event in the Aminabad locality before driving to Ayodhya that night.

The star speaker for that event, however, was a man who had kept himself away from the Ayodhya movement until now. Since Atal Bihari Vajpayee was now a sideshow, his speech was not covered by the media. The only recording that exists is with the Intelligence Bureau. Wearing a white kurta and black jacket, an energetic Vajpayee made sure to say that he was respecting the Supreme Court order. But, Vajpayee told the crowd, there was a way to reinterpret it. 'The Supreme Court has allowed bhajan-kirtan. One man cannot perform bhajan alone. And many people need to gather for kirtan. And kirtan cannot be performed standing up. How long can we stand?' Vajpayee added: 'Sharp stones are emerging from the ground. No one can sit on them. The ground has to be levelled.'[35] *Zameen ko samtal karna padega.*

As Vajpayee finished speaking, a cavalcade of red beacons made an appearance. Murli Manohar Joshi had turned up to speak. Where

Vajpayee was careful to advise the crowd *against* travelling to Ayodhya, Joshi directed them to go.[36]

Vajpayee followed his own advice and returned to Delhi, claiming that he had been ordered not to go to Ayodhya.[37] Had he gone, he may well have never become prime minister. Joshi, on the other hand, followed his own advice and left for Ayodhya, reaching around midnight. Accompanying him was his rival Lal Krishna Advani, who had chosen to go to Ayodhya with Joshi rather than return to Delhi with Vajpayee.

Far from being seen as troublemakers, Joshi and Advani were welcomed by the civil administration. The local bureaucrats were worried, since the crowd around the mosque had swelled from 500 on 25 November 1992 to 175,000 on 30 November and over 200,000 by 5 December.[38] Advani and Joshi assured them that the next day would proceed peacefully.[39] It is not clear on what basis this promise was made, given that neither were really in charge of the arrangements.

They spent the night at Janaki Mahal, a dharmashala or religious guest house located three kilometres from the Babri mosque. The next morning, 6 December 1992, these two rival BJP leaders met the regional satraps who were part of the sangh parivar confederacy. These included Vinay Katiyar (Bajrang Dal), Ashok Singhal (VHP) as well as a host of saffron-clad religious leaders such as Sadhvi Rithambara.[40]

Joshi and Advani then travelled to the Babri Masjid, reaching at 10:30 a.m.[41] The area around the mosque was flooded in a sea of saffron and khaki. Some of those drops were of Ramachandra Paramhans along with sadhus from his akhara. They seemed to be allowing uniformed RSS volunteers to manage them. Some other swayamsevaks were forming lines and standing to attention, while uniformed police milled around them, khaki merging into khaki. The crowd soon reached 150,000.[42]

As Joshi and Advani attempted to part this sea, they needed a ring of volunteers holding hands. They looked like prisoners rather than wardens.[43] Twenty minutes later, they pushed their way to the Ram Katha Kunj, an elevated platform 200 metres in front of the mosque. They settled down on a viewing platform erected there.

Around 12 noon, the chiefs of police and administration for the district made a round of the area. Everything was okay, they relayed back to the home ministry in Delhi. This was conveyed to Narasimha Rao, who was watching on the television in his bedroom along with a friend. Also watching was Atal Bihari Vajpayee in Delhi, seeing on television what Advani was watching live from a podium in front of the Babri mosque. Everything was going to be under control.

Twenty minutes later, a teenager jumped across the security boundary around the mosque and climbed on top of its dome. The police looked on as the central forces guarding the perimeter magically disappeared. The boy was joined by thousands of others, who began to chip away. The idea of India that had prevailed for the past forty years was under attack.

* * *

From the height of the Ram Katha Kunj, Advani saw for himself that 'more and more people appeared to be climbing the dome. Soon I could see them carrying some implements and hammering at the dome.'[44]

At the prime minister's house in New Delhi, 700 kilometres away, the phone began to ring as politician after politician called up Narasimha Rao. But his secretary said that Rao was unavailable. Contrary to later rumours, the prime minister was not praying or sleeping—he was in his room talking to officials.[45] Just a few hundred metres away, N.M. Ghatate was also watching television from his house on Hailey Road in central Delhi. He immediately travelled the ten-minute journey to Vajpayee's house. 'He was all alone, watching TV,' Ghatate remembers. 'He was very, very angry. He could not believe what had happened.'

Vajpayee, far from Ayodhya and far from his party, had the luxury of doing nothing. Not so Advani, who got up and began to use the public-address system to beg the kar sevaks to climb down. 'I spoke with great distress in my heart,' Advani remembers.[46] He was joined by H.V. Sheshadri, that typical RSS polyglot who appealed to the crowds in multiple languages. Rajmata Vijayaraje Scindia, who unlike Vajpayee and Advani had always supported the Ayodhya movement, also used the loudspeakers to tell the mob: 'I am appealing to you as your mother not to do what you are doing.'[47] Swapan Dasgupta was on the podium. He remembers the Rajmata shouting: '*Unko pant se neeche utaaro.*'[48] Pull them down by their pants.

None of these words carried any weight that day. For a movement built on discipline, the scene around the Babri mosque was one of pandemonium. Holes were bored into the mosque, ropes inserted and walls pulled down.

Advani says he climbed down from his platform to look for a phone so that he could talk to Kalyan Singh. He heard a thud. He was told that the first dome of the mosque had collapsed. It was 1:55 p.m.[49] Rather than witness the finale of the journey he had commenced from Somnath in September 1990, Advani spent the next few hours below the podium. The journalist Chandan Mitra was also on the platform. He remembers that Advani 'went downstairs and just sat silently through the evening. Once or twice when he did come up, he kept repeating that it is unfortunate.' Murli Manohar Joshi, Mitra says, was 'absolutely silent', but 'other leaders . . . like Ashok Singhal were, frankly speaking, fairly jubilant about what was going on'.[50]

A new India was emerging from the bedlam below. The public-address system, which had until recently begged the kar sevaks to climb down, now began blaring religious songs. Vinay Katiyar and Sadhvi Rithambara joined the mob, as did RSS workers. Ramachandra Paramhans had spent much of his life preparing for this day. Along with others, 'he went into ecstasy' watching the demolition.[51]

Meanwhile, the thousands of policemen tasked with protecting the mosque watched unmoved. When a paramilitary battalion moved towards the spot, the district magistrate ordered them to stop, citing a written order from the chief minister.[52] All the king's men watched as the third and final dome fell at 6 p.m.

* * *

Forty-five minutes later, at a cabinet meeting in New Delhi, the prime minister of India dismissed Kalyan Singh. 'No one could say anything. We were so shocked,' a minister remembers. 'Then [C.K.] Jaffer Sharief [the senior-most Muslim leader] began to talk. He said what happened was terrible.' Near simultaneously in Lucknow, Kalyan Singh submitted his resignation as chief minister.[53] Advani would soon resign as leader of the opposition in parliament.

The mood was sombre across India, anticipating the riots that would break out through the country and kill more than a 1000.[54] Thousands of Muslims flocked to the Jama Masjid in Delhi, where the Shahi Imam urged all protests to be peaceful. He added: 'It is a major tragedy. Our hearts are broken.'[55]

The atmosphere was just as fearful in the BJP headquarters in Delhi, lightened only by the party's Muslim face Sikander Bakht walking around the office hugging everyone and saying, '*Hindu ne toh kamaal kar diya hai.*'[56] The Hindus have done wonders!

M.G. Vaidya was in Hedgewar Bhavan in Nagpur when he heard the news. He drafted the RSS chief's reaction: 'I am happy that the symbol of outsider's oppression has been removed, even though we were not part of the agitation.'[57] In private, however, the RSS was terrified of being banned again. In a hastily called meeting, one senior leader said: 'This is what happens when sadhus, not pracharaks, take leadership.' The demolition placed the RSS in a quandary. They were delighted that the mosque was gone, but were perturbed that they had lost control.

Later that night Narasimha Rao gave an emergency broadcast to a shaken nation. 'I am speaking to you this evening under the grave threat that has been posed to the institutions, principles and ideals on which the constitutional structure of our republic has been built.' He added: 'I would like to say very clearly that we shall no longer suffer the Machiavellian tactics of the communal forces in this country.'[58] He cast blame on Advani, who he was sure had lied to him. When his secretary told him that he should act against Congressmen such as Arjun Singh for criticizing him over the demolition, Rao replied: 'After what Advani has done to me, what can Arjun Singh do?' Rao ordered the arrest of Advani (along with Joshi and many others).[59] As we shall see, Rao would wait for three more years to extract his full revenge on Advani.

The demolition of the Babri Masjid succeeded in achieving the BJP's aim of uniting the entire non-Congress opposition—however, not alongside the BJP but against it.[60] In a moment reminiscent of the aftermath of Gandhi's murder, the entire political class wanted Hindu nationalism to pay. The RSS and VHP were banned,[61] and the BJP chief ministers of three states were dismissed.[62]

Vajpayee initially seemed inconsolable. So worried was Pramod Mahajan that he called up Ghatate and told him: '*Please Vajpayeeji ko control mein rakhiye.*'[63] Please keep Vajpayeeji under control. Mahajan, who was present at the Babri Masjid, later admitted to Vajpayee: 'All the generals were present there. I don't know what went wrong.'

Vajpayee replied: 'In 1761 in Panipat also there were too many generals, and [the Marathas] still lost.'[64]

* * *

All of this was for private consumption. In public, Vajpayee was careful to avoid making statements criticizing Hindu nationalism for *causing* the demolition. Instead, he said only that 'We are sorry' for the fact that 'we tried to prevent it, but we could not succeed'.[65]

Far from using this moment to separate himself from his party, Vajpayee fell into the familiar pattern of using parliament to defend rather than castigate. He had sensed a turn in his fortunes, and yet another turn in his partnership with Advani. After seven years in which his moderate façade was not required by the movement, he was now back in demand.

In his speech to parliament, Vajpayee reserved much time to defend his old friend. '. . . when the structure fell Advaniji looked sad and had tears in his eyes. It is for this reason that Advaniji tendered his resignation and expressed sorrow for whatever had happened and took responsibility for the same.'[66]

The reason for Vajpayee's U-turn is not hard to divine. As we saw with the 1990 rath yatra and as we shall see with the 2002 Gujarat riots, Vajpayee's first 'liberal' reaction would be followed by the realization that he risked being cast aside by his party. He would then leap to his party's defence, a leap not of faith but of moral acrobatics.

Advani, on the other hand, had a clear-cut response: we wanted the structure to go, but not in the manner it went. For much of his life he had been plagued by self-doubt. The response to his rath yatra in 1990 had briefly assured him of his abilities as a politician. But 6 December had rattled this new-found confidence. It would cause him to once more rely on the old comforts of his old friend. Advani would later describe the demolition as the 'saddest day of my life'.[67]

A few days later, Advani wrote two articles in *The Indian Express*. He blamed a familiar culprit: organizational disunity. But he did not mean the lack of coherence on *his side*. Instead, Advani lumped the reactions to his rath yatra in 1990 with this demolition in 1992 to blame the *other side*. His argument is worth quoting at length: 'Left to himself, Mr. V.P. Singh may not have obstructed the *rath yatra* of 1990. But the internal politics of Janata Dal forced his hand. To prove himself a greater patron of the minorities than Mr. Mulayam Singh Yadav, VP asked Mr. Lalu Prasad Yadav to take action before the Uttar Pradesh Chief Minister did so. Mr. Yadav did as he was told, and became instrumental in terminating VP's tenure. This time around, Mr. Arjun Singh has played a Mulayam Singh to Mr. Narasimha Rao.'[68]

Advani should have applied this analysis to his own party. The Ayodhya movement was a result of a groundswell of Hindu anxiety, nurtured by the VHP–RSS and then Congress; the BJP had only come to the party late in the game. And with the party fractured from within as well as hemmed in by rabid activists and zealous saints, the sangh parivar was not a single army in Ayodhya that December. They were a mishmash of militias.

This view, that the destruction of the Babri mosque was a miscalculation rather than a concerted plan, is challenged by several who were present at the site. A journalist who saw the mosque falling in front of her eyes says: 'Of course there was a conspiracy. Why was Vajpayee not present? It was deliberate. He knew something was going to happen. Advani, Vajpayee, Rao, they all planned it.'

The official investigation, conducted by a commission that took seventeen years and a thousand pages, unearthed a conspiracy involving the BJP, RSS, VHP and Bajrang Dal.[69] The sixty-eight conspirators named included Atal Bihari Vajpayee and Lal Krishna Advani.[70] An astonishing twenty-eight years after the demolition, a special court finally pronounced its verdict in September 2020. The court acquitted all twenty-eight accused, including Lal Krishna Advani. This verdict is unlikely to assuage many, who will allege a fresh conspiracy, this one to cover up the original conspiracy.

But consider, for a moment, an alternative explanation. The evidence tying Advani, let alone Vajpayee, to the crime is circumstantial.[71] And we do know that Advani and Vajpayee had lost control of the movement—the BJP was fighting within, the RSS and VHP were not listening to the BJP, and the sadhus were not listening to the VHP. Improbable though it may sound, what if the events of 6 December were a breakdown of Hindu nationalist ideology rather than its epitome? What if the problem on the battlefield that day was, indeed, too many generals?

11

UNTOUCHABLES (1993–98)

What pint-size chance the BJP had of an embrace by the non-Congress opposition evaporated on 6 December 1992. Three of its chief ministers were dismissed, the RSS and VHP outlawed, and its leaders, Advani included, incarcerated. With its politicians jailed, soundbites were cooked up by sadhus, one of whom even demanded a fresh constituent assembly to anoint a Hindu kingdom.[1] The communist leader Sitaram Yechury spoke for many when he said: 'By mixing religion with politics, the BJP is taking the country back to medieval theocracy.'[2]

The BJP's untouchability was on display in a no-confidence motion pushed by Vajpayee just eleven days after the fall of the mosque. The rare BJP leader to remain free, Vajpayee was back in his favoured location: the centre of the parliamentary stage. The 111 MPs who voted to dismiss the Narasimha Rao government were almost entirely from the BJP; the 336 MPs voting against the motion represented the Congress and the non-BJP opposition.[3] As Advani himself put it: 'The demolition caused a setback because it was not something we bargained for . . . For a democratic party like the BJP, this did contribute to damaging our credibility.'[4] Forty-four years after the murder of Gandhi, Hindutva was once more considered outside the pale.

This loneliness in parliament coincided with an atypical tussle within the party over who its new president should be. As we read earlier, Murli Manohar Joshi was elected in 1991 after twenty-three years of Vajpayee and Advani at the helm. His term was ending soon, and he should normally have received a second term. But these were not normal times. In addition to the reverberations from the mosque's levelling, the BJP was developing the cracks that it abhorred, and Joshi lacked the soothing hands required to spread balm over them. 'Joshi was a strong interfering president,' a BJP leader remembers. 'The strong chief ministers—Patwa, Shekhawat—did not want interference. Advani was great, because he would not intervene. When there was a dispute, he would tell warring CM contenders, "Go to a room and decide."'

The problem was that Advani, now released from prison, was reluctant.[5] His self-confidence had dipped after Ayodhya. He even asked that his name be removed from consideration, since he was 'upset at all the lobbying'.[6] The other option for BJP president was Vajpayee, but those behind the Ayodhya movement vetoed the name.[7]

Eventually, 'tremendous pressure'[8] was exerted on Advani, and, in June 1993, he became president again. An insider says: 'Vajpayee was the one who convinced Advani finally.' An attendee to a national executive held around then described: 'Visible relief at the absence of Joshi, especially by LKA and ABV—both loudly congratulating the other.'[9]

With Advani as party president, his parliamentary position became vacant, since party rules dictated that the same person could not hold two posts. And in the last six months, Vajpayee had demonstrated that the party needed him in parliament. So it came as no surprise when it was Vajpayee who replaced Advani as leader of the opposition a month later. His name was proposed by, again no surprise, Lal Krishna Advani.[10]

Vajpayee's elevation to his cherished role dimmed the BJP's untouchability in parliament, if ever so slightly. Prime Minister Narasimha Rao was confident that his friend would 'uphold parliamentary traditions', a sly reference to the illegal razing of the mosque. Vajpayee hoped the 'winds of change' would reach 'the other side also'.[11]

The return of Vajpayee and Advani as orator and organizer was thus reached through a delicate dance that began with the fall of Joshi, his replacement by Advani and the filling of Advani's post by Vajpayee. Seen from afar, this does seem orchestrated.

But whatever be the source of Vajpayee's resurrection, it was clear that in this new partnership, it was Advani who was boss, Vajpayee his deputy.

A poll of 56,858 voters during this time found that Advani was the most popular leader in the country, the prime minister-in-waiting.[12] He now had the power to take his party in the direction of his choosing. Where would that be?

* * *

The elections to four state assemblies held in early 1993 provided Advani with his answer. The BJP won Delhi, its mainstay. But in the other three states—Uttar Pradesh, Madhya Pradesh and Himachal Pradesh—it forfeited power. These losses were loaded with lessons, given that these were the BJP-run states that Prime Minister Narasimha Rao had dismissed just months ago.

The movement to demolish the Babri mosque had fuelled the BJP's ascent in the 1989 and 1991 national elections. But the state losses in 1993 indicated that the actual demolition had put a lid on this growth. Pratap Bhanu Mehta speculates: 'This is the great puzzle of the Ayodhya movement. Its success actually ended the BJP's ability to mobilize. That's the thing about psychological grievance. As long as the mosque was there, it was a wound that could be exploited. With its demolition, it would not win votes anymore.'[13]

This electoral decline of the BJP after the demolition adds fuel to the theory that 6 December represented the failure of Hindu nationalism rather than its culmination.

L.K. Advani, for one, acted as if he too thought of the demolition as an aberration. In a series of newspaper articles he wrote in late 1993, he did not refer to Ayodhya even once.[14] Speaking to the political scientist Christophe Jaffrelot, the BJP president explained his shift: 'No party can have credibility if it is seen as a one issue party. We would like the BJP to be accepted by the people as a party . . . which is not trying to win power simply on the basis of an emotional issue.'[15]

It was also during this time, after the fall of the Babri Masjid, that Advani reached out to English-speaking journalists such as Swapan Dasgupta and Chandan Mitra. Ajoy Bose says: 'Advani was the guy who made the outreach to English media. Atalji was uncomfortable with English media. He would prefer speaking in Hindi. Advani was fluent in English. He went out of his way.'[16]

Yashwant Sinha, finance minister in the Chandra Shekhar government, says: 'I was at a loose end in [the] early 1990s. A common industrialist friend arranged a lunch with Advani. He wanted people from other parties to join. I was one of the first of these "secularists" to join the BJP. It could well be that after 6 December, Advani wanted to mainstream the party.'[17]

Advani's attempts at making the BJP respectable again were supported by Vajpayee, who was a decades-long specialist at this task. When Vajpayee was awarded best parliamentarian in 1994, he used the occasion to extol the virtues of democracy. 'While the constitution and law are important, the prestige of Parliament is its life-giving strength.' He also had flattering words for Nehru, who 'by his very presence in the house . . . enhanced its prestige . . .'[18]

That same year, Vajpayee led a multi-party delegation to Geneva to prevent Pakistan from tabling a resolution on Kashmir at the UN Commission on Human Rights. Joining him was the minister of state for external affairs, Salman Khurshid, who remembers: 'It was [prime minister] Rao's decision to send Atal Bihari Vajpayee . . . And to his credit, Vajpayee agreed.'[19] Pakistan was unable to garner the numbers to pass the resolution. A photograph of a celebratory Vajpayee and Khurshid hugging was splashed across India. Vajpayee entirely, his party somewhat, seemed to be touchable again.

* * *

This 'moderate' avatar was on display for a series of state elections in 1995 in Maharashtra, Gujarat and Bihar. The BJP campaigned, not on Hindutva, but on 'unemployment, price rise, corruption'. The strategy worked, with the party winning in Maharashtra and Gujarat, and replacing the Congress as the principal opposition party in Bihar.

The most important of these victories was in Gujarat, where the BJP won 121 out of 182 seats, a majority for the first time. Though most legislators wanted Shankersinh Vaghela as chief minister, Narendra Modi lobbied for Keshubhai Patel instead.[20] Advani had appointed Modi as state general secretary in 1993, overruling dozens of MLAs who had threatened to resign over the polarizing pracharak.[21] Advani now backed Modi once more, appointing Keshubhai Patel as chief minister. Keshubhai returned the compliment, crediting the election wins to Modi's 'imagination, strategy and painstaking efforts'.[22]

At the heart of the forty-four-year-old's talent was 'dexterity in formulating arcane caste equations'.[23] In a premonition of his strategies as prime minister, Modi worked with Amit Shah, *his* Advani, to create a Hindu vote bank. They did this, not just by targeting Muslims as the enemy, but by microscopically targeting middle-caste Hindus, blandishing MLA seats, special funds, or just speeches that extolled a local caste hero.

The appointment of Keshubhai as chief minister, however, infuriated Vaghela. Modi and Keshubhai added salt by providing positions of patronage to their supporters alone.[24] The BJP had always strived for consensus from within; Modi's was a different philosophy.

Vaghela had had enough. He split the party on 27 September 1995 along with forty-nine dissident MLAs. They were sent on a chartered flight costing more than four lakh rupees to a luxury resort in Khajuraho (a temple-town in Congress-run Madhya Pradesh known for its erotic sculptures).[25] One rebel legislator described how '[We] spent our time playing table tennis, swimming, listening to music. We were told to relax and enjoy.'[26]

Vajpayee was sent to entice Vaghela, who ignored Advani, saying only that: 'I have every confidence in Atal Bihari Vajpayee. I have placed my demands before him.'[27] As we read in the beginning of this book, the most non-negotiable of those was articulated by Vaghela himself: 'I want Narendrabhai moved out of Gujarat.'[28] Advani had to move Modi to Delhi as national general secretary that very November. Out of this fracas, the only man who emerged victorious was Vajpayee the Peacemaker, able to do what Advani could not.

More than even the Babri demolition, the Vaghela rebellion shook a movement determined to avoid having too many generals. The MLAs who had left for Khajuraho were forever seen as traitors who had not learnt the lessons of the Hindu past. They would be assaulted during party meetings, stripped of their dhotis and nearly set ablaze.[29] One of them was even beaten up in the presence of L.K. Advani.[30] This near-split was a common occurrence in other parties. But Advani was so shattered that he even considered resigning.[31]

Advani had always felt that he was a misfit in his own party, that but for partition he would have pursued a very different calling. This self-doubt was accentuated now, as Advani realized that he lacked the subtleties to handle this inner-party feuding. He also sensed that his party was now in a 'moderate' stage that had less use for him. All this convinced him that the party's prime ministerial candidate had to be a unifier, someone who could appeal to the assorted factions within his party, and assorted parties within parliament.

This was why, in the November 1995 Bombay plenary, held just a month after the truce in Gujarat, Advani announced Vajpayee as the party's prime ministerial candidate. This incident is discussed in the beginning of this book. Having now read eleven more chapters, we are better prepared to grasp its significance.

Part of why Advani acted the way he did might have been love for Vajpayee and doubts about himself. But much of it was an ideology conditioned by Hindu unity, organizational harmony and election victories. This was why Advani had allowed himself to replace Vajpayee as the party's face in 1986. And this was why, a decade later, Advani was allowing himself to be replaced by Vajpayee. Advani's decision was an act of ideology.

* * *

L.K. Advani's largesse of November 1995 was rewarded, two months later, by an act of meanness by Narasimha Rao.

The prime minister was a friend of Vajpayee, but had never warmed to Advani. This chilly air turned to ice after the obliteration of the Babri Masjid. The prime minister met Advani many times in the lead-up.[32] Advani had promised no harm would come to the mosque. Rao had believed him. In the aftermath, the prime minister was convinced that he had been lied to.

Rao got his chance for payback in January 1996. While investigating foreign funds received by Kashmiri terrorists using an alternative system of remittances known as 'Hawala' in 1991, the Central Bureau of Investigation (CBI) had raided the house of a Delhi-based businessman, S.K. Jain. They discovered a diary listing 60 crore rupees worth of payoffs to politicians and bureaucrats.[33] But finding no other evidence, the CBI was unwilling to act. Now, years later, the CBI announced that there was enough evidence to prosecute those named.[34]

The most prominent among them was Lal Krishna Advani, accused of receiving a bribe of rupees 60 lakhs.[35] Advani had taken care to maintain a clean image, and the BJP had sought to segregate itself from the Congress on corruption. 'The party with a difference was now "tarred with the same brush".'[36]

That evening, Advani was in his living room in Pandara Park. He was with family and associates. One of them recalls: '[Advani] paced up and down . . . we were all there . . . some of us said not to resign . . . the old man was adamant.'

Advani vowed that he would not contest elections until he was acquitted. Though Advani would remain party president, any flickers of hope the RSS had of Advani replacing Vajpayee as the party's prime ministerial candidate was extinguished.

If 'Hawala' came as a godsend for Vajpayee, his actions did not show it. At a party meeting held soon after, he cried at the plight of Advani.[37] Vajpayee decided to contest the coming elections both from Lucknow (his current seat) as well as Advani's Gandhinagar, as a symbol of support.[38] Vajpayee explained away the names in the Jain diary as 'donations' to parties. He said: '. . . I am satisfied with Advani's stand . . . All political parties are accepting donations in "black". But it is not fair to target some and leave out the others.'[39] He added with laughter: 'Suppose I had been on my way to Lucknow to contest the election and Jain had come to me and told me to take Rs 1 lakh. Would I have refused it?'[40]

Vajpayee's frank admission of the role of black money reflected a change in the BJP's finances. The Jana Sangh had relied on small donations and volunteers. Nanaji Deshmukh had changed this somewhat, as had Rajmata Scindia and Nusli Wadia. But most businessmen paid money to the Congress and stayed away from the BJP.

By 1996, however, the BJP was seen as being within stone's throw of Raisina Hill, and India's corporates responded in cash. The man facilitating this was Vedprakash Goyal, treasurer of the BJP (his son Piyush would one day also become party treasurer). And assisting him was a man as showy as Goyal was unobtrusive.

Pramod Mahajan had hit the national limelight by organizing Advani's rath yatra. By 1996, he was the chief money man for the BJP at the national level. Mahajan had acquired a reputation for being money-wise, but someone close to Vajpayee rejects this. 'He was collecting money because the party asked him to, not for himself. And he did more than anyone to ensure that Atalji and Advaniji stayed together. Pramod is much misunderstood . . . it's very sad.' One donor describes Mahajan thus: 'With Pramod, the scale of money was very large. And with Pramod, the party became very flashy. He and I never got together because of his money-raising tactics. Advaniji must have told him about my feelings, because Pramod once called me to his house in Delhi. It was one of those MP houses. And it was bare. He told [me]: "I am a poor Brahmin person. Look at how I live." He was implying that the money he collected was for the party, not for him. I think Atalji and Advaniji would have objected had any fundraiser taken the money for personal purposes.'

* * *

Apart from this new money, the BJP's 1996 election campaign was defined by a new face. In just a few months, the spotlight had shifted from Advani to Vajpayee, who emanated a more conciliatory air. Vajpayee took pains to stress that his party was not anti-Muslim: 'For the BJP, all Indians are equal.'[41] Even his opponent in Lucknow, the actor Raj Babbar, emphasized that Vajpayee was the right man in the wrong party. 'I am Arjun in this battlefield, but he's Bhishma Pitamah.'[42]

A magazine described Advani's conundrum thus: 'His supporters feel that politically, he is poised for a soft fade-out. Going by the BJP constitution, he cannot be renominated party president after his term ends in October 1997. Sticking to his own promise, he cannot enter Parliament.'[43] No single image captured this transfer of power more than the release of the party manifesto for the elections. Advani stood alone in the corner of the dais as media-men mobbed Vajpayee on stage for a soundbite.[44] As the BJP stood on the threshold of power, no one was interested in the views of the film director. They only wanted to hear the hero.

Results to the elections were announced on 9 May 1996. The Third Front, a loose coalition of non-Congress non-BJP parties that included the Janata Dal, communists and the DMK, had won 173 seats.[45] The Congress had been reduced to 140 seats, with 96 million Indians voting for it. Though only 68 million Indians had voted BJP, these voters were concentrated in the north and west. As a result, the BJP won 161 seats, making it the single largest party in parliament

The BJP's success was not because of new voters; its vote share had barely increased from the last election in 1991. Instead, the BJP was able to strike better alliances—with the Shiv Sena, Haryana Vikas Party and Samata Party—and had consolidated the upper-caste Hindu vote.[46]

Precedent dictated that it should be invited to form a government. But the BJP was still 111 short of the 272 seats needed to form a stable government, and the three allies Vajpayee had managed to muster provided just twenty-six seats.

Advani and Vajpayee decided to take their chances, and a few days later, on 15 May, President Shankar Dayal Sharma invited Vajpayee to discuss the 'post-poll scenario'. At 1:40 p.m., Vajpayee left his 6 Raisina Road residence to make the five-minute journey to the top of Raisina Hill.[47] He returned soon after, and told his oldest friend: 'The president has fed me laddoos.'[48]

Seventy-six years after India's first general elections had sparked Hindu nationalism, one of its own had become prime minister of India, leader of the world's largest democracy.

* * *

Just before his swearing-in on 16 May 1996, Vajpayee greeted workers in what was likely the party headquarters. Amongst those present was Narendra Modi, recently banished from Gujarat. Modi was Advani's protégé, and had opposed the 'moderate' direction Vajpayee had taken the BJP in the early 1980s. But he too knew that at this moment in Indian history, it was Vajpayee who was best placed to lead the party. As Modi, with salt-and-pepper hair and beard, lunged to hug Vajpayee, the prime minister-elect raised his hand, as if to hit a truant child, then smoothly changed that into a hug. It was playacting amongst the familiar.[49]

A few hours later, at 12 noon, crackers were burst at the BJP headquarters in Nagpur by RSS, Shiv Sena and BJP workers.[50] At this exact moment, Vajpayee stood up in Ashoka Hall in Rashtrapati Bhavan—dressed in white, with an 'orange angavastram marked by a saffron streak'—to take formal oath as the prime minister of India.[51] Eleven other cabinet members were sworn in, including the new home minister (and effective number 2) Murli Manohar Joshi. The overall composition of cabinet were 50 per cent Brahmins[52] (who make up around 5 per cent of India), and one woman.[53]

This was to be expected. What was unexpected was the choice of Jaswant Singh as finance minister.[54] Jaswant was a pro-liberalization voice, closer to Advani than to Vajpayee on economic policy. The appointment indicated that Vajpayee was rewarding a trusted friend and drinking partner. It also showed that he was willing to subdue his Nehruvian instincts and continue the liberalization policies of his other friend, Narasimha Rao.

Also unexpected was the absence of Rajmata Vijayaraje Scindia in the cabinet. As we saw previously, Rajmata was beloved both of the base and the RSS; she could have easily toppled Vajpayee–Advani and taken control of the party through the 1970s and '80s. But she was constrained by loyalty. Her reward was being left out of the first BJP cabinet in Indian history.

The other absent face was L.K. Advani, who had declined to contest elections till he was cleared of the Hawala charges. But he was still party president, and attended the swearing-in ceremony—as part of the audience—wearing a cream kurta and dark cream jacket.[55] And after all these years, Vajpayee's trust in Advani still remained intact. He ensured that Advani was kept in the loop by having all party meetings in Advani's house.[56]

Cheering the new cabinet, Nusli Wadia said: 'I am looking forward to a stable government.'[57] This was the kind of entrepreneur the prime minister wanted to please when he decided to provide a crucial 'counter-guarantee',[58] i.e., green signal, to the Enron power plant in Maharashtra, a showpiece of foreign investment that the state Shiv Sena–BJP alliance had opposed. And in a broadcast to the country on 19 May, Vajpayee made no mention of the three core issues in the BJP's manifesto: a Uniform Civil Code, a Ram temple at Ayodhya and removal of special status for

Kashmir.[59] These were the very issues that separated the BJP from the rest of parliament.

Vajpayee followed this up two days later, by urging the Maharashtra chief minister to revive the Srikrishna Commission.[60] A High Court judge had been tasked with investigating the riots in Bombay after the fall of the Babri mosque in December 1992. When the Shiv Sena–BJP government came to power in 1995, they had disbanded the commission. But now, just a few months later, the new prime minister wanted to parade his 'secular' credentials. The Srikrishna Commission was restored after Vajpayee's elbow nudge.[61]

If this was not enough commitment to Nehruvian India, Vajpayee chose prudence over ideology when it came to the nuclear programme. A nuclear deterrent had been a consistent demand of Hindu nationalists. During the period 1991 to 1996, Prime Minister Narasimha Rao had transformed India's nuclear capability, and by 1996, India had the ability to test both fission as well as hydrogen bombs. Immediately after Vajpayee became prime minister, Narasimha Rao had met him along with scientists associated with the programme. '*Saamagri tayyar hai*,' Rao had told him. The ingredients are ready. Vajpayee even ordered testing. But he then paused to make sure that he had a stable government, even though a mushroom cloud would have energized his cadre, won votes and enticed at least some regional parties. When asked whether he would test, Vajpayee parried: 'Don't ask an interim PM such a loaded question.'[62]

If the aim was to show that the BJP could rule within the four corners of the Nehruvian consensus, this 'moderate' strategy worked. If the aim was to attract regional allies, it failed.[63] The government's numbers still stood at 194, exactly what it was when it was sworn in.[64]

Vajpayee sounded resigned to his own resignation: 'We shall not indulge in horse-trading or manipulation. Everything will be done in broad daylight. If members are willing to support us, the BJP-led coalition will continue. Without their support I don't see any chance.'[65]

Meanwhile, an alternative to the Vajpayee government was shaping up. V.P. Singh and the communists were stitching together regional parties to create a 173-strong non-Congress, non-BJP 'United Front'. The Congress party's 140 MPs promised outside support.

With this United Front having the numbers, the only thing left was to select a prime minister from amongst these parties. After some bickering, the candidate selected was Jyoti Basu, chief minister of West Bengal for nearly two decades. What could have been the first communist prime minister of India was stymied by the communists themselves. The reason for this, the scholar of the third front Sanjay Ruparelia suspects, was that 'it was risky for the CPI(M) to assume formal political responsibility in a diverse governing coalition'.[66]

Jyoti Basu would later term this a 'historical blunder'. But he accepted his party's decision without rebellion. Advani, watching from the other side, confessed that he was 'impressed on two counts—firstly, the party displayed the courage to stick to its own principles even when prime ministership was offered to it on a platter; and, secondly, the discipline that marked the inner working of its highest decision making body'.[67] Advani might have been describing his own resolution to step aside for Vajpayee in 1995.

The United Front finally settled on the Karnataka chief minister, the sleep-induced Deve Gowda. With his replacement named, Prime Minister Vajpayee knew his resignation was a foregone conclusion. The only thing undecided was how well he would sing his swan song.

* * *

Of all the decisions the Vajpayee government made in their thirteen days, the most far-reaching was to allow live telecast of parliament.[68] This was done just in time for the two-day confidence debate over the fate of the government. And so, when the kurta-clad prime minister got up to speak on 27 May 1996, millions were watching live.

All his life, it seemed, Atal Bihari Vajpayee had prepared for this speech. He began by praising Nehru, since it was his thirty-second death anniversary.[69] In his concluding speech the next day, the man who first spoke Hindi in the United Nations, now quoted a Tamil poem, leading a DMK politician to point out that it was the first time a prime minister had spoken Tamil in parliament. Vajpayee said, in English: 'The BJP does not stand for uniformity. We recognize the celebrated India's plural multi-religious, multilingual and multi-ethnic character.'[70] Vajpayee even offered to 'freeze' the provocative issues of a Uniform Civil Code, Article 370 and Ayodhya.[71] 'We understand that a consensus has to be evolved. Everyone has to make some compromise or the other and the BJP is ready for it.'[72]

The Indian summer was made worse by air-conditioning failing the '1500 souls, packed, sardine-like, in the Lok Sabha'.[73] The prime minister's speech was heckled constantly, with 'cat-calls and angry exchanges'. The Speaker had to urge members to 'behave yourself'.[74] All through this cacophony, Vajpayee played the stoic schoolmaster pleading with his wards. The previous television image associated with the BJP was of the domes of the Babri mosque being pickaxed by saffron-clad hoodlums. The new image being beamed across India was of an avuncular moderate being pickaxed by ill-mannered legislators.

Vajpayee made much of the fact that he was resigning before the deadline given to prove his majority. He ended with the famous words: 'Honourable Speaker, I am going to tender my resignation to the Honourable President.'[75]

It was a calculated finish. There was none of Vajpayee's signature flourishes. Instead, he had shown deference to two constitutional functionaries, honoured the House arithmetic, and flaunted his sacrifice, all in one simple sentence. The BJP, millions of viewers were being told, could be trusted with power.

* * *

The new prime minister, H.D. Deve Gowda, was sworn in on 1 June 1996 and soon won the confidence of parliament, helped by 140 Congress MPs. The thirteen constituents of his United Front government had little in common except the desire to keep the BJP out of power.

Meanwhile, the Congress's Narasimha Rao resigned as party president after he was charge sheeted for corruption. His replacement was, to use Deve Gowda's expression, 'an old man in a hurry'.[76] Less than a year into the new prime minister's tenure, Sitaram Kesri pulled the Congress rug from under the Gowda government for reasons that seem more about mismatched chemistry than incompatible policy. The price the United Front had to pay for Congress support was to change prime ministers. In

April 1997, Gowda's foreign minister, the affable I.K. Gujral, became the twelfth prime minister of India.

That the BJP's organizational demeanour was in studied contrast to this disaccord was on view the very month Gujral was made prime minister. On 8 April 1997, the Delhi High Court acquitted Advani in the Hawala case. But any chance that a redeemed Advani would reclaim his mantle from Vajpayee was squashed when the man himself, approaching seventy, hinted at retirement. When asked if he found himself a 'misfit' in a party now marching to Vajpayee's tunes, Advani said: 'Not a misfit, but certainly inadequate. I am guided by the Peter principle. I do not want to reach the height of my inadequacies.'[77]

It was during this time that newspapers carried a story in which BJP general secretary Govindacharya told British diplomats that Vajpayee was only a '*mukhota*' or mask. His words are worth quoting in full: 'As for Atal Bihari Vajpayee, he is not a power within the organisation, he is only the mask for the party. And his importance . . . is akin to that of a mask in a play . . . Advani is the real power in the BJP. Whomsoever be the president of the party, the BJP will be run by him and his decision will be final.'[78]

Though Govindacharya denied the remarks, Vajpayee shot off two letters. The first was to L.K. Advani. It said: 'On returning from my foreign trip I read an interview given by Shri Govindacharya. You must have read it as well. Vijaydashami greetings to you.' The second letter was to Govindacharya, demanding an explanation.[79]

Vajpayee could have picked up the phone and called. But he was well aware that Govindacharya was Advani's protégé, sent to the BJP from the RSS to reduce his influence.[80] Vajpayee had bided his time, but now sensed an opportunity to remind Hindu nationalism that, at this moment, they needed him more than he needed them. Like he had done with Balraj Madhok, M.L. Sondhi, Nanaji Deshmukh and Subramanian Swamy, Vajpayee decided to make an example of Govindacharya.

At a book release by senior BJP and RSS leaders a few days after, Vajpayee complained: 'I wonder why I have been invited to speak here when I am only a mask.'[81] At another function, with Advani sitting next to him, Vajpayee said: 'I am no longer even the face of the BJP, I am only its mask.'[82] Vajpayee even called the RSS leadership to his house. 'Vajpayeeji was glum,' someone present remembers. 'He demanded an explanation.

He wanted to know if [the] RSS felt like this. He wanted action [against Govindacharya].'

Vajpayee was playing a dangerous, clever, even brilliant game. Dangerous because Hindu nationalism abhors such a public show of animosity; Vajpayee's behaviour was more United Front than BJP. Clever because Vajpayee had turned the tables on Govindacharya, accusing *him* of lacking team spirit. And brilliant because, with the BJP at the cusp of power and Advani weakened, Vajpayee had calculated that it was the party that would blink.

He had calculated well; Govindacharya was sidelined. What aided this was disavowal by his backer. Though Advani was fond of Govindacharya, it was nothing compared to his lifelong loyalty to Vajpayee. Sudheendra Kulkarni says: 'Advani never believed that Vajpayee was a mask. He knew that he was much more than that. Vajpayee was both a thought leader as well as its tallest mass leader.'[83]

While the Govindacharya episode was playing out, Sonia Gandhi, until now a private citizen, decided to join the Congress as a primary member in August 1997. Two months later, on 9 November 1997, the media leaked portions of an interim report by a judicial commission investigating Rajiv Gandhi's assassination. The leaks suggested that the commission had indicted the DMK. This put the Congress party in a bind, since the Dravidian party was part of the United Front government they were propping up. Any attempt to patch up this situation was sabotaged by pressure groups forming within both the United Front and the Congress, each determined to pursue self-interest even if it meant sinking the government. They succeeded, and on 28 November 1997, the Congress once again withdrew support from the United Front.[84] Fresh elections were called for, and the BJP prepared for battle once more. But this time around, the sole commander was Atal Bihari Vajpayee. The mask had become the face.

* * *

The BJP's 1998 election operation transmitted the same 'moderate' makeover that it had projected in 1996. Vajpayee even attended an 'iftaar' party wearing a skull cap.[85]

Where the 1998 campaign was distinctive was in the number of allies that now supported the BJP. While only three allies had formed a coalition with the BJP in 1996, the party now attracted many more partners. Three years of a 'Disunited' Front had reconciled these parties to the fact that no coalition without the BJP could last. New friends included the AIADMK's Jayalalithaa from Tamil Nadu, Naveen Patnaik's Biju Janata Dal (BJD) from Orissa, Ramakrishna Hegde from Karnataka and Mamata Banerjee's Trinamool Congress from West Bengal.[86] Advani termed these eastern and southern alliances 'a psychological breakthrough'.[87]

Heading these alliances was Vajpayee, by now the most popular candidate for prime minister.[88] As he travelled to rallies in a 'tiny eight-seater beechcraft airplane', he slept soundly while others struggled to avoid vomiting. When the plane would touch down, Vajpayee would wake up, pop some sugar-candy in his mouth, and go out to speak, extempore.[89]

In these speeches, Vajpayee was careful to stress only 'good governance without prejudice',[90] never ideology. This reticence was not shared by others in the party. The BJP chief minister of Delhi said at a rally: 'Today everyone is saying that party president L.K. Advani should be the party's prime ministerial candidate. But Shri Advani himself says that it should be Vajpayeeji and, because he is saying it, the party is also saying it must be Atal.'[91] Vajpayee responded to comments like this, saying: 'Certain mischievous elements are trying to project the rift between me and Advaniji, that he will be the prime minister immediately after elections.'[92] Advani, once again, had to publicly deny any ambition.[93]

That Vajpayee was at odds with the some in the BJP became the talk of the campaign. It was left to general secretary Narendra Modi to weave together both messages. 'Naturally, in various areas of the country different issues have appeal. As for anybody going "soft" on core issues, that is an incorrect analysis. The point is that the BJP is identified firmly with issues such as Ayodhya and Article 370, so they need not be emphasised like in the past.'[94]

Vajpayee was in his house at Safdarjung Road watching television while L.K. Advani nursed a sore throat when the results were announced in March 1998.[95] The Congress had continued its decline, ending up with its lowest-ever vote share of 25.8 per cent. The BJP's share almost equalled that, though its own seats had improved, from 161 to 179. That and ten extra partners meant that the BJP-led coalition had increased its seats from 187 in 1996 to 251 in 1998. They were now just twenty seats short of a majority.[96]

Apart from allies, the BJP's success was owed to middle-caste Hindus, '42 percent [of whom] had voted for the BJP or one of its allies'. Writing at the time, the political scientist Atul Kohli found 'The growing OBC support—if it turns out to be real and durable— . . . much more perplexing'.[97] While the durable shift would only take place under Prime Minister Narendra Modi two decades later, this support in 1998 indicated that Advani's adroit handling of Mandal and Mandir had kept upper castes within the BJP without alienating middle-caste Hindus.

These expansions made Vajpayee the leader not just of the single largest party but the largest pre-poll coalition. Precedent dictated that he be the natural choice for prime minister. But President K.R. Narayanan, a former Congress minister, demanded formal letters of support from the BJP's allies. This unusual delay triggered the BJP's paranoia that the institutions of India were determined to squelch its popular mandate. Vajpayee's private secretary, Shakti Sinha, says: 'Narayanan wanted to screw [the] BJP, that's why he asked for letters. Narayanan hated the BJP as much as Sonia does.'[98]

The letters came eventually, and so, in March 1998, Vajpayee became prime minister once again. Unlike in 1996, however, he was confident of actually governing this time. And, unlike in 1996, his home minister and number two was L.K. Advani. He anticipated being to Vajpayee what Patel had been to Nehru in the first years of Indian independence.

This was, however, new terrain for their relationship. Vajpayee and Advani's personal chemistry had navigated ideology, movement and party for the last several decades. How would they now navigate power?

PART III

POWER (1998–2004)

12

EXPERIMENT IN GOVERNANCE (1998–99)

The twenty-three parties[1] supporting the second Vajpayee government in March 1998 were christened by L.K. Advani as the National Democratic Alliance or NDA. The name was a salute to Syama Prasad Mookerjee,[2] whose Jana Sangh had fought the 1951 elections as part of the 'National Democratic Front'.

All counted, the NDA was propped up by 179 BJP legislators as well as around ninety-six MPs from nineteen allied parties as well as three independents.[3] Even after all these numbers were tallied, the new government could barely cross the halfway mark in parliament. As Pramod Mahajan described in his customary style: 'Two MPs leaving the House to attend the call of nature can result in the government being reduced to a minority.'[4]

In order to herd this flock, the BJP had erased from the 'national agenda'[5] of the NDA its ideological demands of abolishing Article 370, building a Ram temple at Ayodhya and enacting a Uniform Civil Code. Advani defended these dilutions since 'there is a need for the average party activist to be conscious that the responsibility on us is different now and, therefore, we should be able to change ourselves, our psyche'.[6]

Vajpayee and Advani assumed that this 'moderation' was all that was required to keep their coalition partners content. But they had overestimated the weight of ideology, underestimated the lure of lucre.

The most obdurate of these demands for spoils of power came from Jayalalithaa. The former film star exercised Stalinist control over her

Dravidian party, and carried that attitude to her negotiations with the NDA. As price for her eighteen MPs bolstering the Vajpayee government, Jayalalithaa wanted the dismissal of her rival M.K. Karunanidhi as chief minister of Tamil Nadu. It is to their credit that Vajpayee and Advani, who had made state's rights against a domineering Centre a part of their political identity, refused. Jayalalithaa then demanded that Subramanian Swamy be made finance minister.[7] Swamy had spent the last decade as a one-man Janata army, and was now consigliere to Jayalalithaa. Shakti Sinha says, 'Vajpayee would never have allowed Swamy as FM. He simply didn't trust Swamy.'[8] Swamy, for his part, claims: 'Vajpayee gave me his word. He is a liar.' Jayalalithaa did not pull the rug then, but Swamy seethed. 'Sonia Gandhi once told me, "You are a Sicilian. You never forget an insult."'[9]

Vetoing Swamy as finance minister fitted into Vajpayee's larger design for his inner cabinet. L.K Advani was appointed home minister, their old friend from the Emergency George Fernandes was made defence minister, and Vajpayee planned to make Jaswant Singh and Yashwant Sinha his finance and foreign ministers. One was an army man who had been part of the Swatantra Party, the other a former bureaucrat who had come from the Janata Dal. Yashwant Sinha deciphers Vajpayee's design: 'Not a single member of the cabinet committee on security [i.e., the inner cabinet] was from the RSS.'[10]

One particular RSS man also decoded this pattern. Sparrow-like in build and hawk-like in world view, K.S. Sudarshan had worked his way up the RSS in Vajpayee's Madhya Pradesh. But the two had never warmed to each other. Since Vajpayee had a longer 'sangh aayu' than Sudarshan (i.e., he had joined the RSS before Sudarshan), the prime minister felt no need to genuflect. On his part, Sudarshan lacked the Hindu nationalist etiquette of keeping criticism within the family. He would later say of Prime Minister Vajpayee: 'I don't think he has done anything that great . . . He should have maintained relations with everyone [in the sangh parivar] but he didn't.'[11]

On 18 March 1998, the day before the swearing-in ceremony, Vajpayee had sent his cabinet names to the president of India, as was the custom. He was having dinner with his family that night when an aide told him that Sudarshan was waiting outside. Vajpayee left the table and went to an outer room, where he was closeted with Sudarshan for over an hour. He came out, looking exhausted. One name was removed from the list sent to the president.

Sudarshan had vetoed Jaswant Singh as finance minister because the patrician army officer had contempt for Sudarshan's stick-wielding, khaki-clad amateur militia; Jaswant would even caricature the RSS head as 'Chief Wanga Wanga'. He was also an outspoken liberalizer, something that Sudarshan's 'swadeshi' economics could not countenance.

'Vajpayee won eventually. He waited till December, and made Jaswant foreign minister,' Shakti Sinha says.[12] But right from day zero, his government had been shaken by the RSS, Jayalalithaa and Subramanian Swamy.

Vajpayee had been here before. And in the face of challenges to his authority, he had always been steadied by his oldest friend. Advani simply assumed that he would once more be there for Vajpayee and that their forty-year friendship would spill over into government. He was in for a surprise.

* * *

'When a man gets power, even his chickens and dogs rise to heaven.'[13] From 1986 onwards, it was Advani who ran the party, and it was only through him that any ambitious BJP functionary could rise. But with the new home minister stepping down as BJP president (since the party mandated that the same person could not hold two posts) and with Vajpayee looking like he would be prime minister for a while, the chain of command began to twist.

Protégés of Advani began to cultivate the new prime minister. Pramod Mahajan was given a cabinet rank by Vajpayee. A BJP leader says: 'Pramod was Advani's man. But when Atalji became PM, Pramod never saw Advani for three months.' Sudheendra Kulkarni remembers: '[Advaniji] asked me to come work with him in the home ministry. I said yes. However, on the day Vajpayee was sworn in as PM, he called me and said come work with me in the PMO. I said Advani has already asked me to work with him. Vajpayee said that he will talk to Advani.'[14] The others who had access to the PMO—the colloquial phrase for the prime minister's office—

were N.M. Ghatate, R.V. Pandit and, of course, Nusli Wadia. Swapan
Dasgupta says: 'Nusli could walk into Atalji's house anytime.'[15]

This access to the very top of the party made some in the BJP envious
of Nusli Wadia, a jealousy accentuated by the Bombay businessman's
quarrelsome nature. An insider in the party remembers: 'Many of us didn't
like the way Nusli would throw his weight around. I've heard some people
[in the BJP] snigger "*aakhir Jinnah ka toh khoon hai*".' At the end of the
day, his blood is Jinnah's.

The other presence in the new prime minister's office was Rajkumari
Kaul and her family, who moved along with Vajpayee to the official
residence on 7 Race Course Road. Mr Kaul's student, the IAS officer
Ashok Saikia, was appointed joint secretary. Vajpayee began to host
regular dinners where officers in the PMO and their families were invited
(the home minister and his family was not). 'They were easy affairs,' one of
those present says. 'Mrs Kaul used to come. It was normal. No problem.'

Advani had known Rajkumari Kaul for the last thirty years, and both
had accepted the primacy of the other in their man's life. What Advani
found harder to accept was that Rajkumari Kaul's son-in-law Ranjan
Bhattacharya and daughter Namita began to wield power. A family friend
of the Kauls says: 'In all my years of knowing them, Mrs Kaul never once
said anything negative about Advani. Gunu [Namita] never once said
something positive about Advani.' K.S. Sudarshan would later say '. . . we
had told [Prime Minister Vajpayee] in no uncertain terms to check his
near and dear ones, like Advani did. He never let his son and daughter
get undue advantage of his post. The ideal set by Advani, we expected the
same from Vajpayee. But he did not pay attention.'[16]

More than Vajpayee's family, however, the appointment that really
drove a wedge between Vajpayee and Advani was the bald and laconic
Brajesh Mishra. Unlike Advani, the former diplomat understood how
governmental power worked; his politician father had also taught him to
how to wield it. This was perhaps why Vajpayee appointed him principal
secretary as well as India's first national security advisor.

India has a tradition of principal secretaries playing the second
most important role in the country—P.N. Haksar for Indira Gandhi,[17]
P.C. Alexander for Indira and Rajiv Gandhi, and Amar Nath Varma
for Narasimha Rao. What placed Brajesh Mishra in another orbit was

that he was also a friend and drinking partner of his boss. And unlike Advani, Mishra knew the innards of how policy was made on Raisina Hill. He would later say: 'In every meeting, Vajpayee would listen and let everyone speak. Then before making a decision, he would look at me and say '*Panditji, jail to nahi jayenge na*?'[18] Panditji, we won't go to jail, will we?

Mornings in the Vajpayee household had an indulgent vibe. The prime minister would rise late, and read the *Hindustan Times*, his favourite newspaper. He would sit for breakfast, while the family milled around and his dogs hovered. Mrs Kaul would be busy making breakfast, while Gunu would walk in and out of the room. Vajpayee would be joined by Brajesh Mishra and Ranjan Bhattacharya. Someone present says: 'They would decide the day's work during breakfast. Advaniji never once came, I think.' This person adds: 'This was the most important meeting of the government, and it was between the PM, Brajesh and Ranjan. By the time Advaniji got to know [what was discussed] the match was already fixed.'

* * *

Vajpayee's use of his PMO as a balance to Advani would play itself out gradually, but the signs were visible by April 1998. Vajpayee felt that the party apparatchik lacked the skills to run a national government. While Advani saw this as a personal betrayal by his friend, what continued to keep him loyal was the ideology of teamwork. Advani did not want to jeopardize the first chance his party had of putting at least some of its commitments into practice.

Foremost among these was the belief that India should possess a nuclear deterrent. Though the BJP had watered down other ideological promises to retain allies, Vajpayee and Advani had insisted that the NDA coalition manifesto state: '[We shall] re-evaluate the country's nuclear policy and exercise the option to induct nuclear weapons.'[19] Just before the new government was formed, the journalist N. Ram remembers: 'There was a reception for a visiting French president. Advani and Vajpayee were both there. I asked Advani if they were serious about weaponization [since it was in their manifesto]. He said, "Yes we are."'[20]

As prime minister for thirteen days in 1996, Vajpayee had ordered nuclear testing, but paused when he realized his government would not last. Now, in power for what looked like a longer spell, Vajpayee gave the green signal in April 1998, just a few weeks after becoming prime minister.

Indian nuclear protocols of the time required the prime minister's explicit approval at four stages: T-30 [thirty days prior to testing], T-7, T-3, and finally T-1, i.e., one day before testing.

Around 4 May 1998, T-7, Vajpayee called a minister from his cabinet to his house. He beckoned to his bedroom. It was there that the prime minister told the minister of the test date, 'because [the bedroom] must have been properly secure'. Six days later, Vajpayee said 'yes' at T-1.

That night, Jaswant Singh was at home in 15 Teen Murti Lane. 'I'm going to work tomorrow,' he told his wife.

'But tomorrow is Buddha poornima. It's a holiday,' his wife responded, since she was planning to fast.

'We are going to test tomorrow,' Jaswant told her.

His wife replied: 'I didn't know that was the priority of your government.'[21]

Another non-government source seems to have been tipped off. Within hours of the first nuclear test on 11 May, the RSS had delivered a copy of their latest issue of the *Organiser* to newspaper offices. It was titled 'Nuclear India'.[22]

India would conduct a total of four fission and one fusion explosions over the next three days. The only real surprise seemed to be that the Americans were caught by surprise. Shekhar Gupta jokes that the Americans only take top-secret documents seriously. And the party manifesto was not a top-secret document.

The United States and its allies imposed a range of punishments.[23] The Indian government responded with surefooted diplomacy from a prime minister and principal secretary who had previous experience of how foreign policy worked. Aiding them in mobilizing 'Non-Resident Indians' (NRIs) in the United States was a forty-seven-year-old BJP general secretary.

Ever since Narendra Modi had been banished from Gujarat in 1995, he would travel to the United States, taking buses and trains and staying

Through the 1950s, Vajpayee was the voice of Hindu nationalism. Seen here with M.S. Golwalkar and Deendayal Upadhyaya in the audience.

Vajpayee and Balraj Madhok (behind Vajpayee) accompany Deendayal Upadhyaya's funeral procession in 1968. Their succession fight would draw Vajpayee to Advani.

The under-confident L.K. Advani giving one of his first public speeches soon after Vajpayee made his former secretary party president in 1973.

Nusli Wadia (seen here with wife Maureen and two children) was not just the billionaire grandson of Jinnah, he was also the BJP's early funder.

Vajpayee and Advani announce the formation of a new party, BJP, in Delhi in April 1980.

Vajpayee was injured during campaigning for the 1984 elections.
His electoral loss would begin his long exile from the BJP.

From 1986 to 1995, Advani ran the BJP, aided by loyalists like Narendra Modi—seen here in
Gujarat in 1992.

Vajpayee's fortune changed once again in 1995 when Advani shocked the RSS by announcing him as the party's prime ministerial candidate in Mumbai.

As power came to the BJP, so did the money. R.V. Pandit, one such donor close to Bombay industrialists, only paid by cheque.

Team of Rivals: Murli Manohar Joshi, Advani, Vajpayee and Vijayaraje Scindia.

As power came to Vajpayee, so did BJP general secretary
Narendra Modi—seen here celebrating Holi in 1999.

Prime Minister Vajpayee proved adept at managing his
coalition and cabinet to last a full term in office.

Vajpayee's biggest opponent as prime minister was the RSS.
While he did not back down, neither could he break away
from the family.

Advani's family has always been run by powerful women, first Kamla then Pratibha.

From left: Vajpayee's son-in-law Ranjan, granddaughter, daughter Namita and man Friday Shiv Kumar, at his funeral in 2018.

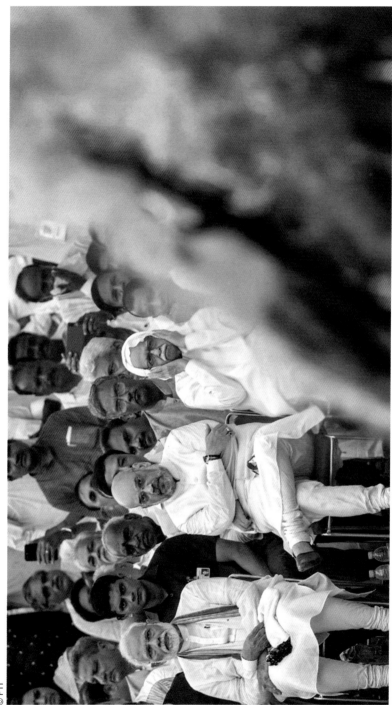

The New Jugalbandi: Modi and Amit Shah with Advani at Vajpayee's funeral.

with NRIs, usually the network of Patels across North America. By the late 1990s, Modi was spending so much time in the US that when Prime Minister Vajpayee met him there on a visit, he joked: 'Do you plan to settle here permanently?'[24] Soon after the nuclear tests, Modi activated his contacts among the diaspora to lobby the US Congress to ease sanctions.

No such lobbying was required within India. A survey across twelve cities found that 87 per cent of those interviewed, across gender and party divides, approved of the tests.[25] Pramod Mahajan proclaimed, 'This is not a nuclear test but a test of nationalism.'[26]

Fifteen days after India's tests, Pakistan carried out six nuclear explosions, one more than India. But this did little to dim the exuberance of Hindu nationalism, for whom the tests were a defensive response to its historical anxiety of invasion. Vajpayee said: 'In any previous war, India lost because of inferior weapons. That's why I supported nuclear weapons.' Talking to journalists after the tests, Advani was seen 'wiping his tears at least twice'.[27] He later quoted the poet Ramdhari Singh Dinkar: '*Kshama shobhati us bhujanga ko jiske paas garal ho.*' Forgiveness befits only that serpent which has venom.[28]

One of the few dissenting voices within the party was a thirty-three-year-old state legislator in Gujarat. Amit Shah was so angry at the tests that he wrote a letter to the prime minister: 'Respected Vajpayeeji, because of your greed for publicity you have forever lost Pakistan Occupied Kashmir.' A puzzled prime minister summoned the writer to Delhi. Amit Shah explained: 'I was in touch with Morarji Desai after he was prime minister. Morarji could have developed nuclear weapons. But Morarji told me that if we both [i.e., India and Pakistan] become nuclear powers, we can never win back POK through war.'[29] Vajpayee was unmoved; he was more interested in global power projection than in reclaiming Akhand Bharat.

'Once the tests were carried out,' former high commissioner to Pakistan T.C.A. Raghavan says, 'the intuitive grasp of the government was that a Pakistan-specific initiative was needed to restore the confidence of the world community . . . to get rid of the belief that there was this delinquent right-wing government in power.'[30] With enough poison in its glands now, India set about forgiving Pakistan.

* * *

The first moves were made when Vajpayee and Pakistani Prime Minister Nawaz Sharif met in Colombo just two months after the nuclear tests. This set the tone for an even more momentous meeting in September 1998, a lunch on the sidelines of the UN General Assembly in New York. Sharif casually mentioned that he had driven his own car from Lahore to Delhi for the 1982 Asian Games. The diplomat Vivek Katju suggested a Lahore–Delhi bus service. Jaswant Singh recalls that Nawaz Sharif 'immediately fancied the idea', while Vajpayee reacted 'not with any Punjabi-style acclaim but with a more reasoned assent'.[31]

Vajpayee was cautious because any such overtures to Pakistan would need the support of the RSS and the VHP, and there was, by late 1998, little love in the Rashtriya Swayamsevak Sangh for the government. 'There was a feeling in the organization,' a senior RSS leader at the time says, 'that there was no point having our government. What was in it for us?' When twenty-six Hindus were killed by Islamic militants in Jammu, the head of the Vishva Hindu Parishad responded: 'Anyone would feel greatly embarrassed to defend the performance of the first BJP government at the Centre in the face of such gruesome killings.'[32]

Through this period, the media reported a rift between the prime minister and his home minister. Vajpayee confirmed these stories by denying them: 'Advaniji and I have worked together as a team for over 40 years. Nothing has happened to change that equation and we are perfect teammates.'[33] Advani and Vajpayee still met for lunch regularly. But the friendship was not what it once was.

Pakistan should have been the one issue where the abandoned Sindhi refugee would stand up to Vajpayee. But, and more than is commonly understood, Advani had always pushed for better relations between India and Pakistan, if only to drive his own ghosts away. And Advani had long felt that only the BJP, not the Congress, could make peace with Pakistan. It's like Nixon going to China, he had told the UK ambassador to Pakistan.[34]

Through the next few months, Vajpayee and Advani spoke several times about overtures to Pakistan. They eventually decided to allow a Pakistani cricket tour of India in early 1999.

The enduring recollection of that series was the first Test match, held between 27 and 30 January 1999 in Chennai. Chasing 271 in the second innings, India was reduced to 82 for 5 before Sachin Tendulkar played the best remembered innings of his career, taking India to within seventeen runs of victory before losing his wicket and India the match.[35] Luckily for India–Pakistan relations, the visual of a crying Tendulkar was somewhat erased by an easy Indian victory in the next Test match.

This cricket diplomacy thawed somewhat the frozen relations between both peoples. But Vajpayee and Advani seemed unable to turn the temperature to a warmer setting, as diplomats from both sides were unwilling to level the roadblocks to the Delhi–Lahore bus service.

A breakthrough came in a circuitous way, when Nawaz Sharif informally invited Vajpayee, through *The Indian Express*'s Shekhar Gupta, to travel on the first bus. Gupta first cleared it with Vajpayee, who sounded out Advani. 'Advani and Vajpayee spoke about this informally, even before the formal cabinet meeting,' Sudheendra Kulkarni remembers, adding, 'Advani supported the idea enthusiastically.'[36] Gupta's story containing the Pakistan prime minister's invitation appeared on the morning of 4 February 1999.[37] Vajpayee said yes that very afternoon.

Even the RSS lent their weight to the bus yatra.[38] An RSS leader of the time says that the deciding factor was that 'both Advaniji and Kushabhaoji [the then BJP president who was close to the RSS] supported the journey. It was not just Vajpayee.'

Two weeks later, on 19 February 1999, the giant gates of the Wagah border check-post were flung open just after 4 p.m. as a golden-coloured Delhi Transport Corporation bus crossed the border near Amritsar to enter Pakistan.[39] The seventy-four-year-old shaky-kneed Vajpayee gingerly got down from the bus steps, and converted a formal handshake with Pakistan's prime minister into a warm embrace. The bus was also carrying twenty-two celebrities, including the actor Dev Anand and the lyricist Javed Akhtar.[40] Advani could well have joined Vajpayee to journey back to the land of his birth. But he had decided that the 'head of the family' should be the one who got the limelight.

The highlight of Vajpayee's visit was a trip to Minar-e-Pakistan, a 200-foot white tower built on the site of the 1940 declaration of the Muslim League advocating a separate country. Here he wrote in the visitor's book: 'A stable, secure and prosperous Pakistan is in India's interest. Let no one in Pakistan be in doubt, India sincerely wishes Pakistan well.'[41]

The wordsmith knew what he was crafting. At a glittering reception with Pakistan's elite, Vajpayee confessed that when he returned to India, people would ask: 'Did you go to Pakistan to certify it?' 'But,' Vajpayee told his audience, 'Pakistan does not need anyone's endorsement [to prove its existence].'[42] In his own elliptical style, Vajpayee was burying, once and for all, the fantasy of an Akhand Bharat or Greater India.

So effective was Vajpayee in charming his audience that Nawaz Sharif said: '*Vajpayee sahab ab toh Pakistan mein bhi election jeet sakte hain.*'[43] Mr Vajpayee can now win elections even in Pakistan.

* * *

He might have been able to gain power in Pakistan, but Vajpayee returned to a Delhi where power was slipping from his government. Jayalalithaa was looking for any excuse to bring it down. An aide to Advani says: 'By March [1999], both Advaniji and Vajpayee had had enough . . .' This aide adds: 'This was also when VHP and Sudarshan were talking against Vajpayee. But they would not cross a line.'

Sensing an opportunity to both unseat Vajpayee as well as become finance minister in the new dispensation, Subramanian Swamy told Jayalalithaa: 'We have an alternative government. But you have to have the Congress [supporting you].' 'I knew that Sonia and Jayalalithaa hated each other,' Swamy remembers, 'so I organized a tea party at the Ashok hotel in Delhi.'[44]

Hundreds of guests, including three former prime ministers, showed up to this 'tea party', held on 29 March 1999. But the stars of the evening were Jayalalithaa and Sonia Gandhi. They spoke to each other for barely ten minutes, but the very public interaction convinced both women that if one played according to script, the other would too. Jayalalithaa eventually announced that her eighteen MPs were withdrawing support to the Vajpayee government.

The vote on the no-confidence motion was set for 17 April 1999. In the interim, aided by the kind of backroom deals that parties in power can afford, the BJP's confidence grew. By the morning of the vote, two new parties, including Jayalalithaa's enemy the DMK, had announced it would support the government. The BSP's Kanshi Ram also called up Vajpayee at 10:45 a.m.[45] to assure him that his five MPs would abstain. Soon after, legislators began filing into parliament as the BJP's floor managers walked up and down the green carpeted aisle, counting their flock.

Vajpayee's speech during this no-confidence motion had the same air of righteous injury that had propelled him to stardom during the 1996 confidence motion. But this time he added barbs for the Congress. The Congress party is divided, he declaimed, 'between the keen greed to remove us, the desire to form a partnership for the sake of power, and the ambition of coming to power on its own'.[46] 'Mrs [Sonia] Gandhi was furious at Vajpayee's tone,' her close advisor remembers. 'She walked up to him angrily. Advani came in the middle. It was almost like he was shielding Vajpayee. Mrs Gandhi shouted at him for what she felt was Vajpayee's insulting tone. Advani simply stood listening, wringing his hand Advani style,' adds this Congressman, imitating Advani's characteristic half-rotating hand massage.

As the time for voting came closer, one of the BJP's floor managers noticed an unusual face in the house. Giridhar Gamang, the Congress MP from Koraput in Orissa, had been made state chief minister in February 1999. Even though he still had six months to formally resign from the Lok Sabha, he had, as convention dictated, not been seen in parliament since.

The vote happened around noon, and after some jittery moments, the Speaker announced: 'Ayes-269, Noes-270. The Noes have it.'[47]

The Vajpayee government had lost by one vote, the closest in the history of parliament. Subramanian Swamy, sitting in the Lok Sabha as the Janata party MP from Madurai, smiled at Vajpayee. 'It was the smile of revenge,' Swamy says. 'I had taught him a lesson.'[48]

Apart from Giridhar Gamang's against-convention vote against the Vajpayee government, the BSP had gone back on its promise given to the prime minister just hours earlier. Saifuddin Soz from the National Conference had also voted against his party diktat.[49]

Vajpayee and Advani walked back to the prime minister's office in parliament.[50] Advani tried to cheer Vajpayee up.[51] The prime minister sat down in his chair. 'He came back with tears in his eyes. He was stunned. He didn't say anything. We were all stunned,' Shakti Sinha remembers.[52]

Sonia Gandhi began to immediately stitch together a Congress–United Front double weave. Three days later, she announced on the forecourt of Rashtrapati Bhavan that 'We have 272 [MPs] and we hope to get more'.[53]

But Sonia Gandhi had misjudged the extent to which the lack of teamwork was endemic to Indian politics. Mulayam Singh Yadav went back on his promise, withdrew the support of his twenty MPs, and prevented Sonia Gandhi from becoming prime minister.[54] Three senior Congressmen would soon rebel against their 'foreign origin'[55] party chief. The Lok Sabha was dissolved on 26 April 1999, with fresh elections scheduled in five months' time.

The political turmoil in these past months were seen by both L.K. Advani and Sonia Gandhi through the lens of organizational unity. Advani later wrote: 'The myth of the "unity of secular forces" was blown to pieces . . . At the same time, I was happy at the manner in which almost all the parties in the NDA stuck together in this hour of crisis.'[56] For Sonia Gandhi, her failure would forever make her cautious in stamping her authority over the party.[57] As the experience of Congress rule from 2004 to 2014 shows, Sonia's solution to the problem of organizational disunity was to let her party heavyweights do what they wanted.

The most significant lesson from the instability of these months in 1999, however, was being drawn by the chief of Pakistan's army. Pervez Musharraf was calculating that Lutyens' Delhi was too distracted to pay him any attention. He was more right than wrong.

* * *

On 3 May 1999, two weeks after the resignation of the second Vajpayee government, a Buddhist shepherd went in search of his missing yak outside his village in the mountainous Kargil region. This part of northern Kashmir was barely a few kilometres from the Line of Control or LoC, the de facto boundary between India and Pakistan. But its rugged and freezing terrain meant that few soldiers guarded the border.

The shepherd chanced upon six Pakistani soldiers in camouflage.[58] He immediately informed the Indian army. Soldiers who went to investigate were ambushed, and an ammunition dump was blown up.[59] It took four more days for Vajpayee, now a 'caretaker' prime minister, to be informally briefed. He immediately called Advani and other senior ministers to discuss 'some urgent matter'.[60]

Around 1500 to 2400[61] fighters had entrenched themselves along a 150-odd kilometre stretch on the Indian side of the LoC at heights of 16,000 feet. They were firing down below at the Srinagar–Leh highway.[62] The highway travelled north from Srinagar, climbed over the Kargil mountains and came within kilometres of the LoC. From here it turned east towards Leh. It was the lifeline for the Indian army to send supplies to northern Kashmir, including the Siachen glacier.

As it became apparent that a majority of the fighters were Pakistani troops—the Indian high commission in Islamabad estimated that around 1700 Pakistanis of the northern light infantry had been deployed in Kargil[63]—the mood began to sour in New Delhi.[64]

'Nawaz saab, what is happening?' Vajpayee called and asked the man he had hugged just months ago. 'Your army is attacking our army. They are fighting against our army.' When Nawaz Sharif denied that any Pakistani troops were involved, Vajpayee told him: 'Nawaz saab, *aap ko pata nahin hai?*' Nawaz saab, do you not know? 'I suppose I should have known about all this,' Sharif would later say. 'But, frankly, I hadn't been briefed.'[65]

Vajpayee and Advani had made a series of miscalculations after the India–Pakistan nuclear tests of May 1998. The lesson they had drawn was that the twin tests provided a chance for an equal peace between the two countries. They did not realize that the Pakistan army had drawn the opposite lesson: that nuclear parity shielded Pakistan from India's conventional military superiority. They had also assumed that Nawaz Sharif was the most powerful Pakistani prime minister in generations, capable of taming his army.

This had blinded them to the fact that, a few months after the nuclear tests, while Vajpayee and Advani were going out of their way to woo Nawaz Sharif, Musharraf and his aides began planning a military incursion across the Line of Control.

Musharraf's idea was to send Pakistani troops disguised as irregulars to cross over to the mountains on the Indian side and shell the Srinagar–Leh highway. Unable to dislodge the intruders or reach supplies to the northern parts of the state, India would be forced to negotiate. The idea had silly written all over it, but Musharraf was confident that Pakistan's nuclear umbrella would prevent India from raining conventional fire.

This was his miscalculation. The Indian army overcame its surprise and reacted as if this was a regular war, deploying thousands of troops and using 250 artillery guns[66] to fire at the mountain tops. Vajpayee also gave permission for the air force to bomb those entrenched at 16,000 feet, something Musharraf did not expect. But Vajpayee balanced this aggression with an explicit order for air force planes to not cross the Line of Control. This was a tactical constraint, since the pilots who flew the 1200 fighter-plane and 2500 helicopter sorties during this period had a corridor as narrow as a pencil to operate in.[67] But it was a strategic showpiece, signalling to the international community that India, unlike Pakistan, respected the sanctity of the Line of Control.

What added to this narrative was the publication by Indian intelligence agencies of a conversation that Musharraf, who was visiting China in late May, was having with his lieutenant general in Pakistan. It was clear to anyone listening that far from being Kashmiri freedom fighters, they were regular Pakistani troops sent by Musharraf.

What made the Pakistani position even more untenable was a series of Indian victories that cleared the mountain tops by early July. With US President Bill Clinton firm that Pakistan should withdraw its troops from the Indian side of the LoC, Pakistan finally ordered its soldiers to return.

Through the Kargil war, 'Advani didn't have much of a role [since he was] home minister', someone present in cabinet meetings says. Advani saw his irrelevance as one of the mistakes that had led to the war in the first place, and had no doubt about who was responsible. He later wrote that Brajesh Mishra should not have been both principal secretary as well as national security advisor: 'In my view the clubbing together of two critical responsibilities, each requiring focussed attention, did not contribute to harmony at the highest levels of governance.'[68]

Advani knew that this was a deliberate choice by the prime minister; he was hurt. A minister loyal to Vajpayee says: 'It was not personal. Advani was very good as a party man but he didn't know governance. A prime minister has to rely on experts. What was Advani an expert on?'

These quibbles, however, remained muted through the war. Unlike Nawaz Sharif–Pervez Musharraf, Jayalalithaa–Sonia–Subramanian Swamy and Sonia–Mulayam, Vajpayee–Advani knew how to remain team players even when they disagreed. And as India declared Kargil Victory Day on 26 July 1999, they prepared to reap the electoral harvest.

* * *

With elections beckoning, L.K. Advani was relevant once more. He was appointed head of the BJP's campaign committee. Whatever Vajpayee's view of minister Advani, he continued to defer to party man Advani. Assisting Advani was general secretary Narendra Modi, who had since returned from the United States in order to play a national role.

Though Advani was still smarting at his treatment in the government, he was realistic enough to shine the campaign light only on Atal Bihari Vajpayee, who, polls showed, was more popular than his party.[69] The BJP's message pitted the 'National Hero of Kargil' against the 'Foreigner' Sonia Gandhi. As Modi put it, 'Atalji has emerged as a leader but Sonia remains a reader.'[70]

When the results were announced on 18 October 1999, the BJP tally had barely increased from the previous elections. But its allies had done better. The NDA now had twenty-seven more seats than required for a majority. No single ally could bring the government down.[71]

During the war, bodies of the Kargil dead had been transported to their villages for ceremonial cremations. This was a strategy that Gujarat chief minister Narendra Modi would implement after the killing of fifty-nine kar sevaks in 2002. Unlike Modi's ploy, however, this use of grief in 1999 does not seem to have helped the BJP electorally. The political scientist Neelanjan Sircar suggests there was only a 'modest' 'Kargil effect'. In the 331 constituencies the BJP contested in 1998 and 1999, for instance, the vote share remained stable. He attributes the BJP's slight improvement to the further decline of the Congress under Sonia Gandhi.[72] More than ire against Pakistan, it was the fury against the Congress that had brought power for the third time to the BJP.

* * *

The previous thirteen months had exposed fault lines between the BJP and its alliance partners, and between Vajpayee and Advani. For the new government to survive for five full years, these fissures needed suturing. Another challenge that awaited the new Vajpayee government was also a hangover from the earlier one. The nuclear tests had shown that 'making India great again' required dexterous management of both foreign policy as well as the domestic economy. But doing this involved measures the RSS was opposed to. And the killing of the Christian missionary Graham Staines and his family in 1999 by a Bajrang Dal activist only furthered the unease that the BJP on Raisina Hill would embolden right-wing thugs on the streets.

A final challenge awaited the new government. A day before Vajpayee was sworn in as prime minister for a third time, Pervez Musharraf deposed Nawaz Sharif as ruler of Pakistan. The interlocutor across the border was now not the warm-hearted Punjabi but the mastermind of Kargil.

Each of these challenges would define the Bharatiya Janata Party's coming five years in office. Accordingly, the next four chapters run in parallel, each covering the period 1999 to 2004, each detailing how the third Vajpayee government dealt with four challenges: of coalition and partnership building, of Pakistan and Kashmir, of economic and foreign policy, and finally, of pressure from the sangh parivar. Taken together, the four chapters that follow paint a miniature portrait of Hindu nationalism's first real exercise of power.

13

COALITION DHARMA (1999–2004)

The third Vajpayee government took office in October 1999. It was more stable than its previous avatar. Though the BJP had won only 182 seats, just three more than in the previous election, its coalition partners had done better. Taken together, the ruling alliance had twenty-seven seats more than a majority in the Lok Sabha, and no single coalition ally had the numbers to topple the government on its own. There was also no Tamil film star to career the prime minister this time around. Instead, he had to duel with a Bengali streetfighter.

The new railway minister, Mamata Banerjee, ran the Trinamool Congress and supplied Vajpayee eight legislators in return for three ministries.[1] Though she alone could not bring down the government, 'Mamata was a mass politician . . . she would never hide her emotions', a minister of the time remembers.

Unlike with Jayalalithaa, Vajpayee's avuncular charm was calibrated for Mamata's temperament. Once when Mamata had submitted her resignation letter for some reason, Vajpayee was travelling to Calcutta for some meeting. Vajpayee was worried that if he accepted the resignation it would look bad. So, when he landed in Calcutta, he made sure to invite himself to Mamata's mother's house for lunch. The RSS's Seshadri Chari remembers: 'Vajpayee had a very good relationship with Mamata Banerjee's mother and he always used to say, "I like your fish very much, so please cook fish for me."' At the lunch, Mamata and Vajpayee didn't talk to each other. But after lunch, when her mother asked how Mamata was doing as minister, Vajpayee replied: 'Sometimes she gets angry over small things, she should not give that too much weight.' Mamata Banerjee withdrew her resignation letter that evening.[2]

Vajpayee alternated these paternal affectations with affectionate fury. The Trinamool's Dinesh Trivedi visited Vajpayee after yet another Mamata bout of resignation. 'It was 3:30 p.m. Vajpayee had woken up; he was waiting in his pyjama and banian. He sat and looked at me, and he shouted, "What do you think? Such childishness. Tell her, nothing is going to happen. Every day, something." I still remember his one-act play.'[3] Trivedi adds: 'Vajpayeeji had a lot of affection for Mamataji. He would ultimately do what she wanted.' A cabinet minister explains: 'He used to behave like an elder brother disciplining his younger sister.'

Techniques such as this delayed Mamata's departure. It also ensured that Vajpayee's other allies—from Chandrababu Naidu in Andhra Pradesh to Nitish Kumar in Bihar—remained loyal to the prime minister even when they were repelled by his party.

* * *

Where Atal Bihari Vajpayee refused to act according to coalition dharma was when it came to his younger brother. As we saw in the last chapter, Vajpayee had cut Lal Krishna Advani to size in the thirteen-month government. The trend persisted into this government, where the home minister's influence was curbed by the prime minister's office run by Brajesh Mishra and Vajpayee's household headed by Ranjan Bhattacharya.

Their political alliance so far had been based on complementary talents. In government, however, Vajpayee was the one attracting voters, mollifying coalition allies and selecting technocrats. It was unclear what talents Advani was bringing to government.

That Advani was not Vajpayee's number two was made clear in October 2000, when Vajpayee had his knees replaced on the top floor of the seven-storey Breach Candy hospital in south Bombay.[4] The prime minister's office moved to Bombay for the surgery 'under the able supervision of his principal secretary, Mr. Brajesh Mishra . . .'[5] Advani, on the other hand, was not made acting prime minister. *The Hindu* noted: 'Indecision? Political compulsion? Call it what you like, the inability of the ruling establishment to officially designate an acting Prime Minister during the knee surgery of Mr. A.B. Vajpayee, has been widely seen as reflecting poorly on the functioning of the polity.'[6]

Advani's shrinking stature was hurried by the fact that his patience in seeking consensus within the party was proving a liability in government. Keshav Desiraju, a senior bureaucrat at the time, remembers: 'There was some dispute between the new Uttarakhand state government and Uttar Pradesh, and both BJP power ministers went to meet Advani. I also went with my minister. It was a simple question . . . but a decision needed to be taken. Advani listened for two hours without saying anything. He ended with: "You discuss among yourselves and come to a decision." As we were walking out, my power minister looked at me and said: "*Aaj Indiraji hoti toh nirnay hota.*" If it had been Indira Gandhi today, we would have had a decision.[7]

Ever since they had ascended the summit of their party three decades ago, the deal had been straightforward: Vajpayee handled parliament while Advani managed the party. But in yet another blow to Advani's power, Vajpayee decided to anoint his own yes-man as party president in August 2000.

That he reported to Vajpayee, not Advani, was not the only thing that made Bangaru Laxman unusual. As a Dalit, Laxman was the first low caste to become president of the historically upper-caste party. He was also from the south, a part of India where the BJP did not have a footprint. As a jubilant Laxman put it: 'I am here to strengthen the coordination between the party and the government as well as to strengthen and expand its geo-social base.'[8]

Vajpayee had found a new partner. As one magazine wrote: 'The buzz is that Ram's party has now entered the Ram-Laxman era with Laxman diligently carrying out the wishes of Ram without any ifs and buts.'[9] With Brajesh Mishra and Ranjan Bhattacharya running the government for Vajpayee and his Laxman running the party, Advani was moving towards redundancy.

* * *

What rebooted Advani's relevance was a sequence of events that began on 13 March 2001, when a scrappy news website announced details of 105 hours of videotape.[10] The Internet era was dawning in India—only 0.66[11] per cent of Indians used the internet in 2001 compared to 36[12] per cent in 2019. But the videos recorded as part of *Tehelka*'s 'sting operation' went viral. They showed politicians and army men accepting money and prostitutes from a fictitious arms dealer in return for candy-coated defence deals. The most prominent of those compromised was Vajpayee's Bangaru Laxman, shown accepting 1 lakh rupees in cash. He was also recorded naming Brajesh Mishra as being involved in defence deals and Ranjan Bhattacharya in 'other deals'.[13]

The videos had also implicated an RSS fundraiser as well as George Fernandes, but Nagpur preferred to deploy the scandal to shrink a prime minister who had grown too big for his boots. It called Laxman a 'failed swayamsevak' and said that 'a headmaster cannot be blamed for a student's failure'.[14] When asked about Mishra and Bhattacharya's role in 'armsgate', the RSS's K.S. Sudarshan demanded that 'extra-constitutional authorities' be removed from the prime minister's office. 'Incompetent people' in the PMO had caused the scam, he added.[15]

A few days later, another magazine, *Outlook*, published a cover story on the 'Tehelka fallout'. It had on its cover the prime minister, Brajesh Mishra, Ranjan Bhattacharya and N.K. Singh. The issue was titled 'The PM's Achilles heel'.[16] The magazine wrote: 'It was said any contract could be bagged or any deal swung, if the interested party won the support of the powerful trio. And what was till then only speculation now appears to have more than a semblance of truth, what with BJP president Bangaru Laxman confirming Ranjan's role in the clearance of power projects.'[17]

If Vajpayee's past was any lesson, he should have abandoned Brajesh and Ranjan. But Vajpayee chose this moment to stay put. He even allowed his officers to hold a press conference, where they denied allegations of influencing defence deals.[18] When asked about the role of Vajpayee's son-in-law in shaping policy, Brajesh Mishra replied: 'I have never seen Mr. Ranjan Bhattacharya in the PMO.'[19] This left undescribed the breakfast meetings that Brajesh would have with Vajpayee and Ranjan in the PM's house.

Vajpayee decided to shoot the messengers. The journalists of *Tehelka* and *Outlook* were made to run through hoops, and their owners were harassed. More than 700 tax officials searched the offices of the proprietor of *Outlook* in twelve cities and 120 premises.[20] As its editor recounts: '[The owner of the magazine] would be summoned to the damp, piss-stinking offices of the Enforcement Directorate and made to wait from 10 a.m. to 6 p.m. He would then be told to come the next day.' The editor was forced to meet Brajesh Mishra and admit 'perhaps some fault on our part!'[21]

While Vajpayee chose not to hear the message about corruption within his government, he was astute enough to see the other fault line the exposé had revealed.

Two months after the scandal, in May 2001, it was the prime minister who drove to the home minister's home for a four-hour lunch.

Advani poured out his hurt. He was being ignored by his oldest friend. Advani complained: 'Not just other members of your family, but even Mrs Kaul is calling me a *saanpnaath* [snake lord].' Vajpayee denied this, but even he knew that, by now, relations between their families had hit a nadir.

When she heard about Advani's complaint to Vajpayee, her friend says, Rajkumari Kaul went out of the way to assuage Advani. As she had done for much of her life, it was left to her to once again cool tensions between the closest man in her life and the closest man in his.

Vajpayee listened to Advani, then poured out *his* hurt: Why were those close to Advani leaking stories in the press against his daughter and son-in-law? And why had the attacks on him by the RSS been so 'vituperative'? Advani replied that it was thanks to his personal intervention that the criticisms had been 'general rather than pointed'.[22] The straight-talking Advani was deploying Vajpayee's roundabout style against the man himself. Vajpayee got the message. He could not sideline both the RSS *and* Advani and expect to survive.

* * *

Nine months later, in April 2002, a guest came to the prime minister's house. His suggestion would set in motion events that would eventually re-energize the Vajpayee–Advani partnership. The president and vice-president of India are largely figureheads who are indirectly elected by legislators. The five-year terms of both incumbents were ending in two months, and the BJP and its allies had nearly enough votes to select their replacements. It was in this context that the visiting RSS chief had a proposal.[23] Why does not Vajpayee become the next president of India and make Advani prime minister?

Those close to Advani insist that he was not privy to this suggestion. An RSS leader at the time also insists that this was not the official RSS view. 'I was in the [RSS] executive council then. There was no discussion in 2002 about making Vajpayee president and Advani PM. But it could have been the private desire of some. Yes, that could be.' The next morning, the RSS head had breakfast with Advani. Here he narrated the suggestion he had made to Vajpayee. Advani asked what Vajpayee's reply was. The sarsangchalak replied: 'He said neither yes nor no. I therefore think that he has not rejected my suggestion.'[24]

Unknown to both of them, a few weeks earlier, industrialist Dhirubhai Ambani had met Vajpayee with potent information. Some journalists close to Advani had told Ambani: 'Advani is going to be the PM and Vajpayee president.' They were hoping to curry favour with India's most wealthy man. Dhirubhai instead chose to curry favour with India's most powerful man.[25] Vajpayee said little then, but ensured that his NDA coalition partners met and resolved to let him decide the next president. All the while saying little, the prime minister had safeguarded his position.

The name of P.C. Alexander was then floated for the post of president. A Malayali Christian and Rajiv Gandhi loyalist, he had endeared himself to the Shiv Sena and BJP during his time as Maharashtra governor. But Sonia Gandhi rejected the name, worried that Alexander had switched loyalties. For L.K. Advani, this incident showed the public culture 'of the Congress leadership, which is habituated to looking at persons in public life through the prism of "our man vs their man" . . .'[26]

A familiar name inserted himself into the race. Sometime during this month, the RSS's M.G. Vaidya got a call from Balraj Madhok. The eighty-two-year-old had spent the last three decades in the suburbs of politics. He asked Vaidya to come to his house in Rajendra Nagar in west Delhi. 'When I went, Madhok asked me to propose his name as president of India.' Vaidya was silent before replying, 'You must ask

Atalji.'[27] Madhok was now silent. The chance that Madhok's old enemy would agree was zero.

The reversals around the presidential nominee showed Vajpayee at his wiliest, manoeuvring without being seen to do it, a trait he had displayed when he had outsmarted Madhok three decades earlier. Now, with the various claimants exhausted, Vajpayee moved to his original preferences.

'Major General Prithviraj',[28] as he was known during the 1998 nuclear tests, was neither an academic nor a nuclear scientist. But the wavy-haired A.P.J. Abdul Kalam had two things most officials lacked: integrity and warmth. For Hindu nationalists, he was also their kind of Muslim. The Ramayana as well as events from the Prophet Mohammad's life were Kalam's bedtime readings; he loved quoting from the Bhagavadgita and the Upanishads, and was an expert in the Rudra Veena.[29] This was a candidature that Vajpayee could push and the RSS could not refuse. With Kalam's candidature certain, Vajpayee chose his friend Bhairon Singh Shekhawat as the next vice-president of India.

With the next president and vice-president certainties, Vajpayee was no more at risk of being promoted to irrelevance. He felt confident enough to reach out to Advani. He announced, at the end of June 2002, that L.K. Advani would become deputy prime minister of India, his official number two.

A beaming Advani gave a press conference with wife Kamla by his side, saying: 'I am the deputy prime minister in the government, but at home I am the deputy home minister.'[30] He was typically straightforward about the reason for his elevation: 'When Mr. Vajpayee first thought of this appointment, the consideration uppermost in his mind must have been to dispel effectively all the canards spread about the rift between him and me.'[31]

* * *

Vajpayee's elevation of Advani eased somewhat one source of tension in his government. But the other remained. As we read in the last chapter, the Vishva Hindu Parishad and Rashtriya Swayamsevak Sangh had begun to wonder: what was the point of coming to power? This question was asked in an even more pointed manner when K.S. Sudarshan replaced the mild-mannered Rajendra Singh as head of the RSS in the year 2000. The new chief did not like Vajpayee. But even he eventually reconciled himself to the fact that on Ayodhya, Article 370, and a Uniform Civil Code, coalition dharma dictated that they wait for an electoral majority, something that would happen only in 2014 under Narendra Modi.

What added to the RSS's reluctance to interfere more directly was that Hindu nationalism, as well as traditional Hinduism, simply did not have a view of the state. On concerns as central to governance as foreign policy and welfare schemes, neither the ideology nor the religion had any shibboleths to proffer the Vajpayee government.

Even on attempts to rewrite the Constitution, the BJP government may have set up a review committee (which the opposition saw as a subterfuge to tinker with the character of India). But the recommendations eventually submitted were cautious, showing that even this was not a priority for the RSS.[32]

The two areas, however, where the sangh parivar insisted on getting its way—despite push back from the media, opposition and coalition parties—were on conversions and the teaching of history. The first hit at Hindu nationalism's source of anxiety, demographics, while the second hit at its source of sustenance, a particular reading of history. These would be the most palpable ways in which the RSS demanded that the Vajpayee government adhere to its dharma.

* * *

Christians constitute less than 3 per cent of India. And unlike with Muslims, Hindu nationalists had never feared their physical prowess. But the RSS had long viewed conversions by missionaries with suspicion. The years 1999 to 2004 saw this suspicion turn to violence. Compared to 1997 (i.e., just before the BJP came to national power), attacks against Christians had increased 800 per cent by the year 2000.[33] The Vishva Hindu Parishad claimed the attacks were a result of the 'anger of patriotic youth against anti-national forces . . . the direct result of the conversion of Hindus to Christianity by the Christian priests'.[34] As the historian Sumit Sarkar explains: 'The competitive logic of numbers made possible by census enumeration acquired greater saliency through the gradual spread of representative institutions . . . [and] even small changes [in demographics] through conversions came to be perceived as ominous.'[35]

Conversions were so central an anxiety to Hindutva that it was one of the few issues where Vajpayee agreed with the RSS. Instead of clearly condemning the violence, he demanded a 'national debate' on conversions.[36]

Perhaps the only Hindu nationalist who did not share this view was, surprisingly, L.K. Advani. While Brajesh Mishra, speaking for Vajpayee, called the attacks 'isolated' and 'aberrational', Advani's response was that attacks on Christians needed to be addressed.[37] 'He loved Christians. He had a lot of respect for them,' Sudheendra Kulkarni says of Advani. 'He was very hurt by the attack on Christians. This was largely because he was educated at St Patrick's School in Karachi.'[38] The man whose service to the RSS was modelled on his own experience of Christian missionaries was making a rare departure from his parent body.

The other area where the RSS was able to extract its pound of flesh was in the teaching of history. As we have read through this book, Hindu nationalism arose as a reaction to one version of history: that despite their cultural glories, Hindus were unable to repel invaders because they were physically weak as well as disunited. The emphasis on institutional unity was a response to this interpretation of history. What infuriated Hindu nationalists was that Indian students were being taught another version, one written by 'Marxists'. These historians, the RSS argued, presented an Indian past devoid of a 'national' (i.e., Hindu) consciousness. They emphasized the foreignness of 'Aryan' Hindus, instead of the foreignness of Muslims.[39]

What helped the RSS rewrite history books was the education minister, Murli Manohar Joshi, an RSS favourite. Sixteen pages from three textbooks were deleted, especially references to historians—such as Romila Thapar and R.S. Sharma—deemed Marxist.[40] Courses such as *jyotirvidya* (Hindu astrology) were made part of the syllabi, and those linked to the RSS were put in charge of cultural and educational bodies such as the University Grants Commission.[41]

The fact that it was demographics and history-writing—not Article 370, the uniform civil code, or even the Ram temple at Ayodhya—that characterized the RSS stamp on the Vajpayee government is telling. It shows the real preoccupations of the ideology. It is similarly telling that the two most enduring ways in which the Narendra Modi government is transforming India is through introducing a national citizen's register as well as changing the character of institutions such as the Jawaharlal Nehru University. The journalist Sheela Bhatt says: 'This is the real face of Modi. It's not 370 or Ayodhya. He will be remembered for changing the character of community living and for changing universities.'[42] The seeds of that vision were sown during the Vajpayee era.

* * *

These two controversies notwithstanding, as the Vajpayee government entered its final year in mid-2003, a precarious equilibrium had been somewhat restored—between the movement and government, between party and government, and between the prime minister and his deputy.

The *Tehelka* exposé had led to the resignation of Bangaru Laxman as BJP president; his replacement was once more an Advani protégé. Venkaiah Naidu only gave voice to this restored reality in what he thought was an innocuous press statement given in June 2003. The party, he said, would approach the coming elections by projecting both Vajpayee and Advani as leaders. 'Vajpayeeji is *vikas purush* [development man] and Advaniji is *lauh purush* [iron man].'[43]

'Vajpayee understood exactly what Naidu was saying,' an aide remembers. The Congress party gleefully called it evidence of an 'unmistakable' power struggle between the prime minister and his deputy. 'Both Mr Vajpayee and Mr Advani are responsible for non-governance, corruption, and deteriorating socio-economic conditions. The multiple-speak is designed to deflect attention from the government's non-performance.'[44]

A few days later, Vajpayee was addressing 250 party leaders at the wood-panelled annexe to his 7 Race Course Road house. With Advani on stage, Vajpayee said: '*Advaniji ke netritva mein vijay ki ore aage badhen* [Let us move towards victory under Advani's leadership].'[45] Shakti Sinha says: 'It was all strategic. Vajpayeeji knew the BJP needed him to win the coming elections.'[46] Vajpayee had used this trick in 1997 after the 'mask' controversy, when he had challenged his party to win elections without him. As Vajpayee had calculated, the party caved in yet again.

Even before the prime minister sat down, Naidu had rushed to the podium and declared: 'Let us clarify this once again . . . Atalji will lead us in the next elections and he will be our prime minister again.'[47]. At the weekly cabinet meeting held soon after, Advani's long-time antagonist Murli Manohar Joshi took the lead and said, to applause, that Vajpayee was the sole leader.[48] Advani was present but said nothing. Even the RSS, which had wanted Vajpayee to be replaced by Advani just a year ago, fell in line.[49] They were applying their own lessons from Panipat: to win in battle, the generals all needed to bury their differences and cohere under the king.

As this chapter shows, the threat to the third Vajpayee government was not external in the form of demanding allies; it was internal in the form of finicky family members. The real coalition dharma was deployed not in keeping the NDA together, but in keeping the sangh parivar and its two charioteers united. The dharma deployed to manage this coalition was the ideology of organizational unity.

Where this Hindu Fevicol was most tested, however, was on Pakistan and Kashmir. Given how the creation of one and the unfinished business of the other had been the bugbear of Hindu nationalism, it was widely expected that the first real BJP government in history would take a harder line than the Congress. The RSS expected, even demanded it. What happened instead was that Vajpayee turned out to be the most pro-Pakistan and pro-Kashmir prime minister in Indian history—and even more astonishing, Advani put aside his recent distrust of Vajpayee and lifelong distrust of Pakistan to support his prime minister. The next chapter follows the story behind this story: the third Vajpayee government's journey from Kandahar to Agra to Srinagar.

14

OH, PAKISTAN (1999–2004)

Two months after the third Vajpayee government was sworn in, the evening of 24 December 1999. Home Minister Lal Krishna Advani was in his office. He got a call around 5 p.m. An Indian Airlines flight travelling from Kathmandu to Delhi had been hijacked by five armed men.[1] IC-814 had 178 passengers and eleven crew members on board. Denied permission in Lahore in Pakistan, the plane landed in nearby Amritsar in India at around 7 p.m. The hijackers were demanding the release of thirty-six Islamist militants being held in Indian jails and a ransom of 200 million dollars.[2]

The prime minister was also mid-air, returning to Delhi from an official tour. An aide on the flight remembers that the aging plane did not have a satellite phone.[3] The prime minister would be told only 100 minutes later, after he had landed in Delhi.

In the prime minister's absence, a crisis management group or CMG was set up with senior officials and the heads of intelligence agencies. Advani was not part of this group, nor, initially, was Brajesh Mishra. A bureaucrat present in the CMG says: 'Advani and Brajesh would never have been in that meeting together, since the line of command would have been unclear. This may also have added [to the confusion].'

It was the cabinet secretary who was formally in charge. But in the absence of the three most senior members of government, the CMG scurried like a chicken whose head had just been sliced off. Instructions were not given to block the runway in Amritsar and prevent the plane from taking off. The commando unit reared for such a scenario was based in Delhi; their departure for Amritsar was delayed. The Punjab police— seasoned after decades of fighting insurgency—could have stormed the plane, but the head of the state police says that Delhi told him: 'No casualties to passengers.'[4]

IC-814 flew off from Amritsar forty-five minutes later, and with it any chance of India regaining control of the plane. An official present in the CMG meeting says: 'Advani, and I think even Brajesh, came into the room only after the plane had taken off [from Amritsar] . . . we were on our own till then.' Another official says: 'I was present in that room, and there was nothing but indecision.' Former national security advisor Shivshankar Menon feels: 'Committees cannot decide. You have to decide. In theory, the decision is with the home minister.'[5]

The hijacked flight flew to Lahore then Dubai and finally landed in Kandahar in Taliban-held Afghanistan. From the Indian point of view, it was the least convenient location possible. The Taliban was an Islamist militia sympathetic to the goals of the hijackers. They were also propped by Pakistan. 'The ISI [Pakistani spy agency] was orchestrating the whole thing,' Jaswant Singh's son says. 'It was revenge for Kargil. My father knew that.'[6]

India's restraints were made tighter by relatives of the passengers who created an unseemly scene. These relatives were given much prominence by the media and even the opposition.[7] Pressure of this kind put the Vajpayee government in a spot: if they gave in, they would be seen as gutless; if they refused, they would be seen as heartless.

Exhausted after a week of negotiations, Vajpayee decided to release three Kashmiri terrorists in return for the passengers and plane.[8] Then finance minister Yashwant Sinha remembers: 'Before any cabinet meeting, Jaswant and Brajesh would meet Vajpayee. When the meeting began, they would come behind him. [On 31 December 1999] we met at the PM's house. It was decided to release the terrorists. I think Brajesh announced it and nobody disagreed. Then Jaswant said, "I will have to leave now." That's when I knew that Jaswant Singh was accompanying the terrorists [to Kandahar]. I assumed he had cleared it with Vajpayee just before the meeting.'[9]

'Advani sat silently throughout the meeting. I heard him muttering "we are a soft state",' another minister adds. 'But he would not dare go against Vajpayee. He was party to the decision.' A few days after, Advani would indulge in an atypical public censure of his own government: 'The hijack episode is a setback to the BJP's image as the party had all along been perceived to be different from other parties by the people.'[10]

He was more wounding in private. He wrote a two-page dissenting note to his oldest friend, the kind of rebellion their friendship had scarcely seen.[11] A seething Advani wrote that the officials Vajpayee had entrusted had proved incompetent. The plane should not have left Amritsar. The government should have driven a better bargain. Advani was venting his frustration at his role as Vajpayee's deputy being usurped. He was also worried that Vajpayee was going too soft on Pakistan and Kashmir.

* * *

The RSS agreed with Advani, saying that the release of militants 'has projected India as a soft state'.[12] The surrender at Kandahar triggered Hindu nationalism's historical paranoia that on the battlefield, the Hindu was too weak to battle the more masculine Muslim. Even Jaswant Singh, who had bravely chosen to besmirch his reputation to prevent any last-minute hitch, kept a memento from IC-814 in his office. 'It was a pair of binoculars left behind by the terrorists. It was black with some brass on it, and he had it mounted,' the director in his office says. 'He wanted to remind himself to be farsighted.'[13]

As we read earlier, Hindutva had been shaped by the desire to emulate the unity that gave Muslims power on the battlefield, both actual and electoral. Fed on this belief their entire lives, Vajpayee had imagined that Muslim Fevicol was the glue that kept Pakistanis together, just like Hindu Fevicol was the glue that kept the sangh parivar together—it was this fantasy of a Muslim Fevicol that, in fact, had been their inspiration. This ideology had blinded him so far to the multiple power centres in Pakistan—to differences between politicians and army men, between Nawaz Sharif and Pervez Musharraf, between Pakistani militants and the establishment, and within Kashmiri secessionists. If the prime minister had chosen to learn from this mistake, he should have spent the next five years staying far away from Pakistan and Kashmir.

Instead, he waited barely a year to announce yet another grand gesture. In November 2000, his government decreed that Indian troops would not launch combat operations against militants, both local and Pakistani, in Kashmir for the next six months. Vajpayee had timed his announcement to coincide with the Muslim holy month of Ramadan.[14] He had also not consulted with Advani, a home ministry official at the time says. 'It was Vajpayee and Brajesh and Jaswant. They were the ones deciding.'

By the splattered standards of Kashmir, the next six months were calm. And as the end of the ceasefire approached, Vajpayee began looking for another grand gesture.

It was in this context that Vajpayee and Jaswant Singh invited Advani for lunch on 23 May 2001,[15] days before the ceasefire was to end. The purpose was to sweet talk Advani into agreeing to another symbolic overture, perhaps an extension of the ceasefire. They were nervous, since relations between Vajpayee and Advani were strained by now, not least by their disagreement over the Kandahar hijack.

But even after playing music together for so many years, Advani was capable of surprising Vajpayee with new tunes. Advani told him: 'Atalji, why don't you invite the General [Musharraf] to come to India for talks? It does not matter if your Lahore initiative failed . . . your invitation to him will be welcomed as an act of statesmanship, both within India and internationally.'[16]

* * *

Unknown to most of the cabinet, Advani had spent the last year laying the groundwork for this invitation to the Pakistani president. Barely a month after Kandahar, when even Vajpayee was lying low, his 'hard-line' deputy began to meet the Pakistani High Commissioner to India, Ashraf Qazi. 'Over the next eighteen months, there were perhaps twenty to thirty such clandestine meetings. The vast majority took place at night.'[17] Had their existence become public in those charged months, Advani would have been branded a 'traitor'. So Advani ensured that Qazi would come to his home on Pandara Road in an unmarked car, away from prying eyes.

Driving Qazi to Advani's house would be Karan Thapar, the television journalist who was at the time trusted by the Advani family. Thapar was also a friend of Qazi—his father had been a colleague of Qazi's father-in-law at Sandhurst when they were both part of the British army in the 1920s.[18] Thapar says: 'I guess Vajpayee would also have known, but the initiative was all Advani's.'

During those meetings, Advani kept asking about the new head of state in Pakistan, someone privy to the meetings says. What kind of man was the architect of Kargil? Advani wondered. Could he be trusted with peace? Was he ready to make a deal? 'Why don't you invite him and see for yourself,' Qazi once suggested. After thinking it over, Advani brought up the idea with Vajpayee and Jaswant Singh on 23 May. As he told an aide: 'Musharraf is the ruler so we have to do business with him.'[19] Karan Thapar says. 'Advani was the architect of the Agra summit. No two ways about it.'[20]

* * *

The summit location was luxury hotels in Agra, home to the Taj Mahal. The head chef set the expectations: 'We will give Musharraf the finest cuisine culled from different parts of India. It will showcase the regional diversity of our country.'[21] Vajpayee was as confident of making a meal of it. He told an aide: '*Hum apne rishtedaaron ko chun sakte hain, padosi ko nahin.*'[22] We can choose our relatives, not our neighbours. The sangh parivar, however, was a family divided. The Rashtriya Swayamsevak Sangh described the summit as 'a good beginning for the future', while the VHP described it as a 'meaningless exercise'.[23]

The Agra invite had all the makings of the Lahore bus invite—back-channel talks, striking symbolism, sudden announcements. T.C.A. Raghavan says: 'Agra outcomes were not planned in advance, unlike other meetings. And unless India–Pakistan meetings are tightly scripted they get taken over by the media and other developments.'[24]

This is what happened from the word go. Soon after his arrival, Pakistan's president Pervez Musharraf met the home minister in Delhi. Advani maddened Musharraf by referring to cross-border terrorism, even asking about the whereabouts of Indian fugitive Dawood Ibrahim.[25]

Musharraf repaid the compliment, referring to the disputed nature of Kashmir.

On the morning of 16 July 2001, the crucial day of negotiations, Musharraf had a breakfast meeting with Indian editors in Agra. He spoke with a soldier's bravado: 'Let us not remain under any illusions that the main issue confronting us is Kashmir . . . There may be some compulsion on your part not to talk about it. There are definite compulsions on my part to talk about it . . .'[26] When asked if he would commit to Pakistan renouncing violence in Kashmir, Musharraf responded: 'We are not encouraging violence there. It is an indigenous freedom struggle.'[27]

Later that day, the foreign ministers of Pakistan and India sat down to work on a joint statement. The version that Pakistan insisted upon was completed around 2:30 p.m. Its words heralded upfront that the 'settlement of the Jammu and Kashmir issue would pave the way for normalisation of relations between two countries'. It mentioned Kashmir two other times, saying that it was 'particularly' discussed in Agra. Terrorism, on the other hand, got just a single token reference, along with 'drug trafficking' as one of the many areas on which 'the two sides will resume a sustained dialogue'.[28]

Jaswant Singh, India's external affairs minister, took this draft to his prime minister, 'who then called his cabinet colleagues to the suite'. Jaswant is at pains to stress that the 'collective view expressed' was that the draft was unacceptable.[29] The Pakistanis were told 'that cross-border terrorism had to be put in'. The Pakistanis then demanded a reference to 'repression and respect for human rights in Kashmir'. The talks broke down.[30]

Angry at the summit being flattened over what he felt was just 'a simple two-three-page English composition',[31] the Pakistani general met the Indian prime minister one last time, at 11 p.m. Vajpayee sat quietly, while Musharraf spoke at length.[32] He told Vajpayee: 'Today you and I have been both humiliated because there is someone above us, sitting above us, who can veto what we decide.'[33]

Musharraf was referring to Advani, and through him, the RSS. He would later say: 'I was certain that Vajpayee would sign the declaration in which the centrality of the Kashmir issue was agreed upon. But the hard-liners prevailed over the Indian prime minister.'[34] This view is shared by the former chief of India's spy agency, A.S. Dulat, who says, 'The Advani of Delhi and the Advani of Agra were different.'[35] Musharraf had erred in investing too much faith in Vajpayee and ignored the 'architect' of the summit. In this telling, Advani, already sensitive at the loss of power in his own government, had wreaked revenge.

But the repeat mention of Kashmir and little of terrorism (in Musharraf's breakfast meeting as well as in the draft) would have been unacceptable to any Indian cabinet—with or without Advani. The Agra summit failed because both sides assumed the other was playing a weak hand.[36] Musharraf had read the Agra visit like he had read the Lahore visit: the BJP needed a deal to buy legitimacy in India and in the international community.[37] But he had not understood the centrality of Kashmir to India's narrative of itself.

Vajpayee and Advani had similarly not understood the centrality of Kashmir to Pakistan's narrative of itself. They had assumed that Musharraf was weak and ready to make compromises. If only they had waited two more months.

* * *

Most people remember where they were on 11 September 2001. Lal Krishna Advani recalls working late in his office in north block when his private secretary came rushing in. 'Sir, there has been a major terrorist attack in the United States.'[38] Advani switched on the television to watch planes crashing into the twin towers of the World Trade Center in New York. Over 3000 people died in the terror attacks,[39] including 117 persons of Indian origin.[40] Musharraf was in Karachi that evening, 'inspecting work at the beautiful gardens of the mausoleum of our founder . . . Muhammad Ali Jinnah'. He recalls: '. . . little did I know that on the other side of the globe yet another event . . . was about to alter the course of my life and the course of Pakistan.'[41]

Ever since Pakistan had failed to wrest Kashmir through conventional wars, support for Islamic jihadis had been its preferred strategy to negotiate with India. But 9/11, as the terror attacks would later be known, would denude Western sympathy for violence by non-state actors in the name of freedom. It would also justify curtailment of civil liberties in the name of combatting terrorism. For instance, the United States adopted fifty-three resolutions and sixty-eight acts in the first year after 9/11, Australia introduced forty pieces of counterterrorism legislation, and Germany amended 'nearly one hundred regulations in seventeen different statutes and five statutory orders'.[42]

In India, the Vajpayee government announced, just weeks after 9/11, a new prevention of terrorism act. The law made it easier to admit evidence in court, as well as detain terror suspects for long periods.[43] Such a law would have provoked international condemnation in the past. But as Advani said soon after: 'After September 11, I don't know of any country which is opposed to stringent laws against terrorism.'[44]

In the long-term, Pakistan would not be able to justify terrorists as freedom fighters. But in the short-term, Pakistan became a valuable Western ally in what Musharraf called the 'frontline of yet another war, a war against shadows'.[45] As the United States and its allies launched an invasion of Afghanistan to topple the Taliban, Musharraf made the opportunistic decision to abandon one ally in order to gain another. Over the next eight years, Pakistan would be the recipient of 19 billion dollars of aid, 75 per cent of which would expressly be for military purposes.[46]

9/11 dealt Vajpayee and Advani a mixed hand. On the one hand, it placed their views of militant Islam on the right side of global opinion. As the VHP's general secretary Pravin Togadia put it: 'Our war with Islamic terrorism began with Mohammad of Ghaznavi's attack on Somnath and it still continues. The only change is that Osama Bin Laden has replaced Ghaznavi.'[47] On the other hand, Musharraf had new leverage with the West to demand concessions on Kashmir. As one Pakistani politician said at the time: 'By sacrificing strategic depth on its western front, Pakistan now hopes that the US may be more supportive on the eastern front by helping break the status quo in Kashmir.'[48] In the first few months after 9/11, no one knew which hand would prove successful. It would take an almost-war between India and Pakistan for the answer to reveal itself.

* * *

The Indian parliament is a circular-shaped building with twelve entry points through large wooden gates. After a heated morning session on 13

December 2001, just two months after 9/11, the session was adjourned around 11 a.m. Prime Minister Atal Bihari Vajpayee and the leader of the opposition, Sonia Gandhi, left parliament in their convoys.[49] The vice-president was also leaving with his entourage.

Suddenly, his cavalcade was hit by a white Ambassador with a red beacon and a home ministry sticker.[50] The car stopped and five men wearing suicide vests stepped out and began firing.

Advani was in his office chamber inside the building.[51] As was the foreign minister, Jaswant Singh. His diary, written later that day, records: 'I was in room 27, doing something routine when there was a rattle of fire. So it has at last happened. Booms of grenade bursts followed, more automatic fire . . .'[52] Alert parliamentary personnel shut the gates, preventing a massacre of an estimated 200 MPs inside.[53] The terrorists were eventually killed, along with eight guards and one gardener.[54]

Politicians across parties were shaken at this attack on the 'temple of Indian democracy'. The phrase would be used non-stop—even Prime Minister Narendra Modi would tweet on the thirteenth anniversary of the attack: 'We salute martyrs who lost their lives protecting the *temple of our democracy* on this day in 2001.'[55] It points to a key aspect of Hindu nationalism: in the absence of any authoritative temple in traditional Hinduism, parliamentary democracy would become the temple through which religious identity would be shaped.

Five days after the attack, the home minister provided a progress report to both houses of parliament. Advani blamed two Pakistan-based militant groups which were controlled by the Inter-Services Intelligence (ISI), Pakistan's spy agency.[56] The lesson that Advani drew from these attacks was the same as he had drawn after the Kandahar hijackings. 'We have allowed ourselves to become a soft society, and our government, being part of the same society, is also too soft.'[57] The prime minister spoke in parliament the next day. Making use of the international reaction to 9/11, he said: 'There should be no double standards in measuring terrorism in different parts of the world.'[58]

There was immense pressure on Vajpayee from the RSS[59] to cross the Line of Control, the effective border, and strike terror camps. A BJP vice-president even suggested that 'we march on the PoK and attack the terrorists' training camps'.[60]

Vajpayee ordered 500,000 troops to mobilize along India's western border. Pakistan responded by deploying 120,000 soldiers. It was the largest build-up of troops in the subcontinent since the 1971 war.[61]

The closest those 620,000 troops came to war was on 14 May 2002, when three Pakistanis crossed the border in Jammu, dressed in Indian army fatigues. They entered an army base in Kaluchak a few kilometres away and killed thirty, including soldiers, their wives, and their children.[62] For an army already mobilized, this attack on its women and children was the last straw. The army chief asked his prime minister for permission to 'let me have a crack at it'.[63] The RSS also put pressure to retaliate. Vajpayee had planned to escape the May heat in Delhi for his favourite Manali, and Advani was planning to holiday in Shimla—both hill stations in Himachal Pradesh. But with war imminent, both cancelled their holidays to remain in Delhi.[64] It was in a similar scenario in 2019 that Prime Minister Narendra Modi ordered warplanes to cross, not just the Line of Control, but the international border and bomb targets in Pakistan proper. But Vajpayee was not Narendra Modi. He refused to cross the line.

Instead, India deployed its superior navy in the Arabian Sea to blockade Pakistan's port town of Karachi.[65] It also asked Pakistan's ambassador, Ashraf Qazi, who had been Advani's interlocutor for an entire year, to leave the country.

Advani invited Qazi for a secret farewell. Had this been publicly known it would have created a furore, not least to the image of India's iron man. As Qazi stretched his hand to say bye, Kamla Advani intervened: '*Galey lago.*' Please embrace. As Advani and the man he was expelling embraced, tears welled in Advani's eyes.[66]

The US assistant secretary of state visited both countries after the attack, worried about 'the continued mobilisation of the two major armies facing each other in close proximity'. But she had little to say about Kashmir. Instead, her main argument was that 'terrorism against India is as unacceptable as it is against America or any other country'.[67] In the Global War Against Islamic Terrorism, Pakistan's narrative on Kashmir had lost currency.

When Musharraf was asked by CNN what he was doing to curb terrorism emanating from his country, he responded: 'I have given a commitment that nothing is happening across the Line of Control. And

I've also said that we will not allow Pakistan territory to be used for any purposes of terrorism across its borders against any country. Now we stand by it, I stand by this.'[68] These were the words that Indians had demanded at Agra. But it had taken an expensive mobilization, two terror attacks, and 9/11 for Musharraf to utter them. India finally drew down its troops in late 2002.

* * *

Vajpayee coincided this order to withdraw troops from the Pakistan border with his decision to hold elections in Kashmir. Over 5000 poll personnel worked alongside 50,000 paramilitaries and 50,000 state police to safeguard 1962 polling booths across the state in September 2002.[69]

There was some expectation that India would rig the elections, like had happened in 1987. But if Vajpayee was not Modi, he was no Rajiv Gandhi either. International observers were allowed free access during the elections, and confirmed they were fair.[70]

With the benefit of hindsight, the clean elections in Kashmir were only one card in Vajpayee's final gamble. In April 2003, he travelled to Kashmir to address a public gathering—the first prime minister to do so after the violence began in 1989.[71]

The routine should have been for Vajpayee to use the occasion to attack Pakistan. But Vajpayee was keeping this card close to his chest. Brajesh Mishra later claimed that even he did not know what his boss was going to say. As Vajpayee walked up on the stage to address an audience of 20,000 at the Sher-e-Kashmir cricket stadium in Srinagar, an official asked for a copy of the speech. 'There is no copy,' came the reply.[72]

The prime minister began speaking behind bulletproof glass. The audience could not believe what they were hearing. The man who had almost gone to war with Pakistan a few months ago now said: 'We are again extending a hand of friendship but hands should be extended from both the sides. Both sides should decide to live together.'[73] Vajpayee then said something no Indian prime minister before or after would ever say. This was a time to change the map, he said, and 'we are busy in Delhi towards that and we need to work together'. To parliament a few days later, he explained: 'Issues can be resolved if we move forward guided by the three principles of *Insaniyat* [Humanism], *Jamhooriyat* [Democracy] and *Kashmiriyat*.'[74]

In his gingerly, elliptical way, Vajpayee had shifted India's decades-long position on Kashmir and Pakistan. Though the speech was in Srinagar, it was addressed to Pakistan, thereby agreeing that Kashmir was the central issue between both countries. Vajpayee's reference to changing the map, though done with his flair for deniability, was explosive. It provided a whiff of the possibility that the boundaries of Kashmir were open to change. And finally, Vajpayee's reference to solving the dispute using the 'three principles' of humanism, democracy, and Kashmiriyat was notable for what it excluded—the claim that the solution to Kashmir lay only within the 'four corners' of the Indian Constitution. Even Vajpayee knew just how much of his career he had staked on the speech. He hinted that he would 'retire' if this third attempt at peace with Pakistan failed.

'Immediately after the 2003 speech, Vajpayee rang me,' the diplomat Shivshankar Menon says. 'He always spoke to me in Hindi, I replied in English. He asked me, "*Pakistan jaoge?*" I said: "Why me? I have not worked on Pakistan for years." But he replied in English: "Because you are innocent." He roared with laughter, but he had a point.'[75]

Vajpayee's 'hand of friendship' infuriated the RSS. They had always felt that it was the 'appeasement' politics of the Congress and the British from 1909 to 1947 that had created Pakistan. This was the lens through which they saw the Congress's concessions on Kashmir since Independence. The RSS chief was alarmed that their own prime minister had not understood this ideological lesson; he accused Vajpayee of 'lacking clarity' on Kashmir and termed any dialogue with Pakistan a 'futile exercise'. The VHP went one step further, egging Advani to resign in protest. Its leader Ashok Singhal said that if Advani abandoned Vajpayee at this stage, 'it would restore the faith of millions of Hindus in him'.[76]

* * *

What the VHP had not grasped was that Advani was Vajpayee's partner in peace, not the obstacle. A few months after his Srinagar speech, in October 2003, Vajpayee told his government to begin talks with the main Kashmiri separatist grouping, the Hurriyat. 'Who will talk from the government's side?' Jaswant Singh asked. Vajpayee replied, 'Advaniji of course.'[77]

Talks began in January 2004, and Hurriyat members became a familiar sight in the citadel of Lutyens' Delhi. 'You could see all these Kashmiris, like the Mirwaiz, in Khan Market,' one journalist remembers. Aware of Advani's reputation as a hardliner, a nervous Hurriyat member asked before the meeting, '*Humara pajama toh nahin uttarvaoge*?'[78] You won't have our pajamas pulled down, will you?

While Advani did not humiliate the separatists, he was unwilling to countenance any dilution of India's sovereignty, something that Vajpayee's 'hand of friendship' speech had hinted at. Advani recalls: '. . . in my very first meeting with the [Hurriyat] delegation, I made it clear that there was no question of the government entertaining any proposal outside the Indian Constitution.'[79]

This plain talk by Advani rendered the meetings moot. The Hurriyat had been created precisely because the Indian Constitution was unable to contain the demands of these nearly two dozen separatist groups. When Advani asked them at the next meeting in March 2004, 'What is it that you want?', the Hurriyat members could think of nothing to say. 'Next time we will come prepared with our ideas.'[80]

There would be no next time. The Vajpayee government would lose the elections held months later, as we shall elaborate in the final chapter. Future governments, both Congress and BJP, would never take up where Vajpayee left. Manmohan Singh was more hard-headed and unsentimental on Pakistan than Vajpayee. And the BJP prime minister who succeeded him has so far used antagonism towards Pakistan to garner domestic votes.

Vajpayee and Advani's outreach from 1998 to 2004 thus remains an unexplained blip in India–Pakistan relations. How did India's first Hindu nationalist government come to do this much to improve ties?

* * *

For Vajpayee, the desire to reach out was part of his yearning for grand gestures that would finally mainstream the BJP. If the party changed its relationship with Pakistanis and Kashmiris, it could gain acceptance in parliament and in the West. For Advani, however, the desire to reach out is psychologically more puzzling. The Sindhi refugee should have balked at any concessions to an idea that had displaced his family. Instead, Karan Thapar says: 'On Pakistan, Advani was very rational. He was never emotional. He only cared about what was good for his party and country. He was not thinking of revenge, I don't think so.' Advani agreed with Vajpayee that Hindu nationalism needed to rid itself of the ghosts of Partition. Thapar adds: 'The thing about Advani was that he was much more liberal than the image he portrayed. He was personally secular. I don't think he had an anti-Muslim bone.'[81]

While Vajpayee deserves credit for being the most pro-Pakistan prime minister India has ever had, Advani's backing was essential. Their teamwork in this regard, especially when personal relations between them soured, says much about their partnership.

Why then, and despite all this, did they fail? We do know that the first two attempts at jumpstarting peace—in Lahore in 1999 and Agra in 2001—were unsuccessful. And there is little to suggest that the concessions India wanted on terrorism and Pakistan on Kashmir would have moved beyond verbiage in their third, final, attempt at peace.

One reason for these repeat let-downs is that Vajpayee and Advani misjudged the centrality of Kashmir to the Pakistani national psyche. But the logic for Pakistan, as we read earlier, had been that Muslim-majority regions of the subcontinent be independent from Hindu-majority India. Even more than Bangladesh, contiguous Kashmir fit into that vision. This means that short of conceding sovereignty over Kashmir, which no Indian government will ever do, there is no solution that will please Pakistan. This is a reality that Hindu nationalists other than Vajpayee and Advani have well understood—that if one were to accept the logic of Pakistan, that logic must extend to Kashmir. When Amit Shah was asked in 2019 about the difference between his government's hard line on Pakistan and Kashmir compared to the Vajpayee government's, he replied: 'International relations runs only according to power. Today we are powerful and Pakistan is weak. That is the only solution to Kashmir.'[82]

15

MAKING INDIA GREAT AGAIN (1999–2004)

Below the thirty-six-metre-high dome of parliament lies Central Hall, in between the Lok Sabha, Rajya Sabha and the member's reading hall.[1] When not in use for special occasions, the green-carpeted room serves as an informal place where parliamentarians relax between sessions. Ministers rub shoulders with current and former MPs, along with select journalists. Friendship across parties are made, gossip across ministries is shared. Central Hall reveals the mood of parliament.

While Lal Krishna Advani preferred to spend time in the party headquarters amidst cadre, Atal Bihari Vajpayee had been a fixture in Central Hall from 1957 onwards. From the hundreds of hours spent here each year, Vajpayee would decode the political 'common' sense of the time, the 'Overton window' of what India would find acceptable. Since Hindu nationalism's cultural project was outside the mainstream for the first four decades of the republic, Vajpayee wanted to ensure that its *other* policies—say, on economics, welfare schemes, or international relations— did not cross a Laxman rekha. Central Hall was where that line was drawn.

He was thus able to sense, in the 1960s, the Nehruvian consensus— on the commanding role of the state, of the need for a non-aligned foreign policy—that even non-Congress parties subscribed to. In the next decade, he saw that Indira Gandhi's tilt towards socialism and the Soviet Union was the flavour of Central Hall. This is what led him to oppose Balraj Madhok's conservative policies during that period. When Vajpayee became foreign minister in 1977, he detected that while Indira Gandhi was unpopular, Indira-ism was not. As he himself put it then: 'Foreign policy is neither decided nor conducted on party lines.'[2]

Now prime minister twenty years later, Vajpayee noticed that Central Hall reflected a new consensus. Narasimha Rao's prime ministership from 1991 to 1996 had overturned the assumptions behind India's economic, foreign and welfare policies. It meant that the state would retreat from the commanding heights of the economy and encourage private, even foreign, participation. And it meant a more 'realist' vision based on national self-interest and a recognition of American primacy in a post-Soviet world. So embedded had this new view become that all prime ministers after Narasimha Rao had operated under this new consensus. The Nehruvian consensus in Central Hall had been replaced by the Narasimha consensus.

Opposing the Narasimha consensus were left parties of course. But, by the late 1990s, they were a peripheral presence in national politics. The real opposition was not within Central Hall in Lutyens' Delhi, but within Hedgewar Bhavan in Nagpur. The RSS chief, K.S. Sudarshan, was focused on Hindu culture and opposed the destabilizing effects of globalization. Govindacharya says: 'We may sound like leftists. But we have always opposed markets deciding everything.' He adds: 'We believe in economic decentralization, on the importance of the village as an economic unit. I know this sounds like Mahatma Gandhi. Our only disagreement with Gandhi was on understanding [the] Muslim psyche. But on [the] economy we completely agreed with him.'[3]

As we read in the previous chapter, Vajpayee and Advani worked as a team when it came to Pakistan and Kashmir. But this chapter deals with the third Vajpayee government's economic and foreign policies from 1999 to 2004. And on these subjects, Vajpayee chose not to rely on Advani, who, he felt, had neither the technical nor ideological expertise.

It was thus for Vajpayee alone to decide whether to operate under the Narasimha consensus of trade deals, private investments and American coalitions—or follow the Rashtriya Swayamsevak Sangh in focusing on cows, temples and culture. Would he align with the United States or with the RSS? The answer would reveal itself most plainly in March 2000.

* * *

In the lead-up to the nineteenth of that month, American aircraft made more than fifty visits to India. They carried 200 secret service officers, 100 marines, thirty bulletproof cars, heavy equipment and cables, twelve choppers, two army trucks and a Labrador with a nose for bombs.[4] On the designated day, 19 March 2000, the person all this equipment was meant for landed in Delhi, accompanied by his daughter, sixty-three officials and more than a hundred journalists.[5]

William Jefferson Clinton was making a presidential visit to India at the apogee of pax Americana. He was also the first US president to enter India since Jimmy Carter was dropped back at Delhi airport in 1978 by the Janata government's foreign minister, Atal Bihari Vajpayee.[6]

Clinton penned a voluble article on the eve of his visit. While he paid lip service to India's diversity and democracy, he was clear about why he was coming. 'India's economy is one of the ten fastest growing in the world . . . There are now more television channels available in Mumbai than in most US cities.'[7] This set the tone for the visit. Though Clinton was careful to meet Advani and others in government, his focus was on business; he even travelled to Hyderabad to see for himself India's software sector.

That Clinton's visit had this motive was not lost on the RSS. Sudarshan had warned just a few months earlier: 'There is a conflict between the US lobby in the government and swadeshi. That is the real struggle.'[8]

At a thirty-five-minute speech to India's parliament under the giant dome of the Central Hall, Bill Clinton seemed to allay some of these fears by offering even more goodies. He had not come to 'mediate the [Kashmir] dispute',[9] he promised. This and other concessions were punctuated with applause and standing ovations. And the US president was 'all but mobbed by Indian parliamentarians after his address'.[10] Once again, Vajpayee had understood the mood of his beloved Central Hall.

Clinton then travelled west. After five days (and five cities) spent in India, he was in Pakistan 'for a few hours'.[11] The historian Ayesha Jalal wrote: in 'sharp contrast to the adoring crowds that had greeted Clinton everywhere in India, the streets of Islamabad were empty'. Clinton used the occasion to make a televised speech to Pakistanis that criticized their leader: 'The answer to flawed democracy is not to end democracy, but to improve it.'[12] And before anyone knew it, he had flown away.

If the 2000 Clinton visit de-hyphenated India from Pakistan for the first time in the American strategic imagination, the year also saw India part of another American hyphen. With the collapse of the Soviet Union, Western anxieties were turning to China. In the past decade, China's reserves had grown twenty-fold to 200 billion dollars, and no country other than the United States was receiving more foreign investment.[13] Self-interested American diplomats began to fashion India as a regional balance to China.

Vajpayee too was seeing this new friendship through the lens of self-interest, just like Narasimha Rao had. He wanted an ancient civilization to rise in the world, and he was realistic enough to understand that in a unipolar order, the only route was through the United States.

That the prime minister would pursue this Narasimha consensus rather than the RSS's 'swadeshi' self-reliance was made even more obvious two months after Clinton left India. This was when Vajpayee appointed a former World Bank employee as his minister for disinvestment.

* * *

Born in 1941 in Jalandhar, Arun Shourie was that rare Hindu nationalist—he was an original thinker. With a deceivingly whispery voice, Shourie had a PhD in economics and had worked in the World Bank, before going on to edit *The Indian Express*. His books railed against socialism, Marxism, judicial activism and reservations,[14] and were required reading for many in the RSS. Vajpayee ensured that Shourie was given a Rajya Sabha ticket in 1998, and in July 2000, made him minister for the newly created ministry for disinvestment.

Under the Nehruvian consensus, socialist India ran several companies—from airlines to telecom to breads to cars—that in most countries would be run by the private sector. The government along with financial institutions had invested nearly 200,000 crore rupees in these public-sector undertakings.[15] And after 1991, the government had ploughed in another 61,968 crore rupees. In return, it had earned a dividend of just 9971 crore rupees.[16] The taxpayer was, quite literally, being looted.

The Vajpayee government was determined to change this. It set a target of selling its stake in twenty-seven government-owned companies,[17] hoping to earn 63,500 crore rupees[18] or nearly 10 billion dollars. With just fifty overworked bureaucrats,[19] Arun Shourie tried to ram through the sale of disparate government-owned business such as Air India, the Maruti car company and the Centaur Hotel in Mumbai. As Montek Singh Ahluwalia, who had served the previous five governments as finance secretary, puts it: 'Vajpayee's policy was bolder on privatization than his predecessors. At least Arun Shourie aimed to do something.'[20]

Shourie's zeal divided Vajpayee's cabinet, with George Fernandes, Ram Naik, Murli Manohar Joshi all opposed to disinvestment. Home Minister L.K. Advani was also not a supporter. Like he had been with Brajesh Mishra on national security, Advani was insecure that Vajpayee was creating his own economic team. The man who had overruled Vajpayee to support liberalization in 1991 now advised caution when it came to disinvestment: '*Hamare hi ministers virodh kar rahe hain.*'[21] Our own ministers are opposing it.

'He was very impressionable,' Shourie counters, 'and on disinvestment he came under the influence of Gurumurthy [from the Swadeshi Jagran Manch].' The journalist Vir Sanghvi had written at the time that Advani was the second most important man in the country. Shourie adds, 'Indeed, Advani was the second most powerful man. The most powerful was the one who met him last.'[22]

The Vajpayee government privatized twelve public-sector companies generating 29,990 crore rupees or 4.6 billion US dollars.[23] What halted this juggernaut was the government's attempts to sell its stake in Bharat and Hindustan Petroleum. Unlike Centaur Hotel or even Air India, these oil companies were seen as profitmaking. Opposition from parliament and even Vajpayee's own cabinet was unrelenting. After several years of breakneck disinvestment, the pragmatist in Vajpayee took over. He finally listened to Central Hall. By 2003, disinvestment had slowed to a crawl.

* * *

If Vajpayee faced disapproval of his disinvestment policies from parliament and even his own party, he also faced hostility from the RSS. As one functionary said at the time: 'We miscalculated on Arun Shourie. We thought he was an upright man who was ideologically committed. We were stupid. We should have seen that he would be equally committed to the free market. Now it's clear that he is very much his own man.'[24] The economy was a particular concern of K.S. Sudarshan. It epitomized all that he abhorred about Vajpayee. He demanded that economic policy be 'overhauled' since it is 'anti-labour, anti-farmer, and anti-poor'.[25]

Vajpayee once sent Shourie and his finance minister Yashwant Sinha to mollify Sudarshan, who told them: 'Why is your foreign exchange in dollars? Why not in rupees? This shows that you lack "*aatma sammaan*" [self-respect].'[26] On another occasion when his ministers requested the prime minister for permission to meet Sudarshan to explain an amendment to the patents act, Vajpayee replied: 'Why are you going? He is a *sarva gyaani*. He knows everything. He is not going to listen.'

Ordinarily, Sudarshan should have relied on Advani to balance Vajpayee. But Advani did not have the interest or appetite to promote swadeshi economics. The two weapons Sudarshan deployed, therefore, were the Swadeshi Jagran Manch—created in 1991 to oppose Advani's support of liberalization—and its founder Dattopant Thengadi. The Swadeshi Jagran Manch called for a 'second freedom struggle' against the Vajpayee government's economics.[27] Thengadi was even more intimidating; the founder of the largest trade union in India was revered within the sangh parivar. So angry was he with Vajpayee's economics that he even said, '*Yeh rashtravirodhi kaam hai*' (this is anti-national work). This being the filthiest abuse within the saffron family, Vajpayee met Sudarshan and demanded an explanation, an RSS old-timer remembers. Sudarshan refused.

The tussle between Vajpayee and Sudarshan reveals that the BJP does not always march to the RSS's tunes. As importantly, it shows that the RSS can withstand the trappings of electoral power. No gift of government—no Rajya Sabha nomination, no state grants, no Ambassador car, no Lutyens bungalow—was able to bend Sudarshan's view.

This worldview mirrors an older strand of Hindu nationalism, where the protection of cultural unity was seen as the key to national power. A wave of Hindu 'history' writing during the twentieth century—by those like K.M. Munshi, V.D. Savarkar and Jadunath Sarkar—had presented Hindus as both militarily weak and culturally divided, leading to invasion and defeat. As Hindus began to think about power, these two strands—

of concerns with physical weakness and with cultural disunity—began to surface.

These anxieties found articulation in a range of 'little' magazines and journals that were published in the early twentieth century—from the *Indian Annual Register* and *Hindu Outlook* to *Arya* and *Brahmavadin*. The scholar Rahul Sagar has categorized 315,000 such articles, culled from 161 libraries.[28] He argues that the writings show two different preoccupations of Hindu nationalism. The first is a pragmatic concern with material power, to catch up with the world. The second set of concerns are more cultural, to do with values and authenticity, by thinkers such as Vivekananda.[29]

K.S. Sudarshan and Dattopant Thengadi were deploying this second strand against Vajpayee's first strand of Hindu nationalism. Their exchange over economics was a family squabble.

* * *

One of the few economic avenues where both strands converged was on road-building. A distinctive feature of the RSS and BJP cadre was that they would constantly travel to organize, a sort of modern teerth yatra, not for salvation but for votes. The cadre took pride at reciting bus and train timetables. A family friend of Advani says: 'He still remembers timings of most trains in and out of Delhi. Till recently, he would have the schedules in his pockets.' This emphasis on travel was often as an end in itself; connecting India would unite it.

A hundred years earlier, British-built railroads had played a similar role in uniting India, allowing people to travel across India's geography and creating a common nationalism.[30] While that was an unintended consequence of British administrative action, the expansion of a 'national' consciousness was part of the *intended* logic of the Vajpayee government's push to build highways.

Under his government, the number of kilometres of roads went from 34,849 in 1996–97 to 58,125 in 2002–03, a 67 per cent increase in just five years.[31] The centrepiece of this effort was the 5800-kilometre 'golden quadrilateral' project that connected New Delhi, Kolkata, Mumbai and Chennai through four- and six-lane highways, allowing a speedy yatra around the four dhams of modern India. *The New York Times* said: 'The journey along the highway offered a before-and-after snapshot of India, of the challenges of developing the world's largest democracy, and of how westernization is reshaping Indian society.'[32] Unlike in the case of disinvestment, the RSS was encouraging, with its number two leader H.V. Sheshadri even formulating routes and policy.

Another area of economic reform that the RSS did not block was telecom, again, because it would improve communication between Indians. Vajpayee's 1999 National Telecom Policy (NTP)[33] allowed more operators into each telecom circle (such as Delhi or Mumbai) as well as shifted the licence regime (i.e., what each operator owed the government) from a fixed amount to revenue sharing.[34] These measures brought more of a market logic, in terms of competition and pricing, into India's hottest sector. As Montek Singh Ahluwalia says: 'The NTP 1999 was absolutely critical. It was a bold decision. Because Vajpayee was changing the terms on which the licences were given, and his minister had even written why this was not the right thing to do.' The changes saved the sector. The first four years of mobile telephony in India, 1995 to 1999, had attracted just 1 million subscribers. But Vajpayee's reforms in 1999 added 12 million more subscribers in the next four years.[35]

The telecom sector, however, became mired in the kind of corruption scandals that the BJP had traditionally accused the Congress of. Reliance Infocomm entered the sector in 2002. A telecom ministry official says: 'It was a mistake. There were a lot of allegations against Reliance. And [telecom minister] Pramod Mahajan was [accused of] tilting everything in favour of Reliance.' The Congress party even made corruption in the telecom sector a political issue.[36] Mahajan had to be shifted from telecom in 2003 and replaced with Arun Shourie, who, in his earlier avatar as a crusading journalist, had taken on Reliance.[37]

The telecom story brought home to Indians that the BJP was no different on corruption than the governments that preceded it. And like the governments that preceded it, its economics was more continuity than change.

For example, while the Vajpayee government did reduce tariff rates from 35 to 29 per cent, this was in keeping with the trend since Manmohan Singh's first budget as finance minister in 1991, one that Vajpayee himself had loudly opposed at the time.[38] And on politically sensitive issues like loosening of labour laws, the government backtracked from its initial determination.[39] In character and strategy, Vajpayee's economics was a carryover from Narasimha Rao's.

Vajpayee shared another trait with Rao. He was not insecure about those who knew more than him. Apart from Arun Shourie, Vajpayee backed Yashwant Sinha from attacks by the RSS as well as certain corporate houses. When pressure to replace Yashwant Sinha as finance minister gained fever pitch in 2002, Vajpayee simply switched him with his foreign minister, Jaswant Singh, and liberalizing reforms continued in the same direction. Yashwant Sinha says: 'In the ministry of finance the most important support you can look for is the prime minister. If he is with you, a lot of things work out. With Vajpayee, it was not that to begin with. But eventually that was the case. That was his great quality. If he liked you he backed you.'[40]

Jaswant Singh, on the other hand, was angry at his removal from his beloved foreign ministry. An aide of his says: 'Jaswant would sit in North Block, in the finance ministry, and he would look out of the window to South Block across the road [where the foreign ministry is housed]. The joke was that it was like Shah Jahan imprisoned in Agra fort looking at his beloved Taj Mahal.' But Jaswant was too loyal a soldier to make his displeasure public.

This handling of the economy makes Vajpayee different from Prime Minister Narendra Modi. Through his tenure, Vajpayee faced withering criticism and alternate points of view—from the RSS, from the opposition, from his own cabinet. But Vajpayee knew when to follow experts, when to follow his own instincts. He knew to always listen to feedback.

* * *

Vajpayee brought this same pragmatism to his international relations. He continued past dealings with the United States, Russia, Iran, and China, following the Narasimha consensus now, just as he had followed the Nehruvian one then.

What might seem like a break from the new consensus was the visit of Ariel Sharon to Delhi in 2003, the first by any Israeli prime minister. This had been preceded by Advani's official visit to Israel, where he was treated like a head of state. Israel of course had been the subject of Hindu nationalist support for decades. As the RSS mouthpiece *Organiser* put it on the eve of Sharon's visit: 'The existence of Israel has important lessons for India especially in the field of defence and on how to influence superpower opinions.'[41] But even this reach out was only a continuation of a growth in ties since 1992, when Narasimha Rao had broken from the Nehruvian consensus and opened full diplomatic relations between both countries.[42] And when Sharon requested Vajpayee to blacklist the head of the Palestinian Liberation Organization (PLO), Yasser Arafat, Vajpayee demurred. Vajpayee was willing to push the boundary, but not cross it.

Another issue on which Vajpayee could have broken from parliament was by sending Indian troops to Iraq in 2003. As part of its war on terror in the aftermath of 9/11, the United States had unilaterally invaded Iraq in March 2003. In a bid to add legitimacy to this occupation, the new US president, George W. Bush, was keen that India send peacekeeping forces.

Deputy Prime Minister L.K. Advani was on an official visit to the United States in June 2003, and would have normally met only his counterpart. But at a meeting between Advani and the US Secretary of State Condoleezza Rice at the White House, the president of the United States decided to 'drop by' and cut straight to the point. Could India send troops to Iraq for peacekeeping?[43] When Advani replied that the cabinet committee on security had met twice to discuss this issue and some questions remained, Bush offered to send a team of experts within a week to Delhi to provide any clarifications.[44]

Advani came back to India, an advocate of sending troops to Iraq. He was backed by Jaswant Singh. 'Advani and Jaswant were totally for sending troops,' Yashwant Sinha remembers, 'I was opposed to it.'[45]

As was much of parliament, which was in a logjam after the Congress and the left insisted that both houses of parliament pass a resolution that would 'condemn' the US invasion. Sensing the attitude of Central Hall, Vajpayee compromised, agreeing to 'deplore' the invasion, a resolution that both houses finally passed.[46]

Vajpayee now decided to pick Central Hall over L.K. Advani and George Bush. The way he did that without upsetting the Americans says much about his political skills.

Jaswant Singh's son Manvendra recalls an incident around 2005, when another prime minister, Manmohan Singh, responded to US pressure and voted against Iran in the International Atomic Energy Agency despite fury from his partners in the left. 'There is a smoking room in parliament. And that is the only classless society I've seen in India—from CPM to Congress to BJP to Shiv Sena, all the way to Vijay Mallya. It's a long room, with wooden doors, and dirty mustard sofas. There is an open door that leads to the courtyard. One afternoon, it was just me and a communist MP. He was in a foul mood. I asked in Bengali, "*Ki hoyechhe?*" He said, "Manvendra, the problem with having a non-political prime minister is that you don't know how to play the political game . . . I remember being part of a delegation to oppose an Indian army division being sent to Iraq [in 2003]. Mr Vajpayee heard of us, and said, '*Aap apna virodh sadakon pe rachaaiyeh.*' Play out your opposition on the streets. And he used our opposition to convey to the West that 'Sorry, our country is against it'."[47]

To his domestic constituency, however, Vajpayee decided to advertise this as his achievement. At an all-party meeting called by Prime Minister Vajpayee in Room 63 in parliament, the Congress president Sonia Gandhi was accompanied by Manmohan Singh and Natwar Singh. Vajpayee began to praise his own government's decision on Iraq. Natwar Singh intervened saying that, 'It was the Congress that prevented you from sending troops to Iraq.' The usually calm prime minister snapped, 'It has become a habit for Natwar Singh to find fault with whatever the government did.' Natwar restrained himself from replying. Three days later a meeting was held at the PM's house. Natwar Singh was also asked to attend. After the meeting, a member of the prime minister's staff came up to Natwar Singh, 'Sir, the PM wishes to meet you.' When he met the PM, Vajpayee said, 'The other day at the meeting in Parliament House, I said too much. I should not have done so.'

'Vajpayeeji was a gentleman politician,' Natwar Singh remembers.[48]

* * *

Vajpayee's foreign and economic policies were shaped primarily by this desire to be liked by parliamentarians. This led to a government that might have been bold on the United States, disinvestment, roads and telecommunication, but took care to remain within the Narasimha consensus. The Vajpayee government's economic and foreign policy showed that it could be trusted to swim in the mainstream.

Like with most other matters of policy (with the exception of Pakistan), Advani was rarely involved here too. And in the few instances in which he expressed a view—on disinvestment, on troops to Iraq—he was overruled. This was of a piece with Vajpayee's treatment of Advani through their years in power. And it was of a piece with Advani's response to other slights and snubs. He chose not to air his wounds. He chose not to take a stand.

This makes the lone instance where the home minister stood up to his prime minister even more noteworthy. As the next chapter shows, the one fight with Vajpayee which Advani refused to back away from was over the newcomer chief minister of Gujarat. It was a tea-seller's son who would burn, and finally extinguish, their five-decade partnership.

16

THE SPECTRE OF
NARENDRA MODI (1999–2004)

The unlikely rise of Narendra Modi began with the kumbh mela, held in Allahabad in January 2001.[1] The twenty million pilgrims and 180,000 sadhus at this edition of the largest religious gathering in the world were an opportune backdrop for the Vishva Hindu Parishad to organize its ninth meeting of spiritual leaders. Resentment at the unkept promises of the Vajpayee government was palpable, and the gathering threatened to build a Ram temple in Ayodhya by the next 'mahashivaratri'.[2] In Gregorian terms, that meant March 2002. A few days later, an earthquake measuring 6.7 on the Richter scale[3] killed 15,000[4] and destroyed 70 per cent of all houses in Kutch in north-west Gujarat.[5]

Though nobody knew it then, these two events—the VHP's call for a temple to be built by March 2002 and the earthquake of January 2001—would set in motion events that would pole-vault Modi to national prominence.

The earthquake was met with a butterfingered response from the heavy-set Gujarat chief minister, Keshubhai Patel. Sudheendra Kulkarni was then an aide to both Vajpayee and Advani. He says: 'In 2001, there was a view that Keshubhai was not an effective administrator. A calamitous earthquake had happened. There was a feeling that the state needed a younger and more capable administrator. I think both Vajpayee and Advani shared this view.'[6]

The other person who shared this view was party general secretary Narendra Modi, who was itching to return to his state after a six-year exile in Delhi. Through this period, Modi had ingratiated himself to L.K. Advani, taking the spot that Govindacharya was vacating. Advani, who took pride in committing train timetables to memory, could relate to Modi's knack for planning. Along with Amit Shah, Modi knew every inch of Advani's Gandhinagar constituency and had helped him win in 1998 and 1999. A friend of Advani says: 'Modi's mentality is pracharak mentality. Advani liked that. He saw politics that way. He was interested in every small detail.'

A colleague at the time says that unlike Govindacharya, Modi took care to never irritate Murli Manohar Joshi or Vajpayee while aligning himself with Advani. Modi had been expelled from Gujarat in 1995 for setting one clique against another, but here in Delhi, he made sure to be everybody's friend. He even cultivated fellow general secretary Arun Jaitley, accompanying him on evening walks in Lodhi Garden. The English-speaking Delhi insider would wear t-shirts, trousers and shoes; Modi would remain in kurta, pajama and chappals.[7] And far from being 'clueless about the ground situation in Gujarat', as he later claimed,[8] Modi kept in touch with the state through Amit Shah, who had become an MLA in 1997. Modi even involved himself in selecting candidates from Gujarat for the 1998 national and state elections, as well as the 1999 national elections.[9]

To the party's leadership, worried about the electoral consequences of the earthquake in Gujarat, Modi presented himself as a consensus figure who could win elections—the very opposite, not coincidentally, of the sitting chief minister.

A few days after the earthquake, Vajpayee and Advani took a flight to Gujarat to survey the extent of the devastation.[10] The Indian Air Force plane was being guarded by the prime minister's Special Protection Group (SPG). A journalist present on the plane remembers, 'We all took the flight from Delhi. In Gandhinagar, we boarded helicopters to see the damage. Narendra Modi was in Gandhinagar airport. But when he went to the helicopter, the SPG did not allow him. They said: "You are not on the list." It was all very embarrassing. Obviously, Modi had inserted himself.'[11]

While Modi was trying his luck in Gujarat, the Vishva Hindu Parishad, formed as a platform for Hindu religious figures, was trying its luck in Ayodhya. In September 2001, the VHP indicated that it had not forgotten its pledge. It once again vowed to build a temple in Ayodhya in six months' time, i.e., by March 2002.[12] Prime Minister Vajpayee responded by promising to settle the dispute by then. Pravin Togadia boasted, 'Media reports on our activities must be weighing on his mind . . .'[13] This was a cat-and-mouse routine. The VHP would announce a specific date to build the temple, then lobby the government for concessions, then, last minute, call off the mobilization.

Two weeks after the VHP's iteration of its resolve, the BJP lost two by-elections in Gujarat. The result in the Sabarmati assembly constituency, where the BJP lost by 18,000 votes,[14] was particularly worrying. L.K. Advani had won that segment of his Lok Sabha constituency by 47,000 votes just two years earlier. He was shaken by this epistle from voters he knew well.[15]

Two days later, a series of meetings were held to discuss Keshubhai's successor as Gujarat chief minister, including a three-hour one at the home of L.K. Advani.[16] While Vajpayee did not consider Advani a partner in government, he was happy to let Advani continue running the party. A decision was made. One of the most senior RSS leaders of the time says: 'It was Advaniji who decided. Vajpayeeji then agreed. But the selection was by Advaniji.'

A few days later, on 1 October 2001, the man selected was asked to meet the prime minister. Atal Bihari Vajpayee began the meeting by joking that Narendra Modi had put on weight, the result of too much 'Punjabi food'. He then asked Modi to go as chief minister to Gujarat to revive the party's electoral fortunes in time for the next assembly elections, scheduled for February 2003.[17]

Modi's own description of the meeting is that 'initially I refused'. The next day he met L.K. Advani, who had already spoken to Vajpayee. Modi recalls: 'Advaniji got angry with me and said why I was being reluctant. How can you refuse after everything has been decided by all of us.'[18]

Yashwant Sinha, then finance minister, says: 'We were worried about losing the state elections in Gujarat. The sanghathan [organization] was always controlled by Advani. Vajpayee was the guest artiste. So it was Advani's bidding to replace Keshubhai, not Vajpayee's.'[19] Arjun Modhwadia, the former Congress leader of the opposition in Gujarat, provides an explanation: 'Advani had been contesting from Gandhinagar for a long time, but he did not control the state [BJP]. Keshubhai . . . Kanshiram [Rana] and others were mass leaders; Advani could not control [them] in the same way. But Narendra Modi was a backroom strategist with no mass base at the time. Advani could control him.'[20]

The selection of Modi as chief minister of Gujarat, so far-reaching for Indian history, was thus based on the two criteria that this book argues defines the Bharatiya Janata Party: an emphasis on organizational unity and an ideology designed to win elections.

In the next few days, Modi signalled that he could meet both benchmarks. He warned of 'harsh decisions' to revive the party's popularity in the state.[21] He also ensured that the outgoing chief minister's favoured ministers were retained in his cabinet.[22]

Unlike in most other parties, Keshubhai acquiesced in his own downfall. He even proposed Modi's name as successor, thereby providing, in the words of the BJP president, 'a shining example of how a *karyakarta* of BJP responds to the call of the organisation'.[23]

In what would, however, mark a break from the muted style of the Bharatiya Janata Party, Modi's inauguration as the fourteenth chief minister of Gujarat was high decibel.[24] Some 50,000 attended, and the oversize purple stage was clothed in flowers. And in a harbinger of Modi's use of technology in the years to come, the function was live-cast on the Internet, a first.[25] Newspapers termed it 'undoubtedly the grandest ever swearing-in ceremony organised for any chief minister'.[26]

* * *

Having, they thought, solved the problem of Gandhinagar through Narendra Modi, Vajpayee and Advani now turned to the problem of Ayodhya, where the VHP was threatening to begin construction of a Ram temple.

Vajpayee invited a group of VHP leaders to meet with him on 27 January 2002. The three-hour meeting was rancorous. A swami told Vajpayee: 'Even the Congress has done more for the Ayodhya cause and the Hindu sentiment than you have.'[27] Vajpayee accused Ashok Singhal of 'threatening' him. As soon as they left the meeting, the VHP held a press conference criticizing Vajpayee and his 'anti-Hindu government'.[28] The BJP replied: 'The VHP can do what it likes, but it'll have to be ready to face legal action.'[29] And on 26 February 2002, the Vajpayee government swore in parliament that no construction would be allowed in the disputed area in Ayodhya.[30]

That very day, a group of VHP activists who had travelled from Gujarat carrying construction material for a new temple boarded coach S-6 of the Sabarmati Express at Ayodhya junction. They were going back to a Gujarat where the ruling party was on the ropes.

Despite the elevation of Modi, the state BJP's electoral fortunes were unimproved. It had lost two by-poll elections to the Congress held barely a week earlier. The third by-poll, from Rajkot, was won by the new chief minister, but with a reduced margin.[31]

The next morning, 27 February 2002, the train carrying these activists halted at Godhra station, 127 kilometres from Ahmedabad. An hour later, Indian politics had fallen off the rails.

* * *

Godhra is a Muslim-majority town in the largely Hindu state of Gujarat. When the train stopped in Godhra station at 7:43 a.m.,[32] local Muslims scuffled with the Hindu activists on board. After one aborted attempt, the train left the platform, but stopped three minutes later. Here a crowd of around 500 Muslims gathered. Soon after, there was a fire inside the train, killing fifty-nine Hindus, most of them activists. While there are competing views on what happened,[33] a government inquiry[34] and the courts of law[35] have held that there was a conspiracy to burn the train conjured the previous night by local Muslims.[36] Saeed Umarji, son of the local preacher and prime accused in the conspiracy, says: 'Yes . . . there was [a] fight, and those around the station who happened to be Muslims may have burnt the train. But why blame all Muslims?'[37]

The new chief minister was informed an hour later. He helicoptered into Godhra to inspect the burnt coach. Families of those dead had begun to reach Godhra. But the bodies were handed over to the VHP, not the

families, who decided to parade them across the state the next day. Such
a move was reminiscent of the Vajpayee government's decision to parade
the bodies of soldiers killed in Kargil three years ago.

Narendra Modi returned to Gandhinagar and called a meeting of
his senior officials that night. The contents of the meeting are disputed.
A senior BJP leader told an unofficial committee of retired judges that
'Mr. Narendra Modi, CM, made it clear that there would be backlash
from the Hindus on the next day and that the police should not come in
their way'.[38] However, the Supreme Court-appointed special investigation
team,[39] the state government-appointed Nanavati commission,[40] and,
finally, the courts[41] found no evidence against Narendra Modi.

An explicit direction was perhaps not necessary. The VHP, RSS and
BJP had called an unofficial shutdown or bandh for the next day, 28
February. The police took this as official. The next morning, VHP youth
began preparing catalogues of shops owned by Muslims. The head of its
Gujarat unit admitted: 'In the morning we sat down and prepared the
list.'[42] The police simply looked on, since 'some of them were Hindus who
thought, let the mob do whatever it wants . . . we were terribly angry. Lust
and anger are blind.'[43]

Hindu nationalism had been created in the 1920s, driven in part by
the fear of effete Hindus being beaten up by tough Muslims on the street.
Eighty years later in Gujarat, fifty-nine Hindus had been burnt to death.
Muslims needed to be taught a lesson.

* * *

Approximately, 944 kilometres away in New Delhi, Vajpayee and Advani
were listening to their finance minister, Yashwant Sinha, deliver his budget
in parliament. They were expecting a battering on the economy by the
opposition. What they had not bargained for was an outburst by their own
MPs, two of whom warned Advani: 'Only those who talk about Hindu
welfare will be able to rule the country.'[44] Some BJP MPs began chanting
inside parliament: 'Hang those who killed the *Ram Bhakts* [in Godhra].'
Advani faced them with folded hands.[45]

At around this time, Hindu mobs began to surround Muslim localities
across Gujarat. They reached Gulbarg Society in Ahmedabad, home to

Ehsan Jaffrey. Jaffrey had been one of the few Congressmen to win a Lok Sabha seat in the 1977 elections. He had watched from the opposition benches while the new foreign minister Atal Bihari Vajpayee orated from the front benches. Still a presence in Gujarat, Jaffrey had campaigned against chief minister Narendra Modi just a few weeks earlier in Rajkot.[46]

As the violence spread that morning, Muslims from elsewhere sought shelter inside Gulbarg Society, leading Jaffrey to make frantic calls to the entire Gujarat establishment. He even called up the chief minister's office. His wife alleges that he got through to Modi, who abused Jaffrey on the phone. This specific allegation was rejected by both the SIT and the trial court.[47] Meanwhile, by 1:30 p.m., the crowd had entered the colony and set the ground floor of Jaffrey's house on fire.

Ehsan Jaffrey stepped out to face the hordes. His daughter described what happened to her father in the minutes that followed: 'They cut his legs and his hands, while he was still alive. Then the final blow, as the witnesses described, was to his head. They hung his head on a "trishul" or trident and paraded it around saying, incredibly, "Jai Shree Ram, Jai Shree Krishna."'[48] According to the court, the mob 'burnt him alive in a fashion that there was no possibility of any remnant of the body'.[49]

Violence had spread across Gujarat by now, but more than any other incident, the murder of Ehsan Jaffrey shocked Lutyens' Delhi. The former parliamentarian was, after all, one of them. L.K. Advani told his aide: 'I do not want a Hindu Taliban.'[50] The next day he would say: 'The killing of Jaffrey and his family members has shaken me.' [51]

A delegation of MPs visited Godhra just a few hours after Jaffrey was dismembered. They included the Trinamool party's Dinesh Trivedi. 'I called up the chief minister and asked: "Narendrabhai, what has happened?" Modi sounded nervous. "Dineshbhai, why hasn't [defence minister] George [Fernandes] sent the army."'[52]

Around the same time in Delhi, a Congress delegation met the prime minister. They asked about sending the army. George Fernandes replied that 'the chief minister has to ask . . . he has not asked'. Under India's Constitution, the army could be deployed only 'in aid of the civil power', i.e., with the consent of the state government.[53]

A few hours after this meeting, a fax arrived at the prime minister's house signed by the chief minister of Gujarat. George Fernandes left early morning for Gandhinagar and headed straight to Modi's office.[54] There he met Modi as well as Lieutenant General Zameer Uddin Shah. The highest-ranking Muslim in the army, and brother of actor Naseeruddin Shah, had been tasked with restoring the peace. Shah handed Modi a list of requirements, such as buses and cars. Troops began to arrive by Indian Air Force planes around 7 a.m. But they were stranded on the airfield as the Gujarat state government delayed providing transport. Shah remembers: 'We just stayed helplessly in the airfield for almost 34 hours. We could hear gunshots but do nothing.'[55]

Modi seemed just as stranded that morning. The journalist Sheela Bhatt went to see him at the chief minister's residence at bungalow number one in Raj Bhavan enclave, Gandhinagar. The house resembled a fortress. Inside, there were just two people, Narendra Modi and the bureaucrat Anil Mukim. She met him in his office, a small building attached to the larger house. 'Modi came out as a person totally shaken up. He had just become CM five months back. We spoke about the government machinery to deal with the riots. Modi was struggling to get a grip on the situation. He was majorly worried that Hindu society was turning against him. He was the first [RSS] pracharak to become CM. And VHP was taunting: "See what has happened to our kar sevaks." Modi was concerned about the Hindu people's wrath. He did not seem like a ruthless operator conducting pre-planned riots. He had been physically hit on the back by an angry Hindu in Godhra when he had gone to inspect the burnt train. I could see that he was really frightened.'[56]

A few hours later on the same day, George Fernandes visited a police kiosk. The police wireless was on when he entered. What he heard stunned him. He later told a friend, 'I heard the voice of some BJP MLAs directing the violence, telling the police not to do anything.' This friend remembers: 'He told me he didn't think Modi was directly involved. He seemed clueless. But his cabinet members, some of them, were directly [involved].'

The anti-Muslim riots would eventually affect 151 towns and 993 villages,[57] and kill 1272 people. These would include 790 Muslims, 254 Hindus, and 228 missing who have now been classified as dead.[58] An estimated 100,000 Muslims and 40,000 Hindus were also displaced.[59] The scholars Raheel Dhattiwala and Michael Biggs have found that the violence was least in areas where the BJP was either electorally weak or strong, but most in areas where the BJP and Congress were in close contest.[60]

Even more telling was the role played by Dalits and Tribals in the violence. Scholars had so far theorized communal violence as an upper-caste Hindu phenomenon.[61] But this time around, hatred of Muslims was unifying Hindus from all castes.[62] Such large-scale participation—unlike in the case of the 1984 anti-Sikh riots in Delhi—led to the supposition, in the initial days at least, that what made these riots different were the sheer numbers of ordinary Gujaratis who took part.

Though there was plenty of anger against the state government, that rage was yet to coalesce around its chief minister. Modi had not held a single government position before becoming chief minister just months ago. And with violence receding and the army gaining control, Modi might have escaped charges of personal culpability.

Any chance of this narrative taking hold evaporated on the morning of 7 March 2002, when an op-ed article appeared in India's most respected national newspaper, *The Hindu*. The article was titled 'The Guilty Men of Ahmedabad'.[63]

* * *

The piece was written by Harish Khare, a journalist who had worked in Ahmedabad and would later become Prime Minister Manmohan Singh's media advisor. He wrote: 'Never before has a State Government been so guilty of siding . . . with the rioter as happened in Ahmedabad and the rest of Gujarat.' He listed three reasons for this collapse of state authority, but minced no words in naming the principal culprit: 'The presence of an activist *kar sevak* in the Chief Minister's post.'[64]

Just a few hours after its publication, Sonia Gandhi led a protest outside the main gate of parliament that attracted politicians from across the opposition. No slogans were raised; instead, placards were wordlessly held demanding the resignation of Narendra Modi.[65] The next day, 8 March 2002, a delegation of MPs from across parties visited Gujarat. They refused to meet the chief minister, claiming that he 'was the culprit in the entire episode and there was no meaning of listening to his explanations'.[66]

From then on, every conversation on the Gujarat riots would be reduced to one facet: the guilt of Narendra Modi. On this, the opposition, the English-language media and the international press seemed united. Even Vajpayee's coalition allies—the TDP and Jayalalithaa—threatened to bring down the central government if Modi wasn't brought down.[67]

The demand to sack Modi united a second group. The VHP, RSS and BJP cadre saw the violence entirely through the prism of Godhra. Of what use was Hindu unity as an electoral strategy if it could not protect Hindus from Muslims on the ground? A senior VHP leader demanded that '. . . the Central and State Governments should own up moral responsibility and resign'.[68] Vajpayee had to personally meet with the RSS chief Sudarshan and VHP head Ashok Singhal. But the conversation was not about bringing these organizations to book for their role in the riots. Instead, the prime minister pleaded that they postpone the kar seva in Ayodhya.[69] When the Supreme Court refused to allow permission,[70] it was left to L.K. Advani to beg the VHP to not violate the law. The mahant he spoke to says: 'I told him to drive some sense into Atalji.'[71]

The VHP finally agreed to postpone the ceremony in Ayodhya. But they had a condition. In meeting after meeting, Advani was told that Modi's ouster was unacceptable. Hindutva politicians such as Bal Thackeray also told him to not sack Modi.[72] The RSS even passed a resolution saying: 'Let Muslims understand that their real safety lies in the goodwill of the majority.' Explaining the resolution, the RSS spokesman defended the Modi government and ruled out the chief minister's resignation.[73]

An Ahmedabad-based journalist says: 'In [the film] *Guide*, Dev Anand is sleeping by a temple during night. It is cold and a sadhu takes pity and puts a shawl over him. The shawl happens to be saffron in colour. Next morning, the villagers come and think Dev Anand is a sadhu. They begin to worship him. [Secular critics of Modi like] Rajdeep Sardesai and others put a saffron shawl on Modi. And suddenly he became a holy man.'[74]

In the space of just a month, the new chief minister, uncertain and afraid, had been elevated to not just the spectre haunting liberal India, but the cause célèbre of Hindu India.

By early March 2002, therefore, the Vajpayee government was caught between two forces. Parliamentary, secular, liberal India was making the sacking of Modi the litmus test for their vision of India. And Hindu nationalist India was making it the test for theirs. Vajpayee and Advani had so far represented each of these conceptions of India. Had they been united on the question of what to do about Modi, they could perhaps have found a way to navigate even this conflict. But, by March 2002, Vajpayee and Advani's fifty-year-long partnership was already under stress. And Narendra Modi was leading it to breaking point.

*　*　*

'The thing about Advaniji,' Ravindra Bhagwat says, 'is that once he makes up his mind, he does not change. He might not insist. But on [a matter of] principle he does not change.'[75] Advani's first reaction to the violence was the same as that of Vajpayee: genuine horror. But a week into the riots, Advani was veering towards defending Narendra Modi, publicly stating that 'never before in Gujarat . . . had such communal violence been controlled within 72 hours'.[76] He even contrasted Modi's actions to the ruling Congress's response during the anti-Sikh riots. While not a single rioter was killed by the police in 1984, the Gujarat police had killed a hundred rioters on the first day itself.[77]

Advani was seeing that the very actions that had horrified liberal India had endeared Modi to the party cadre. A relative provides another reason for Advani's decision to protect Modi. 'We were losing Gujarat. We needed a victory there.'

While Advani's primary audience had always been the party, for Vajpayee it was parliament. The eleven-time MP had been shaped by his forty-five years there, and was sensitive to accusations hurled on the floor of the House. Through March 2002, he sat seething in the front benches as speaker after speaker stood up to ridicule the 'secular' image that Vajpayee had spent decades cultivating. On 20 March, for example, there was uproar in the Lok Sabha that the violence in Gujarat, which seemed to have subsided, was continuing. Action against Narendra Modi was demanded from parties as varied as the Congress, IUML, Samajwadi Party and RJD.[78] A few days later, the National Human Rights Commission slammed Modi for inaction.[79] These comments, by a statutory body headed by a former chief justice, were seized by the opposition as proof that the prime minister was covering up murder. Just as Advani had made up his mind listening to his party, Vajpayee was making up his mind listening to his parliament.

Around this time, Foreign Minister Jaswant Singh got a call. Parliament was in session, and Vajpayee's parliamentary secretary, Pramod Mahajan, begged him to rush across, saying *'sambhaliye, sambhaliye'*. Handle him, handle him. Jaswant hurried to Vajpayee's parliamentary office. In his presence, the prime minister took a piece of paper and started writing his resignation by hand. 'I held his hand,' Jaswant later recounted. 'He looked at me severely and said: "What are you doing."' Somehow, Jaswant Singh persuaded him to remain.[80]

So frequently, in fact, did Vajpayee consider resigning over the Gujarat riots that his daughter Gunu began to joke: 'Baapji, you waited to be prime minister for a long time. And now you are prime minister, you do not want it.'[81]

Vajpayee now contemplated another approach. Through that month, Modi's ouster was debated on television sets. An English-language anchor says: 'Most of the BJP people did not want to come on TV. We only got some sadhus . . . they were not credible.' One of the lone defenders of Narendra Modi on television was Prafull Goradia. To the assertion that Modi must go, Goradia replied: 'Narendra Modi is not your branch manager; he is the elected chief minister of Gujarat.'[82] Soon after, Goradia got a phone call from the prime minister's office. The voice said, 'Modi is no bhai or bhatija, no brother or nephew, of yours; why are you sticking up for him?' Sources in the prime minister's office say that the call was made by Sudheendra Kulkarni, on the express orders of Pramod Mahajan and the acquiescence of Atal Bihari Vajpayee. When asked, Kulkarni does not confirm or deny this allegation.[83]

On 28 March 2002, Vajpayee summoned the Gujarat chief minister for a meeting in Delhi. Modi came armed, not with contrition, but with an opinion poll predicting that if elections were conducted in Gujarat immediately (rather than a year later, when they were scheduled), the BJP would win two-thirds of the assembly seats.[84] Just a month ago, Modi was a newcomer. In the thirty days since, he had become the most popular politician in Gujarat.

Advani agreed with Modi, but Vajpayee did not. Though electoral calculations had also shaped his politics, this was a bridge too far. The prime minister turned down Modi's request for immediate elections.[85]

The rift between Vajpayee and Advani was now complete. What was a frayed personal relationship in the last few years had now become a ruptured professional partnership. Even Advani admits: 'Although Atalji had not expressed his view explicitly on this matter, I knew that he favoured Modi's resignation. And he knew I disfavoured it.'[86]

A few days later, it was announced to the press that Vajpayee would be visiting Gujarat to inspect the rehabilitation efforts personally. Unlike his tour after the earthquake last year, Vajpayee did not ask Advani to accompany him. The message was loud: Vajpayee was setting the scene for the removal of Narendra Modi.

* * *

The Indian air force flight carrying the prime minister took off for Gandhinagar on the morning of Thursday, 4 April 2002. While Advani was absent, Vajpayee was accompanied by other members of his cabinet. They were received at the airport by Chief Minister Narendra Modi. Vajpayee then left for Godhra in a convoy of three helicopters, where he inspected the burnt train carriage numbered S-6.[87]

He flew back to Gandhinagar a few hours later and drove in a large convoy that included Narendra Modi to Shah Alam refugee camp, located in the Muslim quarter of Ahmedabad. Housed here were 9000 Muslims, exiles in their own land.[88] Minutes before the PM's motorcade entered, camp coordinators instructed angry refugees: 'Islam discourages rude behaviour towards a guest. This is your house and Modi is a guest. So control yourselves . . .'[89]

The sight of refugees in their own land unnerved the prime minister. One Muslim told her prime minister how rioters had hacked her brother in bed, bathed him in acid and then burnt him alive.[90] Another described how he had seen fifty people butchered metres from the local police station. 'You must replace the chief minister,' he said.[91] As Vajpayee ran his hand over the head of an orphan child, a young man pointed to Modi, positioned respectfully behind Vajpayee, and screamed: 'He is the killer.'[92]

As the prime minister's convoy left the camp, he could hear the crowds chanting slogans against Modi. Arun Jaitley, who was part of Vajpayee's delegation, heard a different message: 'After we left Shah Alam, our driver told us to roll down the windows. And we heard cries of "Narendra Modi zindabad".'[93] Long live Narendra Modi. While Vajpayee was seeing only a beleaguered minority, the rest of his cabinet were sensing a uniting majority.

At Gandhinagar airport, Modi by his side, Vajpayee was asked by the journalist Priya Sehgal what advice he had for the chief minister. Vajpayee paused, as was his wont. He then chose his words carefully: 'I have only one message for the chief minister, that he follow raj dharma [the king's dharma].' 'Raj dharma,' Vajpayee repeated, as Narendra Modi looked away, in half grimace half grin. 'A king should not discriminate between his subjects.' As the full import of the very public admonishment sunk in, Modi frowned. He interrupted Vajpayee's declamation with, 'That is what we are doing, boss.' Vajpayee paused again. He took his time before adding: 'I trust that this is what Narendrabhai is doing.'[94]

* * *

Vajpayee returned to Delhi still veering towards sacking Modi, but unable to take the final step. He was scheduled to travel to Singapore and Cambodia from 7 to 11 April 2002. The flight to Singapore, from the Palam technical area to Changi airport, is a short one. But it was a long journey for Vajpayee.

The plane had been reconfigured to create a private room for the prime minister—with two-three chairs, a table and a bed—while ministers and bureaucrats sat in a common area outside. Suddenly, Vajpayee's son-in-law Ranjan Bhattacharya came to Arun Shourie, the disinvestment minister who was accompanying Vajpayee, and said: 'Please go and meet him. Baapji is terribly upset.'[95]

Shourie darted into the private room to see the leader of the world's largest democracy slouched on his chair. 'He looked up and signalled for me to sit. [Then] he resumed that posture. He was angry,' Shourie remembers. 'Why am I being sent [abroad]?' Vajpayee said. 'My face has been blackened.' Shourie advised him: 'When you reach [Singapore], call Advani and tell him to ask Modi to resign.'[96]

They reached that evening and checked into the Shangri-La Hotel in central Singapore. At the top of the thirty-eight-floor building is a lounge restaurant called Marco Polo; one side of the restaurant has a glass wall providing panoramic views of the skyscrapers around. The Indian High Commission had booked the entire restaurant for their prime minister and his delegation.

Arun Shourie went to dinner early. Vajpayee was already there, standing by the glass wall, back towards the room, staring down at the urban vista. Shourie walked towards Vajpayee expecting a confirmation that he had called Advani and ordered Modi's sacking. Instead, Vajpayee told the approaching Shourie: 'Look below. *Mein yahaan ayaa karta tha. Yeh Kalkatta ke jaise tha. Dekho, yeh chamatkaar hai. Ek aadmi nein kya kiya hai.*'[97] I used to keep coming here. This place was like Calcutta. See, this is a miracle. See what one man has done.

On every remaining day of the trip, Vajpayee considered but never called Advani to demand Modi's resignation. An upset Shourie asked an accompanying diplomat, 'Why is Atalji not calling Advani.' The diplomat replied: 'He is afraid of being told "no".'

Why was Vajpayee afraid of provoking his oldest friend? Arun Shourie has an answer: 'It's like the daughter-in-law who has suffered for all these years. The mother-in-law fears that if the daughter-in-law is provoked into finally opening her mouth, she won't stop.'[98]

The mother-in-law decided on yet another strategy. On his return flight to Delhi on 11 April 2002, the prime minister held a press conference on board. When asked about Modi, Vajpayee replied that he would 'deliberate on the fate of Gujarat Chief Minister Narendra Modi on his return to New Delhi but would first consult his colleagues'.[99] Vajpayee also referred to the Goa national executive of the BJP to be held in the next two days, 12 and 13 April 2002. Meanwhile, officials leaked to the media that 'the prime minister had decided to replace Modi'.[100] A senior BJP leader says, 'Some of us knew that Vajpayeeji would want Modi's resignation [in Goa]. The one person we knew who did not want it was Advaniji. We didn't know how the two of them would handle [it].'[101]

* * *

The flight to Goa left Delhi the next day, Vajpayee and Advani on board. A last-minute addition was Arun Shourie. Brajesh Mishra had rung him up the previous night. 'You don't know the two of them,' Brajesh told Shourie. 'They won't talk. That's why I am sending you and the Major [Jaswant Singh].'

The air force plane they were travelling in was smaller than the refitted Air India jumbo jets used for Vajpayee's trip abroad. There was no private room for the prime minister, just a small cabin with a table and four chairs. An assortment of the day's newspapers was arranged on the table. Their headlines identified the elephant in that tiny room. *The Hindu* carried three articles on Modi's possible fate in Goa. Its front page declared: 'If several speakers demand [in the Goa meeting] that he [Modi] be thrown out, that would be a signal that perhaps the Prime Minister himself wants to sack him.'[102] *The Times of India* went one step further, quoting officials to say that the PM had decided to sack Modi.[103] *The Indian Express*, read by Lutyens elites, also reported about 'the prime minister having made up his mind to remove chief minister Narendra Modi'.[104] As Vajpayee and Advani sat facing each other on the flight to Goa, the newspapers between them had spoken their minds.

As the flight took off, Vajpayee picked up a Hindi paper and began reading, thus sealing Advani from view. Advani then picked up an English paper, creating another barrier.

After years of being taken for granted by Vajpayee, Advani was taking a stand.

Jaswant Singh and Arun Shourie looked at each other. Then Shourie took the paper from Vajpayee's hand and said: 'You can always read the paper. For the last three days, you wanted to talk to Advaniji. Do it now.'[105]

More silence.

Advani remembers Vajpayee breaking it with '*kam se kam isteefe ka offer to karte*'.[106] Modi should have at least offered to resign. Advani replied tentatively, saying that Modi's resignation would not improve the situation in Gujarat and he was not sure if the party would accept the offer.[107] Jaswant Singh remembers Advani saying that Modi's resignation would result in a '*bawaal*' or 'upheaval' within the party.[108] The flight ended with an agreement that Vajpayee's views would prevail. Advani would work out the modalities of getting Modi to resign.

* * *

The flight landed in Goa and the officials and politicians dispersed. They regathered at the Marriot Hotel that evening, in a hall teeming with around 250 national executive members. Three people sat on stage in front: Prime Minister Atal Bihari Vajpayee, Home Minister L.K. Advani, and party president Jana Krishnamurthy. In the middle of the rows of audience members sat Narendra Modi.

It had been decided that the riots would only be discussed the next day.[109] But right after the president's speech in the beginning, Modi stood up. He gave a long speech defending his actions. Then he said: 'I have taken a decision. No harm should come to the party. So I have decided to give a resignation letter from the position of chief minister.' So far all was going according to Vajpayee's script.

Then all of a sudden, the actors began reading from another script.

Many national executive members began to chant, 'Modi should not go.' Speaker after speaker got up to defend Modi. There were chants of 'Modi, Modi'. In the ensuing commotion, Vajpayee's bemused face on stage was visible. Worried about the evening slipping out of his control, Vajpayee ended the discussion with: 'Let's talk about it tomorrow. Now there is a public meeting.'

Vajpayee had assumed that the evening would be orchestrated by Advani to ensure Modi's resignation. Finance Minister Yashwant Sinha was among those present, and feels that the crowd response betrayed orchestration of a different kind. 'It was not spontaneous. It was planned. We knew beforehand that Modi would offer his resignation and [the] crowd would oppose, and the resignation would not be accepted. Advani knew about it. He planned it [along] with Arun Jaitley, Venkaiah Naidu.'[110] Sudheendra Kulkarni, who was close to both Advani and Vajpayee, says: 'Vajpayee saw the mood and feeling at the national executive. That led him to change his mind, apart from Advani's strong view in this matter. Some of this was orchestrated of course.'[111] As Dinesh Trivedi says, 'With Modi it's never spontaneous. There must have been an orchestration.'[112]

The previous day, Arun Jaitley had flown to Gandhinagar where he had met Narendra Modi in the evening. A BJP insider says that Jaitley was acting on Advani's instructions. Modi and Jaitley had then flown together the next morning to Goa.[113] A BJP leader in Gujarat says, 'I was not there [at the meeting between Jaitley and Modi] but I know the conversation was about the next day's Goa meeting.' Though this leader cannot say for certain, he suspects that Jaitley and Modi identified those who would publicly speak in Modi's favour the next day.

Faced with these protests, Vajpayee backed down. Yashwant Sinha explains: 'One trait of Vajpayee's character I've noticed is that he will push his point till one position, and after that he will go by consensus. Advani represented the consensus within the party.'[114] As Vajpayee told his friend R.V. Pandit, with whom he had dinner in his Cuffe Parade flat on the way back from Goa: 'I wanted Modi gone, but Advaniji was against it.' Pandit adds: 'On organization matters, Vajpayee always deferred to Advani.'[115]

Instead, Vajpayee backed the final resolution of the national executive. In it, the party rejected Modi's resignation, thanked him for his 'firmness and promptitude' in dealing with the violence and agreed with Modi's request that fresh elections be held in Gujarat immediately.[116] Vajpayee had rejected this request two weeks earlier.[117] He now acquiesced.

Vajpayee addressed a public meeting later that evening. The man who just a few hours ago was bent on sacking Modi for violence against Muslims, now had this to say: 'Once Islam meant tolerance and compassion, now it means forcing your opinion through terror . . .'[118] He added: 'They don't mix with the society, they are not interested in living in peace.'[119]

The Congress leader P. Chidambaram wrote: 'It is difficult to believe that a prime minister would actually utter those words.'[120] So uncharacteristic was this speech that it was left to Advani to mollify the government's coalition allies the next day, making it appear that Vajpayee and Advani had swapped roles in Goa.[121]

* * *

Vajpayee's surrender in Goa emboldened the Gujarat chief minister. In a hurried state cabinet meeting on 18 July 2002, Narendra Modi dissolved the state assembly and ordered elections six months in advance. He continued as a 'caretaker' chief minister in the meantime.

L.K. Advani, also emboldened, defended his protégé's decision in parliament a few days later. He argued: 'The manner in which Mr. Modi "firmly" put down violence in Gujarat had never been done during the past 50 years.'[122] A sulking Vajpayee detected yet another conspiracy. A cabinet minister said, 'The PM has told some of us that Narendra Modi would never have tried to pull off this stunt of resigning in between assembly terms if [Arun] Jaitley had not advised him to do so.'[123]

Modi's request for early elections had to be filtered through India's independent Election Commission, led at the time by a man of resolute integrity. Chief Election Commissioner J.M. Lyngdoh sent a team to Gujarat to investigate whether early elections were feasible in a state with continuing violence and Muslim refugees. After visiting the state, the Commission decided against early elections, scheduling them for December 2002 instead.[124]

Breaking the political consensus that the Election Commission was above partisan bickering, a slighted Modi referred to 'James Michael' Lyngdoh's full name to underline his Christian faith and even called him an 'Italian'. Both Vajpayee and Murli Manohar Joshi pulled up Modi for his 'improper language'.[125] Advani, however, continued to back Modi, and wanted the union cabinet to send a presidential reference to the Supreme Court to overturn the Election Commission decision. At a cabinet meeting on 18 August 2002, Vajpayee had to defer to Advani, though he contemplated resigning. This fresh rupture between Vajpayee and Advani was temporarily sutured when the Supreme Court upheld the Election Commission's decision against early polls.[126] A relieved Vajpayee publicly praised the Election Commission.

It was convenient to do so, as the Congress's Jaipal Reddy says. 'In Goa, the fanatics were trying to overtake him. And Vajpayee, when he can't beat them, not just joins the pack but actually leads it.' Vajpayee's backing for the EC now 'is because the poll schedule has been announced and the EC has given a ruling which cannot be questioned. So he can speak up as a liberal'.[127]

* * *

The campaign for the December 2002 Gujarat elections was different from any election in Indian history. A Gujarat-based Congress leader says: 'The 2002 elections were unique. It was an experiment. I would agree that no other election BJP or Jana Sangh had fought until then was like that. The election was all about communalism. It was very clear.' The state BJP saw the elections as an opportunity to avenge the Godhra train burning: 'It's a fight between Hindus and Muslims. We will take revenge for Feb 27 on Dec 12.'[128] The VHP even planned a 'Vijay Yatra' with a replica of the charred S-6 coach.[129] When the Election Commission banned this, the VHP resorted to distributing t-shirts of the Godhra train carnage to voters.[130]

In what would become a recurring pattern in Modi's campaigning, he played up Hindu demographic fears of Muslims producing more children. He declaimed: 'We do not want to continue to run relief camps to produce children', and 'They keep on giving birth to long queues of children, who keep repairing cycle punctures everywhere. We must teach a lesson to those who multiply like this.'[131] The few Muslim leaders in the BJP were told not to campaign.[132] In the last two state elections, the BJP had nominated a lone Muslim candidate for Gujarat's 182 seats. Modi did away with even this tokenism. For the 2002 elections, not a single Muslim was given a ticket by the BJP.

The Congress was caricatured as the 'Muslim League',[133] with the VHP placing front-page ads in Gujarati newspapers reproducing leaflets by the All India Muslim Ulema Council asking Muslims to vote for the Congress.[134] Modi said, 'We brought Narmada waters during *shravan* [monsoons], but the Congress would have wanted it in *Ramzan*.'[135]

In the midst of the campaigning, two Muslim terrorists attacked the iconic Swaminarayan temple in Gandhinagar and killed thirty people. Unlike Godhra, Akshardham did not provoke riots. Narendra Modi, however, used this incident to buttress his credentials as the only man who could protect Gujaratis from Muslims and Pakistan. Voters now began to view national security as a key issue during the elections, with one saying: 'We'll feed ourselves but we need Modi to fight terrorism.'[136]

The Gujarat unit of the Congress party read the writing on the wall. It appointed as its chief ministerial candidate Shankersinh Vaghela, who had been the architect of Hindu consolidation in the state when he was in the BJP. Congress chief Sonia Gandhi even began her campaigning with a trip to Ambaji temple in north Gujarat,[137] and Congress leaders were careful to not be seen with Muslims.[138] Faced with a uniting Hindu vote bank, the Congress behaved like it had in the 1980s.

If Modi's campaign was marked by an unprecedented pandering to religion, it also showed a sophisticated understanding of caste dynamics that both Vajpayee and Advani lacked. As previous chapters have chronicled, the BJP had traditionally treated caste as a problem to be underplayed. Modi, on the other hand, saw it as an electoral opportunity.

The son of a tea-seller, Narendra Modi came from the 'Modh Ghanchi' caste, traditionally engaged in small-scale oil pressing.[139] Though socially middle caste, Modh Ghanchis were categorized as state backward castes only in 1994, and included in the central OBC list in September 2001, one month before Modi became chief minister.[140] Arjun Modhwadia says, 'Modi is not [socially] an OBC. His caste is closer to trader caste.'[141] This is perhaps why Modi did not deploy his OBC status while campaigning in Gujarat. When a Congressman said in the state assembly, 'We are proud our CM is an OBC', Modi made his displeasure known through categorical statements by BJP MLAs.[142]

However much Modi downplayed it at the time, the fact that he was not 'twice-born' made him more sensitive to the psychological pull of caste compared to Vajpayee and Advani. He wooed Dalits by citing Ambedkar,[143] and tribals[144] by chanting Hindutva.

Assisting Modi's reach out to Dalits were Mayawati and Kanshi Ram. The BSP was in alliance with the BJP in Delhi and UP, and as Mayawati's biographer Ajoy Bose says: 'Both Mayawati and Kanshi Ram were clear: "we will do anything to come back to power". So it was a clear quid pro quo with the BJP. Mayawati and Kanshi Ram never bothered about history. They didn't think in those terms—that this would be the rise of Modi. They were functional politicians.'[145] Modi had also learnt from the KHAM (Kshatriyas, Harijans, Adivasis and Muslims) alliance of the early 1980s that his party had to accept caste reservations as the price for middle-caste votes, a learning he would put to use as prime minister when he did more for reservations than any before him.

Narendra Modi had also internalized, indeed lionized, Ram Manohar Lohia's critique of upper-caste Hinduism. Unlike Ambedkar, Lohia had seen the solution to casteism as middle-caste consolidation *within* Hinduism, not without. This was very much Narendra Modi's view. For these elections, he lured middle castes, all the while using the bogey of Pakistan and Muslims to speak to Hindus of all castes.

As the campaigning entered its home stretch in December 2002, it became embarrassingly apparent that L.K. Advani's rallies were attracting thin crowds. The party had to cancel Murli Manohar Joshi's rally for fear of a poor turnout. Even the prime minister's rallies were moved to the evening. Modi rallies, in contrast, were where the crowds were.[146] Helping plan these rallies was the thirty-eight-year-old Amit Shah.[147] A fellow MLA says: 'Shah may not have got a formal post. But he was the only one Modi trusted [in the campaign].'

As voting day approached, the VHP's vice-president, Giriraj Kishore, was asked whether he would support the BJP. He chose his reply with care: 'The VHP is with Chief Minister Narendra Modi.'[148] Outside the party office, a full-length cut-out of Modi glared at party workers. Inside, Arun Jaitley, the man who had plotted to save Modi in Goa, plotted once more to keep Modi in power.[149]

Abetting Modi in his self-projection was television, a medium that had grown from one government channel to 300 private channels in just a decade.[150] The media scholar and journalist Nalin Mehta says: 'Probably the only chief minister in India to have completed a TV management course, Narendra Modi proved particularly adept at manipulating television [during the 2002 elections].'[151] His controversial statements seemed designed to keep him in the news, every day, every hour. He also packaged his provocations in pithy sentences that could be amplified on television. When Modi realized that there were thirty non-Gujarati journalists from Delhi providing 'live' coverage to one of his rallies, he moved from speaking in Gujarati to Hindi.[152] Though his immediate audience struggled to connect, television worked as a 'force multiplier' to broadcast Modi's image nationally. He was everywhere.

The national-level BJP was waking up to the fact that they were being swallowed by a man who, barely a year ago, was a nobody. Vajpayee and Advani had assumed that Modi's fate was a power struggle *between them*; they had not countenanced that it would transform into a power struggle between the two of them on one side, and Modi on the other. When asked to consider the possibility that Modi would soon lead the national BJP, Pramod Mahajan responded: 'Do the rest of us wear bangles? You think we have spent decades in politics to now hand it all over to somebody who walks in through the backdoor?'[153]

Voting began on 12 December at 8 a.m. and ended at 5 p.m., in 36,657 polling booths protected by 55,000 armed guards.[154] Opinion polls suggested a close contest.[155] The *Times of India* presciently argued: 'The state's 32 million voters could well determine the course of national politics in nine hours of polling.'[156]

* * *

When the votes were counted two days later, Narendra Modi's party had won 127 out of the 182 seats in the Gujarat legislature—the highest the BJP has ever won in that state. The demographics of the Modi voter in this election, revealed through surveys, is important to decipher since they would form the template for Modi's vote bank in the years to come.

A majority of Hindus voted for Modi, while Muslims did not. Within Hindus, the more religious the voter, the more likely she was to vote BJP.[157] Upper castes overwhelmingly voted for the BJP, while Dalits, Muslims and Tribals tended to vote Congress. Where the BJP was able to tilt the caste balance was through support among the backward castes.[158] The class composition of the voter in this election was also telling. While the rich and wealthy supported the BJP, the poor voter was split between the Congress and BJP. What cut through all of this was the personal popularity of Modi. Though he had been chief minister for barely a year, voters found him effective and a performer.

The other factor that influenced voters was the lingering effect of the riots. Data shows that the BJP's biggest successes were in areas which had seen the most violence.[159]

The results scotched not just talk of Modi being replaced; they provided a new model for the BJP to replicate nationwide.

Where Vajpayee–Advani had dog-whistled on religion—anxious to appeal to both core voters as well as moderate Hindus—Modi had made his election explicitly about Muslims and Pakistan. Where Vajpayee–Advani ignored caste, Modi catered to caste at the booth level while projecting a pan-Hindu solidarity at the state level. And where Vajpayee–Advani emphasized teamwork and joint leadership, Modi had made the elections about himself alone.

'The success of Vajpayee and Advani,' Prafull Goradia says, 'was that they were able to convince the RSS fellows that we cannot come to power alone. So we have to have moderation as well as Hindutva. For that you need both Advani and Vajpayee.'[160] This was the logic that bound them together, despite so many upheavals in their relationship. Modi's 2002 assembly elections upended that logic.

The Hindu voter of 1971 had changed come 2002. This meant that Hindu nationalism could succeed in its twin endeavours—winning elections and uniting Hindus—without resorting to the playful competition that the jugalbandi of Vajpayee and Advani had resorted to: the 'moderate' and the 'hardliner'. 'You can say that December 2002 elections told us that with ideology you can win elections,' Pravin Togadia says. 'You don't need to dilute ideology to win elections. Yes, you can say that.'[161]

Though it would only play out bit by bit without any breaks to party unity, the December 2002 elections marked the beginning of the end of Vajpayee and Advani. It heralded the rise of Narendra Modi.

POSTSCRIPT

2004 and After

THE LOTUS WITHERS

There were two stories playing out in India by 2004. The first, as we saw in the previous chapter, was the ascendancy of Gujarat chief minister Narendra Modi from nobody to national alternative in two dizzying years. The other reel was being projected 928 kilometres from Gandhinagar, from Lutyens' Delhi. As we read in chapters 14 and 15, Prime Minister Vajpayee and Deputy Prime Minister Advani were selling themselves as a steady pair of hands on foreign policy, Pakistan, infrastructure and, above all, the economy.

This second story reached its climax in late 2003, when data showed the Indian economy growing at a world-beating 10.4 per cent.[1] State elections held during this time went the BJP's way. Though voters had been steered by the shifting tides of local streams,[2] the BJP imagined a deep-water wave gushing through India. And after the December 2002 elections in Gujarat, even Advani, it seems, wanted to follow this economic path to votes rather than the one Modi had charted.

Opinion polls conducted around then suggested that the BJP-led alliance would win 330 seats.[3] In L.K. Advani's words: '[Apart] from our success in these three states . . . our confidence was further buttressed by media reports and opinions polls which predicted a comfortable win for the BJP-led NDA, if elections were held in the first half of 2004.'[4]

What added to Advani's certitude was the party's in-house oracle. The ever-smiling Pramod Mahajan had divined water in 1990 and uncovered a wellspring of voters by placing Advani on a converted chariot. Now, Mahajan convinced Advani to advance the national elections, scheduled for September–October 2004, by five months.

Advani says, 'I was clearly in favour of the idea [of early polls],'[5] though Vajpayee was 'initially not too thrilled'. But the prime minister eventually deferred to his deputy. It made Advani commit his second mistake in the run-up to the elections.

As we have seen in the last few chapters, Vajpayee and Advani's partnership had been tested most over the division of their labour in government. In their first few years in power, Vajpayee had ignored Advani. But by 2004, the eighty-year-old prime minister was of uncertain health and exhausted by repeated attacks from the sangh parivar. And Advani, now deputy prime minister, had managed to claw back some of his clout. He was even able to stare down Vajpayee on Narendra Modi's resignation. A drained Vajpayee had signalled to those close to him that if they won the coming elections, he would retire and Advani would become prime minister. An emboldened Advani now believed he was ready to play his own role as well as Vajpayee's.

Handling allies had been Vajpayee's domain, and the DMK's twelve MPs had supported the Vajpayee government without giving much trouble. Advani's return gift was to abandon them and support their rival AIADMK for the coming elections. 'It was all Advani's doing,' Shakti Sinha says. 'Advani always felt that Jayalalithaa was pro-Hindu.'[6] Vajpayee was sceptical, but went along.[7]

If the brains behind the campaign was all Advani, he was clever enough—and loyal enough—to ensure that the face was all Vajpayee. Fifty-four pictures of the prime minister found their way into the manifesto document.[8] The text did not stress Article 370 or the Ram temple at Ayodhya. Instead, the manifesto cover was titled 'An Agenda for Development, Good Governance, and Peace', with the rest of the pages amplifying that message.[9]

Advani planned to carry that missive across India through a 'Bharat Uday' yatra. The seventy-seven-year-old would travel 12,000 kilometres over thirty-two days and touch 121 constituencies barely a month before the elections.[10] He began from Kanyakumari in south India, 2500 kilometres from Somnath, where he had started his rath yatra in 1990.

Those two launches seemed to have been conducted on different planets. In Kanyakumari, Advani was presented shawls by the dewan of Ajmer Sharif, Christian priests from Tamil Nadu and Kerala, and some Muslim politicians.[11] Throughout the journey his buzzwords were not Ayodhya, Kashmir, or Muslims. It was only: 'Our government has done much in the past six years, and the results of our performance are there for the people to see.'[12] The sadhus and sants in the Vishva Hindu Parishad condemned this as a 'political stunt'; the 'feel-good factor' was incomplete without a Ram temple in Ayodhya.[13]

The long-term legacy of this 'Bharat Uday' yatra was its careless translation. What should have been 'India Rising' was mistranslated as 'India Shining'.[14] Swapan Dasgupta says: 'The inspiration for Advani was [US president] Ronald Reagan's "It's Morning Again in America" ad.'[15] The upbeat tone of that advertisement had highlighted Reagan's first term as president, and helped him get re-elected in 1984.[16] That was what Advani hoped for the BJP in 2004.

Vajpayee knew better. '[He] was not buying India Shining,' Govindacharya says. 'But Advani was, and Vajpayee went along.'[17] By 2004, personal conversations between them had become so strained that it was impacting their political communication.

The yatra bogged Advani down during much of the campaign. 'This was a mistake,' Swapan Dasgupta remembers. 'You couldn't do strategic planning when the leader was on tour.'[18] New opinion polls showed the race closer than expected,[19] and the BJP's own internal report predicted that it would be hard to hold on to its existing 182 MPs, let alone add more.[20] This was obvious towards the end of the yatra itself. A participant remembers: 'We knew we had overshot. There was a problem getting crowds. But it was too late to change track.' Natwar Singh says: 'Vajpayeeji's meetings were being poorly attended. Doordarshan was not showing the empty spaces at his rallies. However, the PM realized that the BJP campaign was failing.'[21]

Meanwhile, the Congress campaigned away from the limelight. Scarred by her brashness in staking claim to power in 1999, Sonia Gandhi was more cautious this time around. She strived to attract smaller parties, and did not project herself as prime minister.[22] The BJP lost eight allies before the elections in comparison.[23] When asked why, Pramod Mahajan was cocky: 'They left due to local issues, not because of leadership or alliance failure.'[24]

If the approach to alliances separated Sonia Gandhi from Advani, so did their styles. While the BJP overextended, contesting twenty-five more seats than in 1999,[25] Sonia Gandhi limited her travel to only those states where the Congress had a shot at winning. Accompanying her was her thirty-three-year-old son, Rahul, who was contesting for the first time— from his father's pocket borough Amethi.

While Sonia Gandhi used her elevated lineage to counter the parvenu BJP, she also mobilized those at the base of society. Her response to the BJP's 'India Shining' campaign was a simple: *Congress ka hath, aam aadmi ke saath*. The Congress hand is with the common man.[26]

Little of this was reported by the media. An editor working for one of India's largest newspapers remembers those elections: 'My owners were sure the BJP would come back. So our coverage was slanted. I was told not to write articles critical of the government.'

India was being led to believe that the lotus would bloom once more.

* * *

The 13th of May 2004 was a torrid day in Delhi, with temperatures reaching 41 degrees Celsius.[27] Vajpayee was in his bungalow at 7 Race Course Road, while Advani tracked the counting of votes on his television at home.[28] He remembers: 'By 10 a.m. it became clear that a shock defeat was in the offing.'[29] Sonia Gandhi was watching television in her home at 10 Janpath. Natwar Singh was with her. 'Sonia and I were both surprised. We didn't expect it.'[30]

The Congress had not just done well, it had won seven more MPs than the BJP. The wider gap, though, was between their political alliances. The NDA had won just 186 seats—around a 100 short of a majority. In contrast, the Congress-led alliance had won 216 seats. With the support of the communists, that number became 278—a stable majority in parliament. A news channel had put up orange and green balloons outside the BJP headquarters on Ashoka Road in anticipation of victory. By 4 p.m., they deflated in isolated silence.[31] *The New York Times* headlined its own astonishment: 'In Huge Upset, Gandhi's Party Wins Election in India.'[32]

This earthquake was attributed, above all, to the arrogance of the slogan 'India Shining'. Montek Singh Ahluwalia says: 'It was urban focused and neglected agriculture. They did not raise procurement prices, and were not sensitive to demands of [the] agricultural sector.'[33] So solid was this narrative that it defined the incoming Congress government for the next decade: rural India needed more than just GDP growth.

The Rashtriya Swayamsevak Sangh offered their own diagnosis: 'The core voter and cadre had developed a disinterest as there was a perception about dilution in its ideology.'[34] The VHP's Pravin Togadia says: 'People didn't feel the party was being consistent in 2004 on ideological issues. The governance was better, but they did not stand by ideology.'[35]

Advani and Vajpayee, on the other hand, blamed too much ideology, not too little. Though it was Advani who had overruled Vajpayee and saved Modi's career, he now realized what he had done. Advani ranted to a family friend soon after: 'The VHP cost us [the elections]. They have become crazy.' Vajpayee also blamed the 2002 Gujarat riots, claiming, 'that is the mistake we made'.[36] At a BJP meeting soon after, he lobbied to sack Modi yet again. But when he was outvoted yet again, Vajpayee went with the party line. Yet again.[37]

There is no way to tell whether it was Narendra Modi who cost Vajpayee–Advani the 2004 election. What we can tell is that the attitude to alliance partners proved costly. The political scientist Yogendra Yadav explains: '[The] BJP on its own dropped 44 seats [compared to the] previous elections . . . the BJP allies lost much more in terms of seats as their tally fell from 114 seats to just 51.'[38] In comparison: 'On their own the allies of the Congress did quite well. Their seats increased from 23 in 1999 to 77 this time.'[39]

The blame for this rickety coalition-building must rest with Advani. He lacked the pragmatism that Vajpayee had displayed when moving the BJP from untouchable in 1993 to being embraced by a dozen parties in 1998. Advani's alliance with Jayalalithaa rather than Karunanidhi in Tamil Nadu alone cost them forty seats.[40] Just those numbers might have brought Vajpayee back to power. If Advani's canniest moment was converting the wrath against Mandal to momentum for his rath in 1990, his most foolish political moment was now.

Six years ensconced in the air-conditioned confines of South Block had disconnected Advani the Grassroots Organizer. Arun Shourie says: 'For six years, the BJP did not focus on organization. Who is [then] going to mobilize people for the election?' He adds: 'Amit Shah and Modi are taking it to the other extreme—where [the] only purpose of organization is to win elections.'[41]

The unexpected loss had upset Vajpayee's succession plan to anoint Advani as his replacement as prime minister. But the thought of clinging to power did not even cross Vajpayee and Advani's mind. When asked what would happen now, Brajesh Mishra said: '*Bistra baandhenge, chalenge.*'[42] We will roll up our mattress, and leave.

The outgoing prime minister bid farewell to the nation that evening. 'My party and alliance may have lost,' Vajpayee said with common grace, 'but India and India's democracy have won.'[43]

The decades-long relationship between Vajpayee and Advani had intertwined the personal, professional and the ideological. Even when one thread frayed, the others held. The result was the greatest political partnership in twentieth century India—one that had planted, nurtured and finally made the lotus bloom. It was now about to wither. That blistering day in May 2004 was the last time they would play music together.

* * *

The British politician Enoch Powell once said, 'All political lives, unless they are cut off in midstream at a happy juncture, end in failure.'[44] Vajpayee began to withdraw from active politics a year after resigning as prime minister. Advani became party president soon after the 2004 elections loss, and in 2005 travelled to his hometown of Karachi in Pakistan. Here he visited the mausoleum of Muhammad Ali Jinnah, called him 'an ambassador of Hindu–Muslim unity' and quoted Jinnah's espousal of 'a Secular State in which every citizen would be free to practise his own religion but the State shall make no distinction between one citizen and another on the grounds of faith'.[45] The fork-tongued Vajpayee could have conveyed the same overtures in woollier language. But Advani slipped once more in assuming he could play Vajpayee's instrument as well as his own. He was accused of being a traitor and asked to resign by the RSS. To be called a betrayer of Hindutva was more than the Sindhi refugee from Pakistan could stomach. 'This was,' Advani recalled, 'quite simply the most agonising moment of my political life . . .'[46]

Meanwhile, and against all expectations, Sonia Gandhi declined to become prime minister in 2004. In a move that would have reminded Advani of his own sacrifice in 1995, Sonia Gandhi nominated Manmohan Singh as the thirteenth prime minister of India.

Family disputes often end with a hug, and L.K. Advani was forgiven for his tactless words in Karachi. For the 2009 elections, the eighty-one-year-old was his party's candidate against Manmohan Singh. Advani rendered himself a decisive leader, in contrast to a prime minister who seemed reliant on Sonia Gandhi. His decisive loss in that election meant that the party had to look for an alternative.

This alternative, as we saw in the previous chapter, was forming in Gujarat. Narendra Modi had fought off the taint of the 2002 riots by rebranding himself as Mr Development. He used this model to win re-election as Gujarat chief minister twice, in 2007 and 2012, though he made sure to also resort to anti-Muslim tropes.

What was aiding his ascent to the top of the BJP was the murder of Pramod Mahajan, shot by his own brother in 2006. Mahajan had been groomed as Vajpayee and Advani's successor. His death cleared the way for Modi to position himself as prime ministerial candidate in time for the 2014 national elections.

A day after Modi was appointed as campaign head for the imminent elections, the man who had spent his life building the Jana Sangh and then Bharatiya Janata Party resigned from all party positions. L.K. Advani's resignation letter is worth quoting in detail: 'For some time I have been finding it difficult to reconcile either with the current functioning of the party, or the direction in which it is going. I no longer have the feeling that this is the same idealistic party created by Dr Mookerji, Deen Dayalji, Nanaji and Vajpayeeji whose sole concern was the country, and its people. Most leaders of ours are now concerned just with their personal agendas.'[47]

Advani was enticed to remain. But the party did not bend on Modi. The 2014 election campaign was all about him, with Vajpayee and Advani barely finding a mention. The new face worked and the BJP won 282 of the 543 parliamentary seats—a majority of its own. Narendra Modi became the second Hindu nationalist prime minister of India, and Amit Shah was appointed party president. The lotus was blossoming once more, but under new gardeners.

As of 2020, most of the leaders in the old BJP are incapacitated, have died, or have been placed on the margins. Apart from Pramod Mahajan, Arun Jaitley and Sushma Swaraj have passed away. Jaswant Singh rebelled from Modi's BJP and was sidelined. He has since passed away. Yashwant Sinha and Arun Shourie have both mutinied. Jinnah's grandson, beloved of Vajpayee and Advani, has moved on. R.V. Pandit says: 'The moment the BJP lost in 2004, Nusli [Wadia] stopped having anything to do with politics.'[48]

Most conspicuous of all, L.K. Advani and Murli Manohar Joshi were denied Lok Sabha tickets in 2019. Though they privately complain of the capture of the party, they make no public criticism. Modi and Shah have responded in kind. Whatever their inner contempt, they make sure to treat the old guard with respect in public. A year into Modi's prime ministership, Vajpayee was conferred the Bharat Ratna, India's highest civilian honour.

Rajkumari Kaul died in 2014 of a cardiac arrest. Indira Gandhi's cousin had chosen to remain publicly invisible for more than fifty years; hardly a photograph exists of her and Vajpayee together. She spent her last moment at the AIIMS in Delhi, where for decades she had helped those in need. The RSS had once threatened to expel Vajpayee over his relationship with Rajkumari Kaul. Now, RSS functionaries attended her funeral.[49]

Five years later, Advani's life partner of more than fifty years died in the same hospital. Kamla Advani had been the initial bread earner and constant family-keeper, allowing Advani the luxury of focusing on politics. Her role as the dominant figure in the Advani household was taken by their daughter Pratibha.

Vajpayee attended neither Rajkumari Kaul's funeral[50] nor Kamla Advani's. Since 2009 he had been confined to his house, suffering a stroke as well as the effects of diabetes and dementia—6 Krishna Menon Marg had been converted into an intensive care unit. A doctor who attended to him says: 'He was alive because of medicines only.' Add to that, son-in-law Ranjan Bhattacharya and daughter Namita. A visitor says: 'Who will take care of someone like that for that long? They see to it that nothing is lacking.' Even though now far away from power, the Bhattacharyas' devotion to Baapji lay undiminished. Once or twice in a week, Vajpayee would be wheeled out of his room, and propped in the wheelchair with his favourite dogs on his lap. 'His eye muscles had weakened. He couldn't see properly,' says N.M. Ghatate, who would regularly visit.

One of the few people Vajpayee seemed to recognize was Advani, but one could not be sure. With both out of power, the warmth in the relationship seemed to have come back somewhat. Advani would visit once a month, and sit by Vajpayee's bed. He would be silent. They would be silent. And then he would leave.[51]

Meanwhile, living and working just minutes away, Modi and Shah were printing the party's foot onto new states. And in the national elections of 2019, the BJP won 303 seats, the highest it has ever received.

Although the BJP under Narendra Modi and Amit Shah has only been in power for six years at the time of this book's publication, the politics they have crafted is already being seen as an alternative to the sixty-year political Hinduism of Vajpayee and Advani. It begs two questions—tentative and yet unfolding. What was it about Vajpayee and Advani that made their relationship work? And how does this older relationship compare with the new one between Narendra Modi and Amit Shah?

* * *

Atal Bihari Vajpayee was an orator, a trait he learnt from his father and honed when he was selected for public relations roles by Deendayal Upadhyaya. Though a middle-rung poet, he sensed not just the structure of sentences but their rhythms. Add to this his extended presence in parliament, where he was almost always the leader of his party. Vajpayee endured by being the most hypnotic political speaker independent India has produced.

If you wear a mask long enough, the mask becomes your face. What parliament did to Vajpayee was to teach him the Nehruvian version of India. It was one which respected India's public institutions, endeavoured to keep Hinduism out of government, was sensitive to the trauma of post-partition Muslims, wanted state control over the economy and veered away from the West on foreign policy. Vajpayee initially followed all of this—not out of love for Nehru (as his right-wing critics alleged), but out of love for the parliament of that period.

Vajpayee's politics was also shaped by the woman in his life. Rajkumari Kaul socialized the provincial Hindu. Their many conversations, most tellingly on Ayodhya, would alter Vajpayee's mind.

This Nehruvian outlook was at odds with the Rashtriya Swayamsevak Sangh. Vajpayee eased this tension in three ways. First, he convinced the RSS that to win elections it needed him to attract the non-Congress opposition as well as the moderate Hindu majority. Second, while he cultivated a liberal air, he was ultimately a party man. On supporting the Ayodhya movement or Modi's continuance as Gujarat chief minister, Vajpayee was torn between principle and party. But his instinct for self-preservation meant that he always chose party. Always.

The third, most striking way, in which Vajpayee was able to balance his liberal demeanour with Hindu nationalist ideology was in his choice of partner.

As we have read, Partition had transformed the English-speaking, tennis-playing Lal Krishna Advani into a grassroots mobilizer, determined to reunite India again. His knack for organizing was made sharp by his decade as a pracharak in Rajasthan. By the time he entered Delhi as secretary to Vajpayee in 1957, Advani's personality had been formed—an eye for detail, a head for the RSS and his heart set on his new boss.

Vajpayee and Advani's relationship since then was held together by love—for each other and for Bollywood films. But it was also based on a division of labour that Hindu nationalism required. On the one hand, the party needed to take its core voter and motivated cadre along. To keep the base, it needed a stern visage. On the other hand, accusations stemming from Gandhi's murder in 1948 had made the ideology untouchable. To come to power, it needed a calming voice. At an election speech Vajpayee once gave in Jaipur, someone threw a snake into the crowd. When the crowd panicked, Vajpayee said, from the podium, there was no snake. The event went on, audience reassured.[52]

After the leadership tussle that followed Deendayal's death, Advani and Vajpayee settled into these complementary roles. When the mood of the nation was for ideological moderation—like in the 1970s or late

1990s—Advani followed while Vajpayee led. When the mood was of anxiety—like in the 1980s and early 1990s—Vajpayee obeyed while Advani steered the party.

Neither Vajpayee nor Advani were intellectuals in the sense that neither had a long-term civilizational vision for their country. But they were able to see the arc of history in the medium-term, i.e., they deciphered the trajectories of the Congress and Hindu nationalism in the first six decades of Indian independence, and their own paired roles through this journey. So conscious were they of the characters they needed to play that they indulged in role play. Advani acted more bigoted than he really was; Vajpayee was adept at performing the role of a Nehruvian liberal. They were wearers of masks, both.

Their alliance worked because they rarely intruded on the other's competence (Advani's coalition-building in 2004 was the exception that proved the rule). Vajpayee seldom visited the party headquarters. He also trusted Advani's judgement on how far the cadre was willing to compromise for the sake of power. The most vivid example of this was when Advani prevailed on Vajpayee to not sack the Gujarat chief minister in April 2002.

In return for this control over the party, Advani ensured that Vajpayee was always given his favoured role: speaking for the party in parliament. He even out-schemed the RSS in the early 1990s to ensure this. And in what must surely be his finest hour, Advani gave the prime ministership of the world's largest democracy to Vajpayee, aware that he himself lacked the soothing smile to keep the BJP in power.

When this division of labour was threatened by others in the party, Vajpayee and Advani backed each other up. Advani supported Vajpayee against Madhok, Sondhi, Swamy and Govindacharya. Vajpayee buoyed Advani against Murli Manohar Joshi. As Shekhar Gupta puts it: 'Advani–Vajpayee are like an old couple you see in the park. They squabble, but if anyone comes in between them, they will defend each other.'[53]

In that sense, it was a genuine jugalbandi: there were different instruments, there was playful competition, there were alternating riffs, and there was, in a profound sense, an *equal* music.

It is easy to fall in love with Vajpayee. An epicurean, a charmer. It is harder to feel for the colourless, odourless Advani. But some of that must surely be because Advani was more a man of principle than Vajpayee, less altered by make-up. Their opponent, a senior Congressman, provides a telling insight: 'Vajpayee was a better actor than Advani. And Modi is a better actor than Vajpayee. With Advani, what you saw is what you got. Sometimes, in politics, you need to be a good actor.'

As their relationship entered the quicksand of government from 1998 to 2004, it frayed. While Vajpayee was happy to let Advani retain control of the party, he saw government as an extension of parliament, i.e., exclusively his domain. But even when their personal relationship suffered during these years, their professional partnership never fully dissolved. In Yashwant Sinha's words: 'Vajpayee and Advani both realized that they were insecure without each other. People were definitely breathing down their neck. They were insecure that if their differences had gone beyond a point, they would have both been hurt. It's MAD. Mutually Assured Destruction.'[54]

Sinha is describing the relationship through self-interest, which there surely was. And there was plenty of affection too. But as we have read through this book, Vajpayee and Advani's ability to work with each other through thick and thin was based on more than just cold calculations and warm feelings. It was also based on an ideology that valued teamwork.

* * *

The longest-serving head of the RSS, M.S. Golwalkar, was so obsessed with teamwork that he worried that having a 'blood' family would distract RSS members from the only cause that mattered: Hindu unity. A telling statistic makes this point forcefully. There is an unwritten rule that the senior leadership of the RSS should be unmarried. Perhaps the only two exceptions to this were Madhukar Rao Bhagwat and M.G. Vaidya. The former explained to Golwalkar that he needed a wife to take care of his aging mother; the latter was already married by the time the rule was instituted. Today, their sons are the number one and number three in the RSS. That they are perhaps the only dynasts in the organization shows why the rule against marriage exists in the first place.

This worry of dynasty has led to the RSS having contradictory views on 'family'. On the one hand, they are suspicious of the nepotism that 'blood' families promote. On the other, they see family 'bonds' and hierarchies as a natural form of team-building in India. The genius of the RSS is to create a bond of family among non-family members, i.e., deploying a traditional form of team-building to a modern, electoral context.

Advani internalized this idiom so much that he even deployed it against the RSS. When criticized for forever deferring to Vajpayee, Advani would reply: 'No family can stay together without a *mukhiya* [head], whose authority is unquestionably accepted by all its members. After Deendayalji, Atalji is the *mukhiya* of our family.'[55]

This emphasis on staying united, above all, came to Vajpayee and Advani through a version of Indian history they were both schooled in. Early Hindu nationalists such as K.M. Munshi (whom both read) as well as the baudhiks at the RSS shakhas (which both attended) taught Vajpayee and Advani that the weakness of the Hindus of past was because of a lack of fellow-feeling. Hindus were divided by caste, region or by egos. This was why, they were taught, Muslims, then the British, and finally the Congress, were able to divide Hindu society in order to rule.

This analysis was applied to organizational strategy. Hindu society could never become unified if the vehicle for this unification—i.e., the Jana Sangh, the BJP, the RSS—was not united itself. This was why Vajpayee and Advani, despite profound personality and policy dissimilarities, never left the party. This was also why they never left each other.

What makes the Vajpayee–Advani relationship even more distinct was their ability to switch places and upturn hierarchies not once, but twice. Between 1957 and 1985, Vajpayee was plainly the leader. But between 1986 and 1995, as the party moved in a more radical direction, Vajpayee served under Advani. A second switch happened in 1995, and for the next decade it was Vajpayee leading the party.

There is no other partnership that switched hierarchies not once but twice without tearing itself apart. Vallabhbhai Patel always served under Nehru, never the other way around. Jayalalithaa and Mayawati always reported to MGR and Kanshi Ram—only claiming power when the other was dead or unwell. Vajpayee and Advani's teamwork stands out in India, a country where bureaucrats and soldiers resign rather than serve someone who once served them. But it also stands out in comparison to the more individualistic West. Imagine Barack Obama once day serving under his former vice-president Joe Biden? Then imagine Joe Biden agreeing to serve once more under Obama?

This unique relationship between Vajpayee and Advani was propelled not just by innate warmth and complementary skills. It was also driven by the creed they belonged to, one that worshipped teamwork. It is no coincidence that of all the political ideologies in the modern world, it was Hindu nationalism that housed Vajpayee and Advani. The glue that kept them together was the ideology itself.

* * *

This brings us to the final question that readers of this book may wish to ask: How does that BJP compare to the current BJP? And how does the Vajpayee–Advani partnership compare with the evolving one between Prime Minister Narendra Modi and his deputy Amit Shah?

To answer that question, one must go back to the periods in which they entered politics. Vajpayee and Advani came of age in the Delhi of the 1950s. It was a time in which the Nehruvian consensus was shared even by the non-Congress opposition. The murder of Gandhi, the leader of India's Hindus, had rendered the RSS and Jana Sangh untouchable. Vajpayee and Advani's primary task was limited to making Hindutva respectable again. This context made both realize that Hindu nationalism had to 'moderate' itself, i.e., reconcile itself to the mores of Nehruvian India, if it hoped to win voters. This was their default position through the next several decades in politics. Even at the height of the rath yatra—with Hindus radicalized like never before—Advani pulled back from the edge. There was a line he would not cross.

In contrast, Modi and Amit Shah had their political education in the Gujarat of the late 1970s and early '80s. Rising lower castes were threatening to split Hindus, and the Congress was rebooting by uniting Muslims and low-caste Hindus against upper castes. Modi and Amit Shah's answer was to radicalize their politics by underplaying caste and overplaying Islamophobia—all in order to fuse enough Hindus into voting for the BJP. Where Vajpayee and Advani sought to appeal to both the moderate and the radical, there was no such electoral incentive for Modi and Shah.

These formative years inform their politics even today. Prime Minister Modi and Home Minister Amit Shah are more astute in catering to low castes microscopically as well as attacking Muslims macroscopically. Though Vajpayee and Advani were as alive to the demographic anxieties that animate the recent Citizenship Amendment Act and National Register of Citizens, they would have both balked from such overt hostility to India's 200 million Muslims. If today's BJP is less upper caste than the BJP of old, it is also more anti-Muslim.

The other reason for this divergence between the two partnerships is that Vajpayee and Advani spent decades in parliament in Delhi. In contrast, neither Narendra Modi nor Amit Shah had held legislative or executive power in Delhi before 2014. They have no training in appealing to the diversity of India as represented in parliament. Their prism is the provincial politics of Gujarat.

The result is that Modi–Shah are more ruthless to political opponents than Vajpayee–Advani ever were. As Advani wrote on an Internet blog after he was denied his Gandhinagar seat for the 2019 elections: 'Right from its inception, the BJP has never regarded those who disagree with us politically as our "enemies", but only as our adversaries. Similarly, in our conception of Indian nationalism, we have never regarded those who disagree with us politically as "anti-national".'[56]

* * *

The political context in which these two relationships began have brought out contrasting attitudes to winning and keeping power. But Vajpayee–Advani and Modi–Shah also share more than is imagined. While there are indeed disparities in their treatment of those outside the party, what both duos share is an emphasis on outward displays of internal unity.

The most visible instance of this was when Vajpayee died in August 2018, at the age of ninety-three. Vajpayee had done much to ruin Modi's career, from trying to get him sacked in 2002, to trying once again after the 2004 election defeat. Yet, Vajpayee's funeral was a national event, with the prime minister accompanying the hearse to its final resting place on foot for six kilometres.[57]

Contrast this with the funeral of P.V. Narasimha Rao in 2004 by the Congress government in power then. Though Vajpayee had done as much to hurt Modi as Rao had done to Sonia, that former prime minister's dead body was denied entry into the party headquarters, was not allowed to be cremated in Delhi, and the funeral pyre was exposed to stray dogs in Hyderabad. This sequence of events is detailed in a biography of Rao written by this author.[58] When Advani read those pages, he responded: 'We also have differences in our party. But we don't treat each other like that.' This, in a nutshell, is why the BJP won then, why it wins now.

Some could argue that this coherence stems from the sangh parivar all being from the same social base, i.e., north Indian Brahmin men. But Vajpayee (UP Brahmin), Advani (Amil Sindhi), Narendra Modi (Gujarati Ghanchi) and Amit Shah (Gujarati Baniya) come from diverse castes and parts of India. And the social base of their party has evolved from upper castes, to tribals, middle-castes and even Dalits.

Besides, caste kinship is no guarantee of teamwork; single-caste parties are as plagued by infighting.[59] Hindu nationalists rely on history, yet again, to grasp this point. To quote Golwalkar: 'The person responsible for the defeat of Prithiviraj, the Hindu King at Delhi, by Mohammed Ghori was his own caste relation Jaichand. The person who hounded Rana Pratap from forest to forest was none other than his own caste-man Raja Mansingh. Shivaji too was opposed by men of his own caste. Even in the last-ditch battle between the Hindus and the British at Poona in 1818, it was a fellow caste-man of the Peshwas, Natu by name, who lowered the Hindu flag and hoisted the British flag.'[60]

It is this analysis of history, not the affective bonds of caste, that have made both partnerships value teamwork above all else.

If Vajpayee–Advani and Modi–Shah share the same attitude to sticking together, even their record in governance is not all that different. On the ideological issues of Article 370 of the Constitution, a Uniform Civil Code and a Ram temple at Ayodhya, the Modi government might seem more determined. But much of this can be explained by the compulsions of coalition politics during the Vajpayee era. In contrast, the Modi government has the freedom, and numbers, to follow ideology.

There are, however, a few areas of governance where the personalities of the two sets of partners have produced divergent results. This is most obviously so on the economy. India's economic performance under Vajpayee was so good that they were even fooled into fighting an election on it. On the other hand, Modi's economic performance, especially in the years 2019–20, has been so bad that Modi never campaigns on it.

Vajpayee was large-hearted enough to allow his own cabinet or party to debate and even criticize his economic policies. He trusted specialists to do their job. In contrast, the man who marketed himself as Mr Development in Gujarat seems to have contempt for economics as a specialist field, trusts few experts and is forever balancing economics with political expediency. Few in his cabinet, let alone his party, are encouraged to speak truth to power. On the flip side, Modi seems to have a better feel for welfare schemes and the farm sector than the Vajpayee government did. This is perhaps why (in addition to Hindutva) Modi–Shah were re-elected in 2019, while Vajpayee–Advani lost in 2004. Modinomics may be bad for the economy, but it seems adept at garnering votes.

Modi's better connect with the voter leads to perhaps the most telling difference between the two eras of the BJP. While Vajpayee was adept at divining the mood of parliamentarians and Advani of the party worker, both lacked the daily contact with ordinary Indians that Narendra Modi has worked on for decades. In that sense, neither Vajpayee nor Advani were mass leaders. They needed a Vijayaraje Scindia to win states, a Pramod Mahajan to spot trends. Narendra Modi, on the other hand, has an almost mystical connect with the voter. The prime minister he is most like is Indira Gandhi.

* * *

This leads to the closing comparison between Vajpayee–Advani and Modi–Shah: How did they treat each other?

Vasundhara Raje Scindia reminds us that both Vajpayee and Advani were sensitive men, capable of crying or laughing at the drop of a hat.[61] Neither Modi nor Amit Shah seem to possess these traits. Their relationship seems more calibrated. It is hard to imagine Narendra Modi one day serving under Amit Shah—the way Vajpayee and Advani were able to swap roles not once but twice. They were able to do this only because they had internalized the teamwork that is at the heart of Hindu nationalism. It is in this sense, and not without irony, that the Vajpayee–Advani relationship seems more 'ideological' than Modi–Shah's.

The ninety-one-year-old Advani was perhaps aware of this when he spoke at an all-party prayer meeting for the soul of Vajpayee in 2018. Wearing a white kurta and cream jacket, the frail Advani's speech was typically dull but atypically illuminating. He said nothing about his own oversize part in Vajpayee's career, or his undersize role in the BJP of the moment. Instead, he thanked Vajpayee of course, but made sure to thank others in the party whom he had learnt from. He ended with: 'I can only say that what all Atalji has taught us and given us, we should take all that and live our lives on that basis. The extent to which we do this . . . we will be able to, in a way, fulfil the values we have learnt in the RSS. And that will give us satisfaction.'[62]

Advani could have described his association with Vajpayee as a labour of love, or even as a productive pairing of contrasting talents. Instead, in Advani's final analysis, their sixty-one-year partnership was simply an act of ideology.

Whether Narendra Modi or Amit Shah will give such a speech for the other, only time will tell. Their relationship is still unfolding, as are the petals of their lotus. But all flowers will wither someday, must wither someday. Then, perhaps, we can write about the music from *their* jugalbandi.

SCHOLARLY CONTRIBUTION

The Bharatiya Janata Party before Narendra Modi, from 1924 to 2004, is the subject matter of this book. And in telling its tale through the story of its two navigators, the book contributes to many academic discussions. Three scholarly debates, in particular, will benefit from the arguments in these pages. They are: What is Hindu nationalism? Does the 'inclusion-moderation' thesis apply to the BJP? And what accounts for the rise of the BJP before Modi? The answers to these questions are summarized, in turn, below.

What is Hindu Nationalism?

One of the main contributions of this book is to explain the BJP as much through events, personalities and contingencies as through structures and ideas. In incorporating these perspectives, the book comes to new conclusions about the nature of Hindu nationalism.

To begin with, it disagrees (in chapters 1 and 2) with scholars such as Antony Copley[1] and Koenraad Elst[2] who categorize Hindu nationalism as religious nationalism. It follows others who define it as a modern invention based on ethnic identity.

These other scholars, however, use the word 'modern' to mean the British colonial state in nineteenth-century India. To give a few examples: Romila Thapar categorizes Hindu nationalism as a creation of the divide-

and-rule policies of the British,[3] R.B. Bhagat[4] follows Nicholas Dirks[5] in arguing that the colonial census constructed religious identity, and John Zavos persuasively shows how the myth of an 'organized' state influenced the organizing of Hindu society.[6] Thus construed, the social reform movements of the nineteenth century are seen (by scholars such as Charles Heimsath)[7] as the origin point of Hindu nationalism.

Late nineteenth-century colonial India did indeed give rise to a quest for a common Hindu consciousness. But group identity alone is insufficient for a phenomenon to be called 'nationalism'. As chapter 1 argues in much detail, what 'nationalism' requires in addition to a theory of the 'people' and an idea of 'territory' is a notion of politics, i.e., a state or homeland. *Nineteenth-century Hindu reform movements did not have this last ingredient.* This cannot be emphasized enough. Neither the early Arya Samaj (as opposed to the later Arya Samajis like Lala Lajpat Rai)[8] nor Vivekananda nor Bankim Chandra conceived of an alternative to British rule. They did not articulate a vision of a 'Hindu state'.

The enunciation of Hindu 'power' occurred only in the early twentieth century, in response to British-induced elections. Since Hinduism had no authoritative conception of power, Hindu nationalists had no 'Hindu' alternative to elections as the way to gain and legitimatize power. And since Hindus were a demographic majority who could form a winning vote bank, Hindu nationalists realized that one-person-one-vote could work to their advantage. *It was modern representative democracy, not the modern colonial state, that created Hindu nationalism.*

By emphasizing the constitutive importance of elections, this book disagrees with scholars such as Jyotirmaya Sharma, A.G. Noorani and many others who portray the BJP and RSS as anti-democratic[9] or even 'fascist'.[10] Fascism arose out of a crisis in liberal democracy in mid-twentieth-century Europe. In applying this historically situated terminology to the rest of the world, scholars have culled out some essential ingredients: ethno-nationalism, monopoly capitalism and total mobilization of the populace (usually for war).[11] But one ingredient is present in all definitions: fascism requires a distrust of parliamentary democracy and a move towards a totalitarian state.[12] Hitler, who came to power through elections only to abolish them, argued that democracy undermined the 'natural selection' of elites who were born to rule.[13]

In contrast, and as every chapter of this book points out, the Hindu nationalists before Narendra Modi were both constituted by and were comfortable with the main ingredient of constitutional democracy: elections. Every time they came to power, critics fretted they would end elections. But every time they lost their mandate, there was never even a murmur of clinging to power. It is entirely fair to argue that Vajpayee and Advani were ethno-nationalists who believed in elections-only democracy, followed the letter of the Constitution without the spirit and underpinned their political liberalism with social majoritarianism. But what is misplaced is the claim that Hindu nationalism from 1924 to 2004 was 'fascist'.

In arguing that Hindu nationalism is shaped and defined by democracy, this book has more in common with Thomas Blom Hansen, Ashis Nandy[14] and Christophe Jaffrelot. As Hansen puts it: 'We have to admit that the movement has grown and come to power largely by obeying the procedures of parliamentary democracy.'[15]

But, even these scholars see the BJP's commitment to democracy as only 'skin-deep'.[16] They describe Hindu Nationalism as a 'conservative' ideology, propagated by traditional elites motivated by 'the felt experience of having power, seeing it threatened, and trying to win it back'.[17]

There is some truth to this argument. The strand of Hinduism that the BJP and RSS have standardized—what Romila Thapar calls 'Syndicated Hinduism'[18]—was associated with the traditional elites: Brahmins and Kshatriyas. The social composition of these organizations were also upper castes like Vajpayee and Advani, as were most of their early voters. And as chapters 7, 8 and 9 chronicle, caste-based reservations did fuel upper-caste anxiety that helped the BJP's first bloom.

But the book lists many more factors—other than just upper-caste fear—that fuelled this rise. And the growth of what Hansen and Jaffrelot themselves call the 'vernacularisation of Hindutva'—i.e., regional variants that incorporate local strands of Hinduism[19]—shows that the ideology is as chameleon-like as Hinduism is. Besides, the changing social composition of the BJP voter even during this first bloom under Vajpayee and Advani (let alone the second bloom under the middle-caste Narendra Modi) proves that its early high-caste air is capable of acclimatization.

Another way in which the BJP can be categorized as conservative is on gender. Many scholars argue that the BJP deploys patriarchal tropes.[20]

And as this book has pointed out, the RSS is an all-male organization, and the percentage of women in Prime Minister Vajpayee's cabinet was low. But unlike, say, in the United States (where women markedly prefer the Democrats over the Republicans), in India, women and men tend to vote in the same direction. For instance, the BJP's recent increase in vote share is reflected in both male and female voters, with a relatively small gender gap. And, though polling of this sort is somewhat recent, there is little evidence to suggest that women and men in India vote for different issues.[21]

The other problem with the label 'conservative' is that Vajpayee, Advani and their ilk saw themselves as victims of the past, rather than lords of it. Their entire twentieth-century project, in fact, was to create a new, united, Hinduism. This translated into an inclusion of low castes as well as a suspicion of Muslims—both of which traditional Hinduism did not have. Rather than conservatives or traditionalists, a better description of the Hindu nationalists of this period would be right-wing radicals.

Thus far, our focus has been on politics. But scholars such as Amrita Basu have analysed Hindu nationalism as a social movement as well.[22] What insights does this book provide about Hindu nationalism in the social sphere?

As admitted right at the outset of the book, one of the blind spots of picking two politicians as conduits to study an ideology is that the focus is more on parties than social movements or the 'public space'. But given this limitation, this book is alive to the context in which the BJP operated—as a party intent on unifying a vote bank and as part of a family of organizations intent on consolidating a social identity in the public sphere. Vajpayee and Advani might have balked when they felt the RSS, VHP and Bajrang Dal were endangering their short-term electoral alliances. But they recognized that in the long term, the movement aim of uniting Hindus socially would also unite them electorally.

Amrita Basu carefully situates this relationship between the social and electoral in perhaps the most studied aspect of Hindutva—its role in anti-Muslim violence.[23] For Hindutva to translate into violence, a particular set of factors need to come together, she argues. In addition, Paul Brass,[24] Steve Wilkinson[25] and Raheel Dhattiwala[26] have all found an electoral logic to Hindu–Muslim riots across India. While this book generally desists from value judgements, it is clear cut about the BJP's complicity in this violence (dealt with in chapters 7–11, and, especially in chapter 16).

This use of what it sees as 'defensive violence' has a historical basis for Hindu nationalists. For them, every Hindu–Muslim riot is viewed through the lens of Hindu defeat at the hands of invading Muslim kings. If one lesson from these beatings is to unite Hindus as a group, the other involves strengthening the puny Hindu against the more martial Muslim. This is the frame through which Hindu nationalism viewed the three acts of violence most associated with it: the killing of Gandhi in 1948, the demolition of Babri Masjid in 1992 and the Gujarat riots of 2002. This book takes a revisionist view of these events, arguing that the actual culpability of the *institutions* of Hindu nationalism is more circuitous than believed. But there is no doubt that the *ideology* saw all three events through the lens of 'defensive violence'; the need to stand up for Hindus in every battle.

Did Power Moderate Hindu Nationalism?

The question of violence leads to the second academic debate to which this book contributes: regarding the 'inclusion–moderation thesis'. This thesis argues that 'when an extremist party contests elections in a democratic framework it accepts institutions that are based on liberal or liberalizing principles . . . and dilutes its ideology to attract voters outside of its own constituency'.[27]

But this book argues that the framing of the BJP before Modi as 'anti-democratic' is a problem to begin with. Though Hindu nationalism is neither socially nor economically liberal, it requires that the political unit be the individual, i.e., one-person-one-vote. Hindu nationalism was created as a response to elections, the primary ingredient of any definition of democracy.

Whether power constrained the BJP before Modi into respecting social individualism, minority rights and counter-majoritarian institutions is more open to debate. Vajpayee and Advani did attempt to make their Jana Sangh (chapters 3 and 4) and their BJP (chapter 11) appear liberal. The privations of the Emergency (chapter 5) also shaped them into respecting civil liberties when they came to power under the Janata government (chapter 6). And the Vajpayee government did attempt to present a socially liberal posture from 1998 to 2004 (chapters 12 to 17).

But as these chapters—and the scholars Sanjay Ruparelia,[28] Christophe Jaffrelot[29] and Lars Tore Flåten—[30] show, there were enough exceptions: above all, the 2002 Gujarat riots. While Vajpayee and Advani's democratic record is durable, their record as liberals is patchy at best.

Why does the BJP win?

The final scholarly debate this book contributes to is an explanation of the BJP's electoral success in its first bloom before Narendra Modi. The popular answer—among politicians, critics and academics such as Pralay Kanungo[31]—is that it is the Rashtriya Swayamsevak Sangh that drives the BJP. The BJP's rise, in this telling, is linked to the slow and steady expansion of the RSS network across India. 'The RSS is the Fevicol that holds the BJP together,' says the Congress's Jairam Ramesh.[32]

The problem with this narrative is that at various points of time—such as the Jana Sangh's shot at power from 1977 to 1980 or the BJP's from 1998 to 2004—the RSS was pitted against party. At other times, of course, the RSS called the shots—in forcing the BJP to accept the Ayodhya movement in the 1980s or in shaping the teenage Vajpayee and Advani's sense of Hindu history. The other problem in identifying the RSS as the glue that holds Hindu nationalism together is to ask the next question: what is the glue that holds the RSS together? To simplify the multifaceted rise of the alternate idea of India to a building in Nagpur misses not just the trees but also the woods.

A second explanation for this electoral growth of the BJP is attributed to the economy. The scholars Stuart Corbridge and John Harriss argue that economic liberalization and Hindu nationalism are both caused by the same variable—an 'elite revolt' against a state increasingly catering to the interests of low castes.[33] But chapters 7 and 8 explain that the factors behind the BJP's rise predated liberalization. And chapter 9 portrays a party more interested in bringing down the Rao government in the early 1990s, than following any convictions on economic reforms.

This book instead relies on scholars such as Ornit Shani[34] and Christophe Jaffrelot[35] to show how apprehensions over backward-caste reservations, the Ram temple movement and Khalistan all played a role in the national rise of the BJP. These are detailed in chapters 7, 8 and 9. What this book does is add to the scholarly literature by providing the chronological sequence in which these factors interacted with each other to help the lotus bloom.

The Hindu anxieties of the early 1980s—fuelled by a doddering economy, caste reservations and anti-Hindu violence by Sikh separatists— did not find an outlet in Vajpayee's new BJP, then being fashioned as a secular socialist party. Into this vacuum jumped the RSS and VHP, radicalizing Hindu voters through the Ram Mandir movement. The BJP supported this only in the late 1980s (and only after the Congress threatened to usurp this Hindu vote bank) and was able to reap votes.

Adding to this new sequence is an altogether novel theory that this book propagates to explain the BJP's first rise to power.

The secret sauce of the BJP, as well as the RSS, was their unbending focus on unity. This meant making Hindus, who number over 80 per cent of India, vote as one. Its strategy of downplaying caste and upping the volume on Islamophobia had this electoral aim in mind. As did its cultural claims, such as a ban on cow slaughter or an emphasis on the vedas and Sanskrit. This was not because Hindu nationalists necessarily believed these to be holy cows; it was because of the need for *some* common definition that united Hindus.

This vote-bank politics, as the BJP never tired of pointing out, was present in other parties too. But where Hindu nationalism won was that despite ideological and personality disagreements between the BJP, RSS and VHP, they did not break up.

In contrast, their competitor parties were weakened by internal splits and factions. Chapter 6 shows how the Janata Party disintegrated because of competing egos. Chapters 7–9 describe how, in the wake of the Congress decline (caused, in part, through faction feuds), the Janata Dal, the communists and the BSP were too inundated by infighting to grow into a national presence. And Chapter 11 describes how the Third Front government was too beset by backbiting to last.

It was the Bharatiya Janata Party alone, led by a Vajpayee and Advani who stayed together, that was able to emerge as the national alternative.

Their idea of India won because they worked as one.

NOTES

PROLOGUE: PRIME MINISTER ADVANI (1995)

1. Dilip Chaware, 'Management and a million man hours make BJP session a reality', *The Times of India*, 12 November 1995, p. 7.
2. Satish Nandgaonkar, 'Saffron security: 6,000 cops deployed at BJP convention venue', *The Times of India*, 8 November 1995, p. 1.
3. Dilip Chaware, 'Management and a million man hours make BJP session a reality', *The Times of India*, 12 November 1995, p. 7.
4. Different Strokes, 'Brokers largesse', *The Times of India*, 12 November 1995, p. 18.
5. Neena Vyas, 'Plenary projects Vajpayee as "Future PM"', *The Hindu*, 11 November 1995, p. 13.
6. See Chapter 8, Section 1 of this book.
7. 'L.K. Advani Declares Vajpayee as next Prime Minister', *India Today*, 30 November 1995.
8. Suhas Phadke, 'Vajpayee's pal is man behind the decor', *The Times of India*, 10 November 1995, p. 2.
9. Ambarish Mishra, 'BJP faces dilemma of reconciling power and principle', *The Times of India*, 10 November 1995, p. 15.
10. 'BJP plagued by factionalism', *India Today*, 31 October 1995.
11. 'Lotus wars', *India Today*, 31 October 1995.
12. 'Shankersinh Vaghela: The Complete Story of Khajuraho', *News Street Journal*. Available at: https://www.newsstreetjournal.com/india/shankersinh-vaghela-the-complete-story-of-khajuraho/

13. Ambarish Mishra, 'BJP faces dilemma of reconciling power and principle', *The Times of India*, 10 November 1995, p. 15.

14. 'A tale of two chiefs', *Outlook India*, 22 May 1996. Available at https://www.outlookindia.com/magazine/story/a-tale-of-two-chiefs/201392

15. Ambarish Mishra, '"Vajpayee is BJP's choice for next PM," says Advani', *The Times of India*, 12 November 1995, p. 28.

16. Available at: https://www.speakingtree.in/blog/saying-abhi-dilli-door-hai

17. Interview with Govindacharya, Delhi, June 2018.

18. Ibid.

19. The BJP leader Subramanian Swamy says that Ashok Singhal said this to him. From an interview with Subramanian Swamy, Delhi, June 2018.

20. Lal Krishna Advani, *My Country My Life* (Rupa Publications, 2008), p. 838.

21. Interview with Swapan Dasgupta, New Delhi, June 2018.

22. Interview with Dinesh Trivedi, New Delhi, May 2018.

23. Interview with Vasundhara Raje Scindia, Delhi, June 2018.

24. Scholars such as Amrita Basu and Thomas Blom Hansen have written about Hindu nationalism as a 'social movement' and as a 'public culture'. This book focuses more on the electoral and political story, without discounting Hindu nationalism in the 'social'. See Amrita Basu, *Violent Conjunctures in Democratic India* (Cambridge University Press, 2015); Thomas Blom Hansen, *The Saffron Wave: Democracy and Hindu Nationalism in Modern India* (Princeton University Press, 1999).

PART I: THE PAST (1924–80)

CHAPTER 1: HINDU FEVICOL (1924–45)

1. Milton W. Meyer, *Asia: A Concise History* (Rowman & Littlefield Publishers, 2000), p. 218.

2. Ullekh N.P., *The Untold Vajpayee: Politician and Paradox* (Penguin Books, kindle edition, 2017), location 196 of 3595.

3. See Manu Bhagwan, 'Princely States and the Hindu Imaginary: Exploring the Cartography of Hindu Nationalism in Colonial India', *The Journal of Asian Studies*, Vol. 67, No. 3 (August) 2008: 881–915. See also: http://www.india-seminar.com/2011/622/622_christophe_jaffrelot.htm

4. N.K. Singh, 'Atal Bihari Vajpayee: A private person with strong dislikes and few close friends', *India Today*, 31 May 1996.

5. Kingshuk Nag, *Atal Bihari Vajpayee: A Man for All Seasons* (Rupa, 2015), p. 20.

6. Tilak Sharma, 'A teacher remembers a student by the name Atal', *The Times of India,* 18 May 1996.

7. Steve Inskeep, *Instant City: Life and Death in Karachi* (Penguin, 2011), introductory chapter titled 'North of North Karachi'.

8. L.K. Advani, *My Country My Life* (Rupa, 2010, paperback), p. 28.

9. Ibid.

10. Ibid., pp. 27–28

11. Kewalram R. Malkani, *The Sindh Story* (Allied, 1984), p. 70.

12. L.K. Advani, *My Country My Life* (Rupa, 2010, paperback), pp. 17–21.

13. Ibid., pp. 31–32.

14. Ibid., p. 293.

15. Benedict Anderson, *Imagined Communities: Reflections on the Origin and Spread of Nationalism* (Verso Books, 2006), p. 60.

16. Available at: http://www.nationalismproject.org/what/anderson.htm

17. See also Lowell W. Barrington, '"Nation" and "nationalism": The misuse of key concepts in political science', *PS: Political Science & Politics* 30, no. 4 (1997): 712–16, at 714.

18. Wendy Doniger, 'Puranas', *Encyclopaedia Britannica.* Available at: https://www.britannica.com/topic/Purana

19. Horace Hayman Wilson, *The Vishnu Purana.* Vol. 9, (Trübner, 1868), https://www.sacred-texts.com/hin/vp/vp060.htm

20. Diana L. Eck, 'The imagined landscape: Patterns in the construction of Hindu sacred geography', *Contributions to Indian Sociology* 32, no. 2 (1998): 165–88, at 168.

21. 'What is India's caste system', *BBC News*, 19 June 2019. Available at: https://www.bbc.com/news/world-asia-india-35650616

22. The Indian census in 2018 estimated that Indians identified 19,500 languages and dialects as their mother tongue. 'India is home to more than 19500 mother tongues', *The Hindu Business Line*, 1 July 2018, https://www.thehindubusinessline.com/news/variety/india-is-home-to-more-than-19500-mother-tongues/article24305725.ece

23. Arvind M. Shah, 'Sects and Hindu social structure', *Contributions to Indian Sociology* 40, no. 2 (2006): 209–48, at 213.

24. Ibid., p. 211.

25. David N. Lorenzen, 'Who Invented Hinduism?', *Comparative Studies in Society and History* 41, no. 4 (1999): 630–59. The author cites the scholars Sheldon Pollock, Chris Bayly and James Laine. Also see Andrew J. Nicholson, *Unifying Hinduism: Philosophy and Identity in Indian Intellectual History* (Columbia University Press, 2010), for the argument that Hinduism was conceptually united between the fourteenth and the seventeenth centuries.

26. David N. Lorenzen, 'Who Invented Hinduism?' *Comparative Studies in Society and History* 41, no. 4 (1999): 630–659, at 655.

27. Charles Herman Heimsath, *Indian Nationalism and Hindu Social Reform* (Princeton University Press, 2015).

28. Norman Barrier's superb study of the Arya Samajis in the turn-of-the-century Punjab Congress advances the argument of this book. It was only in the context of elections (which the British had begun to introduce in the late nineteenth century) that Arya Samajis like Lala Lajpat Rai moved from a purely social reform movement to a political movement with a conception of state power. See Norman G. Barrier, 'The Arya Samaj and Congress Politics in the Punjab, 1894-1908', *The Journal of Asian Studies*, Vol. 26, No. 3 (May 1967): 363–79.

29. Dwight Baker, *Islamic Theory of Statehood* (Indian Institute of World Culture, 1981).

30. Daniel Judah Elazar, *Covenant as the Basis of the Jewish Political Tradition* (Center for the Study of Federalism, Temple University, 1979).

31. Stephen Backhouse, *Kierkegaard's Critique of Christian Nationalism* (Oxford University Press, 2011), p. 60.

32. Pratap Bhanu Mehta, 'World Religions and Democracy: Hinduism and Self-rule', *Journal of Democracy* 15, no. 3 (2004): 108–21, at 114.

33. Valmiki in *Yaddha Kanda in Ramayana*. Available at: https://www.vaachaspathi.com/vedic_library/Ramayana-VOL-3-Yuddha-Kanda.pdf

34. Peter Turchin, Jonathan M. Adams and Thomas D. Hall, 'East-west orientation of historical empires and modern states', *Journal of World-systems Research* 12, no. 2 (2006): 219-229.

35. Swapan Dasgupta, *Awakening Bharat Mata: The Political Beliefs of the Indian Right* (Penguin-Viking, 2019), p. 132.

36. This was the exact analysis that Sir Syed Ahmed Khan had provided in his book *The Causes of the Indian Revolt*. See Madhav Khosla, *India's Founding Moment: The Constitution of a Most Surprising Democracy* (Harvard University Press, 2020), p. 116.

37. Even before 1906, and starting from 1882, the British did make some concessions to the idea of liberal self-representation, by introducing limited elections to municipal councils and rural boards. These councils and boards could now nominate Indians to a limited number of seats to the central legislative assembly and the provincial assemblies. See: James Chiriyankandath, '"Democracy" under the Raj: Elections and Separate Representation in British India', *Journal of Commonwealth & Comparative Politics*, 30 (1) (1992): 39–63, at 40.

38. Maya Tudor, 'Explaining Democracy's Origins: Lessons from South Asia', *Comparative Politics*, Vol. 45, No. 3 (April 2013): 253–72, at 258.

39. The 1911 census, original text available at: http://storage.lib.uchicago.edu/pres/2014/pres2014-0779-1911-01-02.pdf

40. Walter James Shepard, 'Indian Council Act', *The American Political Science Review*, 3 (4) (November 1909): 552–56, at 553.

41. Ibid.

42. The prehistory of the Hindu Mahasabha began with the Punjab Sabha, formed in 1907 to counter Muslim League lobbying in anticipation of the 1909 constitutional reforms. Its failure told the Punjab Sabha that it needed to organize at a national level. Richard Gordon, 'The Hindu Mahasabha and the Indian National Congress, 1915 to 1926', *Modern Asian Studies*, 9, 2 (1975): 145–203, at 146.

43. Madhav Khosla, *India's Founding Moment: The Constitution of a Most Surprising Democracy* (Harvard University Press, 2020), p. 130, footnote 139.

44. Richard Gordon, 'The Hindu Mahasabha and the Indian National Congress, 1915 to 1926', *Modern Asian Studies*, 9, 2 (1975): 145–203, at 151.

45. Ibid., at 164.

46. James Chiriyankandath, '"Democracy" under the Raj: Elections and Separate Representation in British India', *Journal of Commonwealth & Comparative Politics*, 30 (1) (1992): 39–63, at 43, footnote 20.

47. 'Sikhs in Council: Question of Proportion—the Government View', *The Times of India*, 8 May 1920, 14; 'Joint committee: The trouble in Madras Indian Christian representation.' *The Times of India*, 1 August 1919, p. 9.

48. Just three per cent of the population could vote in the provincial elections, and just 1 in 10,000 for the Council of State. James Chiriyankandath, '"Democracy" under the Raj: Elections and Separate Representation in British India', *Journal of Commonwealth & Comparative Politics*, 30 (1) (1992): 39–63, at 44.

49. Ibid., at 43, footnote 22.

50. Ibid., at 42, footnote 18.

51. 1957 candidates contested the 774 seats in the two (central) legislative councils and eight provisional councils. 'The Indian elections: A summary of results', *The Times of India*, 8 June 1921, p. 10.

52. 'Mahomedan Meeting: The Khilafat Movement', *The Times of India*, 1 November 1920, p. 11.

53. S.K. Nair. 'Gandhiji's visits to Kerala: Gandhiji remembered on 30th January', *SpiderKerala*, 30 January 2011. Available at: http://www.

spiderkerala.net/resources/4928-GANDHIJI-S-VISITS-TO-KERALA-GANDHIJI-REMEMBERED.aspx

54. The scholar Manu S. Pillai says that one-fifth of land revenue from the region came from just eighty-six landlords, eighty-four of whom were Hindus. Manu S. Pillai. 'The Mapilla rebellion of Malabar', *Livemint*, 7 September 2018. Available at: https://www.livemint.com/Leisure/rjzd8IKbbcDUEjkJS7uq4M/The-Mapilla-rebellion-of-Malabar.html

55. Ramachandra Guha, *Gandhi: The Years that Changed the World (Volume 2), 1914-1948* (Knopf, 2018), p. 149.

56. Vaibhav Purandare, *Savarkar: The True Story of the Father of Hindutva* (Juggernaut, 2019), p. 193.

57. Nilanjan Mukhopadhyay, *The RSS: Icons of the Hindu Right* (Thomson Press, 2019), p. 68.

58. Rahul Sagar, 'Must liberals oppose Hindu nationalism?' *Indian Express*, 23 April 2018. Available at: https://indianexpress.com/article/opinion/columns/must-liberals-oppose-hindu-nationalism-5147683/

59. Vinayak Damodar Savarkar, *Hindutva: Who Is a Hindu?* (Veer Savarkar Prakashan, 1969).

60. As the political theorist Niraja Jayal says, for Savarkar 'religious minorities should [in the abstract] enjoy equal formal rights of citizenship'. Niraja Gopal Jayal, *Citizenship and Its Discontents: An Indian History* (Harvard University Press, 2013), p. 217.

61. Vaibhav Purandare, *Savarkar: The True Story of the Father of Hindutva* (Juggernaut, 2019), p. 189.

62. Nilanjan Mukhopadhyay, *The RSS: Icons of the Hindu Right* (Thomson Press, 2019), p. 84.

63. Ibid., p. 90, footnote 47.

64. Walter K. Anderson and Shridhar D. Damle, *The Saffron Brotherhood: The Rashtriya Swayamsevak Sangh and Hindu Revivalism* (Westview Press, 1987), p. 33.

65. Ibid.

66. Nilanjan Mukhopadhyay, *The RSS: Icons of the Hindu Right* (Thomson Press, 2019), p. 27.

67. Christophe Jaffrelot, *The Hindu Nationalist Movement in India* (Columbia University Press, 1996), p. 37, footnote 112.

68. Walter K. Anderson and Shridhar D. Damle, *The Saffron Brotherhood: The Rashtriya Swayamsevak Sangh and Hindu Revivalism* (Westview Press, 1987); Christophe Jaffrelot, *The Hindu Nationalist Movement in India* (Columbia University Press, 1996).

69. 'Threatening Letters Received By Hindu Leaders At Nagpur', *The Times of India*, 13 May 1927, p. 11.

70. Walter K. Anderson and Shridhar D. Damle, *The Saffron Brotherhood: The Rashtriya Swayamsevak Sangh and Hindu Revivalism* (Westview Press, 1987), p. 36.

71. Clemens Dutt, 'India Nationalism and the Elections', *Labour Monthly*, Vol. 8, No. 12, December 1926: 733–744. Available at: https://www.marxists. org/archive/dutt-clemens/1926/12/x01.htm

72. Richard Gordon, 'The Hindu Mahasabha and the Indian National Congress, 1915 to 1926', *Modern Asian Studies*, 9, 2 (1975): 145–203, at 150.

73. Clemens Dutt, 'India Nationalism and the Elections', *Labour Monthly*, Vol. 8, No. 12, December 1926: 733–744. Available at: https://www.marxists. org/archive/dutt-clemens/1926/12/x01.htm

74. Farzana Shaikh, *Community and Consensus in Islam: Muslim Representation in Colonial India, 1860–1947* (Imprintone, 2nd edition, 2012); Venkat Dhulipala, *Creating a New Media: State Power, Islam, and the Quest for Pakistan in Late Colonial North India* (Cambridge University Press, 2015).

75. Some scholars have argued that the Hindu princely states of colonial India offered Hindu nationalists an imagination of what a Hindu state looked like. Even if this is accurate, such an imagination was nascent rather than clearly thought out. A Hindu monarchy was never considered as an alternative to an elected state with majority Hindus by Hindu nationalists. Manu Bhagwan, 'Princely States and The Hindu Imaginary: Exploring the Cartography of Hindu Nationalism in Colonial India', *The Journal of Asian Studies*, Vol. 67, No. 3 (August) 2008: 881–915.

76. Nilanjan Mukhopadhyay, *The RSS: Icons of the Hindu Right* (Thomson Press, 2019), p. 90, footnote 47.

77. 'Gwalior home reflects Vajpayee's simple lifestyle', *Hindustan Times*, 18 August 2018. Available at: https://www.hindustantimes.com/ india-news/gwalior-home-reflects-vajpayee-s-simple-lifestyle/story-YjXRJOEcPs0sUihYgc7w3N.html

78. Ullekh N.P., *The Untold Vajpayee: Politician and Paradox* (Penguin Books, kindle edition, 2017), location 210 of 3595.

79. Interview with N.M. Ghatate, Delhi, May 2018.

80. L.K. Advani, *My Country My Life* (Rupa, 2010, paperback), p. 29.

81. Haris Masood Zuberi, 'Through hardships to the stars: St. Patrick's High School turns 150 years old today', *Tribune*, 6 May 2011. Available at: https://tribune.com.pk/story/162698/through-hardships-to-the-stars-st-patricks-high-school-turns-150-years-old-today/%E2%80%99/

82. 'Minute by the Hon'ble T.B. Macaulay, dated the 2nd February 1835'. Available at: http://www.columbia.edu/itc/mealac/pritchett/00generallinks/ macaulay/txt_minute_education_1835.html

83. Interview with Sudheendra Kulkarni, Mumbai, May 2018.

84. Haris Masood Zuberi, 'Through hardships to the stars: St. Patrick's High School turns 150 years old today', *Tribune*, 6 May 2011. Available at: https://tribune.com.pk/story/162698/through-hardships-to-the-stars-st-patricks-high-school-turns-150-years-old-today/%E2%80%99/

85. Interview with T.C.A. Raghavan, New Delhi, May 2018.

86. Kingshuk Nag, *Atal Bihari Vajpayee: A Man for All Seasons* (Rupa, 2015), p. 23.

87. Ullekh N.P., *The Untold Vajpayee: Politician and Paradox* (Penguin Books, kindle edition, 2017), location 369.

88. Interview with Vijai Trivedi, New Delhi, June 2019.

89. Ullekh N.P., *The Untold Vajpayee: Politician and Paradox* (Penguin Books, kindle edition, 2017); Kingshuk Nag, *Atal Bihari Vajpayee: A Man for All Seasons* (Rupa, 2015), p. 62.

90. Srinath Raghavan, *India's War: World War II and the Making of Modern South Asia* (Hachette UK, 2016).

91. Book quoted in Ajai Shukla, 'India's World War II', *Business Standard*, 30 April 2016. Available at: https://www.business-standard.com/article/beyond-business/india-s-world-war-ii-116042901402_1.html

92. Shamsul Islam, *Religious Dimensions of Indian Nationalism: A Study of RSS* (Media House, 2006), p. 213.

93. Ibid.

94. Manini Chatterjee and V.K. Ramachandran, 'Vajpayee and the Quit India Movement', *Frontline*, Vol. 15, No. 3, 7–20 February, 1998. Available at: https://frontline.thehindu.com/static/html/fl1503/15031150.htm

95. Ibid.

96. Ibid.

97. 'Hindu Sangh as "Nazi"', *The Hindu*, 8 March 1934, p. 9.

98. Walter K. Anderson and Shridhar D. Damle, *The Saffron Brotherhood: The Rashtriya Swayamsevak Sangh and Hindu Revivalism* (Westview Press, 1987), p. 38, footnote 74. The figure is for 1939.

99. Kingshuk Nag, *Atal Bihari Vajpayee: A Man for All Seasons* (Rupa, 2015), p. 24.

100. Ibid., p. 23.

101. Ibid., p. 24.

102. Ibid., p. 25.

103. L.K. Advani, *My Country My Life* (Rupa, 2010, paperback), pp. 37–38.

104. Ibid., p. 33.

105. Walter K. Anderson and Shridhar D. Damle, *The Saffron Brotherhood: The Rashtriya Swayamsevak Sangh and Hindu Revivalism* (Westview Press, 1987), p. 84.

106. Christophe Jaffrelot, *The Hindu Nationalist Movement in India* (Columbia University Press, 1996), p. 37.

107. Uday S. Kulkarni, *Solstice at Panipat, 14 January 1761: An Authentic Account of the Panipat Campaign* (Mula Mutha Publications, 2012).

108. L.K. Advani, *My Country My Life* (Rupa, 2010, paperback), p. 41.

109. Ibid., p. 342. Munshi's interpretation is contested by, among others, Romila Thapar in *Somnatha: The Many Voices of a History* (Verso, 2005).

110. Madhav Sadashiv Golwalkar, *We or Our Nationhood Defined* (Kale, 1947), pp. 47–48.

111. Madhav Sadashiv Golwalkar, *Bunch of Thoughts* (Vikrama Prakashan, 1966), p. 176.

112. Phone interview with Sridhar Damle, 2020.

113. 'Golwalkar: Crusader for a Strong India', *The Times of India*, 6 June 1973, p. 10.

114. The scholar on the RSS, Sridhar Damle, says that OTC is a three-step process; however, this source says otherwise. See, Vasudha Venugopal, 'What does it take to be an RSS karyakarta?', *Economic Times*, 30 May 2018. Available at: https://economictimes.indiatimes.com/news/politics-and-nation/what-does-it-take-to-be-an-rss-karyakarta/articleshow/64390472.cms

115. Ibid.

116. Interview with an RSS leader who does not wish to be named.

117. L.K. Advani, *My Country My Life* (Rupa, 2010, paperback), p. 42.

118. 'Vajpayee and his father studied law together in Kanpur', *The Indian Express*, 17 August 2018. Available at: https://indianexpress.com/article/education/when-atal-bihari-vajpayee-and-his-father-were-classmates-in-a-kanpur-college-5312260/

119. Vijai Trivedi, *Haar Nahin Maanoonga* (HarperCollins Hindi, 2016), p. 84.

120. 'Vajpayee and his father studied law together in Kanpur', *The Indian Express*, 17 August 2018. Available at: https://indianexpress.com/article/education/when-atal-bihari-vajpayee-and-his-father-were-classmates-in-a-kanpur-college-5312260/

121. Tilak Sharma, 'A teacher remembers a student by the name Atal', *The Times of India*, 18 May 1996.

122. Ramachandra Guha, *Gandhi: The Years that Changed the World (volume 2), 1914-1948* (Knopf, 2018), p. 757.

123. Ibid., p. 771.

124. Ibid., p. 757.

125. This was particularly so when the Hindu Mahasabha was run by Savarkar from 1937 to 1942, and from 1946 onwards. See Nandini Gondhalekar and Sanjoy Bhattacharya, 'The All India Hindu Mahasabha and the End of

British Rule in India, 1939-1947', *Social Scientist*, Vol. 27, No. 7/8 (July–August 1999): 48–74, at 63.

126. Vaibhav Purandare, *Savarkar: The True Story of The Father of Hindutva* (Juggernaut, 2019), p. 273.

127. Bhimrao Ramji Ambedkar, *Pakistan or Partition of India* (Thacker, 1946).

128. Neeti Nair, *Changing Homelands* (Harvard University Press, 2011).

129. Joya Chatterji, *The Spoils of Partition: Bengal and India, 1947-1967* (Cambridge University Press, 2007).

130. Ayesha Jalal, *The Sole Spokesman: Jinnah, the Muslim League and the Demand for Pakistan*, Vol. 31 (Cambridge University Press, 1994).

131. Gandhi had toyed with the idea of Pakistan in negotiations with Jinnah in 1944. But, using the Rajaji plan, he thought of partition as an option to be discussed only after the British left. Jinnah did not take the discussion any further. See G.S. Chhabra, 'CR formula', *Advance Study in the History of Modern India (Volume-2: 1803-1920)* (Lotus Press, 2005), p. 168.

132. Hindu Mahasabha Papers, 1944, C-60-I, p. 15. Accessed from NMML.

133. Ibid, p. 11.

CHAPTER 2: GHOSTS OF PARTITION (1945–50)

1. The remaining seats (out of 102) were divided as follows: Europeans 8; Landholders 7; Indian Commerce 4; Sikhs 2; General 3. 'Government of India, Return Showing the Results of Elections to the Central Legislative Assembly and the Provincial Legislatures in 1945-46 (Delhi, 1948)', p. 5.

2. This was the Cabinet Mission Plan of the British government, released in May 1946. Though the Congress had some issues with it, they were by and large willing to go with the general principles of the plan.

3. 'Hindus betrayed by Congress: Mr. Savarkar's criticism', *The Times of India*, 31 October 1945, p. 5.

4. Christophe Jaffrelot, *The Hindu Nationalist Movement in India* (Columbia University Press, 1996), p. 73.

5. *Schwartzberg Atlas*, v., 222. Digital South Asia Library. Available at: https://dsal.uchicago.edu/reference/schwartzberg/pager.html?object=260&view=text

6. W.W.J., 'The Indian Elections 1946', *The World Today*, 2(4) (April 1946): 167–75, at 168, Chatham House: The Royal Institute of International Affairs.

7. Ramachandra Guha, *Gandhi: The Years that Changed the World (volume 2), 1914-1948* (Knopf, 2018), p. 772.

8. *Schwartzberg Atlas*, v., 222. Digital South Asia Library. Available at: https://dsal.uchicago.edu/reference/schwartzberg/pager.html?object=260&view=text

9. Ibid.

10. Rupa Subramanya. 'Facts Don't Back The Argument That Most Indian Muslims Wanted Partition', *Huffington Post*, 19 June 2017. Available at: https://www.huffingtonpost.in/rupa-subramanya/facts-dont-back-the-argument-that-most-indian-muslims-wanted-pa_a_22488885/

11. Nilanjan Mukhopadhyay, *The RSS: Icons of the Hindu Right* (Thomson Press, 2019), p. 354.

12. L.K. Advani, *My Country My Life* (Rupa, 2010, paperback), p. 42.

13. Ibid. p. 5.

14. India, The Round Table', *The Commonwealth Journal of International Affairs*, Vol. 37, No. 147 (1947): 262–69, at 262. Available at: https://www.tandfonline.com/doi/abs/10.1080/00358534708451456

15. Yuvraj Krishan, *Understanding Partition: India Sundered, Muslims Fragmented* (Bharatiya Vidya Bhavan, 2002), p. 247.

16. Chandni Saxena, 'Dimensions and Dynamics of Violence during the Partition of India', *Proceedings of the Indian History Congress*, Vol. 74 (2013): 909–20.

17. Ramachandra Guha, *Gandhi: The Years that Changed the World (volume 2), 1914-1948* (Knopf, 2018), p. 861.

18. Ranbir Vohra, *The Making of India: A Political History* (Routledge, 2014, Third Edition), p. 84.

19. 'Indian Independence Act, 1947', chapter 30. Available at: http://www.legislation.gov.uk/ukpga/1947/30/pdfs/ukpga_19470030_en.pdf

20. 'Move to partition Punjab and Bengal: Text of Mr. Jinnah's Statement, I and B Department', New Delhi, 4 May1947. Available at: http://www.nationalarchives.gov.uk/education/resources/the-road-to-partition/jinnah-partition/

21. Tahir Kamran, 'The Unfolding Crisis in Punjab, March-August 1947: Key Turning Points and British Responses', *JPS* 14, no. 2 (2007): 197.

22. Sankar Ghose, *Mahatma Gandhi* (Allied Publishers, 1991), p. 341.

23. S.P. Mookerjee, 'Hindus Will Never Accept Partition', *Organiser*, Vol 1, 1, 3 July 1947, p. 5. Accessed from the Nehru Memorial Museum and Library.

24. L.K. Advani, *My Country My Life* (Rupa, 2010, paperback), p. 8.

25. Ibid., p. 2.

26. Ibid., p. 4.

27. Kingshuk Nag, *Atal Bihari Vajpayee: A Man for All Seasons* (Rupa, 2015), p. 27.

28. Ibid.

29. Interview with Govindacharya, Delhi, March 2018.

30. Prashant Bharadwaj, Asim Khwaja and Atif Mian, 'The big march: migratory flows after the partition of India', *Economic and Political Weekly* (2008): 39–49.

31. Ramachandra Guha, *Gandhi: The Years that Changed the World (volume 2), 1914-1948* (Knopf, 2018), p. 843.

32. Ramachandra Guha, *India after Gandhi: The History of the World's Largest Democracy* (Picador, 2017), p. 86.

33. Arunima Dey, 'Violence against women during the partition of India: Interpreting women and their bodies in the context of ethnic genocide', *ES Review*, No. 37, 2016, p. 106, Universidad de Vallodolid.

34. Ramachandra Guha, *Gandhi: The Years that Changed the World (volume 2), 1914-1948* (Knopf, 2018), p. 843.

35. L.K. Advani, *My Country My Life* (Rupa, 2010, paperback), p. 11.

36. Ibid., p. 109.

37. Ibid., p. 51.

38. Ibid., p. 46.

39. Ibid., p. 67.

40. Ramachandra Guha, *Gandhi: The Years that Changed the World (volume 2), 1914-1948* (Knopf, 2018), p. 864.

41. Interview with Prafull Goradia, Delhi, April 2018.

42. Ranjita Ganesan, 'We Are the Godses', *Business Standard*, 7 February 2015. Available at: https://www.business-standard.com/article/specials/we-are-the-godses-115020600671_1.html

43. Nathuram Godse, *May it Please Your Honour* (Surya Prakashan, Nai Sarak, 1989), p. 50.

44. Ibid., p. 67.

45. A.G. Noorani, 'Savarkar and Gandhi's murder', *Frontline*, Volume 29, Issue 19: 22 September-5 October 2012. Available at: https://frontline.thehindu.com/static/html/fl2919/stories/20121005291911400.htm

46. Interview with M.G. Vaidya, Nagpur, April 2018.

47. L.K. Advani, *My Country My Life* (Rupa, 2010, paperback), p. 72.

48. Ramachandra Guha, *Gandhi: The Years that Changed the World (volume 2), 1914-1948* (Knopf, 2018), p. 867.

49. Nathuram Godse, *May it Please Your Honour* (Surya Prakashan, Nai Sarak, 1989), p. 78.

50. Rajesh Ramachandran, 'The Mastermind?', *Outlook*, 6 September 2004. Available at: https://www.outlookindia.com/magazine/story/the-mastermind/225000

51. Tushar A. Gandhi. 'Nathuram Godse pulled the trigger, but who really killed Mahatma Gandhi?', *Economic Times*, 11 September 2016. Available at: //economictimes.indiatimes.com/articleshow/54270465.cms?from=mdr&utm_source=contentofinterest&utm_medium=text&utm_campaign=cppst

52. Ullekh N.P., 'Savarkar escaped because nobody probed how Godse got an Italian revolver from a Gwalior dealer', *Open*, 20 May 2019. Available at: https://www.openthemagazine.com/article/history/savarkar-escaped-because-nobody-probed-how-godse-got-an-italian-revolver-from-a-gwalior-dealer

53. Prabhash K. Dutta, 'Nathuram Godse was nervous, fearful going to gallows, said judge who heard his appeal', *India Today*, 17 May 2019. Available at: https://www.indiatoday.in/india/story/nathuram-godse-was-nervous-fearful-going-to-gallows-said-judge-who-heard-his-appeal-1527184-2019-05-17

54. Gopal Godse disputes this. On being asked, he said that the words 'Hey Ram' had been uttered by Ben Kingsley, not Mohandas Gandhi, https://www.youtube.com/watch?v=cKiuJnWNaLU

55. Kanika Sharma, 'Spectacular Justice: Aesthetics and Power in the Gandhi Murder Trial', in Awol Allo (ed.), *The Courtroom as a Space of Resistance* (Routledge, 2015).

56. Ibid.

57. The appeal was heard by the Punjab and Haryana High Court. Savarkar's acquittal was not in contention. The judge upheld the rest of the trial court's verdict.

58. Christophe Jaffrelot, 'The retrial of Nathuram Godse: Gandhi assassin's political audience', *Indian Express*, 30 January 2015. Available at: https://indianexpress.com/article/opinion/columns/mahatma-gandhis-assassin-seems-to-have-a-political-audience-once-more/

59. Kanika Sharma, 'Spectacular Justice: Aesthetics and Power in the Gandhi Murder Trial', in Awol Allo (ed.), *The Courtroom as a Space of Resistance* (Routledge, 2015), p. 25.

60. Nathuram Godse, *May it Please Your Honour* (Surya Prakashan, Nai Sarak, 1989), p. 65.

61. Barnik Ghosh, 'The Trial of Nathuram Godse: A Defiant Rebuttal or a Meek Submission', *India Law Journal*, http://www.indialawjournal.org/archives/volume2/issue_2/nathuram_godse_trial.html

62. A.G. Noorani, 'RSS & Gandhi's murder', *Frontline*, 14 October 2016.

63. M.S. Golwalkar, *Collected Speeches (Sri Guruji Samagra), Volume 7* (New Delhi: Suruchi Prakashan), p. 9.

64. Ramachandra Guha, *Gandhi: The Years that Changed the World (volume 2), 1914-1948* (Knopf, 2018), p. 896.

65. A.G. Noorani, *Savarkar and Hindutva: The Godse Connection* (LeftWord Books, 2002), p. 138.

66. A.G. Noorani, 'RSS & Gandhi's murder', *Frontline*, 14 October 2016.

67. Ullekh N.P., 'Savarkar escaped because nobody probed how Godse got an Italian revolver from a Gwalior dealer', *Open*, 20 May 2019. Available at: https://www.openthemagazine.com/article/history/savarkar-escaped-because-nobody-probed-how-godse-got-an-italian-revolver-from-a-gwalior-dealer

68. Vinay Lal, 'Nathuram Godse, the RSS, and the Murder of Gandhi', *UCLA Social Sciences MANAS*. Available at: http://southasia.ucla.edu/history-politics/hindu-rashtra/nathuram-godse-rss-murder-gandhi/

69. Hindu Mahasabha Papers, 1944, C-175 (1948-49), p. 96. Accessed from NMML.

70. From May 1948 to February 1949.

71. Ramachandra Guha, *Gandhi: The Years that Changed the World (volume 2), 1914-1948* (Knopf, 2018), p. 899.

72. A.G. Noorani. 'How Savarkar escaped the gallows', *The Hindu*, 30 January 2013. Available at: https://www.thehindu.com/opinion/op-ed/how-savarkar-escaped-the-gallows/article4358048.ece

73. S. Padmavathi and D.G. Hariprasath. 'Volume VI, Chapter XXV, Bombay investigation, point 25.106', Mahatma Gandhi Assassination: J.L. Kapur Commission Report, Part 2.

74. Krishnadas Rajagopal, 'No material to probe Gandhi assassination again: SC', *The Hindu*, 8 January 2018. Available at: https://www.thehindu.com/news/national/no-material-to-probe-gandhi-death-again-sc/article22398743.ece

75. L.K. Advani, *My Country My Life* (Rupa, 2010, paperback), p. 72.

76. M.S. Golwalkar, *Collected Speech (Sri Guruji Samagra), Volume 1* (New Delhi: Suruchi Prakashan), p. 5.

77. Ibid., p. 6.

78. Ibid., p. 8.

79. Christophe Jaffrelot, *The Hindu Nationalist Movement in India* (Columbia University Press, 1996), p. 88.

80. 'R.S.S. Has Done Nothing To Feel Penitent: Activities to be continued as before', *The Times of India*, 18 July 1949, p. 7.

81. 'Association with R.S.S. May Lead to Dismissal', *The Times of India*, 7 February 1948, p. 9.

82. Omar Rashid, 'RSS is in it and outside it: M.G. Vaidya', *The Hindu*, 13 September 2015. Available at: https://www.thehindu.com/sunday-anchor/rss-is-in-it-and-outside-it-mg-vaidya/article7646310.ece

83. Vijai Trivedi, *Haar Nahin Maanoonga* (HarperCollins Hindi, 2016), p. 50.

84. 'Disturbances spread in Poona: more areas under curfew: Troops called out', *The Times of India*, 2 February 1948, p. 7.

85. 'Hindu sabha office riffled', *The Times of India*, 2 February 1948, p. 7.

86. Interview with M.G. Vaidya, Nagpur, April 2018.

87. L.K. Advani, *My Country My Life* (Rupa, 2010, paperback), p. 75.

88. Ibid., p. 71.

89. Ibid., p. 75.

90. Rakesh Ankit, 'How the Ban on the RSS Was Lifted', *Economic and Political Weekly*, 2012, 47 (16):71–78.

91. Desh Raj Goyal. 'Appendix IV: Text of the government communique of 11 July 1949', *Rashtriya Swayamsewak Sangh*, p. 255, Hindi Shop, 2000.

92. 'Unification Of Hindu Society: New Constitution of R. S. S.', *The Times of India*, 7 September 1949, p. 11.

93. Interview with Ravindra Bhagwat, Chandrapur, March 2018.

94. See, for instance, P.D. Saggi (ed.), *Life and Work of Sardar Vallabhbhai Patel* (Overseas Publishing House, Bombay), p. viii.

95. That this older religious idea of India informed Patel's actions can be seen from this telling comment from V.P. Menon, who assisted the home minister in this task: 'India is one geographical entity. Yet, throughout her long and chequered history, she never achieved political homogeneity . . . Today, for the first time in the country's history, the writ of a single central Government runs from Kailas to Kanyakumari, from Kathiawar to Kamarupa'. V.P Menon, *Integration of the Indian States* (Orient Blackswan, 1956), pp. 7–8.

96. V.P. Menon, *Integration of the Indian States* (Orient Blackswan, 1956), p. 271.

97. G.M. Nandurkar (ed.), Sardar Patel Series, Volume 2, p. 62, https://indianexpress.com/article/explained/sardar-vallabhbhai-patels-views-on-kashmir-problem-what-the-record-says-5060077/

98. Claude Arpi, 'Tragedy of Kashmir that bleeds us to this day', *The Pioneer*, 21 December 2017.

99. The steps were that, first, 'tribesman and Pakistani nationals' were instructed to withdraw from the region. Once they withdrew, India would begin moving its own troops out. It was only once this was done that the

UN would conduct a plebiscite', i.e., elections in Kashmir to determine whether the people wanted to go with India or Pakistan. See UNSCR, Resolution 47. Available at: http://unscr.com/en/resolutions/47

100. The reasons for India and Pakistan's rejections of the UN resolution is provided in detail in Srinath Raghavan, *War and Peace in Modern India* (Palgrave Macmillan, 2010), p. 132.

101. Venkatesh Nayak, 'The Backstory of Article 370: A True Copy of J&K's Instrument of Accession', *The Wire*, 26 October 2016. Available at: https://thewire.in/history/public-first-time-jammu-kashmirs-instrument-accession-india

102. The best book on the legal enactment of Article 370 and its subsequent erosion (prior to 2019) is A.G. Noorani, *Article 370: A Constitutional History of Jammu & Kashmir* (Oxford University Press, 2011).

103. Article 35A of Constitution of India, 1950, which has since been made redundant. The prevention of outsiders buying land in Kashmir predated the Indian Constitution.

104. Neeraja Singh (ed.), *Nehru-Patel: Agreement Within Differences: Select documents and correspondences 1933-1950* (National Book Trust, 2010), p. 167.

105. Rajmohan Gandhi, *Patel: A Life* (Navajivan Publishing House, 1990, kindle edition), location 10773.

106. Romila Thapar. *Somanatha: The Many Voices of a History* (Verso, 2005).

107. K.M. Munshi, *Jai Somnath* (Rajkamal Prakashan, 2016).

108. Christophe Jaffrelot, *The Hindu Nationalist Movement in India* (Columbia University Press, 1996), p. 84.

109. 'Report of the Liberhan Ayodhya Commission of Inquiry', Ministry of Home Affairs, Government of India, 2009, p. 9.

110. Dhirendra K. Jha and Krishna Jha, *Ayodhya The Dark Night: The Secret History of Rama's Appearance in Babri Masjid* (HarperCollins, 2012).

111. Gyanesh Kudaisya, 'Ayodhya in the Time of Jawaharlal', *Outlook*, 10 December 2018. Available at: https://www.outlookindia.com/magazine/story/ayodhya-in-the-time-of-jawaharlal/300943

112. L.K. Advani, *My Country My Life* (Rupa, 2010, paperback), p. 361.

113. Ibid.

114. T.C.A. Raghavan, *The People Next Door: The Curious History of India's Relations with Pakistan* (HarperCollins India, 2017), p. 31.

115. Christophe Jaffrelot, *The Hindu Nationalist Movement in India* (Columbia University Press, 1996), p. 96.

116. T.C.A. Raghavan, *The People Next Door: The Curious History of India's Relations with Pakistan* (HarperCollins India, 2017), p. 33.

117. Ibid., footnote 4.
118. Ibid., footnote 5.
119. Ibid., p. 36.
120. Christophe Jaffrelot, *The Hindu Nationalist Movement in India* (Columbia University Press, 1996), p. 86, footnote 30.
121. Ibid., p. 90.
122. Ramachandra Guha, 'Why Nehru vs Patel', *Indian Express*, 9 February 2018. Available at: https://indianexpress.com/article/opinion/columns/why-jawaharlal-nehru-vs-vallabhbhai-patel-5056609/

CHAPTER 3: IN NEHRU'S SHADOW (1951–67)

1. Interview with N.M. Ghatate, New Delhi, May 2018.
2. M M.S. Golwalkar, *Collected Speeches (Sri Guruji Samagra), Volume 1* (New Delhi: Suruchi Prakashan), p. 117.
3. L.K. Advani, *My Country, My Life* (Rupa, 2010, paperback), p. 86.
4. B.D. Graham, *Hindu Nationalism and Indian Politics: The Origins and Development of the Bharatiya Jana Sangh* (Cambridge University Press, 2008), p. 27.
5. Christophe Jaffrelot, *The Hindu Nationalist Movement in India* (Columbia University Press, 1996) p. 117.
6. Ibid., p. 118, footnote 15.
7. Ibid.
8. Bharatiya Jana Sangh Manifesto, 1951.
9. 'Bharatiya Jan Sangh: Convention in Delhi', *Hindu*, 22 October 1951, p. 6.
10. Ibid.
11. Nilanjan Mukhopadhyay, *The RSS: Icons of the Hindu Right* (Thomson Press, 2019), p. 211.
12. For a representative list of his writings, see https://deendayalupadhyay.org/articles.html
13. B.D. Graham, *Hindu Nationalism and Indian Politics: The Origins and Development of the Bharatiya Jana Sangh* (Cambridge University Press, 2008), p. 76.
14. L.K. Advani, *My Country, My Life* (Rupa, 2010, paperback), p. 88.
15. 'Bharatiya Jan Sangh: Convention in Delhi', *Hindu*, 22 October 1951, p. 6
16. From a 1952 essay in the *Organiser*. Quoted in Ramachandra Guha, 'Rescue Nehru from his descendants, writes Ramachandra Guha,' *Hindustan Times*, 30 July 2017. Available at: https://www.hindustantimes.

com/editorials/can-nehru-be-rescued-from-his-descendants/story-0aXiS7hlFh4fgbKX1SmrSP.html

17. Ramachandra Guha, *India after Gandhi: The History of the World's Largest Democracy* (Picador, 2017), p. 135.

18. Ibid., p. 134.

19. Christophe Jaffrelot, *The Hindu Nationalist Movement in India* (Columbia University Press, 1996), p. 121.

20. 'Dr. Mookerjee Explains Jan Sangh's Objectives: Attitude to Kashmir state issue', *The Times of India*, 30 December 1952, p. 5.

21. 'R.S.S. to launch campaign: Cow slaughter ban', *The Times of India*, 7 October 1952, p. 7.

22. B.D. Graham, *Hindu Nationalism and Indian Politics: The Origins and Development of the Bharatiya Jana Sangh* (Cambridge University Press, 2008), p. 30.

23. Prabhu Chawla, 'United Front stuck with label of instability as parties engage in competitive politics', *India Today*, 15 February 1997. Available at: https://www.indiatoday.in/magazine/cover-story/story/19970215-united-front-stuck-with-label-of-instability-as-parties-engage-in-competitive-politics-832841-1997-02-15

24. Interview with Govindacharya, New Delhi, June 2018.

25. L.K. Advani, *My Country, My Life* (Rupa, 2010, paperback), p. 834.

26. Ibid.

27. Ullekh N.P., *The Untold Vajpayee: Politician and Paradox* (Penguin Books, kindle edition, 2017), location 573.

28. The official version is that Mookerjee lacked the 'permit' required to enter Kashmir. See Kingshuk Nag, *Atal Bihari Vajpayee: A Man for All Seasons* (Rupa, 2015), p. 30. However, Hindu nationalists argue that the arrest was illegal. See Tathagata Roy, *Syama Prasad Mookerjee: Life and Times* (Penguin, 2018), p. 377.

29. Ashok Tandon, 'One day this young man will be PM: Nehru on Vajpayee', *Sify News*, 24 December 2014. Available at: http://www.sify.com/news/one-day-this-young-man-will-be-pm-nehru-on-vajpayee-news-columns-omxua0gfeifdi.html

30. 'Dr. Mookerjee's end followed weakening of heart: 82-year-old mother faints', *The Times of India*, 24 June 1953, p. 5.

31. 'Ibid.

32. Interview with Swapan Dasgupta, March 2018.

33. Kingshuk Nag, *Atal Bihari Vajpayee: A Man for All Seasons* (Rupa, 2015), p. 31.

34. 'Atal Bihari Vajpayee lost his first election in 1953; this is what he did after hearing the news', *DNA*, 17 August 2018.

35. Interview with Govindacharya, New Delhi, June 2018.

36. Syed Muthahar Saqaf, 'Vajpayee's record', *The Hindu*, 26 March 2014. Available at: https://www.thehindu.com/news/national/vajpayees-record/article5832273.ece

37. Vijai Trivedi, *Haar Nahin Maanoonga* (HarperCollins Hindi, 2016), p. 21.

38. N.M. Ghatate (ed.), *Atal Bihari Vajpayee: Four Decades in Parliament*, Volume 1 (Shipra Publications), p. xvi.

39. Vijai Trivedi, *Haar Nahin Maanoonga* (HarperCollins Hindi, 2016), p. 21.

40. L.K. Advani, *My Country, My Life* (Rupa, 2010, paperback), p. 101–02.

41. Interview with N.M. Ghatate, New Delhi, May 2018.

42. Interview with Sudheendra Kulkarni, Mumbai, May 2018.

43. 'Walk-out By M. P.s', *The Times of India*, 21 August 1957, p. 9. See N.M. Ghatate (ed.), *Atal Bihari Vajpayee: Four Decades in Parliament*, Volume 1 (Shipra Publications), p. xviii.

44. L.K. Advani, *My Country, My Life* (Rupa, 2010, paperback), p 103.

45. N.M. Ghatate (ed.), *Atal Bihari Vajpayee: Four Decades in Parliament*, Volume 1 (Shipra Publications), p. 23.

46. Interview with Ullekh N.P., New Delhi, April 2018.

47. Interview with R.V. Pandit, Bengaluru, April 2018.

48. For obvious reasons, this poet did not wish his name to be quoted in the book.

49. Vijai Trivedi, *Haar Nahin Maanoonga* (HarperCollins Hindi, 2016), p. 81.

50. Interview with R.V. Pandit, Bengaluru, April 2018. He says he was told this story by an Indian diplomat.

51. L.K. Advani, *My Country, My Life* (Rupa, 2010, paperback), p. 104.

52. Ibid., pp. 845–46.

53. 'Netra', 'Only a Foreigner Competent to Film Gandhiji's Life, Nehru Says', *Organiser*, Vol. XVII, No. 19, p. 12, 16 December 1963.

54. L.K. Advani, *My Country, My Life* (Rupa, 2010, paperback), p. 110.

55. Interview with Mahesh Rangarajan, New Delhi, January 2019.

56. 'Vajpayee And Subhadra Joshi In Neck And Neck Race', *The Times of India*, 3 February 1967, p. 3.

57. China saw India's 1959 reception of the Dalai Lama as an interference into its internal matters. And China had long rejected the British-drawn border line, claiming some 2,500 square miles of Indian-controlled territory as its own. For the latter argument, see Srinath Raghavan, *War and Peace in Modern India* (Palgrave Macmillan, 2010), p. 266.

58. 'This is a Dharmayuddha', *Organiser*, Vol. 16, No. 13, 5 November 1962, p. 15. Accessed from NMML.

59. Interview with Harin Pathak, Ahmedabad, April 2018.

60. N.M. Ghatate (ed.), *Atal Bihari Vajpayee: Four Decades in Parliament*, Volume 1 (Shipra Publications), p. 69.

61. Kingshuk Nag, *Atal Bihari Vajpayee: A Man for All Seasons* (Rupa, 2015), p 145.

62. 'RSS in R-Day parade: Highlight of Citizens' Group', *Organiser*, Vol. 16, No, 26, 4 February 1963, p. 1. Accessed from NMML.

63. Ibid., pp., 1, 15. Accessed from NMML.

64. The scholars B.D. Graham and Craig Baxter have exhaustively studied the policies of the Jana Sangh through this period. What their studies miss is that these policies had little to do with ideology and everything to do with winning elections. B.D. Graham, *Hindu Nationalism and Indian Politics: The Origins and Development of the Bharatiya Jana Sangh* (Cambridge University Press, 2008); Craig Baxter, *The Jana Sangh: Biography of an Indian Political Party* (University of Pennsylvania Press, 1969).

65. Victor Anant, 'Indians' anxious look at the era after Nehru', *The Guardian*, 28 May 1964.

66. 'When Atal Bihari Vajpayee delivered emotional speech after Jawaharlal Nehru's death', *Economic Times*, 17 August 2017.

67. Craig Baxter, *The Jana Sangh: Biography of an Indian Political Party* (University of Pennsylvania Press, 1969).

68. Interview with Sudheendra Kulkarni, Mumbai, May 2018.

69. Interview with M.G. Vaidya, Nagpur, April 2018.

70. Jacques Maritain, *Integral Humanism: Temporal and Spiritual Problems of a New Christendom*, translated by Joseph Evans (New York: Charles Scribner's Sons, 1968), p. 22. Maritain was writing under the context of the clash between capitalism, fascism and communism in Europe— and the devastation it had caused on family, freedom, as well as on the Catholic church. His solution was to lead the human person towards a full development under the primacy of the spiritual. This conception of a human 'person', free but non-materialistic, was a deliberate reaction to what Maritain calls the 'two opposite errors' of totalitarianism and individualism. To protect democratic freedom from communism and fascism, he argued that it was important that the 'secular' values of the state be grounded in their religious and philosophical basis. Such a state would not be theocratic, but it would acknowledge that the values of secularism, democracy, liberalism and freedom was grounded in a Christian tradition.

71. L.K. Advani, *My Country, My Life* (Rupa, 2010, paperback), p. 120.

72. Ibid., pp. 120–21.

73. Interview with Karan Thapar, New Delhi, November 2019.

74. Interview with Harin Pathak, Ahmedabad, April 2018.

75. Ibid.

76. Vijai Trivedi, *Haar Nahin Maanoonga* (HarperCollins Hindi, 2016), p. 83.

77. Interview with Virendra Kapoor, New Delhi, June 2018.

78. Interview with N.M. Ghatate, New Delhi, May 2018.

79. Balraj Madhok, *Zindagi ka Safar-3: Deendayal Upadhyaya ki hatya se Indira Gandhi ki hatya tak* (Dinman Prakashan), p. 25.

80. Interview with R.V. Pandit, Bengaluru, April 2018.

81. Manjari Katju, *Vishva Hindu Parishad and Indian Politics* (Orient Blackswan, Second Edition, 2010), p. 7.

82. Ibid.

83. 'World Hindu Conference', (WHC I), 22–24 January 1966. Available at: http://vhp.org/conferences/world-hindu-conference/world-hindu-conference-1-whc-i/

84. 'Anti-Cow Slaughter Mob Storms Parliament House: Unprecedented Acts of Violence in Delhi', *The Hindu*, 8 November 1966, p. 1.

85. Ibid.

86. 'Demand for Judicial Enquiry', *The Hindu*, 8 November 1966, p. 1.

87. 'Vajpayee And Subhadra Joshi In Neck And Neck Race,' *The Times of India*, 3 February 1967, p. 3.

88. Interview with Vasundhara Raje Scindia, New Delhi, June 2018.

89. Interview with Virendra Kapoor, New Delhi, June 2018.

90. Estimate compiled by Arpit Gaind from Election Commission data.

91. Interview with Vasundhara Raje Scindia, New Delhi, June 2018.

92. Vijayaraje Scindia and Mridula Sinha, *Royal to Public Life* (Prabhat books, 2008, kindle version), location 2080.

93. L.K. Advani, *My Country, My Life* (Rupa, 2010, paperback), p. 129.

94. Ibid., p. 131.

95. Ibid., p. 124.

96. Interview with R.V. Pandit, Bengaluru, April 2018.

CHAPTER 4: PARTNERSHIP FORGED BY FIRE (1968–73)

1. 'Upadhyaya, Jana Sangh Chief Found Murdered Near Mughalsarai Station', *The Times of India*, 12 February 1968, p. 1.

2. Balraj Madhok, *Zindagi ka Safar 3: Deendayal Upadhyaya ki hatya se Indira Gandhi ki hatya tak* (Dinman Prakashan), p. 11.

3. 'Upadhyaya, Jana Sangh Chief Found Murdered Near Mughalsarai Station', *The Times of India*, 12 February 1968, p. 1.

4. A.G. Noorani, *The Illustrated Weekly of India*, 25 April 1971. Reproduced in https://thewire.in/history/deen-dayal-upadhyaya-death-mystery

5. Ibid.

6. Balraj Madhok, *Zindagi ka Safar 3: Deendayal Upadhyaya ki hatya se Indira Gandhi ki hatya tak* (Dinman Prakashan), p. 11.

7. Ibid., p. 12.

8. 'Upadhyaya's Death: Foul Play Suspected', *The Hindu*, 12 February 1968, p. 1.

9. Balraj Madhok, *Zindagi ka Safar 3: Deendayal Upadhyaya ki hatya se Indira Gandhi ki hatya tak* (Dinman Prakashan), p 16.

10. L.K. Advani, *My Country, My Life* (Rupa, 2010, paperback), p. 142.

11. Interview with Prafull Goradia, New Delhi, April 2018.

12. Interview with Govindacharya, New Delhi, March 2018.

13. Interview with Govindacharya, New Delhi, March 2018.

14. Interview with Govindacharya, New Delhi, March 2018.

15. Balraj Madhok, *Zindagi ka Safar 3: Deendayal Upadhyaya ki hatya se Indira Gandhi ki hatya tak* (Dinman Prakashan), p. 61.

16. M.S. Golwalkar, *Collected Speeches (Sri Guruji Samagra), Volume 7* (New Delhi: Suruchi Prakashan), p. 144.

17. 'Deen Dayal Upadhyay is Cremated', *Times of India*, 13 February 1968, p. 1.

18. Ibid.

19. N.M. Ghatate (ed.), *Atal Bihari Vajpayee: Four Decades in Parliament*, Volume 1 (Shipra Publications), p. 729.

20. Ibid., p. xxxvi.

21. Interview with Srinath Raghavan, Mumbai, 27 June 2018.

22. Balraj Madhok, *Zindagi ka Safar 3: Deendayal Upadhyaya ki hatya se Indira Gandhi ki hatya tak* (Dinman Prakashan), pp. 37–38.

23. See Jacques Maritain, *Integral Humanism: Temporal and Spiritual Problems of a New Christendom* (Joseph Evans translator, Charles Scribner's Sons, 1968).

24. For a dated but influential political science book on Christian democracy, see Stathis N. Kalyvas, *The Rise of Christian Democracy in Europe* (Cornell University Press, 1996).

25. Balraj Madhok, *Zindagi ka Safar 3: Deendayal Upadhyaya ki hatya se Indira Gandhi ki hatya tak* (Dinman Prakashan), p. 66.

26. Roxna Swamy, *Evolving with Subramanian Swamy: A Roller Coaster Ride* (Bahrisons Distribution, 2017), pp. 59–60. Confirmed in interview with Subramanian Swamy, New Delhi, June 2018.

27. Interview with Subramanian Swamy, New Delhi, June 2018.

28. Roxna Swamy, *Evolving with Subramanian Swamy: A Roller Coaster Ride* (Bahrisons Distribution, 2017), p. 45.

29. Interview with Subramanian Swamy, New Delhi, June 2018.

30. Interview with N.M. Ghatate, New Delhi, May 2018.

31. Interview with R.V. Pandit, Bengaluru, April 2018. Confirmed in interview with Govindacharya, New Delhi, March 2018.

32. Interview with R.V. Pandit, Bengaluru, April 2018.

33. This was told to the senior journalist Coomi Kapoor by Nusli Wadia in an interview in November 2019. From an interview with Coomi Kapoor, New Delhi, December 2019.

34. Interview with R.V. Pandit, Bengaluru, April 2018.

35. Interview with Virendra Kapoor, New Delhi, June 2018.

36. Balraj Madhok, *Zindagi ka Safar 3: Deendayal Upadhyaya ki hatya se Indira Gandhi ki hatya tak* (Dinman Prakashan), pp. 47–48.

37. N.M. Ghatate (ed.), *Atal Bihari Vajpayee: Four Decades in Parliament*, Volume 1 (Shipra Publications), p. 41.

38. Bharatiya Jana Sangh, *Party Documents 1951-1972: Resolutions on Economic Affairs* (Bharatiya Jana Sangh Publishers, 1973), Vol. 2, p. 174.

39. 'Bank Bill Voted Unanimously by Rajya Sabha', *The Times of India*, 9 August 1969, p. 1.

40. 'Jana Sangh Talks Next Week on Party Crisis', *The Times of India*, 10 September 1969, p. 1.

41. L.K. Advani, *My Country, My Life* (Rupa, 2010, paperback), p. 161.

42. Balraj Madhok, *Zindagi ka Safar 3: Deendayal Upadhyaya ki hatya se Indira Gandhi ki hatya tak* (Dinman Prakashan), p. 89.

43. Ibid., p. 92.

44. A.S. Dulat, *Kashmir: The Vajpayee Years* (HarperCollins India, 2016), p. 106.

45. See minute 39 of https://www.youtube.com/watch?v=bBTVC7INyws

46. Interview with Govindacharya, New Delhi, June 2018, and interview with one other RSS person who declines to be named. The author spent months attempting to trace the article, but was unable to. But given the fact that two independent sources have confirmed its existence and many in the RSS have confirmed the 'deal' that followed, the author believes in the existence of this article.

47. Interview with Govindacharya, New Delhi, June 2018, and interview with one other RSS person who declined to be named.

48. Balraj Madhok, *Zindagi ka Safar 3: Deendayal Upadhyaya ki hatya se Indira Gandhi ki hatya tak* (Dinman Prakashan), p. 62.

49. Interview with Jairam Ramesh, Kolkata, February 2018.

50. Vijai Trivedi, *Haar Nahin Maanoonga* (HarperCollins Hindi, 2016), p. 20.

51. Interview with Ullekh N.P., New Delhi, May 2018.

52. Interview with Madhuri Sondhi, New Delhi, February 2018.

53. Interview with Govindacharya, New Delhi, June 2018. See also, Christophe Jaffrelot, *The Hindu Nationalist Movement in India* (Columbia University Press, 1996), p. 237.

54. This was said by Balraj Madhok's daughters in a public forum at a talk by the author on Balraj Madhok in India International Centre in New Delhi, April 2018.

55. Balraj Madhok, *Zindagi ka Safar 3: Deendayal Upadhyaya ki hatya se Indira Gandhi ki hatya tak* (Dinman Prakashan), p. 125.

56. Ibid., p. 146.

57. Kingshuk Nag, *Vajpayee: A Man for All Seasons* (Rupa Publications, 2015), p. 71.

58. Balraj Madhok, *Zindagi ka Safar 3: Deendayal Upadhyaya ki hatya se Indira Gandhi ki hatya tak* (Dinman Prakashan), p. 138.

59. Interview with Vasundhara Raje Scindia, New Delhi, June 2018.

60. Balraj Madhok, *Zindagi ka Safar 3: Deendayal Upadhyaya ki hatya se Indira Gandhi ki hatya tak* (Dinman Prakashan), p. 125.

61. Walter K. Anderson and Shridhar D. Damle, *The Saffron Brotherhood: The Rashtriya Swayamsevak Sangh and Hindu Revivalism* (Westview Press, 1987), p. 186.

62. 'Madhok Leaves Kanpur', *The Hindu*, 10 February 1973, p. 7.

63. See: 'RSS reportedly considering admitting non-Hindus in its fold', *India Today*, 30 April 1977. Available at: https://www.indiatoday.in/magazine/indiascope/story/19770430-rss-reportedly-considering-admitting-non-hindus-in-its-fold-823676-2014-08-07

64. Walter K. Anderson and Shridhar D. Damle, *The Saffron Brotherhood: The Rashtriya Swayamsevak Sangh and Hindu Revivalism* (Westview Press, 1987), p. 189.

65. Balraj Madhok, *Zindagi ka Safar 3: Deendayal Upadhyaya ki hatya se Indira Gandhi ki hatya tak* (Dinman Prakashan), pp. 127–28.

66. Ibid., p. 128.

67. 'Madhok Leaves Kanpur', *The Hindu*, 10 February 1973, p. 7.

68. 'Madhok's View Challenged by Vajpayee', *The Times of India*, 9 February 1973, p. 9.

69. Interview with Harin Pathak, Ahmedabad, April 2018.

70. Ibid.

71. Walter K. Anderson and Shridhar D. Damle, *The Saffron Brotherhood: The Rashtriya Swayamsevak Sangh and Hindu Revivalism* (Westview Press, 1987), p. 185.

72. 'Jana Sangh Threatens Action Against Madhok', *The Times of India*, 11 February 1973, p. 1.

73. Interview with N.M. Ghatate, New Delhi, June 2018.

74. 'Jana Sangh Threatens Action Against Madhok', *The Times of India,* 11 February 1973, p. 1.

75. 'Madhok Expelled from Jan Sangh for 3 Years', *The Hindu*, 14 March 1973, p. 1.

76. Interview with Swapan Dasgupta, New Delhi, June 2018.

77. Balraj Madhok, *Zindagi ka Safar 3: Deendayal Upadhyaya ki hatya se Indira Gandhi ki hatya tak* (Dinman Prakashan), p. 138.

78. Interview with Govindacharya, New Delhi, June 2018.

79. 'Golwalkar Dead', *The Times of India*, 6 June 1973, p. 1.

80. M.S. Golwalkar, *Collected Speech (Sri Guruji Samagra), Volume 7* (New Delhi: Suruchi Prakashan), p. 3.

81. 'Touching Farewell to Golwalkar', *The Times of India*, 6 June 1973, p. 1.

82. Interview with Seshadri Chari, New Delhi, April 2018.

83. Christophe Jaffrelot, *The Hindu Nationalist Movement in India* (Columbia University Press, 1996), p. 257.

CHAPTER 5: PERKS OF PRISON (1974–77)

1. The story in this paragraph is common to many developing countries recovering from foreign rule. During colonial rule, all manner of groups unite against the occupiers to forge a 'multi-ethnic' national party. This party then dominates politics in the new country for some years, but sooner or later, people begin to demand parties that singularly cater to their narrow identities. What follows is the breakdown of democracy, electoral fraud, and violence. Alvin Rabusha and Kenneth Shepsle, *Politics in Plural Society: A Theory of Democratic Instability* (Charles E Merrill Publishing Company, 1972), pp. 74–86.

2. Rajni Kothari, 'The Congress "System" in India', *Asian Survey*, 4, no. 12 (December 1964): 1161–73.

3. Atul Kohli, *Democracy and Discontent: India's Growing Crisis of Governability* (Cambridge University Press, 1991).

4. Gyan Prakash, *Emergency Chronicles: Indira Gandhi and Democracy's Turning Point* (Penguin-Viking, 2018).

5. Bipan Chandra, *In the Name of Democracy: JP Movement and the Emergency* (Penguin, 2003), p. 17.

6. Ranabir Samaddar, 'The Indian Railway Workers and the Crisis of 1974', *Working USA: The Journal of Labor and Society*, Vol. 18, December 2016: 575–94, at 575.

7. Rakesh Ankit, 'Janata Party (1974-77): Creation of an All-India Opposition', *History and Sociology of South Asia* 11(1) (2017): 39–54, 53.

8. Bipan Chandra, *In the Name of Democracy: JP Movement and the Emergency* (Penguin, 2003), p. 34.

9. Ibid., p. 37.

10. Ibid., p. 39.

11. Christophe Jaffrelot, *The Hindu Nationalist Movement in India* (Columbia University Press, 1996), p. 260.

12. Vinod K Jose. 'Narendra Modi, Insubordinate', *The Caravan*, 7 April 2014. Available at: http://www.caravanmagazine.in/vantage/narendra-modi-insubordinate

13. See https://www.narendramodi.in/the-activist-3129

14. Rakesh Ankit, 'Janata Party (1974-77): Creation of an All-India Opposition', *History and Sociology of South Asia* 11(1) (2017): 39–54, 53.

15. Ibid., p. 42.

16. Interview with Sadanand Menon, Chennai, June 2018.

17. Bipan Chandra, *In the Name of Democracy: JP Movement and the Emergency* (Penguin, 2003), p. 25.

18. N.M. Ghatate (ed.), *Atal Bihari Vajpayee: Four Decades in Parliament*, Volume 1 (Shipra Publications), p. 394.

19. Interview with Govindacharya, New Delhi, June 2018.

20. Ibid.

21. Interview with Subramanian Swamy, New Delhi, June 2018.

22. The journalist Virendra Kapoor says that Nanaji told this to him. Interview with Virendra Kapoor, New Delhi, June 2018.

23. Rakesh Ankit, 'Jayaprakash Narayan, Indian National Congress and Party Politics, 1934-1954', *Studies in Indian Politics*, 3(2): 149–63, p. 150.

24. L.K. Advani, *My Country, My Life* (Rupa, 2010, paperback), p.186.

25. Ramachandra Guha, *An Anthropologist Among the Marxists and Other Essays* (Orient Blackswan 2001), first page of Introduction.

26. Rakesh Ankit, 'Jayaprakash Narayan, Indian National Congress and Party Politics, 1934-1954', *Studies in Indian Politics*, 3(2): 149–63, p. 161.

27. Bipan Chandra, *In the Name of Democracy: JP Movement and the Emergency* (Penguin, 2003), p. 40.

28. Christophe Jaffrelot, *The Hindu Nationalist Movement in India* (Columbia University Press, 1996), p. 261.

29. Vijai Trivedi, *Haar Nahin Maanoonga* (HarperCollins Hindi, 2016), p. 49.

30. Walter K. Anderson and Shridhar D. Damle, *The Saffron Brotherhood: The Rashtriya Swayamsevak Sangh and Hindu Revivalism* (Westview Press, 1987), p. 211.

31. Ibid.

32. L.K. Advani, *My Country, My Life* (Rupa, 2010, paperback), p. 189.

33. 'Ban Fascist Groups: MPs', *The Times of India*, 30 March 1974, p. 5.

34. Rakesh Ankit, 'Janata Party (1974-77): Creation of an All-India Opposition', *History and Sociology of South Asia* (11) (1) (2017): 39–54, p. 42.

35. L.K. Advani, *My Country, My Life* (Rupa, 2010, paperback), p. 192.

36. Ibid.

37. Rakesh Ankit, 'Janata Party (1974-77): Creation of an All-India Opposition', *History and Sociology of South Asia* (11) (1) (2017): 39–54, 53.

38. Ibid., p. 47.

39. Walter K. Anderson and Shridhar D. Damle, *The Saffron Brotherhood: The Rashtriya Swayamsevak Sangh and Hindu Revivalism* (Westview Press, 1987), p. 211.

40. T. Ramakrishnan, 'The 1975 Gujarat Assembly election', *The Hindu*, 5 December 2017. Available at: https://www.thehindu.com/elections/gujarat-2017/the-1975-gujarat-assembly-election/article21262462.ece

41. Ibid.

42. *State of Uttar Pradesh* v. *Raj Narain*, 1975 AIR 865.

43. Bipan Chandra, *In the Name of Democracy: JP Movement and the Emergency* (Penguin, 2003), p. 65.

44. Ibid., p. 66.

45. Walter K. Anderson and Shridhar D. Damle, *The Saffron Brotherhood: The Rashtriya Swayamsevak Sangh and Hindu Revivalism* (Westview Press, 1987), p. 211.

46. Bipan Chandra, *In the Name of Democracy: JP Movement and the Emergency* (Penguin, 2003), p. 131.

47. B.N. Tandon, *PMO Diary-I: Prelude to the Emergency* (Konark Publishers, 2003), pp. 414–16.

48. L.K. Advani, *My Country, My Life* (Rupa, 2010, paperback), p. 203.

49. Ibid.

50. Ibid., p. 204.

51. Ramachandra Guha, *India after Gandhi: The History of the World's Largest Democracy* (Picador, 2017), p. 493.

52. L.K. Advani, *A Prisoner's Scrap-Book* (Ocean Books, 2003), p. 14.

53. Ibid., p. 16.

54. Ibid., p. 16.

55. Vijai Trivedi, *Haar Nahin Maanoonga* (HarperCollins Hindi, 2016), p. 46.

56. L.K. Advani, *My Country, My Life* (Rupa, 2010, paperback), p. 213.

57. Interview with N.M. Ghatate, New Delhi, May 2018.

58. Ramachandra Guha, *India after Gandhi: The History of the World's Largest Democracy* (Picador, 2017), p. 494.

59. 'Nanaji Deshmukh: The main force behind Jayaprakash Narayan's agitation for total revolution', *India Today*, 30 April 1977.

60. Ramachandra Guha, *India after Gandhi: The History of the World's Largest Democracy* (Picador, 2017), p. 498.

61. Vijayaraje Scindia and Mridula Sinha, *Royal to Public Life* (Prabhat Books, 2008, kindle version), location 2701.

62. N.M. Ghatate, *Emergency, Constitution and Democracy: An Indian Experience* (Shipra Publications, 2011), p. 51.

63. The journalist Coomi Kapoor conducted an interview with Nusli Wadia in November 2019, when he told her this. Interview with Coomi Kapoor, New Delhi, January 2020.

64. Interview with R.V. Pandit, Bengaluru, April 2018.

65. Interview with Virendra Kapoor, New Delhi, June 2018.

66. Interview with Vasundhara Raje Scindia, New Delhi, June 2018.

67. 'RSS, Marg, Jamaat, Among 26 Banned', *The Times of India*, 5 July 1975, p. 1.

68. 'Lethal Weapons in RSS Office', *The Times of India*, 11 July 1975, p. 1.

69. Christophe Jaffrelot, *The Hindu Nationalist Movement in India* (Columbia University Press, 1996), p. 273.

70. Subramanian Swamy, 'Unlearnt lessons of the Emergency', *The Hindu*, 13 June 2000. Available at: https://www.thehindu.com/thehindu/2000/06/13/stories/05132524.htm

71. Christophe Jaffrelot, *The Hindu Nationalist Movement in India* (Columbia University Press, 1996), p. 274.

72. Nilanjan Mukhopadhyay, *Narendra Modi: The Man, The Times* (Tranquebar, 2013), p. 122.

73. Ibid., 121.

74. Ibid., 123.

75. Interview with N.M. Ghatate, New Delhi, May 2018.

76. 'No let-up in activities of banned RSS: P.M.', *The Times of India*, 31 December 1975, p. 14.

77. N.M. Ghatate, *Emergency, Constitution and Democracy: An Indian Experience* (Shipra Publications, 2011), p. 38.

78. Ibid., 39.

79. L.K. Advani, *A Prisoner's Scrap-Book* (Ocean Books, 2003), p. 19.

80. Vijai Trivedi, *Haar Nahin Maanoonga* (HarperCollins Hindi, 2016), p. 47.

81. N.M. Ghatate, *Emergency, Constitution and Democracy: An Indian Experience* (Shipra Publications, 2011), p. 51.

82. Interview with Virendra Kapoor, New Delhi, June 2018.

83. L.K. Advani, *A Prisoner's Scrap-Book* (Ocean Books, 2003), pp. 16–17.

84. L.K. Advani, *My Country, My Life* (Rupa, 2010, paperback), p. 226.

85. N.M. Ghatate, *Emergency, Constitution and Democracy: An Indian Experience* (Shipra Publications, 2011), p. 64.

86. Private papers of N.M. Ghatate, accessed in his house. The papers have since been loaned to the Nehru Memorial Museum and Library, Delhi.

87. Ibid.

88. P.N. Dhar, *Indira Gandhi, the 'Emergency', and Indian Democracy* (Oxford University Press, 2000), p. 264.

89. Bipan Chandra, *In the Name of Democracy: JP Movement and the Emergency* (Penguin, 2003), p. 206.

90. Ibid., p. 205.

91. Ramachandra Guha, *India after Gandhi: The History of the World's Largest Democracy* (Picador, 2017), pp. 500–01.

92. 'Nanaji Deshmukh: The main force behind Jayaprakash Narayan's agitation for total revolution', *India Today*, 30 April 1977.

93. Ramachandra Guha, *India after Gandhi: The History of the World's Largest Democracy* (Picador, 2017), p. 495.

94. M.C. Chagla, 'Foreword', in Atal Bihari Vajpayee, *New Dimensions of India's Foreign Policy* (Vision Books, 1979).

95. N.M. Ghatate, *Emergency, Constitution and Democracy: An Indian Experience* (Shipra Publications, 2011), pp. 54–56.

96. 'Fading Hope in India', *New York Times*, 30 April 1976. Available at: https://www.nytimes.com/1976/04/30/archives/fading-hope-in-india.html

97. Ibid.

98. N.M. Ghatate, *Emergency, Constitution and Democracy: An Indian Experience* (Shipra Publications, 2011) p. 80.

99. L.K. Advani, *A Prisoner's Scrap-Book* (Ocean Books, 2003).

100. 'When you crawl, unasked', *The Indian Express*, 25 June 2015. Available at: https://indianexpress.com/article/opinion/columns/emergency-then-and-now/

101. Vandita Mishra. 'Partition was British guilt. The Emergency is ours, says L.K. Advani', *The Indian Express*, 25 June 2015.

102. Historians are still debating why Mrs Gandhi called elections. Some argue that the Emergency was a required response to the chaos of 1975 and that she always intended to revert to democracy. But another reason could well be that Indira Gandhi—whose friends were Western liberals—was smarting at being labelled a despot by the West. When the Intelligence Bureau predicted her victory, she decided to legitimize her rule and call for elections.

103. 'Non-Communist parties in talks with Congress(I)', *India Today*, 15 January 1977.

104. Rakesh Ankit, 'Janata Party (1974-77): Creation of an All-India Opposition', *History and Sociology of South Asia* (11) (1) (2017): 39–54, p. 50.

105. N.M. Ghatate, *Emergency, Constitution and Democracy: An Indian Experience* (Shipra Publications, 2011), p. 94.

106. Rakesh Ankit, 'Janata Party (1974-77): Creation of an All-India Opposition', *History and Sociology of South Asia* 11(1) (2017): 39–54, at 41.

107. 'Jagjivan Ram's exit from Congress adds new dimension to the Opposition', *India Today*, 28 February 1977; Jitendra Tuli, 'We are confident about getting a two-thirds majority: Jagjivan Ram', *India Today*, 31 March 1977.

108. Rakesh Ankit, 'Janata Party (1974-77): Creation of an All-India Opposition', *History and Sociology of South Asia* 11(1) (2017): 39–54, at 52.

109. Christophe Jaffrelot, *The Hindu Nationalist Movement in India* (Columbia University Press, 1996), p. 286.

110. Dilip Bobb, 'General elections: Can the combined Opposition prove to be a David to the Congress Goliath?', *India Today*, 15 March 1977.

111. L.K. Advani, *My Country, My Life* (Rupa, 2010, paperback), p. 264.

112. Suchitra Behal, 'Congress attacks Janata and Opposition parties with satirical posters', *India Today*, 15 March 1977.

113. Ibid.

114. Ibid.

115. Sunil Sethi, 'A day in the life of a candidate: Atal Bihari Vajpayee', *India Today*, 31 March 1977, https://www.indiatoday.in/magazine/indiascope/story/19770331-a-day-in-the-life-of-a-candidate-atal-behari-vajpayee-823610-2014-07-31

116. Ibid.

117. Interview with Ravindra Bhagwat, Chandrapur, March 2018.

118. Walter K. Anderson and Shridhar D. Damle, *The Saffron Brotherhood: The Rashtriya Swayamsevak Sangh and Hindu Revivalism* (Westview Press, 1987), p. 214.

119. Francine R. Frankel, *India's Political Economy: The Gradual Revolution (1947-2004)* (Oxford University Press, 2006), p. 571.

120. Rakesh Ankit, 'Janata Party (1974-77): Creation of an All-India Opposition', *History and Sociology of South Asia* (11) (1) (2017): 39–54, p. 41.

CHAPTER 6: PRUDENT IN POWER (1977–80)

1. Lloyd I Rudolph and Susan Hoeber Rudolph, 'Rethinking Secularism: Genesis and Implications of the Textbook Controversy, 1977-1979', *Pacific Affairs* 56 (1) (Spring, 1983): 15–37.

2. See https://www.inc.in/en/our-inspiration/babu-jagjivan-ram

3. Richa Taneja, 'Babu Jagjivan Ram, Former Deputy PM, Remembered On Birth Anniversary', NDTV, 05 April 2019. Available at: https://www.ndtv.com/india-news/babu-jagjivan-ram-former-deputy-pm-remembered-on-112-birth-anniversary-2018623

4. Paul Brass, *An Indian Political Life: Charan Singh and Congress Politics, 1967-1987*, Volume 3 (Sage Publishers, 2014), p. 237.

5. Terence C. Byres, 'Charan Singh, 1902-1987: An Assessment', *The Journal of Peasant Studies* 15:2 (1988): 139–89, p. 180.

6. Ramachandra Guha, *India after Gandhi: The History of the World's Largest Democracy* (Picador, 2017), p. 532.

7. Sanjay Ruparelia, *Divided We Govern: Coalition Politics in Modern India* (Oxford University Press, 2015), p. 77.

8. 'Jagjivan Ram's CFD group and Janata party spar over cabinet nominations', *India Today*, 15 April 1977.

9. Arul B. Louis, 'Rashtriya Swyamsewak Sangh gripped in throes of a grave identity crisis', *India Today*, 31 March 1979.

10. Ibid.

11. Interview with Subramanian Swamy, New Delhi, June 2018.

12. Interview with Virendra Kapoor, New Delhi, June 2018.

13. Ibid.

14. Interview with Govindacharya, New Delhi, June 2018.

15. Ibid.

16. Kingshuk Nag, *Atal Bihari Vajpayee: A Man for All Seasons* (Rupa, 2015), p. 90.

17. N.M. Ghatate (ed.), *Atal Bihari Vajpayee: Four Decades in Parliament*, Volume 1 (Shipra Publications), p. 105.

18. Interview with T.C.A. Raghavan, New Delhi, May 2018.

19. T.C.A. Raghavan, *The People Next Door: The Curious History of India's Relations with Pakistan* (HarperCollins India, 2017), p. 138.

20. 'Kashmir discussed in Islamabad Talks', 7 February 1978, *The Times of India*, p. 1.

21. 'Kashmir Not Main Issue at Parleys', 9 February 1978, *The Times of India*, p. 1.

22. T.C.A. Raghavan, *The People Next Door: The Curious History of India's Relations with Pakistan* (Harper Collins India, 2017), p. 140.

23. Kingshuk Nag, *Atal Bihari Vajpayee: A Man for All Seasons* (Rupa, 2015), p. 93.

24. Interview with A.V. Krishnan, Pune, January 2018. Full disclosure: he is related to the author.

25. The video of Atal Bihari Vajpayee's speech about the battle of Plassey is available here: https://www.youtube.com/watch?v=cepVvMvUGsw

26. Madhu P. Trehan, 'PM Morarji Desai USA visit: Doing his own thing', *India Today*, 15 July 1978.

27. Vijai Trivedi, *Haar Nahin Maanoonga* (HarperCollins Hindi, 2016), p. 80.

28. Rakesh Ankit, 'A regional satrap, a Hindu nationalist and a conservative Congressman: Dwarka Prasad Mishra (1901–1988)', *Contemporary South Asia*, 24 (1) (2016).

29. Jaswant Singh, *A Call to Honour: In Service of Emergent India* (Rupa, 2006, kindle edition), location 3309.

30. Interview with Subramanian Swamy, New Delhi, June 2018.

31. 'The Wrecked China Visit', *The Times of India*, 23 February 1979, p. 8.

32. Interview with Shivshankar Menon, New Delhi, June 2018.

33. Interview with Virendra Kapoor, New Delhi, June 2018.

34. L.K. Advani, *My Country, My Life* (Rupa, 2010, paperback), p. 276.

35. Prabhu Chawla, 'No question of not giving autonomy to AIR and Doordarshan: L.K. Advani', *India Today*, 15 December 1978.

36. Christophe Jaffrelot, *The Hindu Nationalist Movement in India* (Columbia University Press, 1996), pp. 284–85.

37. Interview with N. Ram, Kolkata, November 2017.

38. Lashmi Narayan, 'Maharashtra's two most popular women, Durga Bhagwat and Mrinal Gore, part ways', *India Today*, 15 September 1979.

39. L.K. Advani, *My Country, My Life* (Rupa, 2010, paperback), p. 281.

40. Balraj Madhok, *Zindagi ka Safar 3: Deendayal Upadhyaya ki hatya se Indira Gandhi ki hatya tak* (Dinman Prakashan), p. 219.

41. Lloyd I. Rudolph and Susan Hoeber Rudolph, 'Rethinking Secularism: Genesis and Implications of the Textbook Controversy, 1977-1979', *Pacific Affairs* 56 (1) (Spring, 1983): 15–37, p. 19.

42. Walter K. Anderson and Shridhar D. Damle, *The Saffron Brotherhood: The Rashtriya Swayamsevak Sangh and Hindu Revivalism* (Westview Press, 1987), p. 214.

43. Lloyd I. Rudolph and Susan Hoeber Rudolph, 'Rethinking Secularism: Genesis and Implications of the Textbook Controversy, 1977-1979', *Pacific Affairs* 56 (1) (Spring, 1983): 15–37, p. 16.

44. Ibid., p. 30.

45. Ibid., p. 17.

46. Vinay Sitapati, 'Reservations', in Sujit Choudhry, Madhav Khosla and Pratap Bhanu Mehta (eds), *Oxford Handbook of the Indian Constitution* (Oxford University Press, 2016).

47. Shyama Nand Singh, 'Anti Reservation Agitations in Bihar', *The Indian Journal of Political Science*, Vol. 52, No. 1 (January–March 1991): 24–42, p. 33.

48. Sanjay Ruparelia, *Divided We Govern: Coalition Politics in Modern India* (Oxford University Press, 2015), p. 69.

49. Ibid., p. 83.

50. Walter K. Anderson and Shridhar D. Damle, *The Saffron Brotherhood: The Rashtriya Swayamsevak Sangh and Hindu Revivalism* (Westview Press, 1987), p. 215.

51. This figure is for 1979. 'With 53 organizations linked to it, RSS operate in almost every field of human activity', *India Today*, 31 March 1979.

52. Walter K. Anderson and Shridhar D. Damle, *The Saffron Brotherhood: The Rashtriya Swayamsevak Sangh and Hindu Revivalism* (Westview Press, 1987), p. 215.

53. 'Rashtriya Swyamsewak Sangh gripped in throes of a grave identity crisis', *India Today*, 18 March 2014.

54. Ibid.

55. 'Battle-scarred leaders of Janata Party pull out their faded olive branches', *India Today*, 31 May 1979.

56. Christophe Jaffrelot, *The Hindu Nationalist Movement in India* (Columbia University Press, 1996), p. 309.

57. Arul B. Louis, 'Rashtriya Swyamsewak Sangh gripped in throes of a grave identity crisis', *India Today*, 31 March 1979.

58. Christophe Jaffrelot, *The Hindu Nationalist Movement in India* (Columbia University Press, 1996), p. 304, footnote 116.

59. Bhabani Sen Gupta, 'PM Morarji Desai's tour of Russia and Eastern Europe: Predictable as a Siberian winter', *India Today*, 15 July 1979.

60. 'JP Intervenes to Defuse Janata Crisis', *The Times of India*, 29 June 1978, p. 1.

61. Paul Brass, *An Indian Political Life: Charan Singh and Congress Politics, 1967-1987*, Volume 3 (Sage Publishers, 2014, kindle edition), location 250, footnote 58.

62. 'Charan Singh is in office but Mrs Gandhi is in power', *India Today*, 31 August 1979.

63. Rakesh Ankit, 'Janata Party (1974-77): Creation of an All-India Opposition', *History and Sociology of South Asia* 11(1) (2017): 39–54, p. 54.

64. Sanjay Ruparelia, *Divided We Govern: Coalition Politics in Modern India* (Oxford University Press, 2015), p. 87.

65. Sudheendra Kulkarni, 'What made Bharat Ratna Vajpayee an Extraordinary Leader', NDTV, 27 March 2015. Available at: https://www.ndtv.com/opinion/what-made-bharat-ratna-vajpayee-an-extraordinary-leader-750011

66. L.K. Advani, *My Country, My Life* (Rupa, 2010, paperback), p. 305.

67. Sunil Sethi, 'Politicians like Mrs Gandhi cannot find anything against us: Vijayaraje Scindia', *India Today*, 31 December 1979.

68. Vijai Trivedi, *Haar Nahin Maanoonga* (HarperCollins Hindi, 2016), p. 60.

69. http://www.elections.in/parliamentary-constituencies/1980-election-results.html

70. Prabhu Chawla, '1980 Lok Sabha elections see virtual eclipse of Jan Sangh in Parliament', *India Today*, 31 January 1980, https://www.indiatoday.in/magazine/cover-story/story/19800131-1980-lok-sabha-elections-see-virtual-eclipse-of-jan-sangh-in-parliament-821699-2014-12-19

71. Vijai Trivedi, *Haar Nahin Maanoonga* (HarperCollins Hindi, 2016), p. 63.

72. L.K. Advani, *My Country, My Life* (Rupa, 2010, paperback), p. 309.

73. 'Shekhar, 3 Janata secretaries quit', *The Times of India*, 5 April 1980, p. 1.

74. 'Jana Sangh Group to Form New Party', *The Times of India*, 6 April 1980, p. 1.

75. Ibid.

76. Ibid.

77. 'Vajpayee Chief of Bharatiya Janata Party', *The Times of India*, 7 April 1980, p. 1.

78. 'Bharatiya Janata Party', *Organiser*, Vol. 31, 47, 13 April 1980, p. 1. Accessed from NMML.

79. Interview with Subramanian Swamy, New Delhi, June 2018.

80. Interview with R.V. Pandit, Bengaluru, April 2018.

81. Interview with Govindacharya, New Delhi, June 2018.

PART II: THE PARTY (1980–98)

CHAPTER 7: RADICAL HINDUS, MODERATE VAJPAYEE (1980–84)

1. Sumit Mitra. 'BJP convention: Old wine in new bottles', *India Today*, 31 January 1981.

2. 'Impressive show', *The Times of India*, 29 December 1980, p. 1.

3. L.K. Advani, *My Country, My Life* (Rupa, 2010, paperback), p. 311.

4. Ibid., p. 312.

5. 'Biggest-ever procession for Vajpayee', *The Times of India*, 29 December 1980, p. 5.

6. 'RSS secretary visits BJP session venue', *The Times of India*, 31 December 1980, p. 1.

7. 'BJP's Gandhian tag resented', *The Times of India*, 25 December 1980, p. 1.

8. Interview with Seshadri Chari, New Delhi, April 2018.

9. Interview with Pravin Togadia, Ahmedabad, April 2018.

10. L.K. Advani, *My Country, My Life* (Rupa, 2010, paperback), p. 313.

11. Interview with Vasundhara Raje Scindia, New Delhi, June 2018.

12. Vijayaraje Scindia and Mridula Sinha, *Royal to Public Life* (Prabhat Books, 2008, kindle version), location 3237.

13. Interview with Govindacharya, New Delhi, June 2018.

14. Sumit Mitra, 'BJP convention: Old wine in new bottles', *India Today*, 31 January 1981.

15. 'Advani Explains Aims of Party', *The Hindu*, 18 April 1980, p. 12.

16. Vijai Trivedi, *Haar Nahin Maanoonga* (HarperCollins Hindi, 2016), p. 69.

17. Kingshuk Nag, *Atal Bihari Vajpayee: A Man for All Seasons* (Rupa, 2015), p. 97.

18. Atal Bihari Vajpayee's speech at the first BJP Adhiveshan, Mumbai, 1980. Video available at: https://www.youtube.com/watch?v=PGqoA50uiBM

19. Ibid.

20. M.C. Chagla, *Roses in December: An Autobiography* (Bharatiya Vidya Bhavan, 1974), pp. 26, 78–80.

21. 'We are all Hindus by Race', *Bhavan's Journal*, Volume 25, No. 2 (1978): 21.

22. 'BJP only alternative: Chagla', *The Times of India*, 30 December 1980, p. 4.

23. Ibid.

24. Interview with R.V. Pandit, Bengaluru, April 2018.

25. R. Jagannathan. 'Nusli Wadia explains his loss to Ambani in polyester war', *Firstpost*, 14 December 2014. Available at: https://www.firstpost.com/business/nusli-wadia-explains-his-loss-to-ambani-in-polyester-war-514427.html

26. Interview with R.V. Pandit, Bengaluru, April 2018.

27. Results of the 1981 Census of India.

28. V. Srinivas. 'The Economic History of India: India and the International Monetary Fund 1944-2017', Special Lecture at the National Archives of India, 21 July 2017. Available at: http://nationalarchives.nic.in/sites/default/files/new/THE%20ECONOMIC%20HISTORY%20OF%20INDIA.pdf, 9.

29. Ibid.

30. Ibid.

31. Prabhu Chawla, 'Anti-reservation agitation by medicos in Gujarat leaves 16 people dead, several injured', *India Today*, 15 March 1981.

32. Vijai Trivedi, *Haar Nahin Maanoonga* (HarperCollins Hindi, 2016), p. 69.

33. Rajesh Pradhan, *When the Saints Go Marching In: The Curious Ambivalence of Religious Sadhus in Recent Politics in India* (Orient Blackswan, 2014), p. 76.

34. Om Gupta, 'I am not a Guru, only a postman of the Guru: Bhindranwale', *India Today*, 15 July 1981.

35. Madhumita Sharma, 'A study of migration from Bangladesh to Assam, India and its impact', PhD dissertation, 2015. Available at: https://digital. library.adelaide.edu.au/dspace/bitstream/2440/97379/3/02whole.pdf

36. R.B. Bhagat, 'Census and the Construction of Communalism in India', *Economic and Political Weekly*, Vol. 36, No. 46/47 (24–30 November 2001): 4352-4356, at 4355.

37. Christophe Jaffrelot, *The Hindu Nationalist Movement in India* (Columbia University Press, 1996), p. 367.

38. 'Harassment leads to mass conversion', *The Times of India*, 25 May 1981, p. 18. There are varying number of converts, with some saying 1000. See, for example, Manjari Katju, *Vishva Hindu Parishad and Indian Politics* (Orient Blackswan, Kindle edition, second edition, 2012), location 750.

39. H.V. Sheshadri, *Warning of Meenakshipuram* (Jagarana Prakashana, 1981), p. 2. Cited from Gavin Irby, 'A Conviction to Dissent: Reinterpreting Mass Conversion at Meenakshipuram', *Virginia Review of Asian Studies,* 2005.

40. Christophe Jaffrelot, *The Hindu Nationalist Movement in India* (Columbia University Press, 1996), p. 340.

41. V.G. Prasad Rao, 'Why Some Harijans Embrace Islam', *The Times of India*, 1 July 1981, p. 8.

42. 'Harassment leads to mass conversion', *The Times of India*, 25 May 1981, p. 18.

43. Ramachandra Guha, 'A sort of victory: October 14, 1956: the day Ambedkar became a Buddhist', *The Telegraph*, 14 October 2016. Available at: https://www.telegraphindia.com/1161014/jsp/opinion/story_113268.jsp

44. 'Conversions are for personal gain', *The Times of India*, 17 August 1981, p. 7.

45. 'Moopanar moots plan to stop conversion', *The Times of India*, 3 August 1981, p. 13.

46. 'Conversions probe on: Zail', *The Times of India*, 10 August 1981, p. 1.

47. 'Swaminathan blames Arab money: conversion', *The Times of India*, 13 August 1981, p. 14.

48. Mohammad A. Kalam, 'Religious Conversions in Tamil Nadu: Can they be viewed as Protest Movements', *Indian Anthropologist*, 20(1/2) (1990): 39-48, at 47; George Mathew, 'Politicisation of Religion: Conversions to Islam in Tamil Nadu', *Economic and Political Weekly* 17(26) (1982): 1068–72. See more generally: Matthew H. Baxter, 'Two Concepts of Conversion at Meenakshipuram: Seeing through Ambedkar's Buddhism and Being Seen in EVR's Islam', *Comparative Studies of South Asia, Africa and the Middle East* (2019) 39 (2): pp. 264–81.

49. 'Politicisation of Religion: Conversions to Islam in Tamil Nadu', *Economic and Political Weekly* 17(26) (1982): 1068–72, at 1069.

50. Sumit Mitra, 'Virat Hindu Samaj holds massive rally to protest against conversion of Harijans to Islam', *India Today*, 28 October 2013.

51. Interview with Sadanand Menon, Chennai, June 2018.

52. 'Harijans Converted Back to Hinduism', *The Times of India*, 10 July 1981, p. 14.

53. 'Hindus Blamed for TN Conversion', *The Times of India*, 17 July 1981, p. 5.

54. 'BJP's jamboree in Kerala turns out to be a roaring success', *India Today*, 31 May 1981.

55. Chaitanya Kalbag, 'Two-year-old BJP grows like Jack's beanstalk, projects itself as a "national alternative"', *India Today*,15 April 1982.

56. Manjari Katju, *Vishva Hindu Parishad and Indian Politics* (Orient Blackswan, second edition, 2012), p. 7.

57. Interview with Subramanian Swamy, New Delhi, June 2018.

58. 'Ashok Singhal's journey from engineer to VHP chief', *DNA,* 17 November 2015. Available at: http://www.dnaindia.com/india/report-ashok-singhal-s-journey-from-engineer-to-vhp-chief-2146133

59. It was called Sanskriti Raksha Nidhi Yojna. Sumit Pande, 'Long Journey: Meet the Dalit Boy who Laid Foundation Stone of Ram Temple', 5 December 2017. Available at: https://www.news18.com/news/immersive/25-years-of-babri-demolition/such-a-long-journey.html

60. Christophe Jaffrelot, *The Hindu Nationalist Movement in India* (Columbia University Press, 1996), p. 349.

61. Ibid.

62. Raj Chengappa, 'Ayyapuram becomes the flashpoint for one of the worst communal clashes in Tamil Nadu', *India Today*, 15 July 1982.

63. Raj Chengappa. 'Meenakshipuram in Tamil Nadu becomes battleground of Hindu zealots and Muslim fanatics', *India Today*, 15 March 1983.

64. Christophe Jaffrelot, *The Hindu Nationalist Movement in India* (Columbia University Press, 1996), p. 333.

65. Amarnath K. Menon. 'Communal violence burns Hyderabad, leaves 35 people dead and 280 others injured', *India Today*, 15 August 1981.

66. Sreedhar Pillai, 'Kanyakumari communal clashes: Six persons killed, 21 others seriously injured', *India Today*, 31 March 1982.

67. Interview with Sheela Bhatt, New Delhi, May 2018.

68. Interview with Nilanjan Mukhopadhyay, on the phone, May 2018.

69. The 'Patan Trilogy' has been recently translated from the Gujarati to English by Rita Kothari and Abhijit Kothari for Penguin Books.

70. P.R. Ramesh, 'His Master's Mind', *Open Magazine*, 10 April 2014. Available at: https://openthemagazine.com/features/india/his-masters-mind/

71. Interview with Harish Khare, New Delhi, September 2019.

72. Coomi Kapoor, 'There is no single replacement to Congress (I) in all states at the moment: Vajpayee', *India Today*, 28 February 1983.

73. Walter K. Anderson and Shridhar D. Damle, *The Saffron Brotherhood: The Rashtriya Swayamsevak Sangh and Hindu Revivalism* (Westview Press, 1987), pp. 231–32.

74. Christophe Jaffrelot, *The Hindu Nationalist Movement in India* (Columbia University Press, 1996), p. 328.

75. Ibid, p. 329.

76. Coomi Kapoor, 'There is no single replacement to Congress (I) in all states at the moment: Vajpayee', *India Today*, 28 February 1983.

77. Ibid.

78. Sumit Mitra, 'J&K Assembly polls: National Conference poised to sweep Valley, Congress (I) eyes Jammu', *India Today*, 31 May 1983.

79. Ibid.

80. 'Statistical report on general election, 1983 to the legislative assembly of Jammu & Kashmir', Election Commission of India, New Delhi. Available at: https://eci.gov.in/files/file/3792-jammu-kashmir-1983/

81. Sumit Mitra, 'After defeat in J&K polls, BJP to take closer look at its failures, revive its strength', *India Today*, 15 August 1983.

82. P.V. Narasimha Rao, *Ayodhya 6 December 1992* (Penguin, 2006), p. 4.

83. Peter Van der Veer, 'Ayodhya and Somnath: Eternal Shrines, Contested Histories', *Social Research* 59(1) (1992): 85–109, at 98.

84. 'Timeline: Ayodhya holy site crisis', BBC, 6 December 2012. Available at: https://www.bbc.com/news/world-south-asia-11436552

85. That it was Dau Dayal Khanna who came up with the idea is admitted by the VHP on its website. 'Rama Janma Bhoomi', Vishva Hindu Parishad, http://vhp.org/vhp-glance/movements/shriram-janmabhumi-mukti-andolan/; see also Christophe Jaffrelot, *The Hindu Nationalist Movement in India* (Columbia University Press, 1996), p. 365.

86. Sheldon Pollock, 'Ramayana and Political Imagination in India', *The Journal of Asian Studies* 52(2) (1993): 261–97, at 264.

87. Ibid.

88. 'Rama Janma Bhoomi', Vishva Hindu Parishad, http://vhp.org/vhp-glance/movements/shriram-janmabhumi-mukti-andolan/

89. Christophe Jaffrelot, *The Hindu Nationalist Movement in India* (Columbia University Press, 1996), pp. 364–65.

90. Manjari Katju, *Vishva Hindu Parishad and Indian Politics* (Orient Blackswan, second edition, 2012), p. 38.

91. Peter Van Der Veer, 'God Must be Liberated! A Hindu Religious Movement in Ayodhya', *Modern Asian Studies* 21(2) (1987): 283–301, at 292.

92. Shekhar Gupta 'Operation Bluestar: How Army operation unfolded at Golden Temple to quell Punjab terrorism', *India Today*, 30 June 1984.

93. Prabhu Chawla, 'Delhi Police tightens security of VIPs in wake of growing Sikh extremists' threats', *India Today*, 15 May 1984.

94. 'Drive extremists out of Gurdwaras, Akali leaders told', *The Times of India*, 9 April 1984, p. 1.

95. L.K. Advani, *My Country, My Life* (Rupa, 2010, paperback) 363.

96. 'Cong. plea to put off by-elections', *The Times of India,* 10 April 1984, p. 9.

97. Vijai Trivedi, *Haar Nahin Maanoonga* (HarperCollins Hindi, 2016), p. 70.

98. Maya Chadda, *Ethnicity, security, and separatism in India* (Columbia University Press, 1997), p. 135.

99. N.M. Ghatate (ed.), *Atal Bihari Vajpayee: Four Decades in Parliament*, Volume 1 (Shipra Publications), p. 498.

100. Peter Van Der Veer, 'God Must be Liberated! A Hindu Religious Movement in Ayodhya', *Modern Asian Studies* 21(2) (1987): 283–301, p. 291.

101. Farzand Ahmed, 'Ram Janmbhumi: Ayodhya becomes rallying point for start of yet another communal skirmish', *India Today*, 31 October 1984.

102. Peter Van Der Veer, 'God Must be Liberated! A Hindu Religious Movement in Ayodhya', *Modern Asian Studies* 21(2) (1987): 283–301, p. 291.

103. Farzand Ahmed, 'Ram Janmbhumi: Ayodhya becomes rallying point for start of yet another communal skirmish', *India Today*, 31 October 1984.

104. Ashis Nandy, 'A disowned father of the nation in India: Vinayak Damodar Savarkar and the demonic and the seductive in Indian nationalism', *Inter-Asia Cultural Studies* 15 (1): 91–112, p. 95.

105. Ibid., p. 104.

106. Interview with R.V. Pandit, Bengaluru, April 2018.

107. Interview with Sheila Ghatate, New Delhi, June 2018.

108. Interview with Ravindra Bhagwat, Chandrapur, March 2018.

109. Rajesh Pradhan, *When the Saints Go Marching In: The Curious Ambivalence of Religious Sadhus in Recent Politics in India* (Orient Blackswan, 2014), p. 53.

110. Ibid., p. 14.

111. Ibid.

112. L.K. Advani, *My Country, My Life* (Rupa, 2010, paperback), p. 365.

113. Vinay Sitapati. 'Liberal and nationalist', *The Indian Express*, 17 August 2018. Available at: https://indianexpress.com/article/opinion/columns/atal-bihari-vajpayee-liberal-and-nationalist-5310703/

114. Interview with Pravin Togadia, Ahmedabad, April 2018.

115. L.K. Advani, *My Country, My Life* (Rupa, 2010, paperback), p. 841.

116. M.L. Sondhi private papers, letter dated 16 October 1984, sequence no. 67.

117. Coomi Kapoor, 'BJP fails to provide clear-cut sense of direction to its members', *India Today*, 15 November 1984.

118. This distinction between the political and social ends of Hindu unity was made to this author by the scholars Anup Dhar and Pratap Bhanu Mehta. It goes without saying that the author alone is liable for its deployment in this book.

119. Peter Van Der Veer, 'God Must be Liberated! A Hindu Religious Movement in Ayodhya', *Modern Asian Studies* 21(2) (1987): 283–301, p. 299.

120. Ibid., p. 298.

121. Ibid.

122. 'India: No Justice for 1984 Anti-Sikh Bloodshed', *Human Rights Watch*, 29 October 2014. Available at: https://www.hrw.org/news/2014/10/29/india-no-justice-1984-anti-sikh-bloodshed

123. Vijai Trivedi, *Haar Nahin Maanoonga* (HarperCollins Hindi, 2016), p. 72.

124. The evidence for this comes from a testimony by a bureaucrat who was present in the home minister's office at 6:30 p.m. when Narasimha Rao received the call.

125. Manoj Mitta and Harvinder Singh Phoolka, *When a tree shook Delhi* (Roli Books Private Limited, 2013), p. 198.

126. Interview with Virendra Kapoor, New Delhi, June 2018.

127. Zoya Hasan, *Congress After Indira: Policy, Power, Political Change (1984-2009)* (Oxford University Press, 2013), p. 13.

128. James Manor, 'Parties and the Party System', in Atul Kohli (ed.), *India's Democracy: An Analysis of Changing State-Society Relations* (Princeton University Press, 1988), p. 81.

129. Ibid., 83.

130. 'Cong. on the attack: Anandpur resolution', *The Times of India*, 14 December 1984, p. 9.

131. 1984 election manifesto of the BJP. Available at: http://library.bjp.org/jspui/handle/123456789/237

132. R.K Rangan, 'Cassettes used in big way for poll drive', *The Times of India*, 18 December 1984, p. 5

133. 'George Menezes joins BJP', *The Times of India*, 21 December 1984, p. 1.

134. Interview with Govindacharya, New Delhi, June 2018.

135. 'Akali Dal guilty of communalism', *The Times of India*, 19 December 1984, p. 20.

136. Vijai Trivedi, *Haar Nahin Maanoonga* (HarperCollins Hindi, 2016), p. 25.

137. M.L. Fotedar, *The Chinar Leaves: A Political Memoir* (HarperCollins, 2015), p. 202.

138. N.M. Ghatate (ed.), *Atal Bihari Vajpayee: Four Decades in Parliament*, Volume 1 (Shipra Publications), p. xxviii.

139. Shekhar Gupta. 'Gwalior to see epic election battle between Madhavrao Scindia and Atal Bihari Vajpayee', *India Today*, 31 December 1984.

140. Ibid.

141. Gautam S.G. Vohra, 'Close finish likely in Gwalior', *The Times of India*, 22 December 1984, p. 7.

142. 'India: Dates of Elections: 24, 27 and 28 December 1984'. Available at: http://archive.ipu.org/parline-e/reports/arc/INDIA_1984_E.PDF

143. Vijai Trivedi, *Haar Nahin Maanoonga* (HarperCollins Hindi, 2016), p. 73.

144. 'A Massive Hindu Mandate', *Organiser*, Vol 36, 34, 6 January 1985, p. 1. Accessed from NMML.

145. 'Some prominent losers', *The Times of India*, 30 December 1984, p. 13.

146. Ullekh N.P., *The Untold Vajpayee: Politician and Paradox* (Penguin Books, kindle edition, 2017), location 1662.

147. Interview with Ajoy Bose, New Delhi, June 2018.

CHAPTER 8: ADVANI'S BJP (1985–89)

1. M.L. Sondhi private papers, letter dated 6 January 1985, sequence no. 92.

2. M.L. Sondhi private papers, letter dated 3 February 1991, sequence no. 259.

3. Interview with Pravin Togadia, Ahmedabad, April 2018.

4. 'BJP Decides to Forget Jana Sangh', *The Times of India*, 18 March 1985, p. 9.

5. Ibid.

6. Ibid.

7. L.K. Advani, *My Country, My Life* (Rupa, 2010, paperback), p. 321.

8. Ibid.

9. Ibid.

10. N.M. Ghatate (ed.), *Atal Bihari Vajpayee: Four Decades in Parliament*, Volume 1 (Shipra Publications), p. xxvii.

11. Amit Shah has recollected this to a senior journalist who wishes to remain unnamed.

12. Interview with Vasundhara Raje Scindia, New Delhi, June 2018.

13. Vijayaraje Scindia and Mridula Sinha, *Royal to Public Life* (Prabhat Books, 2008, kindle version), location 3251.

14. Shekhar Gupta, 'BJP under Advani expected to move more decisively towards regaining its moorings', *India Today*, 31 March 1986.

15. Interview with Sheila Ghatate, New Delhi, May 2018.

16. Khushwant Singh, *Truth, Love and a Little Malice*. Cited from https://scroll.in/article/732469/operation-blue-star-was-a-well-calculated-and-deliberate-slap-in-the-face-of-an-entire-community-khushwant-singh

17. Ibid.

18. Tania Midha, Inderjit Badhwar and Prabhu Chawla, 'Attempt to assassinate Prime Minister Rajiv Gandhi exposes chinks in his security armour', *India Today*, 31 October 1986.

19. Christophe Jaffrelot, *The Hindu Nationalist Movement in India* (Columbia University Press, 1996), p. 353.

20. Ornit Shani, 'The Rise of Hindu Nationalism in India: The Case Study of Ahmedabad in the 1980s', *Modern Asian Studies* 39 (4) (October 2005): 861-896, p. 867.

21. Rakesh Ankit, 'Caste Politics in Bihar: In Historical Continuum', *History and Sociology of South Asia* 12 (2) (July 2018): 1–22, p. 8.

22. Report of the Mandal Commission.

23. Badri Narayan, *Kanshi Ram: Leader of the Dalits* (Penguin, 2014, kindle edition), location 1626.

24. Yogendra Yadav, 'Ambedkar and Lohia: a dialogue on caste' *Seminar*. Available at: http://www.india-seminar.com/2012/629/629_yogendra_yadav.htm

25. Badri Narayan, *Kanshi Ram: Leader of the Dalits* (Penguin, 2014, kindle edition), location 1586.

26. Ibid., location 1607.

27. Javed M. Ansari and Dilip Awasthi, 'In India, 50 per cent of the media is pro-BJP: Kanshi Ram', *India Today*, 31 December 1993.

28. Atul Kohli, 'Politics of economic liberalization in India', *World Development* 17, no. 3 (1989): 305–28, p. 312.

29. L.K. Advani, *My Country, My Life* (Rupa, 2010, paperback), p. 326.

30. Ibid., p. 332.

31. *Mohd. Ahmad Khan* vs *Shah Bano Begum*, 1985 (2) SCC 556.

32. Simran, 'Case Analysis: *Mohd Ahmad Khan vs Shah Bano Begum*', *Legal Service India*. Available at: http://www.legalserviceindia.com/legal/article-216-case-analysis-mohd-ahmad-khan-v-s-shah-bano-begum.html

33. *Mohd. Ahmad Khan vs Shah Bano Begum*, AIR 1985 SC 945.

34. Ronojoy Sen, 'The Indian Supreme Court and the quest for a "rational" Hinduism', *South Asian History and Culture*, 1 (1): 86–104.

35. 'Tirade Against SC Unfortunate: BJP', *The Times of India*, 5 January 1986, p. 9.

36. Muslim Women (Protection of Rights on Divorce) Act, 1986.

37. Achal Prabhala, 'When India became the first country to ban *The Satanic Verses* much before the Iranian fatwa', *Scroll*, 4 October 2015. Available at: https://scroll.in/article/758288/when-india-became-the-first-country-to-ban-the-satanic-verses-much-before-the-iranian-fatwa

38. Interview with Naresh Chandra, New Delhi, August 2016.

39. Christophe Jaffrelot, *The Hindu Nationalist Movement in India* (Columbia University Press, 1996), p. 375.

40. Interview with Govindacharya, New Delhi, June 2018.

41. Interview with Seshadri Chari, New Delhi, April 2018.

42. Interview with Nilanjan Mukhopadhyay, on the phone, May 2018.

43. Interview with Sheela Bhatt, New Delhi, November 2018.

44. L.K. Advani, *My Country, My Life* (Rupa, 2010, paperback), p. 325.

45. Christophe Jaffrelot, *The Hindu Nationalist Movement in India* (Columbia University Press, 1996), p. 376.

46. L.K. Advani, *My Country, My Life* (Rupa, 2010, paperback), p. 714.

47. Ibid.

48. Ornit Shani, 'The Rise of Hindu Nationalism in India: The Case Study of Ahmedabad in the 1980s', *Modern Asian Studies* 39 (4) (October 2005): 861–96.

49. Inderjit Badhwar. 'Devastating communal riots sweep through Meerut and its adjoining areas in Uttar Pradesh', *India Today*, 15 June 1987; Dilip Awasthi, 'Provincial Armed Constabulary faces flak for controversial role in Meerut riots', *India Today*, 30 June 1987.

50. S.H. Venkatramani, 'Hindu mutts brush aside age-old religious taboos to embrace liberal attitude', *India Today*, 30 June 1988.

51. 'BJP for status quo in quota', *The Times of India*, 21 July 1985, p. 1.

52. Interview with Govindacharya, New Delhi, June 2018.

53. 'Prabhu Chawla, 'Lok Dal-BJP alliance wins by-elections in Haryana', *India Today*, 30 November 1987.

54. 'Winning the Hindu vote', *India Today*, 15 May 1988.

55. Vijai Trivedi, *Haar Nahin Maanoonga* (HarperCollins Hindi, 2016), p. 75.

56. Ibid., 85.

57. Interview with Vijai Trivedi, New Delhi, June 2019.

58. Ullekh N.P., *The Untold Vajpayee: Politician and Paradox* (Penguin Books, kindle edition, 2017), location 1772.

59. Interview with Jairam Ramesh, Kolkata, January 2018.

60. Interview with Subramanian Swamy, New Delhi, June 2018.

61. Vinay Sitapati, 'Liberal and nationalist', *Indian Express*, 17 August 2018. Available at: https://indianexpress.com/article/opinion/columns/atal-bihari-vajpayee-liberal-and-nationalist-5310703/

62. Interview with Karan Thapar, New Delhi, November 2019.

63. Vinay Sitapati, 'Liberal and nationalist', *Indian Express*, 17 August 2018. Available at: https://indianexpress.com/article/opinion/columns/atal-bihari-vajpayee-liberal-and-nationalist-5310703/

64. Kingshuk Nag, *Atal Bihari Vajpayee: A Man for All Seasons* (Rupa, 2015), p. 68.

65. Interview with Ashok Trivedi, New Delhi, June 2018.

66. A.S. Dulat, *Kashmir: The Vajpayee Years* (HarperCollins, 2015), p. 172.

67. Interview with Shakti Sinha, New Delhi, January 2018.

68. Interview with Manvendra Singh, New Delhi, June 2018.

69. Kingshuk Nag, *Vajpayee: A Man for All Seasons* (Rupa Publications, 2015), p. 104. This book quotes V.P. Singh's own memoirs: *Manzil Se Zyada Safar* (2006).

70. Kingshuk Nag, *Vajpayee: A Man for All Seasons* (Rupa Publications, 2015), p. 104.

71. Interview with Ravindra Bhagwat, Chandrapur, March 2018.

72. Video of the speech available at: https://www.youtube.com/watch?v=cepVvMvUGsw

73. Interview with Atul Kohli, Princeton, May 2018.

74. Peter Friedlander, 'Hinduism and Politics', in Jeffrey Haynes, ed., *Routledge Book of Politics and Religion* (2009, second edition, 2016), p. 76.

75. Arvind Rajagopal, *Politics after Television: Religious Nationalism and the Reshaping of the Indian Public* (Cambridge University Press, 2001, kindle edition), location 1186.

76. Simran Bhargava, 'Ramanand Sagar's *Ramayan* is being awarded the sanctity of the original', *India Today*, 30 April 1987.

77. Arvind Rajagopal, *Politics after Television: Religious Nationalism and the Reshaping of the Indian Public* (Cambridge University Press, 2001, kindle edition), location 1214.

78. 'Critics Pan Most Viewed *Ramayan*', *The Times of India*, 30 November 1987, p. 17.

79. Simran Bhargava, 'Ramanand Sagar's *Ramayan* is being awarded the sanctity of the original', *India Today*, 30 April 1987.

80. Ibid.

81. Ibid.

82. 'Stir for *Ramayan* serial's extension', *The Times of India*, 25 July 1988, p. 9.

83. 'Critics Pan Most Viewed *Ramayan*', *The Times of India*, 30 November 1987, p. 17.

84. 'How South, East view *Ramayan*,' *The Times of India*, 1 December 1987, p. 17.

85. Arvind Rajagopal, *Politics after Television: Religious Nationalism and the Reshaping of the Indian Public* (Cambridge University Press, 2001).

86. 'Ram Campaigns at Udhampur', *The Times of India*, 13 June 1988, p. 6.

87. Arvind Rajagopal, *Politics after Television: Religious Nationalism and the Reshaping of the Indian Public* (Cambridge University Press, 2001, kindle edition), location 63.

88. Interview with Govindacharya, New Delhi, June 2018.

89. Interview with Manvendra Singh, New Delhi, June 2018.

90. Pankaj Pachauri, 'Babri Masjid-Ram Janmabhoomi row: Another legal tangle unfolds in Ayodhya', *India Today*, 31 August 1989.

91. '"Shilanyas" peaceful', *The Times of India*, 10 November 1989, p. 1.

92. Badri Narayan, *Kanshi Ram: Leader of the Dalits* (Penguin, 2014, kindle edition), location 2114–15.

93. Vijai Trivedi, *Haar Nahin Maanoonga* (HarperCollins Hindi, 2016), pp. 75–76.

94. Khushwant Singh, 'India at 70: Khushwant Singh on why he shuns men like L.K. Advani', *DailyO*, 15 August 2017. Available at: https://www.dailyo.in/politics/lk-advani-bjp-ram-mandir-modi-vajpayee-khushwant-singh/story/1/18961.html

95. 'Khushwant Singh: 10 Interviews', *Outlook*, 20 March 2014. Available at: https://www.outlookindia.com/blog/story/khushwant-singh-10-interviews/3204

96. Walter K. Andersen, 'Election 1989 in India: The Dawn of Coalition Politics?', *Asian Survey* 30(6) June 1990: 527–40.

97. Ibid.

98. Badri Narayan, *Kanshi Ram: Leader of the Dalits* (Penguin, 2014, kindle edition), location 2287–88.

99. A detailed discussion of these various causes is provided in the end of this book in the section in the 'Scholarly Contributions' titled 'Why does the BJP win?'

100. Yogendra Yadav, 'Electoral Politics in the Time of Change: India's Third Electoral System, 1989-99', *Economic and Political Weekly* 34 (34/35) (21 August– 3 September 1999): 2393–99.

CHAPTER 9: MANDAL, MANDIR, MARKET (1990–91)

1. Interview with Dinesh Trivedi, January 2019.

2. Christophe Jaffrelot, *The Hindu Nationalist Movement in India* (Columbia University Press, 1996), p. 412.

3. 'BJP hardens line on Ayodhya issue' *The Hindu*, 27 August 1990, p. 9.

4. Christophe Jaffrelot, *The Hindu Nationalist Movement in India* (Columbia University Press, 1996), p. 413.

5. Uday Mahurkar, 'Gujarat Janata Dal, BJP oppose Chimanbhai Patel', *India Today*, 31 January 1990.

6. Interview with Harish Khare, New Delhi, September 2019.

7. Sanjay Ruparelia, *Divided We Govern: Coalition Politics in Modern India* (Oxford University Press, 2015), p. 113.

8. Inderjit Badhwar, 'Soft-spoken hardliner L.K. Advani bursts into national limelight', *India Today*, 31 March 1990.

9. Interview with N. Ram, Kolkata, November 2017.

10. Ananth V. Krishna. *India Since Independence: Making Sense of Indian Politics* (Pearson Education India, 2011), p. 364–65.

11. Vinay Sitapati, 'Reservations', in Sujit Choudhry, Madhav Khosla and Pratap Bhanu Mehta (eds), *The Oxford Handbook of the Indian Constitution* (Oxford University Press, 2016).

12. Ibid.

13. Inderjit Badhwar. 'Decision to implement Mandal Commission report threatens to tear India's fabric apart', *India Today*, 15 September 1990.

14. The full text of the 1980 Mandal Commission report is available here: http://www.ncbc.nic.in/User_Panel/UserView.aspx?TypeID=1161

15. Christophe Jaffrelot and Gilles Verniers, 'The representation gap', *The Indian Express*, 24 July 2015. Available at: https://indianexpress.com/article/opinion/columns/the-representation-gap-2/

16. 'Beyond Mandal', *Frontline*, 25 October 1991. Available at: https://frontline.thehindu.com/social-issues/beyond-mandal/article6808404.ece

17. L.K. Advani, *My Country, My Life* (Rupa, 2010, paperback), p. 446.

18. 'Implementation of Mandal Commission report lands PM V.P. Singh in "no-win" situation', *India Today*, 30 September 1990.

19. Sukumar Muralidharan, 'Mandal, Mandir Aur Masjid: Hindu Communalism and the Crisis of the State', *Social Scientist* 18(10) (October 1990): 27–49, p. 36.

20. Nonita Kalra, 'Rajeev Goswami's tragedy provides agitation a rallying point', *India Today*, 15 October 1990.

21. 'Relent, Vajpayee urges VP', *The Times of India*, 28 September 1990, p. 13.

22. Christophe Jaffrelot, *The Hindu Nationalist Movement in India* (Columbia University Press, 1996), p. 415.

23. Pankaj Pachauri, '10-month-old BJP-Janata Dal alliance had not been a harmonious one', *India Today*, 15 November 1990.

24. 'BJP Hardens Line of Ayodhya Issue', *The Hindu*, 27 August 1990, p. 9.

25. L.K. Advani, *My Country, My Life* (Rupa, 2010, paperback), pp. 373–74.

26. 'Twenty Years Too Late: A turning point in Indian history when history refused to turn', *The Telegraph*, 17 September 2010. Available at: https://www.telegraphindia.com/1100917/jsp/opinion/story_12947778.jsp

27. Prabhas Pathan, 'Advani begins Rath Yatra to "promote nationalism"', *The Hindu*, 26 September 1990, p. 7.

28. Ibid.

29. Ibid.

30. 'Overenthusiasm of youth worries Advani', *The Hindu*, 29 September 1990.

31. Christophe Jaffrelot, *The Hindu Nationalist Movement in India* (Columbia University Press, 1996), p. 416.

32. Interview with M.K. Venu, January 2018.

33. 'Overenthusiasm of youth worries Advani', *The Hindu*, 29 September 1990.

34. Christophe Jaffrelot, *The Hindu Nationalist Movement in India* (Columbia University Press, 1996), p. 425.

35. Ibid., p. 430.

36. 'Overenthusiasm of youth worries Advani', *The Hindu*, 29 September 1990.

37. Interview with Swapan Dasgupta, New Delhi, March 2018.

38. Interview with Harin Pathak, New Delhi, March 2018.

39. Interview with Subramanian Swamy, New Delhi, June 2018.

40. Interview with Pravin Togadia, Ahmedabad, April 2018.

41. Interview with Sudheendra Kulkarni, Mumbai, May 2018.

42. Inder Sawhney, 'Vajpayee questions Hindutva policy', *The Times of India*, 4 February 1991, p. 8.

43. Interview with Yashwant Sinha, New Delhi, June 2018.

44. N.M. Ghatate (ed.), *Atal Bihari Vajpayee: Four Decades in Parliament*, Volume 1 (Shipra Publications), p. xxxi.

45. Vijai Trivedi, *Haar Nahin Maanoonga* (HarperCollins Hindi, 2016), p. 107.

46. 'Pressure mounts on VP', *The Times of India*, 23 October 1990, p. 1.

47. 'Advani arrested', *The Times of India*, 24 October 1990, p. 1.

48. 'Advani arrested in nightclothes', *The Times of India*, 24 October 1990, p. 13.

49. Pankaj Pachauri, '10-month-old BJP-Janata Dal alliance had not been a harmonious one', *India Today*, 15 November 1990.

50. L.K. Advani, *My Country, My Life* (Rupa, 2010, paperback), p. 380.

51. Interview with N.M. Ghatate, New Delhi, May 2018.

52. L.K. Advani, *My Country, My Life* (Rupa, 2010, paperback), p. 379.

53. Take, for example, this magazine report that the rath yatra's route in communally sensitive areas was unusually calm: Pankaj Pachauri, '10-month-old BJP-Janata Dal alliance had not been a harmonious one', *India Today*, 15 November 1990.

54. Christophe Jaffrelot, *The Hindu Nationalist Movement in India* (Columbia University Press, 1996), p. 419.

55. Ibid., p. 420.

56. Interview with Vijai Trivedi, New Delhi, June 2019.

57. Amit Shah has recollected this to a senior journalist who wishes to remain unnamed.

58. Ramachandra Guha, *India after Gandhi: The History of the World's Largest Democracy* (Picador, 2007), p. 636.

59. Prasun Sonwalkar, 'Pitched battle in Ayodhya', *The Times of India*, 30 October 1990, p. 1.

60. Christophe Jaffrelot, *The Hindu Nationalist Movement in India* (Columbia University Press, 1996), p. 421.

61. Interview with Sudheendra Kulkarni, Mumbai, May 2018.

62. Interview with Govindacharya, New Delhi, June 2018.

63. M.L. Sondhi private papers, letter dated 30 September 1991, sequence no. 282.

64. 'V.P. Singh, L.K. Advani refurbish their images to project themselves as serious leaders', *India Today*, 15 February 1991.

65. Shahnaz Anklesaria Aiyar, 'Elections 1991: By enticing voters to gamble on an untried party, BJP hopes to improve its Lok Sabha strength', *India Today*, 15 May 1991.

66. 'From helping Advani in filing nomination to replacing him: Amit Shah's life in Gandhinagar comes full circle', *DNA*, 22 March 2019. Available at: https://www.dnaindia.com/india/report-from-helping-advani-in-filing-nomination-to-replacing-him-amit-shah-s-life-in-gandhinagar-comes-full-circle-2731829

67. Prabhash K. Dutta, 'From sticking bills for BJP to managing Union home ministry: Rise and rise of Amit Shah', *India Today*, 31 May 2019.

68. Shahnaz Anklesaria Aiyar, 'L.K. Advani whips up Hindutva fervour, attacks "pseudo-secularism"', *India Today*, 31 May 1991.

69. 'Of Crucial Importance', *India Today*, 31 May 1991.

70. Shahnaz Anklesaria Aiyar, 'Elections 1991: By enticing voters to gamble on an untried party, BJP hopes to improve its Lok Sabha strength', *India Today*, 15 May 1991.

71. Interview with Ravindra Bhagwat, Chandrapur, March 2018.

72. Vijai Trivedi, *Haar Nahin Maanoonga* (HarperCollins Hindi, 2016), p. 112.

73. Ibid., p. 28.

74. N.M. Ghatate (ed.), *Atal Bihari Vajpayee: Four Decades in Parliament*, Volume 1 (Shipra Publications), p. xxix.

75. 'General Election, 1991 (Vol. I, II)', Election Commission of India. Available at: https://eci.gov.in/files/file/4121-general-election-1991-vol-i-ii/

76. Sanjay Ruparelia, *Divided We Govern: Coalition Politics in Modern India* (Oxford University Press, 2015), pp. 104, 148.

77. Interview with Seshadri Chari, Delhi, April 2018.

78. G.V. Ramana and Valsa Raj, 'The Tenth Lok Sabha Elections: Sympathy Swing Helps Congress (I) improve tally by 25 seats (Appendix 11)', in Devendra Thakur (ed.), *Psephology and Elections Forecasting* (Deep & Deep, 1996), p. 296.

79. Interview with Govindacharya, New Delhi, June 2018.

80. Vinay Sitapati, *Half Lion: How P.V. Narasimha Rao Transformed India* (Penguin Random House, 2016).

81. L.K. Advani, *My Country, My Life* (Rupa, 2010, paperback), p. 458.

82. 'BJP flays govt.: foreign loans', *The Times of India*, 8 September 1991, p. 3.

83. N.M. Ghatate (ed.), *Atal Bihari Vajpayee: Four Decades in Parliament*, Volume 1 (Shipra Publications), p. 142.

84. Ibid.

85. M.L. Sondhi private papers, letter dated 30 September 1991, sequence no. 282.

86. Ibid.

CHAPTER 10: TOO MANY GENERALS (1992)

1. The theme for this chapter was provided by the researcher for this book, Arpit Gaind.

2. For a general overview of the third battle of Panipat, see Uday Kulkarni, *Solstice at Panipat: 14 January 1761. An Authentic Account of the Panipat Campaign* (Mula Mutha Publishers, 2011), pp. 224–25.

3. Kaushik Roy, *India's Historic Battles: From Alexander the Great to Kargil* (Orient Blackswan, 2004), p. 86.

4. Ibid., pp. 85–86.

5. Ibid., p. 93.

6. Uday Mahurkar, 'The lost Marathas of third battle of Panipat', *India Today*, 12 January 2012.

7. 'Election 2019 like Third Battle of Panipat: Amit Shah's battle cry at BJP meet', *Hindustan Times*, 11 January 2019. Available at: https://www. hindustantimes.com/india-news/pm-modi-invincible-so-opposition-looks-for-allies-amit-shah/story-nKY5uzsmnD9OqjF4nu4LVP.html

8. Madhav Sadashiv Golwalkar, *Bunch of Thoughts* (Vikrama Prakashan, 1966), p. 184.

9. Dhirendra K. Jha, *Ascetic Games: Sadhus, Akharas and the Making of the Hindu Vote* (Context, 2019), Introductory chapter.

10. William R. Pinch, *Warrior, Ascetics and Indian Empires* (Cambridge University Press, 2006).

11. Dhirendra K. Jha, *Ascetic Games: Sadhus, Akharas and the Making of the Hindu Vote* (Context, 2019).

12. Rajesh Pradhan, *When the Saints Go Marching In: The Curious Ambivalence of Religious Sadhus in Recent Politics in India* (Orient Blackswan, 2014).

13. Report of the Liberhan Ayodhya Commission of Inquiry (Ministry of Home Affairs, Government of India, 2009), para 30.8, pp. 128–29.

14. Ibid., para 30.12, p. 130.

15. Note found amongst P.V. Narasimha Rao's private papers in Hyderabad in 2015.

16. Dilip Awasthi, 'Ayodhya issue: CM Kalyan Singh's fortunes flounder as Hindu hardliners mount pressure', *India Today*, 15 September. 1991.

17. *P.V. Narasimha Rao Selected Speeches, 1992-93* (Government of India Publications Division, New Delhi, 1993), p. 30.

18. Ibid., p. 10.

19. Report of the Liberhan Ayodhya Commission of Inquiry (Ministry of Home Affairs, Government of India, 2009), para 37.57, pp. 186–87.

20. Rajesh Pradhan, *When the Saints Go Marching In: The Curious Ambivalence of Religious Sadhus in Recent Politics in India* (Orient Blackswan, 2014), pp. 160–161.

21. Ibid., pp. 161–62.

22. Yubaraj Ghimire and Dilip Awasthi, 'Ayodhya controversy became BJP's most effective battering ram during two successive polls', *India Today*, 4 January 2013.

23. Note found amongst P.V. Narasimha Rao's private papers in Hyderabad in 2015.

24. Advani met Rao on 12 and 18 November. See Report of the Liberhan Ayodhya Commission of Inquiry (Ministry of Home Affairs, Government of India, 2009), para 41.27 and 41.38, pp. 207, 210. And again around the 25 November. This latter date is from an interview with P.V.R.K. Prasad, Hyderabad, 2015.

25. Naunidhi Kaur, 'Of waffling and double-speak: L.K. Advani's third-round deposition before the Liberhan Commission leaves more questions than answers', *Frontline*, Vol. 18, Issue 11, 26 May–8 June 2001. Available at: https://frontline.thehindu.com/static/html/fl1811/18110310.htm

26. Interview with P.V.R.K. Prasad, Hyderabad, 2015.

27. *Lok Sabha Debates*, Xth Lok Sabha. Available at: https://parliamentofindia. nic.in/ls/lsdeb/ls-archivedeb.htm

28. 'Uproar in Lok Sabha', *The Times of India*, 1 December 1992, p. 1.

29. Report of the Liberhan Ayodhya Commission of Inquiry (Ministry of Home Affairs, Government of India, 2009), para 41.51 and 41.52, p. 215.

30. 'Ayodhya Row Rocks Parliament', *The Times of India*, 3 December 1992, p. 1.

31. Ibid.

32. Ibid.

33. Report of the Liberhan Ayodhya Commission of Inquiry (Ministry of Home Affairs, Government of India, 2009), para 41.68, p. 220.

34. Ibid.

35. Saba Naqvi and Sutapa Mukerjee, 'Hour Of Janus', *Outlook*, 28 February 2005. Available at: https://www.outlookindia.com/magazine/story/hour-of-janus/226634

36. Swapan Dasgupta, 'The Hindu Inflexion', *Open Magazine*, 30 November 2017. Available at: https://openthemagazine.com/cover-stories/ayodhya-25-years-later/the-hindu-inflexion/

37. Saba Naqvi and Sutapa Mukerjee, 'Hour of Janus', *Outlook*, 28 February 2005. Available at: https://www.outlookindia.com/magazine/story/hour-of-janus/226634

38. Zoya Hasan, *Congress After Indira: Policy, Power, Political Change (1984-2009)* (Oxford University Press, 2013). P. 26.

39. Report of the Liberhan Ayodhya Commission of Inquiry (Ministry of Home Affairs, Government of India, 2009), para, 43.16, p. 242.

40. Ibid., para 44.11, pp. 252–53.

41. Ibid.

42. This number comes from the Liberhan Commission report. See also: '1.5 lakh kar sevaks, 2,300 police constables, 1 mosque: How Babri Masjid fell on December 6, 1992', *India Today*, 6 December 2017.

43. Minute 17.15 of 'Babri Masjid demolition: The most comprehensive video coverage from 1992', video available at: https://www.youtube.com/watch?v=k-bhAFsnv2s

44. L.K. Advani, *My Country, My Life* (Rupa, 2010, paperback), p. 401.

45. 'Absurd to say PV was incommunicado during Ayodhya demolition', rediff.com, 9 July 2012. Available at: https://www.rediff.com/news/ report/slide-show-1-arjun-singhs-story-on-ayodhya-demolition-cock-and- bull/20120709.htm

46. L.K. Advani, *My Country, My Life* (Rupa, 2010, paperback), p. 401.

47. Ibid.

48. Interview with Swapan Dasgupta, New Delhi, March 2018.

49. Report of the Liberhan Ayodhya Commission of Inquiry (Ministry of Home Affairs, Government of India, 2009), para 44.21, p. 255.

50. Chandan Mitra's interview at minute 17.20 of 'Babri Masjid demolition: The most comprehensive video coverage from 1992'. Video available at: https://www.youtube.com/watch?v=k-bhAFsnv2s

51. Report of the Liberhan Ayodhya Commission of Inquiry (Ministry of Home Affairs, Government of India, 2009), para 44.51, p. 263.

52. Ibid., para 44.42, p. 260.

53. Ibid., para 44.30, p. 257.

54. 'Bloody aftermath of Babri Masjid demolition across India', *India Today*, 5 December 2011.

55. M.G. Gupta and Vijay Jung Thapa, 'Kar Sevaks Destroyed Babri Masjid', *The Times of India*, 7 December 1992, p. 1.

56. Interview with Swapan Dasgupta, New Delhi, March 2018. He was told this by a senior BJP leader.

57. Interview with M.G. Vaidya. Nagpur, April 2018.

58. *P.V. Narasimha Rao Selected Speeches (1992-93)* (Government of India Publications Division, New Delhi, 1993), pp. 63–65.

59. 'Centre set to Ban Communal Bodies: Advani, Joshi, Singhal Among Others Held', *The Times of India*, 9 December 1992, p. 1.

60. 'Parties demand ban on RSS, VHP', *The Times of India*, 8 December 1992, p. 3.

61. 'Centre set to Ban Communal Bodies: Advani, Joshi, Singhal Among Others Held', *The Times of India*, 9 December 1992, p. 1.

62. Edward A. Gargan, 'India, Acting on Militants, Ousts Local Rulers', *The New York Times*, 16 December 1992. Available at: https://www. nytimes.com/1992/12/16/world/india-acting-on-militants-ousts-local- rulers.html

63. Vijai Trivedi, *Haar Nahin Maanoonga* (HarperCollins Hindi, 2016), p. 111.

64. Ibid.

65. Somak Ghoshal, 'Watch: The Day Atal Bihari Vajpayee Apologised for the Demolition of the Babri Masjid', *Huffpost*, 19 April, 2017. Available

at: https://www.huffingtonpost.in/2017/04/19/watch-the-day-atal-bihari-vajpayee-apologised-for-the-demolitio_a_22045592/

66. 'Speech of Shri Atal Bihari Vajpayee in Lok Sabha on 17-12-92'. *Speeches of Shri Atal Bihari Vajpayee, Swamy Chinmayanand, Shri Lal Krishna Advani on Ayodhya*. Available at: http://www.ataljee.org/digLib/bitstream/1/114/1/2.3%20Atal%20Bihari%20Vajpayee%20on%20Ayodhya%20Issue.PDF

67. 'Advani in image makeover mode; regrets Babri demolition', *Outlook*, 31 May 2005. Available at: https://www.outlookindia.com/newswire/story/advani-in-image-makeover-mode-regrets-babri-demolition/301707

68. Ullekh N.P., *The Untold Vajpayee: Politician and Paradox* (Penguin Books, kindle edition, 2017), location 1981.

69. Report of the Liberhan Ayodhya Commission of Inquiry (Ministry of Home Affairs, Government of India, 2009).

70. Ibid., para 160.6, pp. 922–23.

71. For instance, a later claim by some kar sevaks that Advani ordered the demolition on 3 December 1992 in Ayodhya rings hollow, given that Advani only reached the city two days later.

CHAPTER 11: UNTOUCHABLES (1993–98)

1. Yubaraj Ghimire, 'While senior BJP leaders languish in prison, sadhus hijack party's image and its agenda', *India Today*, 31 January 1993.

2. Ibid.

3. The only exceptions were the forty-seven National Front members, who abstained. See G.C. Malhotra, *Cabinet Responsibility to Legislature: Motions of Confidence and No-Confidence in Lok Sabha and State Legislatures* (Lok Sabha Secretariat, Metropolitan Books, second edition, 2004), p. 86.

4. Yubaraj Ghimire, 'All achievements of BJP, post-1989, have been purely because of our ideology: L.K. Advani', *India Today*, 15 April 1995.

5. 'Kalyan Singh may be next BJP chief', *The Times of India*, 12 April 1993, p. 15.

6. Interview with Govindacharya, New Delhi, March 2018.

7. 'Kalyan Singh may be next BJP chief', *The Times of India*, 12 April 1993, p. 15.

8. 'RSS against Joshi', *The Hindu*, 11 April 1993, p. 6.

9. M.L. Sondhi private papers, letter dated 28 February 1993.

10. 'Vajpayee to head opposition in LS', *The Times of India*, 25 July 1993, p. 9.

11. 'Vajpayee is leader of opposition in LS', *The Times of India*, 27 July 1993, p. 6.

12. 'Assembly polls: BJP emerges as dominant force but Congress(I) shows signs of revival', *India Today*, 30 November 1993.

13. Interview with Pratap Bhanu Mehta, Gurugram, May 2018.

14. Christophe Jaffrelot, *The Hindu Nationalist Movement in India* (Columbia University Press, 1996), pp. 485–86.

15. Ibid., p. 485.

16. Interview with Ajoy Bose, New Delhi, June 2018.

17. Interview with Yashwant Sinha, New Delhi, June 2018.

18. 'Vajpayee "best parliamentarian"', *The Times of India*, 18 August 1994, p. 7.

19. Interview with Salman Khurshid, New Delhi, 2015

20. Yubaraj Ghimire and Bhavdeep Kang, 'Faltering on the Home Stretch', *Outlook*, 18 October 1995. Available at: https://www.outlookindia.com/magazine/story/faltering-on-the-home-stretch/200033

21. Yubaraj Ghimire, 'BJP unleashes its propaganda power for a possible mid-term election', *India Today*, 31 July 1993.

22. Uday Mahurkar, 'Modi's tactics help BJP become first non-Congress (I) party in Gujarat to capture power', *India Today*, 15 July 1995.

23. Uday Mahurkar, 'From a backroom boy, Narendra Modi graduates to a more public profile', *India Today*, 2 March 1998.

24. Uday Mahurkar and N.K. Singh, 'Fate of Keshubhai Patel Govt hangs by a thread as Shankarsinh Vaghela splits ruling BJP', *India Today*, 15 October 1995.

25. 'Shankersinh Vaghela: The Complete Story of Khajuraho', *Newsstreetjournal*. Available at: http://www.newsstreetjournal.com/india/shankersinh-vaghela-the-complete-story-of-khajuraho/

26. Ibid.

27. Yubaraj Ghimire and Bhavdeep Kang, 'Faltering on the Home Stretch', *Outlook*, 18 October 1995. Available at: https://www.outlookindia.com/magazine/story/faltering-on-the-home-stretch/200033

28. 'Shankersinh Vaghela: The Complete Story of Khajuraho', *Newsstreetjournal*. Available at: http://www.newsstreetjournal.com/india/shankersinh-vaghela-the-complete-story-of-khajuraho/

29. Ibid.

30. Priyavadan Patel, 'Sectarian Mobilisation, Factionalism and Voting in Gujarat', *Economic and Political Weekly*, Vol. 34, No. 34/35 (21 August–3 September 1999): 2423-2433, at 2427.

31. Yubaraj Ghimire and Bhavdeep Kang, 'Faltering on the Home Stretch', *Outlook*, 18 October 1995. Available at: https://www.outlookindia.com/magazine/story/faltering-on-the-home-stretch/200033

32. P.V. Narasimha Rao, *Ayodhya 6 December 1992* (Penguin Global, 2006), p. 100.

33. 'Chronology of Hawala Case', *The Times of India*, 17 January 1991, p. 1.

34. 'CBI chargesheets Advani, Arjun, 5 others', *The Times of India*, 17 January 1996, p. 1.

35. L.K. Advani, *My Country, My Life* (Rupa, 2010, paperback), p. 467.

36. N.K. Singh, 'Tarred with the same Brush', *India Today*, 15 February 1996.

37. Ullekh N.P., *The Untold Vajpayee: Politician and Paradox* (Penguin Books, kindle edition, 2017), location 2185.

38. L.K. Advani, *My Country, My Life* (Rupa, 2010, paperback), p. 481.

39. N.K. Singh, 'All political parties are accepting donations in "black": Atal Bihari Vajpayee', *India Today*, 31 March 1996.

40. Ibid.

41. 'Corruption will be the main issue in the coming polls, says Vajpayee', *The Times of India*, 6 February 1996, p. 15.

42. Padmanand Jha, 'A Prime Minister in the Making?', *Outlook*, 17 April 1996. Available at: https://www.outlookindia.com/magazine/story/a-prime-minister-in-the-making/201207

43. Sudeep Chakravarti, '1996 had more than its fair share of both failure and success', *India Today*, 15 January 1997.

44. Ibid.

45. Sanjay Ruparelia, *Divided We Govern: Coalition Politics in Modern India* (Oxford University Press, 2015), p. 154.

46. Pramod K. Kantha, 'BJP Politics: Looking Beyond the Impasse', *Economic and Political Weekly*, 1996.

47. Yubaraj Ghimire, 'In The Saddle, But For How Long?', *Outlook*, 29 May 1996. Available at: https://www.outlookindia.com/magazine/story/in-the-saddle-but-for-how-long/201428

48. Vijai Trivedi, *Haar Nahin Maanoonga* (HarperCollins Hindi, 2016), p. 116.

49. See 'Vajpayee Sworn In As Prime Minister'. Video available at: https://www.youtube.com/watch?v=IEJnqsBbfvU

50. 'Jubilation in Nagpur over new govt.', *The Times of India*, 17 May 1996, p. 3.

51. Janak Singh, 'Vajpayee Sworn in as P.M.', *The Times of India*, 17 May 1996, p. 1.

52. 'All The Prime Minister's Men', *Outlook*, 29 May 1996. Available at: https://www.outlookindia.com/magazine/story/all-the-prime-ministers-men/201430

53. 'All the Prime Minister's men—and a lone woman', *The Times of India*, 17 May 1996, p. 13.

54. Jaswant Singh, *A Call to Honour: In Service of Emergent India* (Rupa, 2006, kindle edition), location 2190.

55. 'Vajpayee Sworn In As Prime Minister'. Video available at: https://www.youtube.com/watch?v=IEJnqsBbfvU

56. L.K. Advani, *My Country, My Life* (Rupa, 2010, paperback), p. 481.

57. 'Leaders, industry enthused by events', *The Times of India*, 16 May 1996, p. 1.

58. Paranjoy Guha Thakurta, 'Ideological Contradictions in an Era of Coalitions: Economic Policy Confusion in the Vajpayee Government', *Global Business Review*, Volume 3, Issue 2 (January 2002): 201–23, p. 203.

59. L.K. Advani, *My Country, My Life* (Rupa, 2010, paperback), p. 481.

60. 'Vajpayee urges Joshi to revive Srikrishna panel: A trick to project secular image, says Congress', *The Times of India*, 27 May 1996, p. 1.

61. It would eventually submit its report, holding the Shiv Sena in large measure responsible for the anti-Muslim violence.

62. Janak Singh, 'BJP is not known for witch-hunting, says A. B. Vajpayee', *The Times of India*, 21 May 1996, p. 7.

63. Anil Saxena, 'BJP makes final pitch to get support of small parties', *The Times of India*, 25 May 1996, p. 1.

64. N.K. Singh, 'Atal Bihari Vajpayee goes down, but with the image of a martyr statesman', *India Today*, 15 June 1996.

65. Janak Singh, 'Candid Vajpayee admits BJP may not win trust vote', *The Times of India*, 21 May 1996, p. 1.

66. Sanjay Ruparelia, *Divided We Govern: Coalition Politics in Modern India* (Oxford University Press, 2015), p. 165.

67. L.K. Advani, *My Country, My Life* (Rupa, 2010, paperback), p. 482.

68. Kingshuk Nag, *Vajpayee: A Man for All Seasons* (Rupa Publications, 2015), p. 122.

69. 'Vajpayee tries to score points as Pawar, Paswan pack punches', *The Times of India*, 28 May 1996, p. 1.

70. Atal Bihari Vajpayee's Speech in Parliament on the Confidence Motion. Video available at: https://www.youtube.com/watch?v=_1n_OIp3EOs

71. 'Conciliation and combat was his flavour', *The Times of India*, 29 May 1996, p. 1.

72. Ibid.

73. 'Historic debate', *The Times of India*, 29 May 1996, p. 11.

74. Ibid.

75. Atal Bihari Vajpayee's Speech in Parliament on the Confidence Motion. Video available at: https://www.youtube.com/watch?v=_1n_OIp3EOs

76. 'Kesri blasts Deve Gowda', Rediff, available at: http://business.rediff.com/news/aug/09cong1.htm

77. Swapan Dasgupta, 'Hindutva will be the dynamo of the new India: L.K. Advani', *India Today*, 23 June 1997.

78. Ishan Joshi, 'So, What's Behind The Mask?: The Govindacharya-Vajpayee tussle over "words" reflects a deeper malaise in the party', *Outlook*, 27 October 1997. Available at: https://www.outlookindia.com/magazine/story/so-whats-behind-the-mask/204448

79. 'A.B. Vajpayee seeks explanation from Govindacharya for calling him mask of party', *India Today*, 27 October 1997.

80. Interview with Govindacharya, New Delhi, March 2018.

81. 'A.B. Vajpayee seeks explanation from Govindacharya for calling him mask of party', *India Today*, 27 October 1997.

82. Ishan Joshi, 'So, What's Behind The Mask?: The Govindacharya-Vajpayee tussle over "words" reflects a deeper malaise in the party', *Outlook*, 27 October 1997. Available at: https://www.outlookindia.com/magazine/story/so-whats-behind-the-mask/204448

83. Interview with Sudheendra Kulkarni, Mumbai, May 2018.

84. For a detailed description of the manoeuvrings within the Congress and United Front that resulted in the fall of the I.K. Gujral government, see Sanjay Ruparelia, *Divided We Govern: Coalition Politics in Modern India* (Oxford University Press, 2015), pp. 272–75.

85. Saba Naqvi Bhaumik, 'BJP aspires for sobriety and respectability, reaches out to audience who shunned saffron', *India Today*, 9 February 1998.

86. 'Hype over new alliance of psychological importance to BJP', *India Today*, 9 February 1998.

87. Swapan Dasgupta and Ashok K. Damodaran, 'In desperation to win Lok Sabha elections, BJP sheds its distinctive character', *India Today*, 29 December 1997.

88. Swapan Dasgupta, 'Major gains for BJP-led alliance, Vajpayee most favoured PM: Poll', *India Today*, 5 January 1998.

89. Ishan Joshi, 'The BJP's Best Man, Ishan Joshi and photographer T. Narayan hop on to Vajpayee's aircraft and trail him around', *Outlook*, 2 February 1998. Available at: https://www.outlookindia.com/magazine/story/the-bjps-best-man/204976

90. Ibid.

91. Ishan Joshi, 'A Deliberate Duality: Vajpayee and Advani adopt varying postures on contentious issues to suit all shades of opinion', *Outlook*, 9 February 1998. Available at: https://www.outlookindia.com/magazine/story/a-deliberate-duality/205007

92. Yubaraj Ghimire, 'Rumblings at the Top: The Advani-Vajpayee "feud" comes to the fore with an RSS-inspired manifesto', *Outlook*, 16 February 1998. Available at: https://www.outlookindia.com/magazine/story/rumblings-at-the-top/205063

93. Ishan Joshi, 'Decoding Advani: The BJP chief's post-poll role becomes a topic of speculation', *Outlook*, 22 December 1997. Available at: https://www.outlookindia.com/magazine/story/decoding-advani/204755

94. Ishan Joshi, 'A Deliberate Duality: Vajpayee and Advani adopt varying postures on contentious issues to suit all shades of opinion', *Outlook*, 09 February 1998. Available at: https://www.outlookindia.com/magazine/story/a-deliberate-duality/205007

95. Swapan Dasgupta and Saba Naqvi Bhaumik, 'PM-aspirant Atal Bihari Vajpayee faces coalition of parties with separate agendas', *India Today*, 16 March 1998.

96. Atul Kohli, 'India Defies the Odds: Enduring Another Election', *Journal of Democracy*, 1998 (3): 7–20, p. 8.

97. Ibid., p. 12.

98. Interview with Shakti Sinha, New Delhi, April 2018.

PART III: POWER (1998–2004)

CHAPTER 12: EXPERIMENT IN GOVERNANCE (1998–99)

1. This figure includes nineteen political parties plus the BJP plus three independents.

2. L.K. Advani, *My Country, My Life* (Rupa, 2010, paperback), p. 534.

3. Sudha Pai, 'The Indian Party System under Transformation: Lok Sabha Elections 1998', *Asian Survey*, Vol. 38, No. 9 (September 1998): 836–52, p. 839.

4. Ashis K. Biswas, Ishan Joshi, Rajesh Joshi and Lekha Rattanani, 'Tough Act: The BJP is poised for its second brush with power. But its sense of destiny may soon drown in the cacophony of coalition politics', *Outlook*, 16 March 1998. Available at: https://www.outlookindia.com/magazine/story/tough-act/205196

5. '"National agenda" adopted', *The Hindu*, 18 March 1998, p. 1.

6. Ishan Joshi, 'We'll Last Longer than the Others', *Outlook*, 18 May 1998. Available at: https://www.outlookindia.com/magazine/story/well-last-longer-than-the-others/205530

7. 'Coalition partner AIADMK gives sleepless nights to BJP-led Government', *India Today*, 20 June 1998.

8. Interview with Shakti Sinha, New Delhi, April 2018.

9. Interview with Subramanian Swamy, New Delhi, June 2018.

10. Interview with Yashwant Sinha, New Delhi, June 2018.

11. Shekhar Gupta, 'When an RSS chief was supremely unimpressed with Atal Bihari Vajpayee', *The Print*, 25 December 2017.

12. Interview with Shakti Sinha, New Delhi, January 2018.

13. Jung Chang, *Wild Swans: Three Daughters of China* (Simon and Schuster, 2008), p. 174.

14. Interview with Sudheendra Kulkarni, Mumbai, May 2018.

15. Interview with Swapan Dasgupta, New Delhi, June 2018.

16. Shekhar Gupta, 'When an RSS chief was supremely unimpressed with Atal Bihari Vajpayee', *The Print*, 25 December 2017.

17. Jairam Ramesh, *Intertwined Lives: P.N. Haksar and Indira Gandhi* (Simon and Schuster, 2018).

18. Interview with Pratap Bhanu Mehta, New Delhi, July 2018.

19. L.K. Advani, *My Country, My Life* (Rupa, 2010, paperback), p. 534.

20. Interview with N. Ram, Kolkata, November 2017.

21. Interview with Manvendra Singh, New Delhi, June 2018.

22. 'Was RSS informed in advance of n-tests?', *The Hindu*, 13 May 1998.

23. Vinay Krishin Gidwani, 'India's nuclear tests: loss of moral stature and courage', *Economic and Political Weekly* (1998): 1312–15, p. 1312.

24. Interview with Sudheendra Kulkarni, Mumbai, May 2018.

25. 'Pokhran nuclear tests: Well done, says a large majority of Vajpayee's fellow Indians', *India Today*, 25 May 1998.

26. Ranjit Bhushan, 'Nuke Harvest: If there's a mid-term poll, the BJP says it has a clear advantage, thanks to its bold N-strategy', *Outlook*, 25 May 1998. Available at: https://www.outlookindia.com/magazine/story/nuke-harvest/205577

27. Ibid.

28. L.K. Advani, *My Country, My Life* (Rupa, 2010, paperback), p. 545.

29. Amit Shah has recollected this to a senior journalist who wishes to remain unnamed.

30. Interview with T.C.A. Raghavan, New Delhi, May 2018.

31. Jaswant Singh, *A Call to Honour: In Service of Emergent India* (Rupa, 2006, kindle edition), location 3472, 3477.

32. Harinder Baweja and Sumit Mitra, 'With BJP firmly in the saddle, RSS wants more say in govt's policies and functioning', *India Today*, 28 September 1998.

33. Prabhu Chawla, 'We are not authoritarian like the Congress: A.B. Vajpayee', *India Today*, 2 November 1998.

34. Interview with Sudheendra Kulkarni, Mumbai, May 2018.

35. Siddhartha Vaidyanathan, 'India. Pakistan. Chennai. 1999', *The Cricket Monthly*, 31 January 2019; 'When Sachin Wept After Losing to Pakistan in Chennai', News18, 31 January 2018.

36. Interview with Sudheendra Kulkarni, Mumbai, May 2018.

37. Celia W. Dugger, 'Indian Leader Accepts Pakistani Offer to Take a Ride to Lahore', *The New York Times*, 4 February 1999. Available at: https://www.nytimes.com/1999/02/04/world/indian-leader-accepts-pakistani-offer-to-take-a-ride-to-lahore.html

38. L.K. Advani, *My Country, My Life* (Rupa, 2010, paperback), p. 551.

39. K.K. Katyal, 'Vajpayee arrives in Pak., steps into history', *The Hindu*, 21 February 1999.

40. 'In 1999, Nawaz Sharif said, "Vajpayee sahab can now win an election even in Pakistan"', *The Indian Express*, 17 August 2018. Available at: https://indianexpress.com/article/lifestyle/books/atal-bihari-vajpayee-dead-nawaz-sharif-delhi-lahore-bus-book-excerpt-5310123/

41. Srijan Shukla and Sajid Ali, 'The Bus Ride That Almost Helped Vajpayee, Sharif Rewrite History of South Asia', *The Print*, 1 July 2019.

42. Ibid.

43. 'In 1999, Nawaz Sharif said, "Vajpayee sahab can now win an election even in Pakistan"', *The Indian Express*, 17 August 2018. Available at: https://indianexpress.com/article/lifestyle/books/atal-bihari-vajpayee-dead-nawaz-sharif-delhi-lahore-bus-book-excerpt-5310123/

44. Interview with Subramanian Swamy, New Delhi, June 2018.

45. 'BJP's one-vote defeat in 1999 was narrowest in history', *The Times of India*, 22 July 2008.

46. See 0.51 seconds onward at 'DNA rewinds: How Congress toppled Vajpayee government on this day 20 years ago'. Video available at: https://www.youtube.com/watch?v=ykiXjYKhBsM

47. 'BSP's revenge spelt doom for govt.', *The Times of India*, 18 April 1999, p. 8.

48. Interview with Subramanian Swamy, New Delhi, June 2018.

49. 'BSP's revenge spelt doom for govt.', *The Times of India*, 18 April 1999, p. 8.

50. L.K. Advani, *My Country, My Life* (Rupa, 2010, paperback), p. 554.

51. Ibid.

52. Interview with Shakti Sinha, New Delhi, June 2018.

53. 'The last time Sonia Gandhi said "we have the numbers"', *The Times of India*, 19 July 2018.

54. L.K. Advani, *My Country, My Life* (Rupa, 2010, paperback), p. 556.

55. Rasheed Kidwai, 'May 15, 1999: The Day Tariq Anwar Joined Sharad Pawar's Revolt Against "Foreign Lady" Sonia', News18, 27 October

2018. Available at: https://www.news18.com/news/opinion/opinion-tariq-anwar-may-be-back-in-congress-19-years-after-joining-sharad-pawars-revolt-against-foreign-lady-sonia-gandhi-1892971.html

56. L.K. Advani, *My Country, My Life* (Rupa, 2010, paperback), pp. 558–59.

57. Vinod Mehta, *Lucknow Boy: A Memoir* (Penguin Books India, 2011), p. 303.

58. Shoumojit Banerjee, '13 years on, a good shepherd awaits recognition', *The Hindu*, 6 August 2014.

59. Jaswant Singh, *A Call to Honour: In Service of Emergent India* (Rupa, 2006, kindle edition), location 3637.

60. L.K. Advani, *My Country, My Life* (Rupa, 2010, paperback), p. 562.

61. Kargil Review Committee (ed.), *From Surprise to Reckoning: The Kargil Review Committee Report* (SAGE Publications Pvt Limited, 2000), p. 96.

62. Ibid., pp. 83–86.

63. Ibid., p. 96.

64. T.C.A. Raghavan, *The People Next Door: The Curious History of India's Relations with Pakistan* (HarperCollins India, 2017), p. 234.

65. Raj Chengappa, 'I seriously wanted Kargil War to come to an end, says former Pakistan PM Nawaz Sharif', *India Today*, 26 July 2004.

66. Gen. V.P. Malik, 'Lessons from Kargil', *Indian Defence Review*, Volume 16 (5) 2002: 2.

67. Ibid.

68. L.K. Advani, *My Country, My Life* (Rupa, 2010, paperback), p. 575.

69. Swapan Dasgupta, 'BJP banks on Prime Minister Vajpayee to bring in votes in the coming elections', *India Today*, 2 August 1999.

70. Saba Naqvi Bhaumik, 'Once a BJP mask, Vajpayee's popularity today makes him bigger than party itself', *India Today*, 2 August 1999.

71. Rob Jenkins, 'Appearance and reality in Indian politics: Making sense of the 1999 General Election', *Government and Opposition* 35, no. 1 (2000): 49–66.

72. In constituencies where the BJP went head-to-head against the Congress, its vote share increased from 44 per cent in 1998 to 48 per cent in 1999. Neelanjan Sircar, 'Lok Sabha election 2019: The gains for BJP were not uniform across all states after the Kargil war', *Hindustan Times*, 14 March 2019.

CHAPTER 13: COALITION DHARMA (1999–2004)

1. Alistair McMillan, 'The BJP coalition: partisanship and power-sharing in government', in Katharine Adeney and Lawrence Sáez (eds), *Coalition Politics and Hindu Nationalism* (Routledge, 2007), p. 27.

2. 'Rare moments with Atal Ji with Seshadri Chari'. Video available at: https://www.youtube.com/watch?v=97XtD1lO0BQ

3. Interview with Dinesh Trivedi, New Delhi, May 2018.

4. Supriya Bezbaruah, 'Prime Minister Vajpayee's knee surgery to be most watched medical event in Indian history', *India Today*, 16 October 2000.

5. K.K. Katyal, 'Why is Delhi without an acting PM?', *The Hindu*, 10 October 2000.

6. Ibid.

7. Interview with Keshav Desiraju, New Delhi, 2016.

8. Farzand Ahmed, 'Vajpayee tightens his grip on BJP, picks Bangaru Laxman as party chief', *India Today*, 14 August 2000.

9. Farzand Ahmed, 'In a departure from the past, Vajpayee's pronouncements become a new theme song of BJP', *India Today*, 22 January 2001.

10. 'CBI asks Tehelka for unedited "sting" tapes', *The Economic Times*, 13 December 2004.

11. 'Individuals using the Internet (% of population)', The World Bank. Available at: https://data.worldbank.org/indicator/IT.NET.USER.ZS?end=2017&locations=IN&start=2001

12. Megha Mandavia, 'India has second highest number of Internet users after China: Report', *The Economic Times*, 26 September 2019.

13. 'Rid PMO of incompetent officers, says Sudarshan', *The Times of India*, 19 March 2001, p. 1.

14. Rajesh Ramachandran, 'Bangaru is a "failed swayamsevak": RSS', *The Times of India*, 17 March 2001, p. 1.

15. 'Rid PMO of incompetent officers, says Sudarshan', *The Times of India*, 19 March 2001, p. 1.

16. 'The PM's Achilles Heel', *Outlook*, 26 March 2001. Available at: https://www.outlookindia.com/magazine/issue/282

17. Ajith Pillai and Murali Krishnan, 'Reign of The Triad: The Prime Minister has three blind spots. and everybody seems to see them but he', *Outlook*, 26 March 2001. Available at: https://www.outlookindia.com/magazine/story/reign-of-the-triad/211150

18. Harish Khare, 'I didn't dabble in defence deals: Brajesh Mishra', *The Hindu*, 20 March 2001.

19. Ibid.

20. Vinod Mehta, *Lucknow Boy: A Memoir* (Penguin Books India, 2011), p. 202.

21. Ibid., p. 205.

22. Smita Gupta, 'PM meets Advani in bid to make peace at home', *The Times of India*, 3 May 2001, p. 1.

23. There is some confusion on the name of the RSS chief since Advani in his memoirs says that it was RSS chief 'Rajju Bhaiiya' who met him in 2002 with this suggestion. But Rajju bhaiiya, i.e., Rajendra Singh, had retired in 2000. So it was likely Sudarshan who made the suggestion. See L.K. Advani, *My Country, My Life* (Rupa, 2010, paperback), pp. 839–40.

24. L.K. Advani, *My Country, My Life* (Rupa, 2010, paperback), pp. 839–40.

25. Interview with Virendra Kapoor, New Delhi, June 2018.

26. L.K. Advani, *My Country, My Life* (Rupa, 2010, paperback), p. 599.

27. Interview with M.G. Vaidya. Nagpur, April 2018.

28. Krishna Prasad, 'Two Out Of Five: India's Mr Nuclear is also an all-too-human Kalam Iyer', 24 June 2002. Available at: https://www.outlookindia. com/magazine/story/two-out-of-five/216160

29. S.S. Dhawan, 'Why Kalam—despite being a Muslim—is a favourite of Hindu Right', *DailyO*, 2 August 2017. Available at: https://www. dailyo.in/voices/apj-abdul-kalam-hindutva-bjp-rss-hindu-right-muslims/ story/1/18721.html

30. 'Play second fiddle at home', *The Times of India*, 2 July 2002, p. 1.

31. 'Advani says his appointment as deputy PM has silenced rift-mongers', *The Times of India*, 5 July 2002, p. 1.

32. V. Venkatesan. 'A cautious exercise', *Frontline*, 13 April 2002. Available at: https://frontline.thehindu.com/static/html/fl1908/19080260.htm

33. This figure comes from the National Commission of Minorities. Cited from 'India: Treatment of Christians by Hindus, particularly the treatment of Christians who have converted from Hinduism; and the protection available to them', *Canada: Immigration and Refugee Board of Canada,* 12 September 2002, IND39529. Available at: https://www.refworld.org/ docid/3f7d4da823.html

34. Sumit Sarkar, 'Conversions and politics of Hindu Right', *Economic and Political Weekly* (1999): 1691–1700, p. 1691.

35. Ibid., p. 1696.

36. Celia W. Dugger, 'Attacks on Christians Unsettle Rural India', *The New York Times*, 23 January 1999. Available at: https://www.nytimes. com/1999/01/23/world/attacks-on-christians-unsettle-rural-india.html

37. Robert Marquand, 'In India, a pattern of attacks on Christians', *The Christian Science Monitor*, 29 June 2000. Available at: https://www. csmonitor.com/2000/0629/p1s2.html

38. Interview with Sudheendra Kulkarni, Mumbai, May 2018.

39. For some essays critical of this move, see Atishi Marlena, *The Politics of Hindutva* and the NCERT Textbook, *Revolutionary Democracy*, Vol. X, No. 2, September 2004; Mridula Mukherjee and Aditya Mukherjee,

'Communalisation of Education, The History Textbook Controversy: An Overview', Delhi Historians' Group, Delhi (2001).

40. Marie Lall, 'Indian Education Policy under NDA government', in Katharine Adeney and Lawrence Sáez (eds), *Coalition Politics and Hindu Nationalism* (Routledge, 2007), p. 161.

41. Ibid., p. 160.

42. Interview with Sheela Bhatt, New Delhi, May 2018.

43. Ashok Damodaran, 'Vajpayee is our undisputed leader, Advani is No. 2: Venkaiah Naidu', *India Today*, 16 June 2003.

44. 'Congress gleefully watches pre-poll "power struggle"', *The Times of India*, 7 June 2003, p. 6.

45. Prabhu Chawla, 'A.B. Vajpayee creates a political storm by announcing L.K. Advani as heir apparent', *India Today*, 16 June 2003.

46. Interview with Shakti Sinha, New Delhi, January 2018.

47. Prabhu Chawla, 'A.B. Vajpayee creates a political storm by announcing L.K. Advani as heir apparent', *India Today*, 16 June 2003.

48. 'Cabinet, party rally behind Vajpayee', *The Hindu*, 6 June 2003.

49. 'Vajpayee is supreme leader, says RSS', *The Times of India*, 5 June 2003.

CHAPTER 14: OH, PAKISTAN (1999–2004)

1. L.K. Advani, *My Country, My Life* (Rupa, 2010, paperback), p. 621.

2. Ibid., p. 622.

3. Kanchan Gupta, 'The Truth Behind Kandahar', *Sulekha*. Available at: http://creative.sulekha.com/the-truth-behind-kandahar-an-article-by-kanchan-gupta_435997_blog

4. Sarabjit Singh, 'Once upon a hijack', *The Indian Express*, 21 March 2019. Available at: https://indianexpress.com/article/opinion/columns/indian-airlines-ic-814-flight-hijack-kandhar-jaish-e-mohammad-masood-azhar-5636551/

5. Interview with Shivshankar Menon, New Delhi, June 2018.

6. Interview with Manvendra Singh, New Delhi, June 2018.

7. Kanchan Gupta, 'The Truth Behind Kandahar', *Sulekha*. Available at: http://creative.sulekha.com/the-truth-behind-kandahar-an-article-by-kanchan-gupta_435997_blog; Vir Sanghvi, 'Hijacked Logic: As politics over 1999's IC 814 rages now, are we really different today?', *DailyO*, 14 March 2019; Rachna Pratihar, 'Media complicated Kandahar', *Hindustan Times*, 1 September 2009.

8. T.C.A. Raghavan, *The People Next Door: The Curious History of India's Relations with Pakistan* (HarperCollins India, 2017), p. 237.

9. Interview with Yashwant Sinha, New Delhi, June 2018.

10. Uday Mahurkar and Farzand Ahmed, 'BJP-led Government's trade-off at Kandahar provokes RSS into hardening its attitude', *India Today*, 24 January 2000.

11. 'Crisis and mismanagement', *Frontline*, 8 January 2000. Available at: https://frontline.thehindu.com/cover-story/article30253142.ece. The content of this note has been confirmed by a close friend of Vajpayee who does not wish to be named.

12. Uday Mahurkar, 'India needs to take a strong line against Pakistan: H.V. Sheshadri', *India Today*, 24 January 2000.

13. Interview with T.C.A. Raghavan, New Delhi, May 2018.

14. T.C.A. Raghavan, *The People Next Door: The Curious History of India's Relations with Pakistan* (HarperCollins India, 2017), pp. 247–48.

15. Jaswant Singh, *A Call to Honour: In Service of Emergent India* (Rupa, 2006, kindle edition), location 4474.

16. L.K. Advani, *My Country, My Life* (Rupa, 2010, paperback), pp. 696–97.

17. Karan Thapar, *Devil's Advocate* (HarperCollins India, 2018), p. 183.

18. Interview with Karan Thapar, New Delhi, November 2019.

19. Interview with Sudheendra Kulkarni, Mumbai, May 2018.

20. Interview with Karan Thapar, New Delhi, November 2019.

21. George Iype, 'Jiggs to provide food for summiteers' thoughts', rediff.com, 14 July 2001. Available at: https://www.rediff.com/news/2001/jul/14inpak18.htm

22. 'Rare moments: Atal Ji with Sheshadri'. Available at: https://www.youtube.com/watch?v=97XtD1lO0BQ

23. 'Cancel summit, says VHP', *The Hindu*, 14 July 2001.

24. Interview with T.C.A. Raghavan, New Delhi, May 2018.

25. Sheela Bhatt, 'Advani destroyed Agra summit with Pakistan: A.S. Dulat', rediff.com, 6 July 2015. Available at: https://www.rediff.com/news/report/exclusive-advani-destroyed-agra-summit-with-pakistan-a-s-dulat/20150706.htm

26. 'Musharraf-Speak', *Outlook*, 16 July 2001. Available at: https://www.outlookindia.com/website/story/musharraf-speak/212640

27. Josy Joseph and Sheela Bhatt, 'Musharraf blindsides Vajpayee with media blitz', rediff.com, 16 July 2001. Available at: https://www.rediff.com/news/2001/jul/16inpak8.htm

28. 'Draft Agra declaration' *Frontline*, 29 July 2005. Available at https://frontline.thehindu.com/static/html/fl2215/stories/20050729002304800.htm

29. Jaswant Singh, *A Call to Honour: In Service of Emergent India* (Rupa, 2006, kindle edition), location 4638.

30. Seema Guha, 'Officials were having major problems in agreeing to a draft', *The Times of India*, 21 July 2001, p. 7.

31. 'Good evening India: Gen Musharraf seeks audience across the border', *The Times of India*, 21 July 2001, p. 1.

32. Interview with A.S. Dulat, June 2018.

33. Pervez Musharraf, *In the Line of Fire: A Memoir* (Simon & Schuster, 2006), p. 299. Exact quote is in: 'Musharraf's comment on failed Agra Summit: "Hidden Hand" says "Maine Dekha Hai"', *The Economic Times*, 7 December 2010.

34. B. Muralidhar Reddy, 'Musharraf blames it on Advani', *The Hindu*, 31 August 2001.

35. Sheela Bhatt, 'Advani destroyed Agra summit with Pakistan: A.S. Dulat', rediff.com, 6 July 2015. Available at: https://www.rediff.com/news/report/exclusive-advani-destroyed-agra-summit-with-pakistan-a-s-dulat/20150706.htm

36. T.C.A. Raghavan, *The People Next Door: The Curious History of India's Relations with Pakistan* (HarperCollins India, 2017), p. 250.

37. Ibid.

38. L.K. Advani, *My Country, My Life* (Rupa, 2010, paperback), p. 627.

39. Thomas H. Kean and Lee H. Hamilton, *The 9/11 Commission Report: Executive Summary*. National Commission on Terrorist Attacks upon the United States (2004), pp. 1–2.

40. L.K. Advani, *My Country, My Life* (Rupa, 2010, paperback), p. 628.

41. Pervez Musharraf, *In the Line of Fire: A Memoir* (Simon & Schuster, 2006), p. 199.

42. Benedikt Goderis and Mila Versteeg, 'Human rights violations after 9/11 and the role of constitutional constraints', *The Journal of Legal Studies* 41, no. 1 (2012): 131–64, p 132.

43. Jayanth K. Krishnan, 'India's Patriot Act: POTA and the Impact on Civil Liberties in the World's Largest Democracy', *Law & Ineq.* 22 (2004): 265–300.

44. 'Our society, our government is too soft', *The Times of India*, 16 December 2001, p. 14.

45. Pervez Musharraf, *In the Line of Fire: A Memoir* (Simon & Schuster, 2006), p. 199.

46. Zaidi, S. Akbar, 'Who benefits from US aid to Pakistan?', *Carnegie Endowment for International Peace*, 21 September 2011, p. 103–09, p. 5. Available at: https://carnegieendowment.org/files/pakistan_aid2011.pdf

47. 'Togadia urges Hindus to back US', *The Times of India*, 14 September 2001.

48. Mushahid Hussain, 'By sacrificing bin Laden it expects US help on the core issue', *India Today*, 1 October 2001.

49. 'Vardaat: 2001 Indian Parliament attack (Part 1)'. Video available at: https://www.youtube.com/watch?v=kXl2-hLoWZA

50. This information is provided, in main, from the Delhi High Court in *State vs Mohd. Afzal and Ors*, 003 VIIAD Delhi 1.

51. L.K. Advani, *My Country, My Life* (Rupa, 2010, paperback), p. 628.

52. Jaswant Singh, *A Call to Honour: In Service of Emergent India* (Rupa, 2006, kindle edition), location 4725.

53. 'Terrorists attack Parliament; five intruders, six cops killed', rediff.com, 13 December 2001. Available at: https://www.rediff.com/news/2001/dec/13parl1.htm

54. This information is provided, in main, from the Delhi High Court in *State vs Mohd. Afzal and Ors*, 003 VIIAD Delhi 1.

55. 'PM salutes the martyrs who lost their lives during attack on Indian Parliament in 2001', Press Information Bureau, Government of India, Prime Minister's Office, 13 December 2014.

56. 'ISI planned to wipe out top political leadership: Advani', *The Times of India*, 19 December 2001, p. 1.

57. Mohua Chatterjee. 'Our society, our government is too soft', *The Times of India*, 16 December 2001, 14.

58. 'All options open in war against terror: The Dividing Line Preach', *The Times of India*, 20 December 2001, p. 1.

59. Dilip Chaware, 'Destroy terrorist camps in PoK, RSS tells Centre', *The Times of India*, 15 December 2001, p. 2.

60. 'Advani to spell out Govt. stand in Parliament today', *The Hindu*, 18 December 2001.

61. Hemant Kumar Pandey and Manish Raj Singh, *India's Major Military and Rescue Operations* (Horizon Books, 2017), p. 210.

62. 'Terror at Dawn', *The Times of India*, 15 May 2002, p. 1; Manoj Joshi, 'Attack is bid to derail J&K polls', *The Times of India*, 15 May 2002, p. 1.

63. Interview with T.C.A. Raghavan, New Delhi, May 2018.

64. Mohua Chatterjee, 'No holidays for Vajpayee and his ministers', *The Times of India*, 19 May 2002.

65. T.C.A. Raghavan, *The People Next Door: The Curious History of India's Relations with Pakistan* (HarperCollins India, 2017), p. 257.

66. Karan Thapar, 'The untold Advani story', *Hindustan Times*, 2 April 2008. Available at: https://www.hindustantimes.com/columns/the-untold-advani-story/story-wNChlh8dbIzKbYEARdMEHK.html

67. 'Infiltration into J&K from Pak must stop: Rocca', *The Times of India*, 15 May 2002.

68. 'Transcript of CNN interview with Musharraf', cnn.com, 1 June 2002. Available at: https://edition.cnn.com/2002/WORLD/asiapcf/south/06/01/musharraf.transcript/

69. See the following two sources for this data: 'Jammu and Kashmir Assembly Elections 2002 Phase 1, 16 September 2002', 16 September 2002, Ministry of External Affairs, Government of India. Available at: https://mea.gov.in/in-focus-article.htm?18974/Jammu+and+Kashmir+Assembly+Elections+2002+Phase++1+16+September+2002; 'Jammu and Kashmir: Assembly Elections 2002: Under the Shadow of Fear', *Economic and Political Weekly*, Vol. 37, Issue No. 43 (2002).

70. 'Assembly Elections 2002: Under the Shadow of Fear', *Economic and Political Weekly*, Vol. 37, No. 43 (26 October–1 November 2002): 4357–60, at 4359.

71. Shujaat Bukhari, 'PM extends "hand of friendship" to Pakistan', *The Hindu*, 19 April 2003.

72. Interview with A.S. Dulat, June 2018.

73. Shujaat Bukhari, 'PM extends "hand of friendship" to Pakistan', *The Hindu*, 19 April 2003.

74. 'Statement by Prime Minister Shri Atal Bihari Vajpayee in Lok Sabha on his two day visit to Jammu & Kashmir', Ministry of External Affairs, 22 April 2003. Available at: https://mea.gov.in/Speeches-Statements.htm?dtl/4351/Statement+by+Prime+Minister+Shri+Atal+Bihari+Vajpayee+in+Lok+Sabha+on+his+two+day+visit+to+Jammu+amp+Kashmir

75. Interview with Shivshankar Menon, New Delhi, June 2018.

76. 'BJP stays firm as Sangh steps up attack on PM', *The Times of India*, 30 June 2003, p. 1.

77. A.S. Dulat, *Kashmir: The Vajpayee Years* (HarperCollins, 2015), pp. 264–65.

78. Ibid., p. 266.

79. L.K. Advani, *My Country, My Life* (Rupa, 2010, paperback), p. 689.

80. A.S. Dulat, *Kashmir: The Vajpayee Years* (HarperCollins, 2015), p. 267.

81. Interview with Karan Thapar, New Delhi, November 2019.

82. Amit Shah has recollected this to a senior journalist who wishes to remain unnamed.

CHAPTER 15: MAKING INDIA GREAT AGAIN (1999–2004)

1. Bulletin, *National Legislators Conference, 2018*, 10 March 2018. Available at: http://164.100.47.193/Intranet/1Day2018.pdf

2. N.M. Ghatate (ed.), *Atal Bihari Vajpayee: Four Decades in Parliament*, Volume 1 (Shipra Publications), p. 105.

3. Interview with Govindacharya, New Delhi, June 2018.

4. Raj Chengappa, 'US President Bill Clinton's India visit holds promise of a major change in Indo-US ties', *India Today*, 27 March 2000.

5. Jaswant Singh, *A Call to Honour: In Service of Emergent India* (Rupa, 2006, kindle edition), location 5635.

6. Vijai Trivedi, *Haar Nahin Maanoonga* (HarperCollins Hindi, 2016), p. 138.

7. Bill Clinton, 'Restraint, Respect, Dialogue: What I Hope to Accomplish in South Asia', *The Times of India*, 20 March 2000, p. 1.

8. Swapan Dasgupta, 'NDA Government and RSS work in tandem, but simmering tensions remain', *India Today*, 21 February 2000.

9. 'Goals of the Journey to Asia', President Clinton, *The Washington Times*, 21 March 2000. Available at: http://www.acronym.org.uk/old/archive/spvisit.htm.

10. Srinath Raghavan. *The Most Dangerous Place: A History of the United States in South Asia* (Penguin Random House, 2018, kindle edition), location 5904.

11. Jane Perlez, 'Clinton Decides to Visit Pakistan, After All', *The New York Times*, 8 March 2000. Available at: https://www.nytimes.com/2000/03/08/world/clinton-decides-to-visit-pakistan-after-all.html

12. T.C.A. Raghavan, *The People Next Door: The Curious History of India's Relations with Pakistan* (HarperCollins India, 2017), pp. 245–46.

13. Tilak Abeysinghe and L.U. Ding, 'China as an economic powerhouse: Implications on its neighbors', *China Economic Review* 14, no. 2 (2003): 164–85, at 165.

14. Arun Shourie, *A Secular Agenda: For Saving Our Country, for Welding it* (ASA Publications, 1993); Arun Shourie, *Worshipping False Gods: Ambedkar, and the facts which have been erased* (ASA publications, 1997); Arun Shourie, *Religion in Politics* (Roli Books, 1989); Arun Shourie, *Symptoms of Fascism* (Vikas Publishing House, 1978).

15. Swapan Dasgupta, 'Government must grasp that disinvestment is good politics', *India Today*, 7 February 2000.

16. Ibid.

17. Swapan Dasgupta, 'Don't let secrecy and cronyism jeopardise the end of socialism', *India Today*, 12 March 2001.

18. Jyotindra Dubey, 'Disinvestment got boost under Vajpayee-led NDA govt. Here's how public sector companies fared post-privatisation', *India Today*, 6 July 2019.

19. Siddharth Srivastava, 'Shourie's ministry has just 50 people', *The Times of India*, 8 December 2002, p. 5.

20. Interview with Montek Singh Ahluwalia, New Delhi, March 2018.

21. Rohit Parihar and Rajeev Deshpande, 'How politics, corporate rivalry led Vajpayee government to undo privatization', *India Today*, 23 September 2002.

22. Interview with Arun Shourie, New Delhi, June 2018.

23. Jyotindra Dubey, 'Disinvestment got boost under Vajpayee-led NDA govt. Here's how public sector companies fared post-privatisation', *India Today*, 6 July 2019.

24. 'Very Much His Own Man', *Outlook*, 2 September 2002. Available at: https://www.outlookindia.com/magazine/story/very-much-his-own-man/217032

25. Arup Ratan Lala, 'RSS chief says govt's economic policies are against the poor', *The Times of India*, 20 March 2000, p. 7.

26. Interview with Yashwant Sinha, New Delhi, June 2018.

27. Farzand Ahmed, 'Swadeshi Jagran Manch attacks NDA Government for "mortgaging India's economic security"', *India Today*, 10 July 2000.

28. Ragul Sagar, 'Ideas for India website', available at: https://www.ideasofindia.org/

29. Maya Mirchandani, 'Wide Angle Episode 17: What is Hindu Nationalism?', *The Wire*, 6 January 2018. Video available at: https://thewire.in/politics/wide-angle-episode-17-hindu-nationalism

30. Bruce T. McCully, 'The origins of Indian nationalism according to native writers', *The Journal of Modern History* 7, no. 3 (1935): 295–14, at 304–05.

31. Arup Roychoudhury, Megha Manchanda and Sanjeeb Mukherjee, 'Atal Bihari Vajpayee's approach to economic issues had the common touch', *Business Standard*, 18 August 2018.

32. Amy Waldman, 'Mile by Mile, India Paves a Smoother Road to Its Future', *New York Times*, 4 December 2005. Available at: https://www.nytimes.com/2005/12/04/world/asia/mile-by-mile-india-paves-a-smoother-road-to-its-future.html

33. 'New Telecom Policy, 1999', Department of Telecommunication, Government of India. Available at: http://dot.gov.in/new-telecom-policy-1999

34. Priyanka Kokil and M.K. Sharma, 'Sap Lap Analysis of National Telecom Policy: India', *India Journals*. Available at: http://www.indianjournals.com/glogift2k6/glogift2k6-1-1/theme_1/Article%2010.htm

35. 'A Twenty Year Odyssey 1997-2017', Telecom Regulatory Authority of India, 2017. Available at: https://main.trai.gov.in/sites/default/files/A_TwentyYear_Odyssey_1997_2017.pdf

36. 'Telecom lobby swayed TRAI, allege consumer groups', *The Times of India*, 28 January 2003, p. 2.

37. Smita Gupta, 'Mahajan puts on brave face', *The Times of India*, 30 January 2003, p. 1.

38. See chapter 9, section 7 of this book.

39. Rob Jenkins, 'The NDA and the politics of economic reform', in Katharine Adeney and Lawrence Sáez (eds), *Coalition Politics and Hindu Nationalism* (Routledge, 2005), p. 187.

40. Interview with Yashwant Sinha, New Delhi, June 2018.

41. Indrani Bagchi, 'Israeli PM Ariel Sharon's India visit a watershed event, both nations to sign several pacts', *India Today*, 15 September 2003.

42. Shekhar Gupta, 'A pragmatic peace', *India Today*, 21 June 2013.

43. Sridhar Krishnaswami, 'Bush, Advani discuss issue of troops for Iraq', *The Hindu*, 11 June 2003.

44. C. Raja Mohan. 'Decision on Iraq remains open', *The Hindu*, 17 June 2003.

45. Interview with Yashwant Sinha, New Delhi, June 2018.

46. Yashwant Sinha, 'When Vajpayee Summoned Sushma Swaraj and Me', NDTV, 25 March 2018. Available at: https://www.ndtv.com/opinion/when-vajpayee-summoned-sushma-swaraj-and-me-1828400?pfrom=home-lateststories

47. Interview with Manvendra Singh, New Delhi, June 2018.

48. Interview with Natwar Singh, New Delhi, January 2018.

CHAPTER 16: THE SPECTRE OF NARENDRA MODI (1999–2004)

1. Kama Maclean, 'Seeing, being seen, and not being seen: pilgrimage, tourism, and layers of looking at the Kumbh Mela', *Cross Currents* 59, no. 3 (2009): 319–41, pp. 320, 324.

2. 'Dharma sansad 9', Vishva Hindu Parishad. Available at: http://vhp.org/conferences/dharmasansads/dharma-sansad-9/

3. 'Weak at the base', *Economic and Political Weekly*, Volume 36, issue 4 (2001), p. 251.

4. Ibid.

5. Prakash Louis, 'Gujarat: Earthquake and After', *Economic and Political Weekly*, Vol. 36, Issue No. 11 (2001).

6. Interview with Sudheendra Kulkarni, Mumbai, May 2018.

7. Interview with Sheela Bhatt, New Delhi, May 2018.

8. Nilanjan Mukhopadhyay, *Narendra Modi: The Man, The Times* (Tranquebar, 2013), p. 247.

9. V. Venkatesan, 'A pracharak as Chief Minister', *Frontline,* Volume 18 (21), 13–26 October 2001.

10. Manas Dasgupta, 'PM grants Rs. 500 cr., toll may cross 30,000', *The Hindu*, 30 January 2001.

11. That Modi wanted to get into the helicopter at Gandhinagar has been confirmed by a journalist, who does not wish to be named, and who adds that Modi was not permitted by the SPG.

12. 'Ram Temple After March 12, 2002', *The Times of India*, 11 September 2001, p. 1; 'Mandir Countdown', *The Times of India*, 4 September 2001, p. 10.

13. Sharad Gupta, 'Hindus are not ready to compromise anymore: VHP leader Pravin Togadia', *India Today*, 10 September 2001.

14. Neena Vyas, 'Keshubhai may be replaced', *The Hindu*, 25 September 2001.

15. Nilanjan Mukhopadhyay, *Narendra Modi: The Man, The Times* (Tranquebar, 2013), p. 245.

16. Neena Vyas, 'New Chief Minister Likely', *The Hindu*, 27 September 2001.

17. Ullekh N.P., *The Untold Vajpayee: Politician and Paradox* (Penguin Books, kindle edition, 2017), location 3045–46.

18. Nilanjan Mukhopadhyay, *Narendra Modi: The Man, The Times* (Tranquebar, 2013), p. 247–48.

19. Interview with Yashwant Sinha, New Delhi, June 2018.

20. Interview with Arjun Modhwadia, June 2019.

21. 'Modi warns of harsh measures in Gujarat', *The Times of India*, 5 October 2001, p. 8.

22. Manas Dasgupta, 'Modi sworn in Gujarat CM amidst fanfare', *The Hindu*, 8 October 2001.

23. Nilanjan Mukhopadhyay, *Narendra Modi: The Man, The Times* (Tranquebar, 2013), p. 246.

24. 'Modi warns of harsh measures in Gujarat, *The Times of India*, 5 October 2001, p. 8.

25. '50,000 watched Modi's ascent to power in splendid style', *The Times of India*, 8 October 2001, p. 7.

26. Ibid.

27. Ranjit Bhushan, 'Gun to the Temple', *Outlook*, 11 February 2002. Available at: https://www.outlookindia.com/magazine/story/gun-to-the-temple/214496

28. Ibid.

29. Ibid.

30. 'Ayodhya: 'Govt. duty-bound to maintain status quo', *The Hindu*, 26 February 2002.

31. Nilanjan Mukhopadhyay, *Narendra Modi: The Man, The Times* (Tranquebar, 2013), p. 249.

32. 'Timeline of the Riots in Modi's Gujarat', *The New York Times*, 19 August 2015. Available at: https://www.nytimes.com/interactive/2014/04/06/world/asia/modi-gujarat-riots-timeline.html#/#time287_8514

33. Since the fire had taken place on the premises of the Indian Railways, a central organization, the railway minister appointed the Justice U.C. Banerjee Commission in 2004 to inquire into the cause of the fire. The commission report, submitted in 2006, held the fire to be an accident. The political context is critical. The commission was appointed by the central railway minister soon after the BJP lost in the 2004 elections, and he came to power.

34. Report by Commission of Enquiry Consisting of Justice Nanavati and Justice Mehta. Available at: http://www.home.gujarat.gov.in/homedepartment/downloads/godharaincident.pdf

35. 'Godhra Sabarmati Express burning case: Gujarat HC commutes death sentence to 11 convicts into life imprisonment', *Economic Times*, 9 October 2017. Available at: https://economictimes.indiatimes.com/news/politics-and-nation/godhra-sabarmati-express-burning-case-gujarat-high-court-may-pronounce-verdict-today/articleshow/61001281.cms

36. Manoj Mitta, *The Fiction of Fact-Finding: Modi and Godhra* (Harper Collins Publishers India, 2014), p. 7.

37. Interview with Saeed Umarji, in April 2014, in Godhra town (Gujarat).

38. Zakiya Jafri protest petition against SIT report, p. 53.

39. Report in Compliance to the Order dtd 12.09.2011 of the hon'ble Supreme Court of India of the complaint dtd 8/06.2006 of Smt. Jakia Nasim Ahesan Jafri.

40. G.T. Nanavati and A. H. Mehta, The Nanavati-Mehta Commission: Report by the Commission of Inquiry Consisting of Mr Justice G.T. Nanavati and Mr Justice Akshay H. Mehta (2008).

41. 'Gujarat court accepts clean chit to Narendra Modi in 2002 riots', NDTV, 26 December 2013.

42. Sheela Bhatt, 'It had to be done, VHP leader says of riots', rediff.com, 12 March 2002. Available at: http://m.rediff.com/news/2002/mar/12train.htm

43. Ibid.

44. 'Gujarat incident: Angry scenes in Lok Sabha', *The Hindu*, 1 March 2002.

45. Ibid.

46. 'Compounding Injustice: The Government's Failure to Redress Massacres in Gujarat', Chapter IV, Human Rights Watch, July 2003, Vol. 15 (3).

47. 'SIT report on riots in court; Modi optimistic', News 18, 13 February 2012. Available at: https://www.news18.com/news/politics/modi-ff-modi-446215.html; 'Jafri didn't call me, Modi told commission', *The Times of India*, 12 December 2019. Available at: https://timesofindia.indiatimes.com/city/ahmedabad/jafri-didnt-call-me-modi-told-commission/articleshow/72482075.cms

48. 'Nishrin Hussain, The Daughter of Ehsan and Zakiya Jafri Writes: My Mother, My Motherland', *The Wire*, 8 September 2018. Available at: https://thewire.in/communalism/the-daughter-of-ehsan-and-zakiya-jafri-writes-my-mother-my-motherland

49. Satish Jha, 'Gulbarg Society massacre verdict: "Mob dragged out Ahsan Jafri, burnt him alive"', *Indian Express*, 18 June 2016.

50. Interview with Sudheendra Kulkarni, Mumbai, May 2018.

51. Sheela Bhatt, 'Ex-MP Jaffrey's widow relives a day of terror', rediff.com, 2 March 2002. Available at: https://www.rediff.com/news/2002/mar/02train.htm

52. Interview with Dinesh Trivedi, May 2018.

53. Entry 2A of List I of the 7th schedule to the Indian Constitution.

54. Jaya Jaitley, *Life Among the Scorpions: Memoirs of a Woman in Indian Politics* (Rupa, 2017), p. 257.

55. Sunetra Choudhury, '"300 Could Have Been Saved": Ex-General's Revelation On Gujarat Riots', NDTV, 10 October, 2018. Available at: https://www.ndtv.com/india-news/army-lost-1-day-waiting-in-airfield-ex-general-on-2002-gujarat-riots-1929445

56. Interview with Sheela Bhatt, New Delhi, May 2018.

57. Christophe Jaffrelot, 'Gujarat 2002: What Justice for Victims? The Supreme Court, SIT, the Police and the State Judiciary', *Economic and Political Weekly*, Vol. 47, No. 8 (2012): 77–89.

58. Raheel Dhattiwala and Michael Biggs, 'The Political Logic of Ethnic Violence: The Anti-Muslim Pogrom in Gujarat, 2002', *Politics and Society*, Vol. 40, No. 4, 2012: 481–514, p. 491.

59. Parvis Ghassem-Fachandi, *Pogrom in Gujarat: Hindu Nationalism and Anti-Muslim Violence in India* (Princeton University Press, 2012), p. 283, note 1.

60. Raheel Dhattiwala and Michael Biggs, 'The Political Logic of Ethnic Violence: The Anti-Muslim Pogrom in Gujarat, 2002', *Politics and Society*, Vol. 40, No. 4, 2012: 483–516. These towns where the BJP was electorally neck-and-neck, according to the economist Saumitra Jha, were ones 'founded by Muslims, housed Muslim mints or political capitals, or faced a longer history of Muslim political rule'. Saumitra Jha, '"Unfinished

business": Historic complementarities, political competition and ethnic violence in Gujarat', *Journal of Economic Behavior & Organization* 104 (2014): 18–36, p. 21.

61. See the 'Scholarly Contribution' towards the end of this book, in the section titled 'What is Hindu nationalism'.

62. Howard Spodek, 'In the Hindutva laboratory: Pogroms and politics in Gujarat, 2002', *Modern Asian Studies* 44, no. 2 (2010): 349–99, at 375–76.

63. Harish Khare, 'The guilty men of Ahmedabad', *The Hindu*, 7 March 2002.

64. Ibid.

65. 'Oppn demands Modi, Advani's resignation', *The Times of India*, 8 March 2002, p. 7.

66. Manas Dasgupta, 'All Party team refuses to meet Modi', *The Hindu*, 9 March 2002.

67. 'Naidu in dilemma, seeks face-saver', *The Times of India*, 14 April 2002, p. 1.

68. 'VHP seeks resignation of Central, Gujarat Govts', *The Hindu*, 28 February 2002.

69. Bhavdeep Kang, 'The Arson Within', *Outlook*, 11 March 2002. Available at: https://www.outlookindia.com/magazine/story/the-arson-within/214851

70. Arvind Lavakare, 'A question of "squaring up"', rediff.com, 2 April 2002. Available at: https://www.rediff.com/news/2002/apr/02arvind.htm

71. Murali Krishnan, 'I Told Advani To Drive Some Sense Into Atalji', *Outlook*, 25 March 2002. Available at: https://www.outlookindia.com/magazine/story/i-told-advani-to-drive-some-sense-into-atalji/214978

72. 'Walk the Talk with Bal Thackeray (Aired: January 2007)', NDTV, 18 January 2018. Available at: https://www.ndtv.com/ndtv-at25/classics/walk-the-talk/307189

73. 'Don't become pawns, RSS tells Muslims', *The Hindu*, 28 March 2002.

74. Interview with Sheela Bhatt, New Delhi, May 2019, who says she was told this story by the Ahmedabad-based journalist Arvind Bosamia.

75. Interview with Ravindra Bhagwat, Chandrapur, March 2018.

76. 'Modi need not quit: Advani', *The Hindu*, 12 March 2002.

77. 'Advani admits riots a blot, but rejects call for resignation', *The Times of India*, 12 March 2002, p. 7.

78. 'Modi should quit, says Opposition', *The Hindu*, 21 March 2002.

79. 'It's horrible: NHRC chief', *The Hindu*, 24 March 2002.

80. 'Vajpayee wanted to sack Modi: Walk the Talk with Jaswant Singh', NDTV. Video available at: https://www.youtube.com/watch?v=05MVcOfbVMY

81. Interview with R.V. Pandit, Bengaluru, April 2018.

82. Prafull Goradia, 'Modi is no bhai or bhatija of yours, why are you defending him?', rediff.com, 16 January 2017. Available at: https://www.rediff.com/news/special/modi-is-no-bhai-of-yours-why-are-you-defending-him/20170116.htm

83. Interview with Sudheendra Kulkarni, Mumbai, May 2018.

84. Priya Sahgal, 'Minor Modification', *Outlook*, 15 April 2002. Available at: https://www.outlookindia.com/magazine/story/minormodification/215185

85. 'PM opposes snap poll in Gujarat', *The Times of India*, 29 March 2002, p. 7.

86. L.K. Advani, *My Country, My Life* (Rupa, 2010, paperback), p. 842.

87. Anil Pathak and Raja Bose, 'PM visits site of attack on Sabarmati Express', *The Times of India*, 4 April 2002.

88. Uday Mahurkar, 'A.B. Vajpayee's visit to riot-torn Gujarat fails to have a balming effect', *India Today*, 15 April 2002.

89. Priya Sahgal, 'Minor Modification', *Outlook*, 15 April 2002. Available at: https://www.outlookindia.com/magazine/story/minormodification/215185

90. 'Replace Modi, victims implore PM, *The Times of India*, 5 April 2002, p. 7.

91. Ibid.

92. 'Modi has blood on his hands PM told', *The Times of India*, 5 April 2002, p. 1.

93. Priya Sahgal, 'Minor Modification', *Outlook*, 15 April 2002. Available at: https://www.outlookindia.com/magazine/story/minormodification/215185

94. 'Vajpayee Raj Dharma for Modi in 2002'. Video available at: https://www.youtube.com/watch?v=6_vAgb364Ik

95. Ullekh N.P., *The Untold Vajpayee: Politician and Paradox* (Penguin Books, kindle edition, 2017), location 2977.

96. Interview with Arun Shourie, New Delhi, June 2018.

97. Ibid.

98. Ibid.

99. Ritu Sarin, 'Half the night is over, half is left: PM', *The Indian Express*, 12 April 2002.

100. 'Kashiram Rana may replace Modi', *The Times of India*, 12 April 2002, p. 1.

101. Interview with Harin Pathak, New Delhi, March 2018.

102. Neena Vyas, 'What will happen to Modi?', *The Hindu*, 12 April 2002.

103. 'Kashiram Rana may replace Modi', *The Times of India*, 12 April 2002, p. 1.

104. 'Vajpayee wanted Modi to quit over Gujarat riots, but party said no: Venkaiah Naidu', *The Indian Express*, 9 March 2014.

105. Arun Shourie's version is contested by an anonymous source who agrees with Shourie's description, but says that he very much wanted to protect Modi, not sack him.

106. L.K. Advani, *My Country, My Life* (Rupa, 2010, paperback), p. 843.

107. Ibid.

108. 'LK stopped Atal from sacking Modi over Guj Riots', *The Times of India*, 23 August 2009.

109. Ranjit Bhushan, 'His Second Phase', *Outlook*, 29 April 2002.

110. Interview with Yashwant Sinha, New Delhi, June 2018.

111. Interview with Sudheendra Kulkarni, Mumbai, May 2018.

112. Interview with Dinesh Trivedi, May 2018.

113. 'Modi feels the heat, friend Jaitley drops in', *The Indian Express*, 12 April 2002.

114. Interview with Yashwant Sinha, New Delhi, June 2018.

115. Interview with R.V. Pandit, Bengaluru, April 2018.

116. Smita Gupta, 'Seek fresh mandate Modi told: BJP meet rejects offer by Gujarat CM to quit', *The Times of India*, 13 April 2002, p. 1.

117. 'PM opposes snap poll in Gujarat', *The Times of India*, 29 March 2002, p. 7.

118. Priya Sahgal, 'PM's Spin Quantum Number', *Outlook*, 29 April 2002. Available at: https://www.outlookindia.com/magazine/story/pms-spin-quantum-number/215369

119. Sheela Bhatt, 'Muslims don't want to live in harmony, says Vajpayee', rediff.com, 12 April 2002. Available at: https://www.rediff.com/news/2002/apr/12bhatt.htm

120. P. Chidambaram, 'Vajpayee's speech at Goa signals his rebirth as a true swayamsevak', *India Today*, 29 April 2002.

121. Smruti Koppikar and Pradeep Kaushal, 'In Goa drama, Advani and Vajpayee swap their roles', *The Indian Express*, 14 April 2002.

122. K.V. Prasad, 'Conditions in Gujarat conducive for polls: Advani', *The Hindu*, 25 July 2002.

123. 'Unhappy Atal Thinks of Quitting', *Outlook*, 2 September 2002. Available at: https://www.outlookindia.com/magazine/story/unhappy-atal-thinks-of-quitting/217031

124. J. Venkatesan, 'EC rules out early polls in Gujarat', *The Hindu*, 17 August 2002.

125. 'PM raps Modi for remarks on Lyngdoh', *The Times of India*, 24 August 2002.

126. 'Supreme Court upholds EC decision on Gujarat polls', *The Hindu*, 3 September 2002.

127. Ranjit Bhushan and Bhavdeep Kang, 'The Flip Flop PM', *Outlook*, 2 December 2002. Available at: https://www.outlookindia.com/magazine/story/the-flip-flop-pm/218145

128. Milind Ghatwai, 'Last lap: C in BJP campaign stands openly for communal', *The Indian Express*, 10 December 2002.

129. J. Venkatesan, 'EC takes note of Godhra pictures', *The Hindu*, 2 December 2002.

130. Ibid.

131. Darshan Desai, 'Dark Descent', *Outlook*, 23 September 2002. Available at: https://www.outlookindia.com/magazine/story/dark-descent/217313

132. Neena Vyas, 'BJP only guarantor of security for minorities', *The Hindu*, 8 December 2002.

133. 'Cong donning mantle of Muslim League: BJP', *The Times of India*, 10 December 2002.

134. Manas Dasgupta, 'VHP strategy', *The Hindu*, 11 December 2002.

135. Darshan Desai, 'Dark Descent', *Outlook*, 23 September 2002. Available at: https://www.outlookindia.com/magazine/story/dark-descent/217313

136. Smita Gupta, 'How Modi's appeal works', *The Times of India*, 9 December 2002.

137. Manas Dasgupta, 'BJP creating atmosphere of fear: Sonia', *The Hindu*, 4 December 2002.

138. Milind Ghatwai, 'Cong paints self pro-Hindu', *The Times of India*, 7 December 2002.

139. Sheela Bhatt, 'Is Narendra Modi really an OBC?', rediff.com, 5 June 2014. Available at: https://www.rediff.com/news/column/ls-election-sheela-says-is-narendra-modi-really-an-obc/20140510.htm

140. Ibid.

141. Interview with Arjun Modhwadia, New Delhi, May 2019.

142. Ibid.

143. 'Modi primes pitch for polls', *The Times of India*, 15 April 2002, p. 1.

144. Bharat Desai, 'Hindutva strikes a chord with tribals', *The Times of India*, 5 December 2002.

145. Interview with Ajoy Bose, June 2018.

146. 'Modi, the big draw', *The Hindu*, 6 December 2002.

147. Anirban Ganguly and Shivanand Dwivedi, *Amit Shah and the March of BJP* (Bloomsbury, 2018), p. 49.

148. 'VHP supports Modi, says BJP not nationalist', *The Times of India*, 3 December 2002.

149. Smita Gupta, 'BJP election campaign revolves around Modi', *The Times of India*, 2 December 2002, p. 8.

150. Nalin Mehta, 'Modi and the Camera: The Politics of Television in the 2002 Gujarat Riots', *South Asia: Journal of South Asian Studies* 29(3) (2006): 395–414, pp. 395–96.

151. Ibid., p. 409.

152. Ibid., p. 410.

153. Shekhar Gupta, 'If Modi wins on Sunday', *The Indian Express*, 11 April 2014.

154. 'Gujarat assembly polls could chart future of India's politics, *The Times of India*, 12 December 2002, p. 7.

155. Sanjay Kumar, 'Gujarat Assembly Elections 2002: Analysing the Verdict', *Economic and Political Weekly*, 25 January 2003: 270–75, p. 270.

156. 'Gujarat assembly polls could chart future of India's politics', *The Times of India*, 12 December 2002, p. 7.

157. Sanjay Kumar, 'Gujarat Assembly Elections 2002: Analysing the Verdict', *Economic and Political Weekly*, 25 January 2003: 270–75, pp. 274-275.

158. Ibid.

159. Raheel Dhattiwala and Michael Biggs, 'The political logic of ethnic violence: The anti-Muslim pogrom in Gujarat, 2002', *Politics & Society* 40, no. 4 (2012): 483–516. See also Sanjay Kumar, 'Gujarat Assembly Elections 2002: Analysing the Verdict', *Economic and Political Weekly*, 25 January 2003: 270–75, p. 271.

160. Interview with Prafull Goradia, New Delhi, April 2018.

161. Interview with Pravin Togadia, Ahmedabad, April 2018.

POSTSCRIPT: 2004 and After

THE LOTUS WITHERS

1. This figure is for the third quarter of 2003. See: Carole Spary and Andrew Wyatt, 'The general election in India, May 2004', *Electoral Studies* 2, no. 25 (2006): 398–404, p. 398.

2. Elections were held in November–December 2003 for Chhattisgarh, Madhya Pradesh and Rajasthan. The BJP's success in these elections were due to a combination of local factors like anti-incumbency and unemployment, rather than a national wave. See, for example, N.S. Gehlot, 'Reflections on the 12th assembly elections of Rajasthan', *The Indian Journal of Political Science*, Vol. 64, No. 3/4 (July–December, 2003): 191–202, pp. 191–92.

3. Ajit Kumar Jha, 'NDA rides on Vajpayee's popularity, appears set to sweep elections 2004: India Today poll', *India Today*, 30 November 1999.

4. L.K. Advani, *My Country My Life* (Rupa, 2008), pp. 762–63.

5. Ibid., p. 763.

6. Interview with Shakti Sinha, New Delhi, April 2018.

7. 'Vajpayee was in two minds over poll timing', *The Times of India*, 15 May 2004, p. 7.

8. Rajeev Deshpande, 'BJP's Vision 2004 document marks significant shifts on Hindutva issues', *India Today*, 12 April 2004.

9. '2004 Manifesto: NDA, An Agenda for Development, Good Governance and Peace'. Available at: http://library.bjp.org/jspui/ bitstream/123456789/245/1/NDA%20MANIFESTO%202004.pdf

10. 'Advani hits the "shining" path, again', *The Times of India*, 3 March 2004, p. 1.

11. Smita Gupta, 'Advani hardsells BJP with Atal as USP: "Smiling India, Shining India"', *The Times of India*, 11 March 2004, p. 11.

12. L.K. Advani, *My Country, My Life* (Rupa, 2010, paperback), p. 765.

13. Smita Gupta, 'Rein in VHP, BJP tells parivar: Rath Row', *The Times of India*, 6 March 2004, p. 7.

14. Interview with Sudheendra Kulkarni, Mumbai, May 2018.

15. Interview with Swapan Dasgupta, New Delhi, June 2018.

16. 'Ronald Reagan: It's Morning in America 1984'. Available at: https://www. youtube.com/watch?v=fa8Qupc4PnQ

17. Interview with Govindacharya, New Delhi, June 2018.

18. Interview with Swapan Dasgupta, New Delhi, June 2018.

19. Ajit Kumar Jha, 'Elections 2004 promises close finish between NDA and Congress-led alliance', *India Today*, 26 April 2004.

20. Smita Gupta, 'Party not shining, says BJP report: "Seat count likely to dip"', *The Times of India*, 4 March 2004, p. 5.

21. Interview with Natwar Singh, New Delhi, January 2018.

22. Lakshmi Iyer, 'Sonia Gandhi, Congress strategists plan aggressive poll strategy to take on NDA', *India Today*, 2 February 2004.

23. 'Maneka and Varun Gandhi want to be in national politics so they joined BJP: Pramod Mahajan', *India Today*, 8 March 2004.

24. Ibid.

25. Yogendra Yadav, 'The elusive mandate of 2004', *Economic and Political Weekly* (2004): 5383–98, p. 5385.

26. Prabhu Chawla, '14th Lok Sabha polls: Sonia Gandhi performs electoral miracle, brings Congress back to power', *India Today*, 24 May 2004.

27. 'New Delhi, Delhi, India Weather History', *Weather Underground*. Available at: https://www.wunderground.com/history/daily/in/new-delhi/VIDP/date/2004-5-13

28. L.K. Advani, *My Country, My Life* (Rupa, 2010, paperback), p. 766.

29. Ibid.

30. Interview with Natwar Singh, New Delhi, January 2018.

31. 'Deathly quiet at BJP headquarters', *The Times of India*, 14 May 2004.

32. Amy Waldman, 'In Huge Upset, Gandhi's Party Wins Election in India', *The New York Times*, 13 May 2004. Available at: https://www.nytimes.com/2004/05/13/international/asia/in-huge-upset-gandhis-party-wins-election-in-india.html

33. Interview with Montek Singh Ahluwalia, New Delhi, March 2018.

34. 'Absence of ideology led to loss', *The Times of India*, 13 May 2004.

35. Interview with Pravin Togadia, Ahmedabad, April 2018.

36. A.S. Dulat, *Kashmir: The Vajpayee Years* (HarperCollins India, 2017), p. 272.

37. Interview with a journalist who wishes to remain unnamed.

38. Yogendra Yadav 'The elusive mandate of 2004', *Economic and Political Weekly* (2004): 5383–98, p. 5385.

39. Ibid.

40. 'Vajpayee was in two minds over poll timing', *The Times of India,* 15 May 2004, p. 7.

41. Interview with Arun Shourie, New Delhi, June 2018.

42. A.S. Dulat, *Kashmir: The Vajpayee Years* (HarperCollins India, 2015), p. 270.

43. L.K. Advani, *My Country, My Life* (Rupa, 2010, paperback), p. 766. See also: Neena Vyas, 'Vajpayee quits, offers cooperation to new government', *The Hindu*, 14 May 2004.

44. 'Enoch Powell', *The Economist*, 12 February 1998. Available at: https://www.economist.com/obituary/1998/02/12/enoch-powell

45. 'When LK Advani lost his job as BJP president for calling Jinnah a "great man"', *DNA*, 4 May 2018.

46. L.K. Advani, *My Country, My Life* (Rupa, 2010, paperback), p. 785.

47. 'Full text of L.K. Advani's resignation letter', NEWS18, 10 June 2013. Available at: https://www.news18.com/news/politics/full-text-of-lk-advanis-resignation-letter-614958.html

48. Interview with R.V. Pandit, Bengaluru, April 2018.

49. 'Mrs Kaul, Delhi's most famous unknown other half, passes away', *The Indian Express*, 4 May 2014.

50. Ibid.

51. Interview with N.M. Ghatate, New Delhi, May 2018.

52. Vijai Trivedi, *Haar Nahin Maanoonga* (HarperCollins Hindi, 2016), p. 30.

53. Interview with Shekhar Gupta, New Delhi, May 2018.

54. Interview with Yashwant Sinha, New Delhi, June 2018.

55. L.K. Advani, *My Country, My Life* (Rupa, 2010, paperback), p. 841.

56. 'Never regarded those who disagreed with us politically as enemies . . . anti-national: LK Advani', *The Economic Times*, 5 April 2019.

57. Anvit Srivastava and Karn Pratap Singh, 'PM Modi's decision to walk at Vajpayee's funeral surprised all', *Hindustan Times*, 18 August 2018.

58. Chapter 1 of Vinay Sitapati, *Half-Lion: How P.V, Narasimha Rao Transformed India* (Penguin, 2016).

59. The Bahujan Samaj Party, Samajwadi Party or the Republican Party of India, for instance.

60. Madhav Sadashiv Golwalkar, *Bunch of Thoughts* (Vikrama Prakashan, 1966), pp. 98, 99.

61. Interview with Vasundhara Raje Scindia, New Delhi, June 2018.

62. 'L.K. Advani's Speech: All-party prayer meet to mourn Vajpayee's demise'. Available at: https://www.youtube.com/watch?v=BYOCQxea8IQ

SCHOLARLY CONTRIBUTION

1. Antony Copley (ed.), *Hinduism in Public and Private: Reform, Hindutva, Gender, and Sampraday* (Oxford University Press, 2009).

2. Koenraad Elst, 'Hindu Activism outside the Sangh Parivar', 18 August 2011. Available at: https://samvada.org/2011/articles/hindu-activism-outside-the-sangh-parivar-dr-koenraad-elst/

3. Romila Thapar, 'In defence of history', *Seminar* (2003): 65–72. Available at: http://www.india-seminar.com/2003/521/521%20romila%20thapar.htm; see also, Chandra Mallampalli, 'Evaluating Marxist and Post-Modernist Responses to Hindu Nationalism during the Eighties and Nineties', *South Asia Research* 19, no. 2 (1999): 161–190.

4. R.B. Bhagat, 'Census and the Construction of Communalism in India', *EPW Commentary*, 24 November 2001. Available at: http://www.sacw.net/2002/CensusandCommunalism.html

5. Nicholas B. Dirks, *Castes of Mind: Colonialism and the Making of Modern India* (Princeton University Press, 2001).

6. John Zavos, *The Emergence of Hindu Nationalism in India* (Oxford University Press, 2000).

7. Charles Herman Heimsath, *Indian Nationalism and Hindu Social Reform* (Princeton University Press, 2015).

8. Norman Barrier's superb study of the Arya Samajis in the turn-of-the-century Punjab Congress advances the argument of this book. It was only in the context of elections (which the British had begun to introduce in the late nineteenth century) that Arya Samajis like Lala Lajpat Rai moved from a purely social reform movement to a political with a conception of state power. See Norman G. Barrier, 'The Arya Samaj and Congress Politics in the Punjab, 1894-1908', *The Journal of Asian Studies*, Vol. 26, No. 3 (May, 1967): 363–379.

9. Jyotirmaya Sharma, *Hindutva: Exploring the Idea of Hindu Nationalism* (Penguin Books India, 2011), p. 8.

10. A.G. Noorani, 'The RSS is at war with India's past', *The Hindu*, 1 May 2019.

11. For a discussion on the history of definitions of 'fascism', see: Joachim Scholtyseck, 'Fascism—National Socialism—Arab Fascism: Terminologies, Definitions and Distinctions', *Die Welt des Islams* 52, no. 3–4 (2012): 242–89.

12. Joachim Scholtyseck, 'Fascism—National Socialism—Arab Fascism: Terminologies, Definitions and Distinctions', *Die Welt des Islams* 52, no. 3–4 (2012): 242–89, at 249–50. See also, Juan J. Linz, 'Some Notes Toward a Comparative Study of Fascism in Sociological Historical Perspective', in Walter Laqueur (ed.), *Fascism: A Reader's Guide* (University of California Press, 1976), pp. 3–121.

13. 'Fascism, Opposition to parliamentary democracy', *Encyclopaedia Britannica*. Available at: https://www.britannica.com/topic/fascism/Opposition-to-parliamentary-democracy

14. Ashis Nandy, 'The twilight of certitudes: Secularism, Hindu nationalism, and other masks of deculturation', *Alternatives* 22, no. 2 (1997): 157–76. Available at: http://dx.doi.org/10.1080/13688799889969

15. Thomas Blom Hansen, *The Saffron Wave: Democracy and Hindu Nationalism in Modern India* (Princeton University Press, 1999), p. 6.

16. Ibid.

17. This definition of conservatism is taken from Corey Robin, *The Reactionary Mind: Conservatism from Edmund Burke to Sarah Palin* (Oxford University Press, 2011), p. 4.

18. Romila Thapar, 'Syndicated Hinduism', *Hinduism Reconsidered* 4 (1997): 54–81; Chandra Mallampalli, 'Evaluating Marxist and Post-Modernist Responses to Hindu Nationalism during the Eighties and Nineties', *South Asia Research* 19, no. 2 (1999): 161–90.

19. Thomas Blom Hansen, 'The Vernacularisation of Hindutva: the BJP and Shiv Sena in rural Maharashtra', *Contributions to Indian Sociology* 30, no. 2 (1996): 177–214.

20. See, for instance, Prem Kumar Vijayan, *Gender and Hindu Nationalism: Understanding Masculine Hegemony* (Routledge Studies in South Asian Politics, 2019).

21. Data from the Lokniti-CSDS National Election Surveys. Compiled at: https://scroll.in/article/893869/how-india-votes-has-the-bjp-gained-enough-women-voters-under-narendra-modi-to-seal-2019

22. Amrita Basu, 'Mass movement or elite conspiracy: The puzzle of Hindu nationalism', in *Contesting the Nation* (Oxford India Paperbacks, 1996), pp. 55–80.

23. Amrita Basu, *Violent Conjunctures in Democratic India* (Cambridge University Press, 2015).

24. Paul R. Brass, *Theft of an Idol: Text and Context in the Representation of Collective Violence* (Princeton University Press, 1997).

25. Steven I. Wilkinson, *Votes and Violence: Electoral Competition and Ethnic Riots in India* (Cambridge University Press, 2004) 293.

26. Raheel Dhattiwala and Michael Biggs, 'The Political Logic of Ethnic Violence: The Anti-Muslim Pogrom in Gujarat, 2002', *Politics and Society*, vol. 40, no. 4 (2012): 481-514, at 491.

27. Christophe Jaffrelot, 'Refining the moderation thesis. Two religious parties and Indian democracy: The Jana Sangh and the BJP between Hindutva radicalism and coalition politics', *Democratization*, 20, no. 5 (2013): 876–94, at 876.

28. Sanjay Ruparelia, 'Rethinking institutional theories of political moderation: the case of Hindu nationalism in India, 1996-2004', *Comparative Politics* (2006): 317–36.

29. Christophe Jaffrelot, 'Refining the moderation thesis. Two religious parties and Indian democracy: The Jana Sangh and the BJP between Hindutva radicalism and coalition politics', *Democratization*, 20, no. 5 (2013): 876–94.

30. Lars Tore Flåten, 'The Inclusion-Moderation Thesis: India's BJP', in *Oxford Research Encyclopaedia of Politics*, 2019.

31. Pralay Kanungo, 'Myth of the monolith: The RSS wrestles to discipline its political progeny', *Social Scientist* (2006): 51–69.

32. Interview with Jairam Ramesh, Kolkata, January 2018.

33. Stuart Corbridge and John Harriss, *Reinventing India: Liberalization, Hindu Nationalism and Popular Democracy* (John Wiley & Sons, 2013).

34. Ornit Shani, *Communalism, Caste and Hindu Nationalism: The Violence in Gujarat* (Cambridge University Press, 2007).

35. Christophe Jaffrelot, *The Hindu Nationalist Movement in India* (Columbia University Press, 1996), pp. 485–86.

Index

ACKNOWLEDGEMENTS

This is one of those books where so many who gave their voices, memories and sweat demanded to remain in the shadows. So let me state upfront that all controversies are of my choosing, and the few named in these pages carry no responsibility for its contents. The same disclaimer applies to a crew of brain-pickers who disinfected, brushed and polished the manuscript. This acknowledgement is for them.

I come from a family with words to spare. Kamala Ganesh read each sentence with a fine-toothed comb that created the perfect middle-parting of academic arguments and popular style. I owe who I am to her. Aditi Sriram, a writer's writer, partnered this book through the three years it took to write it. She added flair to the manuscript while making the story pertinent to even those who don't shop at Bahri Sons. Sudhir Sitapati, genius marketeer, read each chapter as I wrote them. He has shaped the vision and tone of the book more than any other. Krishna Sriram read much of the book, correcting errors as well as flagging where the narrative sagged. R. 'Ambi' Srinivasan ran his *meethi chhuri* through the early chapters; his attentive support and inspirational life have made the book and its author what they are. Priya Krishnan subtly left her fingerprint on every page, the same skill she generously provided for my previous book.

My publisher Meru Gokhale from Penguin reminded me what courage and composure look like. She read the draft multiple times, adding external markers and demanding more emotion between Vajpayee and Advani. I can be fastidious and obsessive, as those who know me will unhappily vouch. Tarini Uppal dealt with that throughout, being the sutradhaar for this entire project. Thanks also to Shantanu Ray Chaudhuri for expert copy editing and Gunjan Ahlawat for an enticing cover.

A battery of academics shone their light on this book. Years after mentoring me through a vexing PhD, Atul Kohli continues to keep a watchful eye on my words and ideas. Lawrence Liang, lateral thinker par excellence, encouraged my storytelling to be understated and my theory more pronounced. Shivaji Sondhi mixes the analytical clarity of a Princeton physicist with the upbringing of a Jana Sanghi. Not just his details, but his insights have shaped this book. Anup Dhar brought his eclectic training to every chapter; the double doctor clinically sewed together parts that were left hanging. It seems repetitive to thank Pratap Bhanu Mehta for so many contributions to my life. Two of the main arguments of the book—of Hindu nationalism's comfort with elections, and of its need for defensive violence—are owed to him.

This academic rigour was the perfect jugalbandi to the comments of four practitioners. Human rights expert Sunitha Rangaswami despises all that the BJP stands for, but read each sentence with a fair mind; she is more objective than she is willing to admit. M.R. 'PRS' Madhavan is my model for unfussy public service. He brought his daily exposure to politics and nightly exposure to fiction to bear on every chapter. Ashoka University's 'most valuable player', Eshwara 'Venkat' Venkatesam, was the first person I bounced this book idea off, as well as the last to read the manuscript. He prodded words as well smoothened ideas. Nandini Mehta in some sense invented the genre of serious non-fiction in India. Her surgical hand has made for a well-sutured book.

A quintet of lawyers gave the manuscript pro bono vetting. Aman Ahluwalia produced twenty-eight pages of comments: no mistake was too small to redline or too big to correct. The only thing more admirable than his ample intelligence is how lightly he wears it. Not so much Neel Maitra, who helped conceptualize the book and read early chapters. When his normally acid tongue began to hurl praise, I sensed I was on to something. Govind Naidu went through each page (his legal acumen disguised by light green crocs), ensuring balance and preventing a descent into polemics. Suhaan Mukerji read the entire manuscript during the Covid lockdown, providing me with seven hours worth of comments on the telephone. His swift slices have cut a lot of the flab. And the ever-diligent Abhishek Nath Tripathi kept me on my toes with regard to more tenuous claims on the Jana Sangh. Since I have left law as a profession, I endlessly wondered why lawyers charge 60,000 rupees for an hour of reading. Now I know.

For newspaper archives, ProQuest provided a trial subscription of the entire *Times of India* archive. N. Ravi, N. Murali and A. Sankaran from *The Hindu* made available their physical archives in Chennai. Prafulla Ketkar helped with *Panchajanya* and *Organiser* archives, as did the Nehru Memorial Museum and Library. They also provided a host of private archives which the endnotes set in ink. Neeraj Priyadarshi and Renuka Puri helped with the back issues of *The Indian Express* and *Janasatta*. Thanks are also due to the BJP's swanky new library in New Delhi, as well as the idiosyncratic material on Hindu nationalism at Princeton University's world-beating library (thank you, David Magier). For providing their private (and hitherto unseen) papers, I thank N.M. Ghatate, R.V. Pandit and the family of M.L. Sondhi. Rahul Sagar's website IdeasofIndia.org provided lists of rare Indian publications. Ganesh Iyer sent me a valuable book on Rajpal Puri (Advani's early mentor), and Andrea Costabir aided a long (and alas futile) search to locate an interview of Vajpayee's daughter in *Savvy* magazine.

Helping me sieve through this mass of material were two research assistants. Nabhojeet Sen is a classic scholar—brilliant, painstaking and late! His natural turn for historical research has made the book bulletproof. Shivani Bajpai also helped with archival work in the Nehru Memorial and the National Archives.

When it came to providing introductions, a shout out to J.P. Singh and his encyclopaedic son Shubhranshu, K. Raju, Arvind Subramanian and Suman Dubey. Ashutosh Salil, raja of eastern Maharashtra, rotated his rolodex of contacts. The many others who vouched for my 200 interviews have exacted a promise that they remain anonymous.

Over the three years I wrote this book, I have learnt from conversations with many. These are: Sandipto Dasgupta (who refused to read the draft since he claimed to know all about fascism already), Satyam Viswanathan (market research guru, who helped structure the chapters), Madhav Khosla (both for his ground-breaking work on constitutional representation and for his Germanic work ethic), Naresh Fernandes (for being a genuinely liberal trampoline to bounce ideas off), Geoffrey Sigalet (on comparisons to Western conservatism), Ramachandra Guha (on the use of a particular reading of Indian history by Hindu nationalists), Bipin Aspatwar (who listened—nothing more, nothing less), EMESCO Vijaykumar (for the initial idea of focussing on Advani), Sudipta Kaviraj (on Muslim and Hindu anxieties in the late nineteenth century), Nabanjan Maitra (on the history of Hindu ascetics and sanyasis), Ashis Nandy (on elaborating on his original claims on Hindu nationalism while walking in Jhula Park), Coomi Kapoor (for her long-brewed insights into both the Jana Sangh and the BJP), Kanta Murali (for her stress on the demand-side explanations for the BJP's rise), Devesh Kapur (for forcing me to follow facts, rather than fickle academic fashion), Srinath Raghavan (on Hindu nationalism's foreign policy), Dinsha Mistree (on nestling the argument in comparative politics), Jan-Werner Mueller (for conversations on populism, as well as on Christian Democracy), Shekhar Gupta (on the need to tell this story in an accessible way), Vivek Trilokinath (for loaning me his mind and his apartment), and to Raj Kamal Jha (for suggesting that the book lead up to Narendra Modi's BJP).

In addition to this specific assistance, a number of people helped during the writing of this book. Thank you: Alia and Naira Allana, Vishnu Shankar, Seetha Druva, Niraja Gopal Jayal, Satyajit Banerjee, Keshava Guha, Sushant Sachdeva, Abu Mathen George, Mahesh Rangarajan, Rudrangshu Mukherjee, Mini Kapoor, Abir Bazaz, Rita Kothari, Malabika Sarkar, Kaushik Vaidya, B. Chandrasen Rao, K. Vivek Reddy, Dinyar Patel, Srinivasan 'Murali' Krishna, Akshaya Mukul, Rajesh Krishnan, Gowri Tirumurti, Sunil K. Gulati, Matthew H. Baxter, Rushabh Sanghavi, FEA's Deepak Chopra, Sadanand Menon, Ashutosh Varshney, Patrick French, Shishira Rudrappa, Deepika Mahidhara, Darshana Narayanan, Malay Duggar, Suketu Mehta, M.K. Venu, Jayadev Calamur, Radhika Herzberger, Pranav Ullal, Kim Lane Scheppele, Mohit Abraham, Ezra Suleiman, Rachel 'Tina' Immanuel, Saurabh Seth, Kartick Maheshwari, Azza Cohen, Milan Vaishnav, Rohit Lamba, Steven Wilkinson, Gautam Sabharwal, Sunil Khilnani, Alex Travelli, Anusha and Aparaajit Sriram, Max Rodenbeck, Parul Bhandari, Shoumitro Chatterjee, Anisha Sharma, Averi Banerjee, Kanishka Gupta, Ashish Dhawan, Neelanjan Sircar, Khushdeep Kaur Malhotra, Ashok Trivedi, Adarsh and Yamini Aiyar, Parth Mehrotra, Shilpi and Pavan Jambagi, Ananth Padmanabhan, Vandita Mishra, Asif Ali, Anand Bhatkar, Pushpaji, Sonam Masta, Santosh Mali, Surjit Singh and Balbir.

Ashoka University was kind enough to give me leave for a year while I worked on the book. And what nutritious soil to grow this project, from support by senior faculty to camaraderie from the political science department (in addition to those mentioned earlier, they include Malvika Maheshwari, Gilles Vernier, Ali Khan Mahmudabad and Bann Seng Tan). I thank especially those students who took the courses on 'Right Wing Politics' (2017), 'Religion & Politics' (2017) and 'Introduction to Indian Politics' (2020), as I do my teaching fellows Mahima Malik and Rohith Jyotish.

A word now on the two without whom this book would never have reached the finish line. Arpit Gaind spent two years as a researcher on this book. In our jugalbandi, no detail was too small for him to crosscheck, no idea too repugnant to consider. I may never again find someone as diligent a researcher and tireless a manager. The other person this book owes a weighty debt to is the journalist Sheela Bhatt—her generosity, contacts and labyrinthine memory. She has taught me much about India and its Indians.

Families are what you have above all. Thank you: Chellam Ramanathan, T.S.R. Subramanian, Parvathy Narayanan, Janakiram Sitapati, Harish Khosla, Rukmani Sriram, Ketki Sitapati, the Sachdevs, the Krishnans (of the tennis; police; and Shadow varieties), and the Mannars. And to the next generation: Sahaana, Siya and Kabir.

Finally, I dedicate this book to Sitapati Ganesh. He's up there somewhere, whisky in hand, grumbling about the book while secretly pleased that I wrote it.